EU Digital Copyright Law and the End-User

Giuseppe Mazziotti

EU Digital Copyright Law and the End-User

Springer

ISBN 978-3-540-75984-3 e-ISBN 978-3-540-75985-0

DOI 10.1007/978-3-540-76985-0

Library of Congress Control Number: 2008920730

Production: le-tex Jelonek, Schmidt & Vöckler GbR
Cover design: WMX Design GmbH, Heidelberg

Printed on acid-free paper

9 8 7 6 5 4 3 2 1

springer.com

For my parents,
Lorenzo and Adonella

Preface

This book draws on the contents of the Ph.D. dissertation I wrote and defended at the European University Institute (EUI) of Florence. At the beginning of my research, I did not expect to write a book on the intersection between copyright law and digital technologies and, in particular, on the implications that digitisation presents for the interests of users of copyrighted works. At that time, I was neither an expert on new technologies nor an avid user who viewed the Internet as a "no copyright land" where anyone should download whatever content for free. Before graduating from the University of Perugia School of Law, I had established myself as a clarinet player who performed mostly chamber music and the symphonic repertoire. I had also worked extensively as a radio speaker, music critic and writer with the Italian public broadcaster RAI-Radio3. In performing all these music-related activities, I developed a considerable interest for copyright issues and, when choosing my dissertation topic, I immediately opted for a work on copyright law that examined the economic rights of music performers under the Italian and the EU legal systems. I was very curious to see how and to what extent the law sought to protect the subtle, particular kind of creativity and originality embodied in musical performances. That was my first step towards writing a book on copyright law. However, my background as a musician and writer naturally made me more sympathetic to the interests of copyright owners than to those of users of protected works. So, my initial research interests were focused on the analysis of copyright *protection* rather than on that of copyright *restrictions*.

My study was consequently stimulated, at the beginning, by a reflection on how the law could preserve the rationale of copyright protection when controlling the unauthorised digital copying and use of copyrighted works seemed to be unfeasible and utopian. At a time when the economic and moral rights of copyright owners were objectively endangered by the advent of the digital society, the spectacular rise of Digital Rights Management (DRM) technologies and other measures of technological protection started modifying the state of the art in the field of digital copyright. It became clear in the relevant literature on the future of copyright that the risk of "digital abandon", which was widely perceived as imposing a structural change on copyright policy, would soon be replaced by the risk of "digital lock-up". This stemmed from the technical assumption that DRM systems and similar technologies would provide efficient systems of control and management of digitised information. My analysis has focused on the consequences of the directive that the European Union enacted in May 2001 as a legal tool that sought to adapt copyright law to the digital environment and to harmonise national regulations with the institutional objective of developing pan-European markets in copyright-related markets. By the enactment of Directive 2001/29/EC, European law-makers harmonised the rights of copyright owners at European Union level and conferred legal protection to technologies such as DRM systems without considering that such digital means sought to transform the public, which has been the traditional addressee of copyrighted works, into a chain of single users, whose legitimate and socially valuable purposes of personal copying, quotation, teaching and research, parody, and so on, should be effectively enabled and preserved notwithstanding the wide adoption of access control and rights management mechanisms. I maintain that the pursuit of objectives of public policy can be achieved only by ensuring a reasonable breadth of the copyright scope even in the digital world. For instance, the objective of protecting the user's private sphere from the increasingly pervasive capabilities of control and monitoring enabled by DRM technologies and "Trusted Computing" platforms requires careful reflection upon the suitability of the private copying exception, which would avoid expanding the enforcement of copyright to the realm of personal uses. Similarly, the policy goal of fostering cumulative creativity in fields where the user is often a potential follow-on creator would require the statutory grant of rights of uses with the consequence of limiting the power of access- and copy-control technology to the benefit of qualified classes of users. Such concerns, as well as many others, do not have a place within today's EU copyright legislation. By testing the legislation enacted in 2001 in the most contested digital settings (*i.e.*, peer-to-peer networks, DRM-based protection of access to and use of digital works), I develop a critical review of the EU copyright system by seeking to emphasise why the legislation enacted a few years ago would need to be reformed and why the important goal of copyright enforcement targeted at end-users should be reconciled with the pursuit of other strategic policies such as the implementation of human rights law, consumer protection law, competition law and privacy protection law in copyright-related scenarios.

Rome, November 2007

Giuseppe Mazziotti
giuseppe.mazziotti@gmail.com

Acknowledgments

First of all, I wish to thank all the members of the examining board of my PhD thesis defence, which took place at the Department of Law of the European University Institute (EUI) on 18 June 2007: Hanns Ullrich (EUI, supervisor), Thomas Hoeren (University of Muenster), Bernt Hugenholtz (University of Amsterdam) and Giovanni Sartor (EUI). I would like to thank them for their insightful remarks, suggestions and criticism they provided in their reports and during the public discussion we held one very hot and sunny day in Florence. In particular, I wish to express my sincere gratitude to my supervisor, Hanns Ullrich, who provided me with firm guidance and criticism during the years of study and research spent at the EUI, while letting me choose and concentrate on the research issues which most stimulated my interest and curiosity. I thank Prof. Ullrich very much for his patience in waiting for the final draft of my thesis, for his continuous support during my stay at the EUI, and for his quick and in-depth reading of my work, especially in the final stages of the writing process.

The autumn of 2004, which I spent at the School of Law of the University of California at Berkeley, was a turning point in my PhD research. Here, I had the opportunity to meet and learn from Robert Merges, Peter Menell, Molly van Howeling, Howard Shelanski and François Lévêque. I wish to thank them for their brilliant teaching, the very useful discussions I had with them and their comments on my research project. I owe much to Robert Merges for his kindness, continuous encouragement and appreciation of my work. Upon my return to Italy, I had the chance to meet two people who helped me greatly in developing my research ideas with confidence and optimism, at a time when I needed to be confident and optimistic, given my delay in bringing the writing process to its conclusion within the time schedule. These people were Séverine Dusollier and Giovanni Sartor. Without their helpful comments and intellectual support, my work would have missed much and might never have reached a happy end.

I would like to thank the Italian Ministry of Foreign Affairs and the EUI for the financial support they provided during these years, and for the freedom they allowed me in pursuing my research interests without having to please any Italian law professor. This is something unusual for an Italian doctoral student, and I am fully aware of having benefited from a very privileged situation. In addition, I would like to express all my gratitude to the board of the prize "Borsa di studio in memoria dell'Avvocato Leonello Leonelli", awarded by the law firm Leonelli Duranti e Associati of Perugia and by the Italian Law Society (*Consiglio Nazionale Forense*). This prize was not only an honour for me, but also gave me financial support during the last months of work at the EUI. In particular, I would like to thank Fabrizio Leonelli, who, at the time of the award, encouraged my professional and academic career with enthusiasm, trust and friendship. I am also very grateful to Giandomenico Magrone, Livia Magrone Furlotti and Gianmatteo Nunziante for the confidence they gave me and their understanding during the preparation of this book while practising law with their outstanding firm in Rome.

Once completed, much support was provided to me by the EUI Language Centre, whose teaching and staff I will never forget, and by such friends as Mel Marquis, Ana Vrdoljak and Chris Engert, without whose help the book would never have been written (at least not in English). A very special thank you goes to Ana Vrdoljak, for her advice on the formal organisation of the various chapters and for her careful and enlightening support in reviewing and commenting on my drafts. An equally important acknowledgment goes to my publisher, Springer, which is offering me the opportunity to publish this work all over the world, and in particular to Anke Seyfried and Manuela Ebert, who greatly helped me in editing the final proofs of the book.

It is impossible to mention here all the EUI friends who deserve my gratitude for having established a sort of second, huge family. Within the EUI world, I wish to address a very special thank you to Irene Sobrino Guijarro, without whose support this work would never have been accomplished; and to Marta Arespa Castelló, who helped and gave me much support in the final stages of the writing and editing process. Out of the EUI world, I am particularly indebted to Davide Berretta, a long-term but very young friend from Perugia who has supported me during these years while sharing also the experience of a new project of on-line dissemination of classical and jazz music (http://www.musikethos.org); and all the flatmates of my last years in Florence and Rome, especially Massimo Delfino, Fiorella Triscritti, Carmen Bullón, Elena Roveglia, Barbara Mottura and Amedeo Barletta. A very special thank you goes to all the friends who allowed me to feel deeply linked to the environment of music and musicians, a state of mind that I still feel as mine own: Filippo Fanò, Alessia Rullo, Filippo Farinelli, Stefano Micheletti, Matteo Fossi, Guido Zaccagnini, Sabina Sacchi and Jacopo Pellegrini; Gabriele Mirabassi, who granted me the privilege of his friendship by letting me discover in person his geniality as a musician and clarinet player, which stimulated reflections on formerly neglected or undeveloped musical interests; and Ciro Scarponi, my clarinet teacher and mentor at the Perugia Music Academy, an extraordinary performer and man of enormous generosity and charisma, whose unexpected, premature death one year ago has created a huge gap in my life: without his teaching and his invitation to join his class in Perugia in autumn 1994 my life would have followed a completely different path.

Finally, for their continuous support, love and teaching, I wish to thank my parents Lorenzo and Adonella, to whom this book is dedicated; my sister Anna Maria and my brother Raffaele, my grand-mother Maria, my aunt Lorena and my cousin Allan, who have been very close to me during these years notwithstanding the painful and premature losses of my beloved *nonno* Mario and *zio* Giorgio, whom I remember with great love.

Giuseppe Mazziotti

Table of contents

List of abbreviations

CD	Compact Disc
Community	European Community
DMCA	Digital Millennium Copyright Act
DPRL	Digital Property Rights Language
DRM	Digital Rights Management
DVD	Digital Video Disc
EC Treaty	Treaty establishing the European Community
EIPR	European Intellectual Property Review
EU	European Union
IIC	International Review of Intellectual Property and Competition Law
IP	Internet Protocol
InfoSoc Directive	Directive 2001/29/EC on the harmonisation of certain aspects of copyright and related rights in the information society
IPRs	Intellectual Property Rights
ISO	International Organisation for Standardization
ISP	Internet Service Provider
LAB	Legal Advisory Board of the European Commission
MPAA	Motion Picture Association of America
MPEG	Motion Picture Experts Group
MP3	MPEG-1 Audio Layer 3 (digital audio encoding standard)
OJ	Official Journal
REL	Rights Expression Language
RIAA	Recording Industry Association of America

RIDA	Revue Internationale du Droit d'Auteur
TC	Trusted Computing
TCG	Trusted Computing Group
TCPA	Trusted Computing Platform Alliance
TPM	Trusted Platform Module
TRIPS	Agreement on Trade-Related Aspects of Intellectual Property Rights
U.S.	United States of America
VCR	Video Cassette Recorder
VHS	Vertical Helical Scan (recording and playing standard for VCR)
WIPO	World Intellectual Property Organisation
WTO	World Trade Organisation
XML	eXtensible Mark-up Language
XrML	eXtensible Rights Mark-up Language

PART I
COPYRIGHT AND DIGITISATION

1. Introduction

1.1. The research question

Since the last decade of the 20th Century, the advent of digital technology and the establishment of a networked environment, such as the Internet, have had an immense impact on the patterns of production, modification, dissemination and consumption of creative works packaged in digital formats. Within this new, borderless environment, Internet users and, more generally, owners of cheap digital devices (such as modern personal computers) have been able to play the role of creator, re-creator and extensive distributor of this particular kind of information. The advent of digitisation has changed the economics of creativity, dissemination and copyright by:

- reducing dramatically the cost of making perfect reproductions of a work;
- allowing these reproductions to be disseminated quickly, easily and cheaply; and
- making available technological tools and devices that make creativity much cheaper and easier than at any other time.[1]

---

1 See Shapiro and Varian, *Information Rules, A Strategic Guide to the Network Economy*, Harvard Business School Press, Boston 1999, pp. 84-85 (who argued that "digital technology is uniquely potent precisely because it sharply lowers both copying and distribution costs. Each of these new capabilities offers a different set of challenges to rights management and require a different set of responses."). The authors of this excellent business guide consciously disregard the third type of change which is mentioned in the text and relates to the changes that digital technology has brought to the economics of creativity. An account of how digital technologies made users' creativity easier and cheaper is provided by Benkler, 'From Consumers to Users', 52(3) *Federal Communications Law Journal* 2000, p. 561, at p. 568; Lessig, *The Future of Ideas, The Fate of the Commons in a Connected World*, Vintage Books, New York 2002, p. 8 ("Digital technology has radically reduced the cost of digital creations [...] the cost of filmmaking is a fraction of what it was just a decade ago. The same is true for the production of music or any digital art. Using what we might call a 'music processor', students in a high school music class can compose symphonies that are played back to the composer. Imagine the cost of that just ten years ago [...]"); and more recently by Fisher, *Promises to Keep. Technology, Law and the Future of Entertainment*, Stanford University Press, Stanford 2004, p. 11; and Van Howeling, 'Distributive Values in Copyright', 83(6) *Texas Law Review* 2005, p. 1535.

Today, such technology-enabled diffusion of digital creativity appears to be colliding with modern copyright legislation (such as the 2001 EU Information Society Directive[2] and the 1998 U.S. Digital Millennium Copyright Act[3]), which allows digital copyrighted works to be sealed, while outlawing the production, marketing, possession and use of technologies which have the potential to circumvent and/or decrypt technological protection measures and so-called digital rights management (DRM) systems.

This collision is the primary research question of this book: to what extent does European copyright law, as shaped by the InfoSoc Directive, accommodate the interests of end-users to interact with copyrighted works in the digital world?

This research question is broken down into the following issues which have concrete significance for producers and users of digital content:

- How can contemporary end-users obtain access to copyrighted digital works and engage in uses that copyright law permits if technological measures restrict the use of such works?
- How can they creatively re-use and "tinker" legitimately with embedded copyrighted content if the law forbids the reproduction and transformation of copyrighted materials?
- How can end-users benefit from the new flow of out-of-copyright and free-to-disseminate information enabled by peer-to-peer networking on the Internet if the availability and permissibility of powerful communication technology is conditioned and threatened by the implementation of copyright enforcement measures?

1.2. Terminology

This book uses an open notion of "end-user". Depending on his or her position and purpose in the digital environment, the single user can alternatively be seen as a potential consumer of the protected digital works, as a user of copyrighted works on the Internet, or as a possible follow-on creator building upon pre-existing copyrighted works in order to make new copyrightable creations. In this book, the end-user is defined as a natural person, that is, an individual, easily distinguishable from institutional users such as broadcasters, content suppliers, libraries, archives, and so forth. At the same time, the end-user is a consumer of digital goods and services who benefits from consumer protection law when contracting with professional traders. Finally, the end-user is an individual (*e.g.*, a single music com-

2 See Directive 2001/29/EC of the European Parliament and of the Council of 22 May 2001 on the harmonisation of certain aspects of copyright and related rights in the information society (hereinafter "InfoSoc Directive"), OJ, L 167, 22.6.2001, 10.

3 See the U.S. Digital Millennium Copyright Act signed into law by President Clinton on 28 October 1998, which amended the U.S. Copyright Act: see U.S. Code, Title 17, Chapter 12, §1201.

poser, a film-maker, a blogger, a teacher, a scientist, *etc*) who makes transformative uses of pre-existing copyrighted materials enabled by digital technologies.

Before outlining the structure of the book, this introduction will briefly focus on how digital technology and the network society have changed the role of the user in the value-creating chain concerning digital content. As pointed out by Boyle, digital production techniques blur the line between listening, editing, and re-creating.[4] As a consequence of the new economics of digitisation, the opportunities of violating digital copyright (*i.e.*, the exclusive rights of copying and modifying digital works) by acts of transformative (*i.e.*, productive) or non-transformative use have been broadened immensely. Due to the easy, cheap and far-reaching opportunities of digital production techniques, the user can establish himself or herself as a follow-on creator or as a massive distributor of unauthorised works covered by property rights. As a result, digital technologies have replaced a world in which copyright operates upstream, as a form of industrial unfair competition policy, with a world where *all* creative, communicative, and just plain consumptive acts performed in everyday life implicate copyright protection (and its potential violation).[5]

In the book, broad reference will be made to the concept and to the effects of so-called "technological protection measures" and, in particular, Digital Rights Management (DRM) systems. These devices have been developed at a rapid pace in order to enable content suppliers (mainly, the content industry) to control the access to and the use of digital works perfectly. Appendix I to this book provides an overview of the invention and development of "digital rights languages" and of the technological perspectives concerning the fast-changing world of DRM systems. In this Appendix, it is briefly explained that DRM and other similar technologies have the potential to transform digital *works* (*i.e.*, goods) into digital *services*, whose use can be regulated under the contractual terms which come with the product. This new situation collides with the *ratio* of copyright exceptions and may result in a great restriction of the legitimate opportunities of free, unauthorised uses while confining the user's role to that of an ultimate consumer.

In this book the term "exceptions" is used interchangeably with expressions such as "restrictions" and "limitations". This term is intended to refer to certain categories of acts which are exempted by law from the copyright scope, with a view to achieving a number of public policy objectives (*e.g.*, allowing criticism, research, teaching, news reporting, parody, and so on).[6] As convincingly observed by Guibault, copyright exceptions may encompass different types of statutory provisions, including full copyright exemptions, statutory licences, compulsory li-

---

4 See Boyle, 'The Second Enclosure Movement and the Construction of the Public Domain', (66) *Law and Contemporary Problems* 2003, p. 33, at p. 40. This article can be downloaded at:
http://www.law.duke.edu/boylesite/.

5 See Boyle, 'The Second Enclosure Movement', op. cit., p. 40.

6 See Guibault, *Copyright Limitations and Contracts, An analysis of the contractual overridability of limitations on copyright*, Kluwer Law International, The Hague 2002, p. 16.

cences, and cases of so-called mandatory collective administration of copyrights.[7] What makes these provisions similar to each other is that, in all of these cases, users are entitled to access, copy, quote, extract, manipulate and tinker directly with copyrighted material without the authorisation of the copyright owner.

Moreover, the analysis of digital copyright legislation contained in this book will not focus on other kinds of structural limitations of copyright, such as the temporary duration of copyright protection, which has lasted 70 years *post mortem autoris* both in the U.S. and in the EU.[8] Nor does this analysis deal with the limitation of the scope of copyright embodied in the so-called idea/expression dichotomy, which impedes any copyright owner from appropriating ideas and principles and from restricting the development of the same ideas in further creative work and expression.

Finally, when speaking of "copyright" or "copyright owners", this book will make undifferentiated reference to all rights and related rights created by copyright law in favour of authors, performers, producers of phonograms and broadcasters.

1.3. The value of transformative and non-transformative uses in the copyright system

To highlight precisely how today's end-user, equipped with cheap digital technologies (for example, a general-purpose personal computer), can vigorously interact with and build upon pre-existing work, it is useful to distinguish two different kinds of use of copyrighted work: transformative and non-transformative (*i.e.*,

7 See Guibault, *Copyright Limitations and Contracts*, op. cit., p. 20. As this author explains, "the most common form of limitation recognised in favour of users consists of a full exemption from the scope of the right owner's exclusive right, where the right to prohibit is withdrawn without monetary compensation to rights owners for the use of their work". Under a statutory licence, instead, "the copyrighted material may be used without authorisation from the rights owner but against payment of an equitable remuneration. Contrary to negotiated licenses, the amount of remuneration to be paid to rights owners under a statutory licence is fixed by the legislator or by some regulatory authority". In Guibault's classification, the third category (compulsory licences) is distinguished from the previous one (statutory licences) on the assumption that the former requires a rights owner to grant an individual licence at a price and under conditions determined either with the user or by authorities where an agreement cannot be reached. The fourth category, finally, addresses a much less constraining form of limitation, under which copyright law requires that certain rights must be exercised through authors' collecting societies.

8 In the EU, the term of copyright protection was harmonised and set out by the Council Directive 93/98/EEC, OJ L 290, 24.11.1993, 9. In the U.S., the term was extended from 50 to 70 years by the 1998 Copyright Term Extension Act, which amended the U.S. Code, Title 17, §§302-304.

consumptive).[9] This book uses a merely descriptive notion of "transformative use". It does not encompass all of the legal implications created by transformative purposes under copyright law. In particular, the book does not deal in depth with the scope of the author's exclusive right of authorising the translation, adaptation or other alteration of the work, whose enforcement is undoubtedly endangered by the wide spread of digital technologies.[10] The reason for this exclusion is circumscribed by the EU InfoSoc Directive, which sets out the fundamental legal framework of our analysis. The Directive does not take any harmonisation measures with regard to the scope and the exceptions to this right.[11]

The distinction between transformative and non-transformative uses covers both traditional works (such as music, films, books, research contributions and photography) and newer modes of expressions (*e.g.*, multimedia works and software). Transformative use takes place when the user creates a new work incorporating an earlier one into it. Derivative works, such as caricatures, parodies, and pastiches, as well as uses such as quotations for teaching, criticism and scientific research, exemplify this transformative use. In contrast, non-transformative use takes place when the user accesses the work without embedding it into a new creation. Non-transformative use includes activities such as reading, watching, listening to, and copying for purposes of entertainment, private study, information and communication.

Senftleben has recently drawn on this descriptive distinction to shed light on the ultimate purpose of copyright exceptions which enable transformative and non-transformative uses.[12] He emphasises the assumption that intellectual production, as a fruit of the human intellect, is an iterative (*i.e.*, cumulative) process that requires an author "to allow subsequent creators to use and enjoy the fruit of his labour in the same way as he was permitted to access already existing works".[13] This requirement, which is described as "intergenerational equity", is justified by

---

9 This distinction was proposed and relied upon mainly in the U.S. by scholars such as Netanel, 'Copyright and a Democratic Civil Society', (106) *Yale Law Journal* 1996, p. 283, at p. 311 (who spoke of "consumptive" and "transformative" use); Samuelson, 'Fair Use for Computer Programs and Other Copyrightable Works in Digital Form: The Implications of Sony, Galoob and Sega', (1) *Journal of Intellectual Property Law* 1993, p. 49, at p. 61 (who referred to the same categories as "intrinsic" and "productive"); and Dowell, 'Bytes and Pieces: Fragmented Copies, Licensing, and Fair Use in a Digital World', (86) *California Law Review* 1998, p. 843, at p. 866 (who distinguished "end-uses" from "secondary uses").

10 The author's exclusive right of authorising the translation, adaptation or other alteration of the work is recognised internationally under Articles 8 and 12 of the Berne Convention for the Protection of Literary and Artistic Works.

11 The wording of the Directive is very ambiguous on this issue, because it includes the exception of caricature, parody and pastiche (which is an exception to the above-mentioned right) in the list of copyright exceptions provided under Article 5 of the Directive: see Article 5(3)(k). I owe this insight to a comment made by Bernt Hugenholtz.

12 See Senftleben, *Copyright, Limitations and the Three-Step Test. An Analysis of the three-Step Test in International and EC Copyright Law*, Kluwer Law International, The Hague 2004, pp. 34-41.

13 *Ibidem*, p. 38.

the notion that intellectual production is a public good which cannot be depleted and which is constantly renewed by new ideas and forms of expression. Using this premise, Senftleben convincingly argues that it is highly desirable, in order to promote scientific and cultural progress, for transformative and non-transformative uses of works of the intellect to be able to draw upon more than just the public domain, which is formed by all the pre-existing ideas and works of former authors which are unprotected (either because of the non-eligibility of mere ideas for copyright protection, or due to the expiration of the term of protection of the copyrighted material in question).[14] To a certain extent, this opportunity also concerns the works of contemporary authors who still enjoy copyright protection.

The opportunity for new authors to build upon the pre-existing stock of works still protected by copyright is ensured by certain exceptions built into copyright law. These exceptions are intended to strike a balance between providing incentives and rewards for individual creation, and providing too much protection and thereby stifling intellectual innovation. Senftleben and Heide have argued that copyright exceptions that facilitate "transformative" or "productive" uses of copyrighted works should be ranked above all the other exceptions.[15] According to Senftleben, this conclusion is grounded in the constitutional protection of freedom of expression, which guarantees public access to quotations and enables other transformative uses of copyrighted works, such as caricatures, parodies and pastiches. Similarly, Heide stresses that copyright exceptions which allow transformative uses must be considered to be more important than those which enable mere reproductive (and hence non-transformative) uses because only the former promote the creation of competing works by leaving follow-on users free to share ideas or parts of pre-existing works.[16]

This distinction is useful for the purpose of identifying the justification behind each copyright exception. Nonetheless, Senftleben's view that the creation of new works of authorship would never be possible without the opportunity of engaging in non-transformative uses of copyrighted works (for example, personal use for the purpose of private study), which serve as an indispensable source of inspiration and information for contemporary authors and end-users wishing to become new creators, must be shared.

It will be argued that, by opening up new scenarios for the use of copyrighted works, the advent of digital technology has considerably strengthened the need for society to have an effective system of copyright exceptions.

---

14 *Ibidem.*

15 See Senftleben, *Copyright, Limitations and the Three-Step Test*, op. cit., p. 39; Heide, 'Copyright, Contract and the Legal Protection of Technological Measures – Not "the Old Fashioned Way": Providing a Rationale to the "Copyright Exceptions Interface"', 2003, available at: http://www.ssrn.com.

16 See Heide, 'Copyright, Contract and the Legal Protection of Technological Measures', op. cit., p. 2, who referred to a distinction proposed in the U.S. by Landes and Posner, 'An Economic Analysis of Copyright Law', (18) *Journal of Legal Studies* 1989, p. 325, at p. 360.

1.4. New kinds of transformative use

Excellent examples of the transformative use allowed by digital devices have recently caught the attention of scholars in the U.S., provoking a debate on whether the fair use doctrine[17] could apply in cases of independently created, derivative creations which "mix, rip, and burn" pieces of pre-existing copyrighted work.[18] These cases showed that poorly-equipped artists and creators have been able to create highly appreciated works of art by re-using pieces and extracts from pre-existing films and songs, and inserting them into independently created works whose production and release costs were low thanks to new digital technologies and software. For instance, the film "Tarnation", which received great acclaim at the 2004 Cannes and Sundance film festivals, was made by Jonathan Caouette, an unemployed actor from New York, who worked as a doorman, on a borrowed Apple Macintosh by editing and combining his own home movies with other video-clips and music.[19] Caouette spent $218 on the production of the film, but would have had to pay a further $400,000 if rights to use copyrighted music and video-clips had been obtained. The same happened with an album created by DJ Brian Burton, "The Grey Album", by mixing vocals from hip-hopper Jay-Z's "The Black Album" and rhythms that appeared in songs from the Beatles' "White Album" with $400 of software.[20] According to the *Rolling Stone* Magazine, the album, which resulted from the creative combination, was "an ingenious hip-hop record that sounds oddly ahead of its time". Unfortunately for Brian Burton and hip-hop lovers, the owner of the rights to the Beatles' sound recordings, EMI, claimed that Burton's work amounted to copyright infringement and sent a "cease and de-

17 U.S. copyright law first developed and then codified in 1976 an open system of copyright exceptions - the so-called fair use doctrine - that is much wider than the sets of narrow copyright exceptions characterising the French and the other *droit d'auteur* regimes. After the 1976 reform of copyright law, the U.S. Code, Title 17, §107, provides a non-exhaustive list of fair use factors to be considered by courts when reviewing cases of copyright infringements. These factors include: (1) the purpose and character of the use, including whether such use is of a commercial nature or is for non-profit educational purposes; (2) the nature of copyrighted work; (3) the amount and substantiality of the portion used in relation to the copyrighted work as a whole; and (4) the effect of the use upon the potential market for or value of the copyrighted work.

18 Lessig, *The Future of Ideas*, op. cit., p. 9, significantly recalls that "Mix, rip and burn" was the instruction of a 2001 Apple Computer's advertisement urging "consumers" to do more than simply consume. As proudly admitted by Apple, devices such as Macintosh personal computers allow users to "mix" creative work ("meaning to reform it however the user wants"), to "rip" it ("meaning to copy it") and, more importantly, to "burn" it, that is "to publish it in a way that others can see and hear". Lessig stresses that, while Apple's devices provide technological tools to engage in transformative use, traditional copyright law and right holders' licences require end-users to ask permission to do all these things.

19 This example is owed to Van Howeling, 'Distributive Values in Copyright', op. cit., p. 1536.

20 See Van Howeling, 'Distributive Values in Copyright', op. cit., p. 1563.

sist letter" to the author and others who distributed "The Grey Album" in record stores and on the Internet.

Although much depends on the room left by national copyright legislation for the derivative work to be exempted from the original owner's permission, works such as "Tarnation" and "The Grey Album" might - in principle - qualify as pastiches, parodies or caricatures, in other words, uses that could turn out to be allowed under statutory copyright law when certain requirements are met. Where under U.S. law such requirements are enshrined in the fair use doctrine;[21] under the laws of the Member States of the European Union the identification of the same requirements depends mainly on different statutory or judicial interpretations of the author's exclusive right to authorise derivative works. This right (and its protection) is out of the scope of the InfoSoc Directive.[22]

1.5. Non-transformative use

As will be explained in more depth in the course of this book, laws forbidding the circumvention of technological protection measures (hereinafter "anti-circumvention laws"), such as those embodied in both the EU InfoSoc Directive and the U.S. Digital Millennium Copyright Act, do more that merely pre-empt transformative use. This new form of copyright protection for the digital era even limits non-transformative personal use, which - by definition - excludes uses which aim at direct commercialisation. This kind of non-commercial use is unregulated in the analogue world, but is subject to copyright control in the digital environment. The Free Software Foundation's creator, Richard Stallman, has predicted how the future enforcement of digital copyright law could impede end-users from engaging in the most inoffensive non-transformative use of creative works (*i.e.*, reading itself). In his "The right to read",[23] by projecting current trends in copyright protection, Stallman sets a fictional story in 2047 and pictures a world in which access to information is strictly controlled. In this world, Stallman tells us, the idea of "trusted" computing is wholly deployed: no one is allowed to read another's books without a licence, and each book has a copyright monitor that reports when and where a book is read, and by whom, to a hypothetical "Central Licensing" authority.[24] The time when anyone could go to a library and read journal articles and books without having to pay a fee has become a distant memory going

[21] See Title 17, §107, U.S. Code. In *Campbell* v. *Acuff-Rose, Inc.*, 841 U.S. 419 (1994) [114 S.Ct 1164 (1994)], the U.S. Supreme Court held that a rap version of the copyrighted song "Oh, Pretty Woman!" was a transformative work and could therefore be covered by the exception of fair use.

[22] See §3.3.1, see *infra*.

[23] See Stallman, 'The Right to Read', in *Free Software Free Society: selected essays of Richard M. Stallman*, GNU Press (Free Software Foundation), Boston 2002, p. 73.

[24] A brief overview of the concept of "trusted computing" is provided in Appendix I, §D, see *infra*.

back to the 1990s, when commercial and non-profit publishers started charging fees in exchange for permission to "access" printed materials.

As provocatively envisaged by this tale, digital copyright confers on right holders the exclusive right to authorise any access to and copying of protected information. This is a pervasive extension of proprietary regulation of use which has remained unregulated in the "real" or analogue world. As Lessig has noted, the core of regulation under traditional copyright law is copying, and extending the same legal approach conceived for real space to the digital world and to the Internet has had the effect of regulating what copyright law had previously left unregulated, namely, all uses that did not create a copy in real space (unless otherwise permitted as fair use).[25] This situation is not completely due to digitisation and technological protection measures, but to the copyright concept of "reproduction", which operates as an access "gate".[26] The consequent extension of the copyright scope in the digital world effectively means that simple, non-transformative use such as reading, studying, quoting, private copying and lending are not permitted without the contractual consent of the copyright owners and without the availability of code bypassing digital locks. In this new context, therefore, regulation of exceptions and limitations to a *de facto* draconian system of copyright protection is left to a complex interface established by copyright law, electronic contracts (or click-licences) which take place between copyright owners and end-users, and even more sophisticated technological measures which manage access to, and use of, copyrighted work. The expression "copyright exceptions interface" comes from Heide, who used it to refer to the inter-relationship between copyright, on the one hand, and contract and legal protection extended to technological measures used by copyright holders, on the other.[27]

---

25 See Lessig, *Free Culture: How Big Media Uses Technology and the Law to Lock Down Culture and Control Creativity*, The Penguin Press, New York 2004, pp. 139-40; ("[F]or while it may be obvious that in the world before Internet, copies were the obvious trigger for copyright law, upon reflection, it should be obvious that in the world with the Internet, copies should not be the trigger for copyright law [...] My claim is that the Internet should at least force us to rethink the conditions under which the law of copyright automatically applies, because it is clear that the current reach of copyright was never contemplated, much less chosen, by the legislators who enacted copyright law [...]").

26 See *infra*, §3.3.3.1.

27 Heide, 'Copyright, Contract and the Legal Protection of Technological Measures', op. cit., p. 1. According to this author, the above-mentioned expression refers to "how legislators envisage that users of copyright material can benefit from copyright exceptions despite attempts to restrain or prevent certain uses either through contract or technology [...] For users, the interface indicates what contractual restrictions can be considered to be null or void, and in what instances they can circumvent right-holders' technological measures".

1.6. The structure of the book

Given the situation described above, end-users' new expressive opportunities and enhanced expectations will be pre-empted if legislators do not ensure that the new interface established by digital-era copyright law, e-contracts and technological measures guarantees the effectiveness of uses which are lawful according to traditional copyright law. This book will attempt to analyse whether and how EU harmonisation of national copyright law for the digital environment accommodates copyright exceptions by permitting end-users to engage in both transformative and non-transformative use of copyrighted content.

It will be argued that the interface resulting from EU digital copyright law, e-contracts and technological protection, as currently envisaged by the InfoSoc Directive, leads to an implicit transfer of regulation, formerly provided by traditional copyright law, from public to private hands. It will be shown that this private legislation may dramatically diminish the freedom of end-users to interact with copyrighted work released in digital formats, despite the enhanced possibilities that these formats present for creative expression.

The book is structured in four parts. In Chapter 2, it is explained how, from a theoretical point of view, the increasing implementation and operation of technical measures and rights management technologies (such as DRM systems and "trusted" computing platforms) have the potential to restrict dramatically both the old and the new opportunities open to end-users to interact lawfully with copyrighted work in digital formats. Part Two examines the InfoSoc Directive, the legal framework established in the European Union in the face of the technological and economic change related to digitisation. This analysis demonstrates how the harmonisation process undertaken in the EU in order to afford stronger and immediate protection to copyright holders does, in fact, ignore the constitutional provisions and objectives laid down in the Treaty Establishing the European Community ("EC Treaty"). These include clauses on culture and consumer protection as well as the achievement of a European Internal Market for information goods.

These inconsistencies between the harmonisation of copyright law and the EC Treaty lead to the discussion, in Part Three, of two case studies that shed light on the still-unsettled issues concerning the accommodation of the interests of certain end-users within two technological settings that are particularly troublesome. The first specifically concerns the Internet as a digitally networked environment in which end-users are increasingly able to engage in peer-to-peer transfer of creative works. The second scenario concerns all digital settings in which the operation of encryption and DRM technologies may preclude the effective enforcement of statutory copyright exceptions.

In Part Four, possible reforms of the EU copyright system will be analysed in order to propose specific solutions with regard to the definite issues raised by online copyright enforcement against unauthorised peer-to-peer transfer and the operation of DRM technology at the expense of end-user opportunities of free, legitimate use. This analysis will show that EU copyright law, as it stands, is unfit to accommodate end-user interests in digital settings, and would, as a consequence, need to be revised. This conclusion will be achieved after having clarified that, in the presence of copy- and access-control mechanisms enabled by DRM and similar technologies, EU law fails to provide legal tools which ensure the effective accessibility of digital copyrighted works for uses that are specifically permitted by law. Emphasis will be given to the fact that the InfoSoc Directive does not specify whether copyright exceptions which exempt certain socially-valuable uses from the copyright scope are to be treated (in the same way as certain rights of the consumer under consumer protection law) as having a non-derogable or "mandatory" nature, and, possibly, the character of subjective *rights*. In the analysis of this delicate issue, some guidance will be given by the fact that Article 6(4) of the InfoSoc Directive already imposes a duty upon copyright holders and Member States to ensure the effectiveness of certain free uses, notwithstanding the operation of technological protection measures.[28] It will therefore have to be ascertained as to whether and how (*i.e.*, by means of which legal tools) the EU copyright law embodied in the InfoSoc Directive may be reformed in order to establish a fair balance between copyright protection and the accommodation of free uses that may continue to preserve the public interest by fostering the cultural enrichment of society even in the digitally networked environment.

28 See Article 6(4) of the InfoSoc Directive.

2. The impact of digitisation on the desirability of copyright exceptions

2.1. An economics-based introduction to the book problem

In the Introduction, the most important changes that digitisation has brought to the economics of creativity and to the dissemination of information were focused upon. The purpose of this chapter is to shed light on how the operation of technological protection measures and rights management technologies, such as DRM systems, has impacted upon the social desirability of copyright exceptions.

2.1.1. Works of intellect as public goods

Rights management technologies seek to eliminate the non-excludability of copyrighted information. Non-excludability is one aspect that makes works of intellect that are protected under copyright law a public good from an economic point of view. The economics of intellectual property effectively demonstrates that information is a public good which is characterised by concerns of under-production and under-utilisation.

The problem of underproduction stems from the non-excludable nature of information goods. A good is non-excludable when, once it is produced, it is impossible to exclude an individual from using that good even if he or she does not contribute to the cost of producing it. A classical example is that of a publisher who cannot stop the same book from being borrowed and read by several people.[29] This creates a risk that the creator will not have sufficient incentives to engage in creative invention and production. By making the good excludable (for some limited time), intellectual property rights aim to foster production by allowing creators to charge customers royalties for the consumption of that good.

While solving the problem of under-production, excludability addresses another fundamental characteristic of information goods: non-rivalry. To say that a good is "non-rival" means that its consumption by an individual does not reduce the quan-

---

29 The example is taken from Leveque and Ménière, *The Economics of Patents and Copyright*, Berkeley University Press, p. 4. This book is available at: www.cerna.ensmp.fr/PrimerForFree.html.

tity of the same good available to other people.[30] For instance, watching a film on TV does not prevent other viewers from consuming the same movie. In economic terms, non-rivalry implies that the marginal cost of serving an additional consumer is zero.[31]

If marginal cost is assumed to be zero for non-rival goods, then property rights permitting royalties to be charged to additional consumers lead to an inevitable "deadweight loss" to society. Indeed, if the good is made available at a price that is higher than the marginal cost (where the marginal cost is zero), only consumers who are willing to pay the price set by the right holder (that is to say, a price higher than zero) are allowed to benefit from the good. Consumers whose willingness to pay is higher than zero but lower than the price set by the right holder are thereby excluded from consumption, even if they would have consumed the good at no cost to anyone.

Like patent law, copyright law purports to solve the under-utilisation problem by granting exclusive rights only for a limited time, after which copyrighted creations fall into the public domain and become available to everyone.[32] It is generally acknowledged that the economic analysis of intellectual property started with Arrow, who considered works of intellect in the light of the two above-mentioned problems (*i.e.* non-excludability and non-rivalry) which goods covered by intellectual property rights present in terms of allocation of resources.[33] According to Ar-

---

30 It must be noted that non-rivalry of use and non-consumption by use are characteristics of *intellectual* goods. There are other public goods that, although non-rival, can be consumed (*e.g.*, military defence).

31 See Leveque and Ménière, *The Economics of Patents and Copyright*, op. cit, at p. 5. However, Lemley, 'Property, Intellectual Property, and Free Riding', John M. Olin Program in Law and Economics, Stanford Law School, Working Paper No. 291, August 2004, available at http://ssrn.com/abstract=582602, p. 29, points out that it is an oversimplification to say that the marginal cost (*i.e.* the cost to produce an additional unit) of non-rival goods is (always) zero ("Producing and selling copies of a CD requires manufacturing the disc and the case, producing copies of the cover and liner notes, wrapping the whole thing in plastic, delivering it to a store, and engage in a sales transaction. These costs may be low relative to the fixed costs of recording the CD, but they are not zero. The same is true for books, DVDs, and the machines or products that embody patented inventions [...]").

32 See Leveque and Ménière, *The Economics of Patents and Copyright*, op. cit., p. 5, who explain that, by offering an exclusive right for a limited period, intellectual property law solves "sequentially" the problems of non-excludability and non-rivalry ("Initially, the legal mechanism of protection makes the good excludable. Users are required to pay for the services offered, through royalties. Subsequently, when the work passes into the public domain, all consumers can access it free of charge. Intellectual property thus attempts to strike a balance between the incentive to create and innovate, and the diffusion of the results obtained.").

33 See Arrow, 'Economic Welfare and the Allocation of Resources for Inventions', in: Nelson (ed), *The Rate and Direction of Economic Activity: Economic and Social Factors*, Princeton University Press, Princeton 1962, p. 609, at pp. 614-16. For a recent account of these characteristics of information goods, see Leveque and Ménière, *The Economics of Patents and Copyright*, op. cit., p. 4; and Lemley, 'Property, Intellectual Property, and Free Riding', op. cit., p. 30.

row's taxonomy, many people can consume public goods without depletion, and it is difficult to identify those who will not pay and to prevent potential free riders from using those goods.

2.1.2. From imperfect to perfect excludability

Basic economics explains that creative works are non-excludable and non-rival. By providing an incentive to would-be creators, copyrights attached to works of intellect make new pieces of work excludable for a limited time. As recently pointed out by Lemley, intellectual property:

"is a conscious decision to create scarcity in a type of good in which it is ordinarily absent in order to artificially boost the economic returns to innovation [...]".[34]

In the non-digital world, though, the artificial excludability created by copyright law is limited not only in time, due to the limited duration of copyright, but also in scope, given that positive externalities make excludability highly imperfect.[35]

The non-rival nature of information ensures that the excludability provided by copyright, even in the most individualistic systems, does not amount to perfect control over protected work. Lemley has recently drawn upon such imperfect excludability to argue "in defence of free-riding".[36] In his view, the traditional attempt of intellectual property law to eliminate free-riding is, at least from a U.S. law perspective, groundless and has harmful consequences. He claims that such an attempt is a consequence of the inappropriate extension of the *real* property rhetoric to that of *intellectual* property. Unlike a finite natural resource, he argued, the subject matter of intellectual property, namely, information, is a non-rival good that cannot be depleted.[37] In economic terms, intellectual property is said not to generate negative externalities, as tangible property does. Consequently, why

---

34 See Lemley, 'Property, Intellectual Property, and Free Riding', op. cit., at p. 31. The artificial nature of scarcity of goods under intellectual property law was also strongly emphasised by Cohen, 'Lochner in Cyberspace. The New Economic Orthodoxy of "Rights Management"', (97) *Michigan Law Review* 1998, p. 462, at pp. 495-515.

35 An externality is positive when the benefits of an exchange or a use decision spill over to parties other than those explicitly engaged in the exchange or in the decision. A positive externality is generated, for instance, if landlords plant beautiful flowers in their front lawns: they are not able to capture the full benefit of those flowers, given that passers-by can enjoy them too. As explained by Cooter and Ulen, *Law and economics*, (fourth edition), Addison-Wesley, Boston 2004, p. 165, "when the utility or production functions of different people are interdependent, they impose benefits or costs on each other, regardless of whether or not they have agreed [to do so]. Such interdependence is called an externality, because the costs and the benefits are conveyed outside the market [...]". The rhetoric of property has regarded exclusively negative externalities, the costs of which are internalised by property rights. The classic example of a negative externality is given by pollution affecting air or water.

36 Lemley, 'Property, Intellectual Property, and Free Riding', op. cit., p. 17.

37 *Ibidem*, p. 25.

should exclusive rights on information goods be expected to share the same rationale? Given that an externality is conveyed outside the market and is not priced, internalising externalities amounts to pricing them.[38] The economic theory of property rights set out by theorists such as Coase, Demsetz and Hardin views property as a tool that internalises the negative externalities generated by transaction costs.

The well-known Coase Theorem demonstrates that the efficient use of resources would not depend on the assignment of property entitlements if transaction costs were non-existent.[39] In doing so, Coase implicitly specifies that property law becomes important only when there are transaction costs.

Demsetz explained that property rights are valuable in society because they limit the creation of uncompensated externalities: since multiple users of a common good impose costs on each other, giving control over the common good to a single owner ensures that that particular owner pays the full cost of his or her use of the property.[40] Hardin pictures joint or public ownership of a piece of property as an inefficient model, under which non-owners who use the property have no incentive to take care of it and may, therefore, overuse it.[41] Lemley stresses that none of these commentators has taken into account the specific non-excludable and non-rival nature of intellectual property, whose common use generates a "comedy", in which everyone can enjoy the good, rather than a "tragedy".[42] This is why Lemley concludes that the extension of the real property rationale to intellectual property is inappropriate.[43] On this view, most positive externalities produced by intellectual property are, and should remain, uncompensated.

Even if Lemley's claim best fits the U.S. utilitarian approach to copyright protection, it shows very clearly what harmful consequences would emerge if intellectual property law compensated virtually *all* of the positive externalities.[44] Such

---

38 See Cooter and Ulen, *Law and Economics*, op. cit., pp. 165-66.

39 The Coase Theorem was first elaborated in Coase, 'The Problem of Social Cost', (3) *Journal of Law and Economics* 1960, p. 1. According to this theorem, negotiation leads to an efficient allocation as long as property rights are clearly defined and there are no obstacles to deals among interested parties. In a hypothetical world where transaction costs are non-existent, each asset could be assigned a property right and an owner and each user would be compelled to pay to be able to use it.

40 See Demsetz, 'Toward a Theory of Property Rights', (57) *American Economic Review Papers and Proceedings* 1967, p. 347.

41 See Hardin, 'The Tragedy of the Commons', (162) *Science* 1968, p. 1243.

42 See Lemley, 'Property, Intellectual Property, and Free Riding', op. cit., pp. 8-11 and p. 26,

43 For a very similar explanation, see Lessig, *Code and Other Laws of Cyberspace*, Basic Books, New York 1999, pp. 130-135.

44 See Lemley, 'Property, Intellectual Property, and Free Riding', op. cit., pp. 26-27, who argues that "information goods create only positive externalities, and there is no general reason to worry about uncompensated positive externalities. Indeed, part of the point of intellectual property is to promote uncompensated positive externalities, by ensuring that ideas and works that might otherwise be kept secret are widely disseminated". The same argument is made by Lessig, *The Future of Ideas, The Fate of The Commons in a Connected World*, op. cit., p. 97 (who holds that producers are given a limited exclusive

a hypothetical excludability would raise social costs, both in terms of static and dynamic efficiency. According to economic theory, *static* efficiency is an economic objective that is achieved when the allocation of resources maximises surpluses.[45] To achieve this objective, the copyright system should be understood as promoting the use of works of intellect by the greatest number of users. Given that, by definition, copyright allows owners to raise prices above marginal costs, it creates deadweight losses by raising the prices paid by consumers. Such losses, which cause static inefficiency, therefore depend upon the duration and the scope of the exclusive rights.[46] If the notion of perfect excludability were effectively implemented, overly broad property rights would increase the deadweight loss inevitably generated by the granting of temporary monopoly rights under copyright law.

As regards *dynamic* efficiency, this notion refers to the improvement and renewal of creation techniques and intellectual works over time.[47] In this respect, perfect excludability of copyrighted works would diminish and delay the disclosure of new creations by stifling cultural and scientific progress and its incremental nature. The social cost of wholly eliminating free-riding on copyrighted content is dynamic because it results in giving creators control over all the positive externalities associated with their creations, including improvements and new uses that might be made of or to their works.[48] Benkler described this dynamic effect by saying that, considering that copyrighted information is both an input and an

right over their intellectual property, in such a way that "they can recover the costs of producing that property and receive a sufficient return to give them the incentives to produce that property. A 'sufficient return', however, is not perfect control, and intellectual property does not, therefore, give authors or inventors perfect control [...]").

45 See Leveque and Ménière, *The Economics of Patents and Copyright*, op. cit., pp. 5-6.

46 See Benkler, 'A political economy of the public domain: markets in information goods versus the marketplace of ideas', in: Dreyfuss, Zimmermann and First (eds), *Expanding the boundaries of intellectual property: innovation policy for the knowledge society*, Oxford University Press, Oxford-New York 2001, p. 266, at p. 271, who stresses that, in a static analysis, property rights that increase excludability reduce efficient consumption of information by permitting its price to be raised above its efficient demand price. See, also, Lemley, 'Property, Intellectual Property, and Free Riding', op. cit., pp. 35-36, who recalls how, in principle, this deadweight loss could be avoided if intellectual property owners had the power to perfectly price discriminate. This condition is rarely fulfilled, because it requires intellectual property right holders to have adequate information about the willingness to pay of their various customers. Although not always, the information costs are normally too high to be able to apply perfect price discrimination. However, as it is pointed out below (see §2.2.1) rights management technologies enhance the information supplier's ability to price discriminate by enabling suppliers to charge for all uses of the information valuable to users.

47 See Leveque and Ménière, *The Economics of Patents and Copyright*, op. cit., p. 6.

48 See Lemley, 'Property, Intellectual Property, and Free Riding', op. cit., p. 37 (who pointed out the eminently cumulative nature of innovation: "inventions are not created in a vacuum. They build on existing technology and ideas. But those ideas themselves were once new [...]").

output of the process of intellectual creation, a conflict exists between first and second-generation producers:

"the greater the rights (and hence incentives) of the first generation, the greater the costs (and hence the lower the incentives, or benefits net of costs) of the second generation."[49]

The conclusion of this reasoning is that the elimination of healthy free-riding would dramatically restrain the use of copyrighted information as an input to further creativity. In fact, only those whose willingness to pay equals the monopoly price charged by copyright holders would have the opportunity to access and build upon the protected ideas and the material embedded in the pre-existing work.[50]

2.1.3. Perfect lock-up of copyrighted information

DRM technologies bundled with copyrighted digital goods aim at establishing perfect excludability in the digital world. From an economic point of view, the excludability enabled by DRM systems, and, even more so, by trusted computing technologies, relies on the traditional principle of bundling a private good, for example, a given DRM technology, with content such as songs, texts or films. Bomsel and Geffroy have emphasised that, by making the content excludable and forcing people to pay for access, DRM systems work in the same way as a ticket system.[51] However, control and rights management technologies are different from other delivery goods and services, since they are not necessary for consumption. These authors have stressed that, whereas traditional physical formats and services can bring some additional value to the bundle (for example, where further information concerning the good is included, as in the case of disc designs, or where the physical format itself has an intrinsic artistic value, such as in the architecture of a concert hall), DRM systems are merely an exclusion tool, having "no other utility or additional value to the consumer than making him pay".[52]

Authors such as Wagner and Merges have expressed skepticism about the applicability of the notion of perfect excludability to the situation of copyrighted goods bundled with control and DRM technologies that exclude unauthorised parties from accessing and using such goods.[53] Merges argues that:

---

49 See Benkler, 'A political economy of the public domain', op. cit., p. 271.

50 The fact that information is both an input and on output in its production process was firstly emphasised by Scotchmer, 'Standing on the Shoulders of Giants: Cumulative Research and the Patent Law', (5) *Journal of Economic Perspectives* 1991, p. 29; and then by Benkler, 'A political economy of the public domain', op. cit., pp. 270-72; and Cohen, 'Lochner in Cyberspace', op. cit., p. 512 and pp. 547-48.

51 See Bomsel and Geffroy, *Economic Analysis of Digital Rights Management systems (DRMs)*, MediaNet Project Paper, reviewed version of 10 February 2005, available at: http://cerna.ensmp.fr, p. 14.

52 *Ibidem*.

53 See, generally, Wagner, 'Information Wants to Be Free: Intellectual Property and the Mythologies of Control', (103) *Columbia Law Review* 2003, p. 995; and Merges,

"[E]ven the strongest digital rights management system one might contemplate falls far short of total control over the information it protects from unwanted copying [...] there are many manifestations of digital content that cannot be effectively controlled by a right holder [...]".[54]

When referring to such uncontrollable aspects, however, Wagner and Merges rely on a rather weak (and, in my view, inappropriately market-oriented) example. In particular, for Wagner and Merges, perfect control is inconceivable because of the prohibitive costs which, for instance, the owner of a digital copyrighted film would face in order to prevent users from talking about the film with friends, or speaking about it while teaching a classroom full of students, or borrowing broad themes from the film in writing a short story, and so on.

The achievement of perfect (or almost perfect) excludability was not easy to predict when digital technology and its new media *par excellence*, the Internet, emerged, came to the fore and became diffused. Since that time, technology has evolved at a very rapid pace, running in two opposite directions. At a time when encryption and DRM technologies were not yet wholly developed, information became much easier and cheaper to produce and disseminate than in the analogue world. In the Internet's infancy, due to the peculiar, highly decentralised architecture of the new medium, web users were able to obtain enormous benefits from the unstoppable flows of creative work made available at no cost through a borderless, networked environment. At this stage, digital technology celebrated the non-excludable and non-rival nature of information to its greatest extent. The cost of copying and disseminating information approached zero, while the increasing ease in bypassing the hurdle of copyright protection and right holder intermediation gave users the firm conviction that the Internet was a land without copyright.[55]

Since the mid-1990s, it has been widely accepted that traditional copyright law would be unenforceable unless digital technologies could make protected information virtually inaccessible to unauthorised parties. It was considered that digital technology would have to provide the tools which created scarcity in relation to copyrighted digital work.[56] To this end, the copyrighted content that flooded onto the Internet (as well as other easily reproducible media) had to be packaged in secured digital boxes in order to be distributed commercially, in the same way that wine needs bottles to be sold on the market.[57] With the implementation of DRM

'Compulsory Licensing vs. the Three "Golden Oldies"', (508) *Policy Analysis*, 15 January 2004, available at: http://www.cato.org, p. 5.

54 See Merges, 'Compulsory Licensing vs. the Three "Golden Oldies"', op. cit. at p. 5.

55 See, generally, Farchy, *Internet et le droit d'auteur, La culture Napster*, CNRS Editions, Paris 2003.

56 See the prophetic view expressed by Clark, 'The Answer to the Machine is in the Machine', in: Hugenholtz (ed), *The Future of Copyright in a Digital Environment*, Kluwer Law International, The Hague 1996, p. 139.

57 The metaphor is taken from Barlow, 'The Economics of Ideas. Selling Wine Without Bottles on the Global Net', downloaded at: http://homes.eff.org/~barlow/EconomyOfIdeas.html.

technologies, and, even more so, with the possible implementation of trusted computing platforms on end-user computers, it is possible to conclude that, what once flowed freely, may now be sold in bottles.[58] Modern technological protection and rights management capabilities give copyrighted information an unprecedented degree of excludability. Most importantly, access to and use of digitally embedded information can be both restricted and licensed in accordance with price-discrimination schemes, which allow right holders to exploit better consumer willingness to pay in exchange for flexible ranges of permission or uses.

2.2. Legal consequences

While commenting on the virtually perfect lock-up of digital copyrighted information, the views of economists and legal scholars divided into two fronts.[59] On the one hand, the supporters of a "freedom of contract" view of copyright welcomed the implementation of DRM systems by arguing that technology would finally provide an unprecedented environment for frictionless market transactions, in which information goods could be marketed at a very flexible range of prices which reflect the different degrees of willingness, on the part of the users, to pay for access to and use of copyrighted works.[60] On the other hand, defenders of a "public domain" view of copyright have claimed that such privatisation, in the absence of legislative re-adjustments and monitoring systems, could erase the balanced nature of the public law of copyright.[61] Privately enforceable licences would create access and usage conditions which, in the past, were subject to public regulation and whose enforcement was ultimately guaranteed by means of judicial review. According to the "public domain" approach, only by means of public regulation could the complexity of the subject matter of copyright be better understood without being reduced to a simple commodity.

Drawing upon issues raised by both the "freedom of contract" camp and the "public domain" camp, it will be pointed out that technological protection and management of copyrighted material does not necessarily weaken the need for so-

---

[58] An overview of the notion of "trusted computing platforms" is provided in the Appendix I, §D, see *infra*.

[59] See O'Rourke, 'Copyright Pre-emption After the ProCD Case: A Market-Based Approach', (12) *Berkeley Technology Law Journal* 1997, p. 53.

[60] The views of the above-mentioned front are oversimplified and do not give a detailed account of the differences existing among the contributions of authors such as Hardy, 'Property (and Copyright) in Cyberspace', *University of Chicago Legal Forum* 1996, p. 217; O'Rourke, 'Copyright Preemption After the ProCD Case', op. cit., p. 53; Merges, 'The End of Friction? Property Rights and Contract in the "Newtonian" World of On-line Commerce', (12) *Berkeley Technology Law Journal* 1997, p. 115; Bell, 'Fair Use vs. Fared Use: The Impact of Automated Rights Management on Copyright's Fair Use Doctrine', (76) *North Carolina Law Review* 1998, p. 557.

[61] The opposite view is well represented by authors such as Cohen, 'Lochner in Cyberspace', op. cit.; and Benkler, 'An Unhurried View of Private Ordering in Information Transactions', (53) *Vanderbilt Law Review* 2000, p. 2063.

ciety to have a system of effective copyright exceptions in the digital environment. Instead, it is maintained that the new technologies pose a dilemma about whether private actors should be entitled to establish licence and sale conditions that preempt the enforcement of fair use rights.

2.2.1. In search of a public policy without free access to copyrighted works

Scholars who support a "freedom of contract" view of copyright have argued that the possible restriction of the rights of users by means of electronic, self-enforceable licences should not give rise to particular concern. In their view, such a model of dissemination for copyrighted content would leave end-users and society better off by pursuing the objectives that were formerly ensured by copyright exceptions.[62] As Bell has advocated, if social welfare is defined as the sum of the wealth generated by private transactions, the replacement of "fair" use by "fared" use in the digital world would best serve the public interest.[63] Thus, most scholars from the law and economics movement have argued that the unlimited control ensured by control and rights management technologies is likely to permit the most efficient allocation of entitlements over intellectual creation.

The efficiency of perfect control over copyrighted goods is said to stem from a number of considerations. First, it is argued that the ability of suppliers to license by price-discriminating among different typologies of access to and use of digital goods would allow a better extraction of the willingness of users to pay and thereby mitigate the deadweight losses inevitably created by copyrights.[64] For instance, Wagner has argued that, in a regime where tight digital control over downloaded content is practicable, copyright owners may have an incentive to distribute their work more widely than they do in environments characterised by easy copying. Consequently, under a regime of greater control, the total amount of cultural information made available to the public might ultimately increase.[65]

Second, it is said that if suppliers are able to charge for *all* uses that are valuable to users, then users can use price signaling to inform suppliers as to which goods they value most. This signaling would, in turn, enable suppliers to increase the production of those goods for which users are willing to pay most. As Goldstein has argued:

---

62 Exponents of the "freedom of contract" approach have contended that its model would increase the value realised by both producers and consumers of information by enabling the formation of markets. See Hardy, 'Property (and Copyright) in Cyberspace', op. cit., pp. 242-52; O'Rourke, 'Copyright Preemption After the ProCD Case', op. cit., pp. 70-71; Bell, 'Fair Use vs. Fared Use', op. cit., pp. 601-08; and Merges, 'Compulsory Licensing vs. the Three "Golden Oldies"', op. cit., pp. 6-10.

63 See Bell, 'Fair Use vs. Fared Use', op. cit., pp. 587-90.

64 See Easterbrook, 'Cyberspace vs. Property Law?', (4) *Texas Review of Law and Policy* 1999, p. 103.

65 See Wagner, "Information Wants to Be Free", op. cit., p. 1009.

"the logic of property rights dictates their extension into every corner in which people derive enjoyment and value from literary and artistic works. To stop short of these ends would deprive producers of the signals of consumer preference that trigger and direct their investments."[66]

Third, it is maintained that the combination of strong property rights, control and rights management technologies, and electronic contracts gives both the suppliers and the consumers of copyrighted goods the opportunity to achieve the most efficient allocation of price and access. According to Merges, the crucial assumption is that private parties are in a better position to know the correct level of access and use at a given price than public officials (*i.e.*, legislators, judges, and regulatory agencies).[67]

However, supporters of the "public domain" view of copyright have widely criticised this market-based approach.[68] In their opinion, notwithstanding the advent of technologies that ensure perfect excludability, the economic nature of copyrighted goods remains the same: as Benkler has persuasively pointed out, the fact that encryption technology eliminates (partial) non-excludability does not affect the assumption that information goods are non-rival and that their marginal costs remain zero. If we assume, as Benkler does, that creators will produce a good because they will be able to exclude *all* consumers and sell it at a price that covers their investments in the production of the good, that is to say, a price that is higher than its marginal costs, the good will be under-utilised when it is sold.[69] Standard economics explains that a good is produced and consumed efficiently only when it is sold at its marginal costs. Therefore, it is incorrect to conclude that perfect exclusion enables an efficient production of the good.[70] Benkler's criticism examines other assumptions of the "freedom of contract" view and finds that they cannot be proved. There is no empirical evidence, he argues, that private parties can identify, any better than public officials, the most efficient allocation of control over the access and use of copyrighted information.[71] The argument defending the supposed superiority of contracts in designing the solution that seems best to private parties would be particularly ill-suited if one takes into account the fact that the terms of all mass-market transactions regarding copyrighted goods are not individually negotiated, but are instead fixed by the suppliers who hold intellectual property rights and who thus (probably) enjoy market power.[72] Nor is it certain

66 See Goldstein, *Copyright's Highway: The Law & Lore of Copyright from Gutenberg to the Celestial Jukebox*, Hill and Wang, New York 1994, pp. 178-79.

67 See Merges, 'Compulsory Licensing vs. the Three "Golden Oldies"', op. cit., at pp. 6-10.

68 See Cohen, 'Lochner in Cyberspace', op. cit., pp. 495-515; Benkler, 'An Unhurried View', op. cit., pp. 2066-76.

69 Benkler, 'An Unhurried View', op. cit., p. 2066.

70 *Ibidem*, p. 266.

71 See Benkler, 'An Unhurried View', op. cit., pp. 2067-69.

72 See Benkler, 'An Unhurried View', op. cit., pp. 2078-79, who specifies that the above-mentioned "market power" refers to a necessary design feature of intellectual property rights over information goods. Indeed, as Benkler argues, if such rights were designed "in a manner that failed to give their owners some power to control price, they would

that deadweight losses for society would be reduced by price discrimination. The social gain attained by the increase in the number of the consumers who can afford to pay for access to copyrighted work under price-discriminating licences should be compared with the social loss caused by the exclusion from access of all those potential consumers whose willingness to pay exceeds the marginal costs of the good, but does not match the lowest of the prices set by the suppliers.[73] It would, thus, be a matter of empirical analysis to assess whether the social gain ensured by price-discrimination outweighs or not the loss determined by the subsequent foreclosure of the previously non-excludable aspects of copyrighted goods.

A brief comparison of these two lines of reasoning clearly defines the question raised, as regards public policy, by the introduction and operation of encryption and management technologies.[74] The question is whether private actors should be legally entitled to establish technical and contractual conditions which transform the above-mentioned *imperfect* excludability of copyrighted goods into *perfect* enclosure, with the consequential foreclosure of information which was previously available to anyone in the public domain, and which ensured the compatibility of copyright law with constitutional, non-market values such as freedom of speech and expression. Under the private ordering regime pictured by Bell, access would depend exclusively on the willingness of users to pay, which would leave no room for the intervention of public law to safeguard social values that imperfect control over information generates in the non-digital world. The private ordering regime would even eliminate statutory copyright exceptions on the assumption that pure market mechanisms would produce the most desirable conditions under which users would be allowed to access and use copyrighted goods.

In the absence of statutorily mandated public access, users willing to engage in either transformative or non-transformative uses for both commercial and non-commercial purposes might be caught in a paradoxical situation in which they would not know for what they were paying.[75] The value of any given piece of digitally-protected information, if not provided free of charge through commercial samples, would be so uncertain that most users would not have an incentive to pay

fail, for the price of information would be driven to its marginal cost of zero, and the incentive effect [...] would be lost". Benkler firmly believes that, "in the presence of market power we have no systematic reason to think, *a priori*, that the terms of access negotiated will be socially optimal, any more than we have reason to think that the price of access will be socially optimal [...] This may be an empirically determinable question, but it is not determined as a matter of theory by noting that private parties have better information about their own interests than public officials [...]".

73 See Benkler, 'An Unhurried View', op. cit., pp. 2075-76.

74 See, generally, Lessig, *Code and Other Laws of Cyberspace*, op. cit., pp. 122-141.

75 See Cohen, 'Lochner in Cyberspace', op. cit., at p. 548 ("If the public is willing to pay the prices set by copyright owners, we must ask what the public believes it is paying for, and what copyright owners believe they are selling. Any answer to that question must take existing statutorily-mandated public access and use rights into account."); and Benkler, 'An Unhurried View', op. cit., p. 2076 (who argues that, from a social policy perspective, the high uncertainty as to the value of any given piece of information is one of the most interesting reasons that might result in users being unwilling to pay enough to gain access to more perfectly excluded information).

in order to discover what lies behind the encryption technology. This potential foreclosure of access to copyrighted digital works might have the consequence of stifling the "spiral" process of intellectual production by depriving users, including follow-on authors, of the primary sources of knowledge and input for the creation of new works. This situation of enclosed digital works would lead to a *de facto* commodification of information which copyright protection was unable to cover before the advent of access-control technologies and anti-circumvention laws.[76] This kind of potentially foreclosed information, which was previously available to everyone for subsequent uses and whose free accessibility is threatened now, is indicated, especially in the U.S. legal scholarship, as information "commons".[77]

In this respect, Cohen has argued that perfect lock-up of copyrighted information, enabled by contracts and by "code", would ensure the economic compensation of previously uncompensated positive externalities or benefits. This change, she emphasises:

"[w]ould not simply re-allocate a fixed, immutable surplus from consumers to producers. Instead, the property-and-contract-based model [...] would fundamentally alter the social welfare equation. The change would be both (re-) distributive and qualitative; some shared social benefits would be replaced by privately-appropriated ones."[78]

Additionally, the property-and-contract-based model mentioned by Cohen would raise high costs in terms of public policy by considerably restricting both transformative and non-transformative uses. With non-transformative use, the fact that the rights of users might rest exclusively upon the provision of electronic, self-enforceable contracts would encourage the granting of narrow, standardised licenses regarding non-commercial use.[79] Benkler is right that strict budget constraints are likely to typify users who seek access to information for non-commercial reasons. In the absence of free access, the mere "right to read" advocated by Stallman would be regarded as the cheapest form of permission.[80] As for transformative use, the new expressive opportunities open to users would hardly be accommodated at all. Indeed, the more "pieces" of protected work that users need in order to engage in transformative use, the more expensive (and the more unlikely) their opportunity to play the role of second-generation authors by building upon original work will become. The inexpensiveness of creativity ensured by the recourse to digital devices which enable an unprecedented degree of interaction with pre-existing content would be wholly offset by the increasing cost that would result from billed access and the re-utilisation of digitally locked-in material. In my view, first of all, the generalisation of pay-per-access and pay-per-use

76 See Boyle, 'The Second Enclosure Movement', op. cit., pp. 37-38.

77 See Lessig, *The Future of Ideas*, op. cit., pp. 19-20, where this author defines the "commons" as a resource to which anyone within the relevant community has a right without obtaining the permission of anyone else.

78 See Cohen, 'Lochner in Cyberspace', op. cit, p. 550.

79 See Benkler, 'An Unhurried View', op. cit., p. 2076.

80 See *supra*, §1.5.

patterns would encourage only *passive* consumption (if any) at the expense of the proactive use of quotations, extracts, parodies, pastiches and other re-creations (which would hardly be appreciated or enthusiastically authorised by the copyright owners of the original works). But most importantly, the commercial enclosure of digital copyrighted content would alter the iterative character of innovation in science and the arts by billing access and lessening the degree of disclosure of new creations to the public. Consequently, it is submitted that law-makers must reflect upon and then adopt an explicit position on the expansion of the reach of copyright in the new digital environment and how it may be counter-balanced with legislative measures which safeguard the old goals of public policy.

2.2.2. DRM and the economics of copyright exceptions

In the last section, it was pointed out that the non-market values traditionally preserved in copyright law might be erased if DRM technologies were understood to be a good reason to abandon public monitoring of the dissemination of copyrighted work. The following analysis of the economics of copyright exceptions intends to show how DRM technologies have an impact upon these economics.

2.2.2.1. Transaction costs and the market failure behind private copying

Copyright systems have usually taken account of particular cases in which transaction costs exceed the benefits of deals which authorise the use of protected material. In the field of intellectual property, the problem raised by transaction costs refers to whether such costs are higher or lower than the gain of the negotiation.[81] Transactions are costly in the real world because potential buyers and sellers need to be identified, the drafting of a sale or a licence contract requires time and expertise, performance is difficult to measure, and the agreements have to be enforced.[82] If these costs are expected to exceed the gain of the parties involved, then deals are likely to fail, and consequently, transferable assets will not be allocated in the most efficient way.

The problem of transaction costs was enhanced dramatically by the increasing availability of copying devices (for example, video cassette recorders in the 1990s), which empowered end-users to engage in private copying while eroding the copyright holders' monopoly in the dissemination of copyrighted work. Such

---

81 See Leveque and Ménière, *The Economics of Patents and Copyright*, op. cit., pp. 11-12; Cooter and Ulen, *Law and Economics*, op. cit., pp. 85-99. Copyright law provides creators with exclusive, transferable and enforceable entitlements over their work. Law and economics theorists explain that transferability ensures that each resource is used by the party who values it most. The effects on efficiency of property rights negotiation are the subject of the well-known Coase Theorem referred to earlier in the main text.

82 See Merges, 'The End of Friction? Property Rights and Contract in the "Newtonian" World of On-line Commerce', op. cit., p. 116 (where the author focuses on "Varieties of Transaction Costs").

private use would (absurdly) have made it necessary for right holders to enter users' households in order to license an endless number of private reproductions. The unbearable costs implied by this hypothetical bargaining, together with the fact that copyright enforcement would have faced the obstacle of end-user privacy, led to market failure because the transaction costs of a voluntary transfer were so high that a consensual transfer was unlikely to take place spontaneously.[83] In the face of market failure, the law-makers' reactions proved to be quite different. Germany and other European countries sought to establish alternative forms of compensation to classical property rights through the implementation of statutory licences which took the form of levies on copying equipment and recordable formats. In the United States, in contrast, the discussion on the effects of uncontrollable home-taping upon markets for copyrighted goods gave rise to a rationalisation of the theory of fair use. In her article "Fair Use as Market Failure", Gordon relied upon one of the fair use factors listed in Section 107 of the U.S. Copyright Act – the impact of the supposedly fair use on the (potential) market for and value of the copyright[84] – to argue that private copying of copyrighted material was fair when users were unable to purchase the desired use on the market and where the transfer of the control of the use served the public interest without impairing the incentives of the copyright owners.[85] Gordon's theory highlighted that the application of the fair use doctrine made sense when no functioning market for copyrighted goods existed. Under this innovative view, private copying was wholly exempted from the reach of copyright, with no room for the economic compensation of copyright owners.

2.2.2.2. *Why the market failure rationale behind private copying is losing its significance*

It seems undisputable to me that Gordon's market failure argument is considerably weakened by today's increasing implementation of access-control and copy-control technologies. In cyberspace, at the very least, copyrighted goods may be marketed directly to the end-user under contractual and technological conditions which prevent the public from engaging in unauthorised use, and provide information suppliers with systems to monitor such use. In 1997, Merges observed that:

> "because electronic exchange potentially eliminates the market failure rationale for digital content, fair use law will significantly shrink, or an alternative basis for fair use will be rediscovered."[86]

---

83 See Merges, 'The End of Friction', op. cit., p. 130.

84 See U.S. Code, Title 17, Charter 1, §107: "[…] In determining whether the use made of a work in any particular case is a fair use the factors to be considered shall include […] (4) the effect of the use upon the potential market for or value of the copyrighted work."

85 See Gordon, 'Fair Use as Market Failure: A Structural and Economic Analysis of the Betamax Case and Its Predecessors', (82) *Columbia Law Review* 1982, p.1600.

86 See Merges, 'The End of Friction', op. cit., p. 130.

In discussing how digital technology and cyberspace have had an impact on transaction costs, Merges expressed his skepticism regarding the assumption that the on-line environment would make such costs negligible.[87] However, he admitted that technologies which provide encryption and self-reporting content would considerably reduce the monitoring and enforcement costs associated with information exchanges. If these technologies worked perfectly, this author argued, the market failure approach to fair use would have a very limited future because creators could craft individualised restrictions on use in bilateral relations built upon property rights.[88]

Given that Gordon's theory was based on the likelihood of market formation, the fair use defence was applicable to pursue the public interest better in areas where no functioning markets existed. But the fact that new technology enables unprecedented markets to form does considerably narrow the breadth of the market failure. In principle, as long as control and rights management technologies allow copyright owners and end-users to enter smoothly into licences regarding pieces of copyrighted work, the rationale for allowing "fair use" cannot apply. In this respect, the fact that two U.S. judgments have concluded that the fair use defence, as interpreted by Gordon's theory, is not applicable where market-making institutions exist and provide would-be users with the possibility of seeking and obtaining permission to engage in certain use of copyrighted work needs to be considered here. In *American Geophysical Union* v. *Texaco, Inc.*,[89] the U.S. Second Circuit found that corporate photocopies of the plaintiff's scientific publications could not be excused under the fair use doctrine because there was an institution organised as a clearing house for photocopying royalties, and because the clearing house had established a viable market for licensing the rights of reproduction and distribution for individual journal articles. Then, in *Princeton University Press* v. *Michigan Document Services, Inc.*,[90] the Sixth Circuit dismissed the fair use claim of a copy shop for the sale of university course packets assigned by University of Michigan professors because the plaintiffs had set up specific permission departments. Both judgments declined to uphold these fair use claims because of the absence of market failure. Indeed, in the view of these courts, the existence of an established derivative market for licences implied that the plaintiffs deserved protection from economic harm in accordance with the fourth factor contained in Section 107 of the U.S. copyright statute with regard to fair use (*i.e.*, as noted above, the effect of a given use upon the potential market for and value of the copyrighted work).[91]

---

87 *Ibidem*, p. 130.

88 *Ibidem*, p. 128.

89 *American Geophysical Union, et al.* v. *Texaco Inc.*, 60 F.3d 913 (2nd Circuit 1994).

90 *Princeton University Press, Macmillan, Inc., et al.* v. *Michigan Document Services, Inc., et al.*, 99 F.3d 1381 (6th Circuit 1996).

91 See §1.4., footnote 17, see *supra*. Beyond the market failure argument, it must be admitted that, in both the examined cases, the two U.S. courts could have dismissed the above-mentioned fair use claims even by considering, on the grounds of the first factor of the doctrine codified under §107 of the U.S. Copyright Act, that in both the examined cases the unauthorised copying had no private (*i.e.*, personal) character. The first

Considering that DRM systems promise to ensure the establishment of easier, cheaper and perfectly enforceable contracts between the users and the suppliers of copyrighted information, situations of market failure would disappear in the hypothetical situation in which these technologies of control were effectively implemented on the vast majority of hardware and digital media. In Merges' review of fair use, Gordon's theory still remains valid, although it must be developed in order to apply to the fast-changing markets that are emerging in the digital world. As Merges points out, Gordon's rationalisation of fair use did not specify how permanent the market failure must be for the defence to be activated.[92] Drawing upon Gordon's model as understood in *American Geophysical Union* v. *Texaco, Inc.* and *Princeton University Press* v. *Michigan Document Services, Inc.*, Merges contends that, "where a market could develop if copyrights are enforced, the absence of an initial market should not automatically lead to the implementation of the fair use defence".[93] From this point of view, fair use should apply only when market development is unlikely, bearing in mind that the likelihood of market development must be assessed carefully and within a reasonable period of time. If the market failure rationale were applied without any determination of whether or not new markets have a chance of developing, new forms of commercial exploitation could be killed by an inappropriate application of fair use. Interestingly, at the end of his article, Merges goes beyond the position taken earlier in reviewing the validity of Gordon's model for the realm of cyberspace. First, he suggests that:

"[I]f we are unsure whether a market for a certain use of copyrighted works will develop, why not fully enforce the rights and see whether the market follows? At the very least, we should grant the firms and individuals in the field an opportunity to explore the creation of a market mechanism. If, after some reasonable period of time, no potential market takes shape, then perhaps fair use is in order [...]".[94]

Later, after having commented on the two above-mentioned cases, and having shown deference to Gordon's theory, Merges concluded, perhaps too optimistically, that Gordon's reasoning has to be abandoned for cyberspace by assuming that a market for the copyrighted work will certainly form.[95]

2.2.2.3. The persistence of "bargaining breakdown" problems

Gordon's model is not the only rationalisation of the fair use doctrine based upon a market failure argument. Interestingly enough, another purely market-related model persuasively demonstrates that the doctrine of fair use in the U.S. and the

---

factor of the fair use doctrine requires courts to consider the purpose and character of the use, including whether such use is of a commercial nature or is for non-profit educational purposes.

92 See Merges, 'The End of Friction', op. cit., pp. 130-31.

93 *Ibidem*, p. 131.

94 See Merges, 'The End of Friction', op. cit., p. 131.

95 *Ibidem*, p. 135 ("Rather than focusing on whether a market might form for the copyrighted work, we should assume it will.").

exemptions of transformative uses from the scope of copyright in *droit d'auteur* systems can still play an important function in the digital environment. Scholars such as Merges, Parisi and Depoorter have emphasised that control and rights management technologies do not eliminate all the transaction costs from digital markets for copyrighted goods. Such costs are dramatically reduced on markets for non-transformative uses, where end-users of copyrighted material behave essentially as consumers and the establishment of electronic permission systems reduces only search or tracing costs.[96] But savings are not expected with regard to bargaining costs which affect markets for derivative works, where users have the potential to behave as second-generation authors.[97] As noted earlier, new technology empowers most users to engage easily in the production of complex derivative work. If users had to seek and obtain permission from all copyright holders over the materials they wished to include in their derivative creations, bargaining costs would increase proportionally to the number of original copyright owners involved in the negotiation.[98] In the absence of copyright exceptions which exempt transformative uses (*e.g.*, quotations, parodies, *etc*) under certain circumstances, the risk of breakdown in the bargaining between first- and second-generation authors would lead to failures in the markets for derivative creations. Depoorter and Parisi explain that such failures are more likely to take place where different pieces of pre-existing work, seen as factors of production, are strictly complementary (that is, when they are not substitutable with other comparable sources of material) and where copyrights belong to different holders. They argue that, from an economic point of view, when original works built upon pre-existing works are strictly complementary, market failures mainly depend upon the fact that copyright owners can impose external costs on the sellers of other complementary input, due to the cross-price effects between the goods.[99] Under this condition, which replicates the so-called "Tragedy of the Anti-commons", the owners of original copyrighted work might be unable to co-ordinate the price(s) of granting permission among themselves, and the subsequent unsatisfactory pricing may lead

96 See Depoorter and Parisi, 'Fair Use and Copyright Protection: a Price Theory Explanation', George Mason Law & Economics Research Paper No. 01/2003, available at: http://papers.ssrn.com/sol3/papers.cfm?abstract_id=259298, p. 10.

97 See Merges, 'The End of Friction', op. cit., p. 133 ("Where market failure is based on factors other than locating a right holder and proposing a deal, the logic of fair use still makes sense; some varieties of market failure exist beyond the simple case of costly market-making.").

98 See Depoorter and Parisi, 'Fair use and copyright protection', op. cit., pp. 14-20 and pp. 25-26. The point made by these authors draws on the economic theory of so-called "double marginalisation" in the presence of complementary goods, which was spelt out firstly by Cournot, *Recherches sur les principes mathématiques de la théorie de la richesse*, Hachette, Paris 1838.

99 See Depoorter and Parisi, 'Fair use and copyright protection', op. cit., pp. 17-19, showing that independent pricing of copyright licences for the production of a final derivative work results in a sub-optimal equilibrium as long as original inputs are strictly complementary. In contrast, in the case of perfect substitutability of the various copyrights as factors of production, the owner of the copyright covering a "piece" of original work is unable to impose any external cost on the owners of other copyrighted material.

to bargaining failure.[100] In the field of copyright protection, Deporter and Parisi have examined the problem of the "anti-commons" by considering the case of two copyright holders having autonomous exclusion rights over two distinct original works. In their hypothesis, if such works are non-substitutable (*i.e.*, complementary) input for the production of a derivative work (*e.g.*, an anthology or a critical review), each copyright owner enjoys the right to exclude others from taking advantage of not just his own original work, but also of the original work of the other right holder.[101]

However, according to Merges, the problem of possible "bargaining breakdown" on the markets for transformative use, in particular parodies, stems from the fact that the original right holders are likely to refuse permission to parodists (or other second-generation authors) on non-rational grounds.[102] Pursuant to this view, market failure unrelated to legitimate reservation prices (*i.e.*, the willingness of users to pay) is understood as a good reason for removing copyright protection in order to justify the legal coercion of a transfer that ultimately serves social goals.[103] Merges makes the crucial point that, by exempting parodies from having to obtain the permission of the rights holder, the application of the fair use doctrine avoids the depletion of social commentary and ends up pursuing "redistributive" objectives. He concludes that, from this perspective, fair use can profitably be understood as a "tax" on copyright holders for the benefit of certain classes of users. The only relevant questions, in his view, are how to identify which class(es) of users should be allowed to bypass the presumptive market, and how much revenue the copyright holder should be obliged to forego to serve the redistributive goals of fair use.[104]

---

100 The "Tragedy of Anti-commons" – a mirror-image of Hardin's "Tragedy of the Commons" - is a concept recently revitalised by Heller, 'The Tragedy of the Anticommons: Property in the Transition from Marx to Markets', (111) *Harvard Law Review* 1998, p. 621, with regard to the transition to market institutions in contemporary Russia. Heller argued that the under-use of storefronts in Moscow was due to the presence of too many players (local, regional, federal government agencies, *etc*) holding the right to prevent their use.

101 See Depoorter and Parisi, 'Fair use and copyright protection', op. cit., pp. 14-15.

102 See Merges, 'The End of Friction', op. cit., p. 133, arguing that, on the market for parodies "…market exchange fails to occur for reasons other than because buyers and sellers cannot cost-effectively find each other […] the failure to agree occurs for reasons that a rational party would not entertain. A parodist willing to pay reasonable compensation may be turned away […]".

103 As put by Merges, 'The End of Friction', op. cit., p. 133, "a voluntary bilateral exchange, in other words, is important – but exchange itself (which might be better called dissemination) is more important still".

104 See Merges, 'The End of Friction', op. cit., p. 135.

2.2.2.4. Which justifications are affected by the implementation of DRM?

The above-mentioned analysis of the economic justifications behind copyright exceptions which enable private copying and transformative uses, such as quotations and parodies, shows that the ultimate purpose of these exceptions was the pursuit of the public interest, at least when the markets for copyrighted goods failed to form or function effectively. This conclusion was derived by scholars who focussed on the U.S. copyright system and the fair use doctrine, which developed basically as a judge-made doctrine (later codified) that identifies and excludes, *ex post,* certain uses from the copyright scope in order to protect certain principles, such as freedom of expression.

From a market-based perspective, the exemption of certain uses under the fair use doctrine was deemed to solve either the problem of transaction costs (that is, unenforceable private copying), or cases of "bargaining breakdown" (in the case of transformative uses). With respect to transaction costs, the limitation of copyright served the purpose of enabling the dissemination of copyrighted works when market mechanisms failed to form. As for bargaining breakdown, the exemption for uses such as parodies and quotations facilitated original, derivative works of authorship to the benefit of end-users who acted as second-generation authors.

The economic analysis of the impact of control and rights management technologies on the social desirability of copyright exceptions provides evidence of two different conclusions. With regard to private copying, the market failure rationale upholding this exception considerably diminishes in importance because these technologies have the potential to enable copyright owners to monitor and license private copying opportunities. For instance, the Fairplay DRM system implemented by Apple Computer on the iTunes online music platform allows the consumers of music downloads to make personal copies of each purchased download on a limited number of personal computers.[105]

As far as transformative uses are concerned, the above analysis shows that the implementation of DRM technologies does not address and solve problems of bargaining breakdown. This is particularly unfortunate if it is considered that the main characteristics of digital settings, and especially the Internet, while immensely enhancing the opportunities for wide, cheap and easy commentary upon copyrighted works, increase the social desirability of transformative use exemptions. However, the implementation of DRM technologies has the potential to prevent in a systematic manner end-users from engaging in lawful transformative uses by disabling (and contractually prohibiting) all unauthorised operations, for example, quoting, extracting, editing and so forth, without which any transformative purpose regarding protected materials is simply not viable. An example of this situation is given by the encrypting and management possibilities enabled by the rights management technology recently released by Adobe Systems.[106]

---

[105] See "Usage rules" at: http://www.apple.com/legal/itunes/us/service.html.

[106] See Patrizio, 'Adobe Right Management Server Extends to Office', available at: http://www.internetnews.com, 17 November 2006. For instance, the last product launched by Adobe (called "LiveCycle Policy Server 7.2") is an update to its enterprise

As pointed out below,[107] the lack of adequate consideration under the InfoSoc Directive for the effective enforcement of copyright exceptions in the presence of DRM technologies has the consequence of foreclosing valuable uses of copyrighted works, while at the same time forbidding courts from examining *ex post* the conformity with the law of such uses through a case-by-case analysis.[108]

2.2.3. Privacy concerns

In Germany and other European legal systems, the statutory exception of private copying was accompanied by the legislative implementation of remuneration schemes based on levies to be charged on various copying equipment and recordable formats. Despite the occurrence of the same situation of market failure which was highlighted above, the main policy objective of this statutory exception was that of protecting the privacy of end-users from copyright infringement claims while ensuring compensation for copyright holders in the face of unauthorised copying of their works. As noted by Hugenholtz, Guibault and van Geffen, the potential elimination of unauthorised private copying enabled by control and by DRM technologies should lead to the phasing-out of levy systems.[109] Indeed, if use of copyrighted material can be traced and remunerated by recourse to these technologies, charging fees on the sale price of copying machines and recordable formats would amount to asking for the same remuneration twice. Through the extension of digital copyright to the realm of personal use, it has finally become feasible to enforce property rights which, despite their practical unenforceability, were legally recognised by the German Supreme Court in 1955.[110] At that time, the German authors' collecting society (GEMA) successfully made a legal claim against a producer of tape recorders to the effect that authors held the exclusive right to prohibit private recordings and to obtain remuneration for the private exploitation of their works. However, this attempt to enforce copyright against private users was unsuccessful because home-taping could not be monitored without copyright owners being physically able to enter individuals' homes.

---

rights management software that allows an organisation to attach specific privileges to individual documents, dictating if and how they may be stored or distributed, who can access them, and who can edit or change them. This software can update or revoke usage rights to access a document, regardless of where the information is stored or if it has been distributed.

[107] See §7.2., see *infra*.

[108] See Articles 6 and 7 of Directive 2001/29/EC of the European Parliament and of the Council of 22 May 2001 on the harmonisation of certain aspects of copyright and related rights in the information society, OJ L 167, 22.6.2001, p. 10.

[109] See Hugenholtz, Guibault and van Geffen, *The Future of Levies in a Digital Environment*, Final Report, Institute for Information Law, Amsterdam 2003, available at: http://www.ivir.nl/staff/hugenholtz.html.

[110] See Guibault, *Copyright Limitations*, op. cit., pp. 50-54.

In 1964, the German Federal Constitutional Court acknowledged that the implementation of measures of control over copyright infringement caused by home-taping would have conflicted with the privacy of end-users and, specifically, against the inviolability of the home as guaranteed by Article 13 of the German Basic Law.[111] Interestingly, the Federal Constitutional Court declined to uphold the plaintiffs' request for an order compelling suppliers of home-taping equipment to disclose the identity of their customers in order to permit GEMA to verify whether such customers engaged in unlawful uses. Guibault noted that it was largely because of the two judgments just described that the German Copyright Act of 1965 was amended to include the first statutory right to equitable remuneration in favour of authors, performers and phonogram producers for home-taping through the imposition of levies on the sale of sound recording equipment.[112]

The clash between copyright enforcement regarding personal use and end-user privacy has grown immensely with the advent of today's control and DRM technologies. Pioneering contributions by American scholars such as Cohen and Lessig have argued for many years that the operation of technologies capable of monitoring end-user behaviour and consumption patterns could threaten the right of users to use copyrighted information anonymously.[113] Cohen has pointed out that reading anonymously is so intimately connected with the freedom of speech and of thought that it should be protected under the shield of the First Amendment of the U.S. Constitution, which guarantees freedom of expression. Lessig suggests that end-user privacy is not excluded by encryption technology itself. Instead, it is sacrificed only when such technology is programmed in such a way that user identity and consumption patterns cannot be hidden from information suppliers.[114] According to Lessig, privacy protection mainly depends on the architecture of encryption and management technologies. Consequently, the only measure at the disposal of law-makers is that of compelling the producers of such technologies to design them in compliance with forms of regulation that afford protection to personal data.

---

111 See Guibault, *Copyright Limitations*, op. cit., p. 51.

112 *Ibidem.*

113 See Cohen, 'A Right to Read Anonymously: A Closer Look at 'Copyright Management' in Cyberspace', (28) *Connecticut Law Review* 1996, p. 981; Lessig, *Code and Other Laws of Cyberspace*, op. cit., p. 140.

114 See Lessig, *Code and Other Laws of Cyberspace*, op. cit., p. 140 ("Cohen, it seems to me, is plainly right about anonymity [...] [W]e should certainly architect cyberspaces to ensure anonymity – or more precisely, pseudonymity – first. If the code is going to monitor just what I do, then at least it should not know that it is 'I' that it is monitoring. I am less troubled if it knows that '14AH342BD7' read such and such; I am deeply troubled if that number is tied back to my name. Cohen is plainly right for a second reason as well: all of the good that comes from monitoring could be achieved while protecting privacy as well. It may take a bit more coding to build in routines for breaking traceability; it may take more planning to ensure that privacy is protected. But if those rules are embedded up front, the cost would not be terribly high. Far cheaper to architect privacy protections in [sic] now rather than retrofit for them later.").

The increasing recognition in Europe of the need to create technological mechanisms which ensure respect for privacy interests (the so-called "privacy-enhancing technology"), particularly in the on-line world, is demonstrated by Recital 57 of the InfoSoc Directive.[115] This provision first of all acknowledges that:

> "[A]ny such rights-management information systems [...] may, depending on their design, at the same time process personal data about the consumption patterns of protected subject matter by individuals and allow for tracing of on-line behaviour."

However, it subsequently provides that:

> "[...] these technical means, in their technical functions, should incorporate privacy safeguards in accordance with Directive 95/46/EC of the European Parliament and of the Council of 24 October 1995 on the protection of individuals with regard to the processing of personal data and the free movement of such data."[116]

As pointed out by Bygrave, the "soft" law nature of Recital 57 does not seem to mandate the implementation of privacy-enhancing technologies ("PET's"). Nor does its outdated and ambiguous wording help to identify which technologies should be made subject to this technological mandate.[117] Indeed, the text of the provision merely refers to rights management information systems, and does not extend to the design and operation of technological protection measures. Thus, modern DRM technologies which provide both functions (*i.e.*, management information *plus* technological protection) may easily be found not to be subject to the obligation.

Notwithstanding its crucial importance to the welfare of end-users in the digital world, privacy protection will not be further dealt with in this book. Given that this analysis is solely concerned with the protection of the interests of users with respect to copyright law, a detailed focus on how copyright enforcement in the digital environment interplays with the complex regulation of personal data protection in the EU would excessively expand the breadth of this work. However, privacy concerns will be taken into account in examining the legal treatment of personal use in the digital environment under the InfoSoc Directive.

2.3. The legal framework: copyright exceptions under EU law

EU supranational law-making does not seem to ensure an adequate consideration of the public interest when it touches upon both market and public policy aspects of national copyright law. In this book, it will be shown that the copyright legisla-

[115] See Bygrave, 'The Technologisation of Copyright: Implications for Privacy and Related Interests', (24) *EIPR* 2002, p. 51.

[116] See Recital 57 of the InfoSoc Directive.

[117] See Bygrave, 'The Technologisation of Copyright', op. cit., p. 56.

tion resulting from the InfoSoc Directive of May 2001 is unfit to pursue the objective of an effective enforcement of statutory copyright exceptions in the face of the increasing implementation of DRM and other technologies of control.

The problem basically stems from the assumption that, according to Article 295 of the EC Treaty, the European Community has no direct competence to legislate in the field of copyright law.[118] According to this Article, intellectual property law is - in principle - a matter of national law. This lack of direct competence implies that, when legislation is not enacted on the grounds of the so-called "implied powers" conferred by Article 308 of the EC Treaty, the harmonisation of copyright law is undertaken on the grounds of Article 95, the objective of which is to favour and reinforce market integration. The fact that EU copyright law is shaped as internal market legislation implies that the adoption of harmonisation measures in this field is intended mainly to help remove disparities between national provisions that hinder the free movement of goods, or to help remove disparities that cause distorted conditions of competition.

This basic purpose of the Treaty was identified in the first case in which the conflict between the national protection of intellectual property and the community-wide free movement of goods was addressed by the European Court of Justice (hereinafter "ECJ").[119] As explained in depth below, before the enactment of the InfoSoc Directive in 2001, harmonisation measures in the field of copyright were concerned, at least from a formal perspective, with facilitating or enabling intra-Community trade in goods embodying copyrighted works.[120] In two examples of EU copyright legislation, the institutional pursuit of the objective of market integration was used as a pre-text to re-direct copyright in accordance with the development of common industrial policies. This was the case of the 1991 Directive on the Legal Protection of Computer Programs and of the 1996 Directive on the Legal Protection of Databases, whose evident purpose, along with market integration, was that of fostering the industrial production of these information goods and afford them an equal legal protection throughout the Community in order to avoid conditions of distorted competition.[121] This kind of legislative action by EU lawmakers in the field of copyright law has resulted in an imbalance between the accommodation of market and non-market (that is to say, cultural) values. The analysis of EU copyright harmonisation provided below will show that, with the

---

118 See Article 295 of the EC Treaty: "The Treaty shall in no way prejudice the rules in Member States governing the system of property ownership."

119 See *Deutsche Grammophone* v. *Metro-SB-Grossmärkte*, C-78/70, ECR 1971, 487. On that occasion, the ECJ held that: "[T]he essential purpose of the Treaty, which is to unite national markets into a single market [...] could not be attained if, under the various legal systems of the Member States, nationals of those States were able to partition the market and bring about arbitrary discrimination or disguised restrictions on trade between Member States [...]".

120 See §3.2.1., see *infra*.

121 See Council Directive 91/250/EEC of 14 May 1991 on the legal protection of computer programs, OJ L 122, 14.06.1991, 42 (hereinafter "Software Directive"); and Directive 96/9/EC of the European Parliament and of the Council of 11 March 1996 on the legal protection of databases, OJ L 077, 27.03.1996, 20 (hereinafter "Database Directive").

InfoSoc Directive, this imbalance in copyright legislation reached its greatest degree. This directive provided for the harmonisation of certain aspects of copyright for the digital society. Notwithstanding the fact that its horizontal nature applied, for the first time, to all substantive aspects of the copyright law of all the Member States, in both the digital and the non-digital copyright environments, the directive provided no legal tools with which to preserve the effective enforcement of copyright exceptions in the digital society. In my view, this basic failure has the consequence of upholding an unlimited expansion of digital copyright protection at the expense of end-user interests which enjoy specific protection and consideration under the EC Treaty. If the directive had truly sought to achieve the objective of facilitating intra-Community trade, it would have provided harmonisation measures with regard to the legal definition of both the exclusive rights of copyright and its exceptions. Instead, it was accepted (most probably on the grounds of the nature of internal market legislation) that exceptions could only be harmonised where there was plain evidence that differences in protection between Member States affected trade within the internal market.[122] In spite of the original purpose of making copyright exceptions strict, the directive ended up providing an extensive (and exhaustive) list of non-mandatory exceptions that Member States were familiar with, regardless of whether these exceptions concretely affected cross-border trade in the eminently trans-national Information Society.[123] The resulting legislation raises specific problems that will be analysed in Part Two of this book:

- it restricts the cultural policies of the Member States by prohibiting the adoption of copyright exceptions other than the ones included in the directive's (exhaustive) list;
- it does not provide a copyright exception "interface" to ensure that exceptions are not systematically overridden by means of electronic licences which automatically impose DRM and other technologies; and
- it does not solve the problem of how (that is, by virtue of which mechanisms, monitoring systems and procedures) copyright exceptions should be enforced if control and DRM technologies operate effectively.

2.4. Summary

This chapter has argued that the mere possibility that technological protection enables electronic licences to enforce contractual conditions which restrict access to and use of digital copyrighted materials does not call for the demise of publicly mandated protection of end-user interests under copyright law. On the one hand,

[122] See Cornish and Llewelyn, *Intellectual Property: Patents, Copyright, Trade Marks and Allied Rights*, Sweet and Maxwell, London 2003, p. 441.

[123] See Cornish and Llewelyn, *Intellectual Property*, op. cit., p. 441 ("In the case of photocopying, for instance, it was hard to see that case, since the practice did not result in cross-border trading […]").

the fact that copyright law confers certain rights (or privileges) of use to end-users on *non-market* grounds suggests that, at least under national copyright systems, control and DRM technologies should not be allowed to interfere with, and ultimately pre-empt, statutory end-user rights and privileges. On the other hand, it has been acknowledged that, under the operation of technologies which enable the marketing of copyrighted goods directly to the end-user, the market failure rationale behind the exception of private copying has acquired less importance. This new assumption calls into question the desirability of copyright compensation measures, such as continental-European levies on copying machines and recordable formats.

In contrast, another market failure rationale which is still valid in digital settings is the exemption of certain transformative uses from the exclusivity of copyright when these uses (*e.g.*, quotations, extracts, parodies, *etc*) might be blocked because of non-coordination between multiple copyright owners of original materials or for reasons unrelated to permission prices (*i.e.*, non-rational decisions). In this respect, it has been concluded that these uses should be preserved, especially since digital technologies enhance the expressive opportunities of end-users.

At the end of the chapter, it has been explained why the horizontal harmonisation of copyright law provided by the InfoSoc Directive creates a troublesome scenario for the effective enforcement of copyright exceptions. The following parts of this book will aim at analysing the above-mentioned scenario in detail, and, at the same time, highlighting its most unfortunate characteristics, and will also propose policy alternatives for the accommodation of the legitimate purposes of end-users.

PART II
EU DIGITAL COPYRIGHT LAW FROM THE END-USER PERSPECTIVE

3. Copyright harmonisation according to technological dictates

3.1. Introduction

In a recent review of the EU legal framework in the field of copyright, the European Commission presented the 2001 InfoSoc Directive as the "most horizontal" (*i.e.*, comprehensive) measure ever adopted in this field.[124] In spite of its title and apparent objectives, the InfoSoc Directive provides EU law with a horizontal regulation of copyright which goes far beyond the framework of digital settings, and involves all dimensions of artistic and literary property. In accordance with the field of application of the Directive, this analysis will not deal directly with earlier copyright regulations addressing specific subject matters such as software and database protection. The exclusion of software is specifically provided by Recital 50 of the InfoSoc Directive, according to which the Directive does not affect the specific provisions on protection provided for by the Software Directive.

To understand the purpose of this ambitious piece of legislation, it is worth engaging in a short overview of the origins of EU copyright law. To this end, this chapter focuses on the legal basis and the objectives which support the development of a copyright policy by the European Community. The analysis deals with the re-definition of copyright protection provided by the Directive and gives a short account of the expansion of property rights over the digital reproduction and the communication to the public of copyrighted works. Finally, the chapter discusses the effects of the controversial "anti-circumvention" law concerning technological protection measures and electronic rights management information.

3.2. Legal basis and objectives of copyright harmonisation in the EU

In commenting upon the proposal for the InfoSoc Directive, Cohen Jehoram pointed out that the European Community was about to replace "maybe two-thirds

---

124 See Commission of the European Communities, Commission Staff Working Paper on the review of the EC legal framework in the field of copyright and related rights, SEC (2004) 995, Brussels, 19.7.2004, p. 3.

of national copyright laws".[125] In doing so, the Commission and the Parliament ceased to approach copyright legislation in a piecemeal fashion and moved decidedly towards a horizontal approach in the harmonisation of copyright law. None of the former interventions of the Community in this field were as wide as the legislative reform of 2001, which encompassed all the rights and all the exceptions in copyright, in the digital, as well as in the analogue, world.[126]

3.2.1. The progressive development of a Community copyright policy

Until the early 1990s, copyright law remained untouched by Community action. National copyright rules came into consideration exclusively under the jurisprudence of the ECJ regarding the EC principles of the free movement of goods and services, and unrestricted competition. It was from the early 1970s that national courts started to seek clarification concerning the conflict between the protection of national property rights (Articles 30 and 295 of the EC Treaty), and the rules covering the free movement of goods and competition (Articles 28, 81 and 82).

3.2.1.1. Free movement of goods and the exhaustion principle

The free movement of goods immediately found an exception in the circulation of intellectual property rights within the Community. The exercise of these rights (which, despite being property, are not "goods" in themselves) could allow companies to partition the Common Market in order to prevent the free movement of goods between Member States. National law reserves the exclusive right to exploit a protected process or product within a Member State's territory to the owner of an intellectual property right; and thereby confers to this owner, expressly or implicitly, the right to oppose the importation of a good which enjoys an identical or similar right from another Member State. With regard to copyright, the ECJ analysed such a conflict for the first time in the case of *Deutsche Grammophone* v. *Metro-SB-Grossmärkte*.[127] In this case, a German manufacturer of gramophone records sought to enforce its exclusive right as the proprietor under German copyright law in order to oppose the importation of records, manufactured and sold under licence in France by its French subsidiary, into Germany by a third party. The Court held that, although Article 295 reserved the creation and definition of the subject matter of an intellectual property right (in the Court's terminology: the *existence* of the right) to Member State law, the *exercise* of the right nevertheless fell within the field of the application of the Treaty. Moreover, the Court clarified that Article 30 did shield the exercise of an intellectual property right from the full rigour of Article 28, but only in so far as it was necessary for the protection of the specific subject matter of that right. The ECJ pointed out that the right was "ex-

---

[125] See Cohen Jehoram, 'European Copyright Law – Even More Horizontal', (32) *IIC* 2001, p. 532, at p. 545.

[126] *Ibidem.*

[127] See *Deutsche Grammophone* v. *Metro-SB-Grossmärkte*, C-78/70, 1971, ECR, 487.

hausted", and could not be relied upon in a manner which inhibited the free movement of goods. This meant that, once a copyright holder exercises his or her exclusive right of distribution by putting the copyrighted product on the Community market for the first time, Community law prevents the right holder from using the copyright to prevent parallel trade. In this way, Community law ends up respecting the existence of copyright, while restricting its exercise for the attainment of the objective of free movement of goods.

Having been defined by the ECJ, the principle of exhaustion progressively found legislative recognition in Article 4(c) of the 1991 Software Directive, which regards the right of distribution.[128] Similar provisions are embodied in Article 5(c) of the 1996 Database Directive, and Article 4(2) of the InfoSoc Directive.

3.2.1.2. National copyright protection under Article 30 of the EC Treaty

Subsequently, the ECJ refined its definition of the exhaustion principle in several decisions concerning Article 30, according to which restrictions on imports and exports could be justified upon the grounds of national copyright protection.

In *Coditel, and others* v. *Ciné Vog Films and others*,[129] the ECJ excluded that the principle of free movement of goods and services could allow a Belgian trans-border cable re-transmission of a film, broadcasted in Germany, without the authorisation of the copyright owner of the film. The Court made it clear that the principle of Community-wide exhaustion applied only to the physical dissemination of copyrighted goods, without extending it to intangible forms of commercial exploitation such as re-transmissions.

In *Warner Brothers Inc. and Metronome Video ApS* v. *Erik Viuff Christiansen*,[130] the Court declined to apply the exhaustion rule to a case of unauthorised rental of a videocassette in Denmark that had been marketed in the United Kingdom, on the assumption that Danish law, as opposed to UK law, did provide a rental right in favour of copyright owners. Even if the Court recognised that the protection of the Danish rental right had the effect of restricting the intra-Community market for videocassettes, it held that such protection was justified on the grounds of Article 30 of the EC Treaty.

In *EMI Electrola GmbH* v. *Patricia Im- und Export and others*,[131] then, the ECJ argued that the national protection of intellectual property based on Article 30 allowed a copyright owner of sound recordings to obtain an injunction in Germany

---

128 Article 4 (c) of the 1991 Software Directive provides as follows: "The first sale in the Community of a copy of a program by the right-holder or with his consent shall exhaust the distribution right within the Community of that copy, with the exception of the right to control further rental of the program or a copy thereof [...]".

129 See *Coditel and others* v. *Ciné Vog Films and others*, C-62/79, 1980, ECR 881 (hereinafter *Coditel*).

130 See *Warner Brothers Inc. and Metronome Video ApS* v. *Erik Viuff Christiansen*. C-158/86, 1988, ECR 2605 (hereinafter *Warner Brothers*).

131 See *EMI Electrola GmbH* v. *Patricia Im- und Export and others*, C-341-87, 1989, ECR 79 (hereinafter *EMI/Electrola*).

against the unauthorised importation of records from Denmark, where copyright on such recordings had already expired.

3.2.1.3. Copyright legislation as a tool fostering market integration

Fiercely opposed to any restriction on the principle of the free movement of goods, the European Commission started to react to each of the above-mentioned ECJ decisions with directive proposals aimed at harmonising specific aspects of national copyright law. The Commission's harmonisation measures in the field of copyright law sought, on the one hand, to remove distortions at the level of *primary* exploitation of exclusive rights. On the other, the Commission's reaction intended to remove national disparities - under copyright law - that opened a breach in the application of both the free movement of goods and of the exhaustion principle, which affected internal trade at a *secondary* level (*i.e.*, the level of the free circulation of copyrighted goods after their primary exploitation by their proprietors within the Community territory). Cohen Jehoram referred to the proposed directives as "incidents" which occurred as a consequence of the above-mentioned ECJ decisions.[132] This author emphasised that the Commission's reaction to such incidents consisted of specific legislation that would have brought the conflict provoked between the free movement of goods and the protection of national copyright to an end. From this perspective, the adoption of Directive 93/83/EEC on the co-ordination of certain rules concerning copyright in satellite broadcasting and cable re-transmissions[133] has to be understood as a (late) remedy to *Coditel*, Directive 92/100/EEC on rental and lending rights[134] must be linked to the *Warner Brothers* decision, and Directive 93/98/EEC on the harmonisation of the term of copyright protection[135] should be viewed as an answer to the problem outlined by *EMI/Electrola*. By proposing specific adjustments in Member State copyright law, the Commission did not intend to create an entire European copyright system. The publication of the 1989 Green Paper on copyright and the challenge of technology[136] shows that the Commission mainly wanted to put an end to the undesirable outcome of the ECJ's decisions, "and only for very particular subjects, such as computer software, databases, term of protection and resale rights [...]". This

---

[132] See Cohen Jehoram, 'European Copyright Law', op. cit., pp. 533-34.

[133] See Council Directive 93/83/EEC of 27 September 1993 on the co-ordination of certain rules concerning copyright and rights related to copyright applicable to satellite broadcasting and cable retransmission, OJ L 248, 6.10.1993, p. 15.

[134] See Council Directive 92/100/EEC of 19 November 1992 on rental right and lending right and on certain rights related to copyright in the field of intellectual property, OJ L 346, 27.11.1992, p. 61, which has been repealed and replaced by Directive 2006/115/EC of 12 December 2006, OJ L 376, 27.12.2006, p. 28.

[135] See Council Directive 93/98/EEC of 29 October 1993 harmonising the term of protection of copyright and certain related rights, OJ L 290, 24.11.1993, p. 9, whose later amendments have been codified by Directive 2006/116/EC of 12 December 2006, OJ L 372, 27.12.2006, p. 12.

[136] Commission of the European Communities, *Green Paper on Copyright and the Challenge of Technology*, COM (88), 172, Final of 7.06.1988.

Commission's document explicitly emphasised that EU law should have abstained from enacting horizontal (*i.e.*, general) provisions.[137]

Nonetheless, an incomplete view of the Commission's purposes in the field of copyright would be provided if the industrial policy objectives pursued by copyright directives were overlooked. Copyright legislation in the EU also aimed to pursue the objectives of avoiding competitive distortions in internal trade and of strengthening the industrial development and the international competitiveness of European industry, especially in the strategic sectors of computer programmes and databases.[138] The evident pursuit of these industrial policies, which follows directly from the recitals of the copyright directives themselves, is also demonstrated by the fact that the first Community copyright statute, *i.e.*, the Software Directive, defined one of the most horizontal aspects of copyright law, namely, the standard of originality as a basic requirement for the protection of software as literary work.[139] By adopting a standard of originality taken from continental-European *droit d'auteur* (*i.e.*, the author's right) tradition, Article 1(3) of the Software Directive forced Member States such as the UK and Ireland to change their copyright laws on a basic point.[140] Before the enactment of the 1991 Directive, British and Irish laws afforded copyright protection to computer programmes in which "skill, labour or investment" were involved. In contrast, under German law, the originality test required, at least for certain categories of work such as designs and computer programmes, that further qualitative or aesthetic requirements were met before copyright protection was granted.

The Commission continued to act as a copyright legislator and to pursue the objectives of internal and external industrial policy even in the case of the 1996 Database Directive, which was adopted with the object of removing the existing differences in the standard of originality required for a database to enjoy copyright protection.[141] On this occasion, the Commission reasoned that the difference between the lower copyright standard that applied in common law Member States (often referred to as "sweat of the brow" standard, involving the aforementioned "skill, labour and investment") and the higher standard of intellectual creation applying in *droit d'auteur* Member States created market distortions in database products. Hence, the Commission pursued the policy goal of creating horizontal rules which granted a high level of copyright protection to certain databases ("original" databases, which would presumably obtain protection under *droit*

137 *Ibidem*, p. 536.

138 See Ullrich, 'Legal Protection of Innovative Technologies: Property or Policy?', in: Grandstrand (ed), *Economics, Law and Intellectual Property - Seeking Strategies for Research and Teaching in a Deeloping Field*, Kluwer Academic Publishers, Boston, 2003, p. 439, at p. 471.

139 See Article 1(3) of the Software Directive ("A computer program shall be protected if it is original in the sense that it is the author's own intellectual creation. No other criteria shall be applied to determine its eligibility for protection.").

140 See Cohen Jehoram, 'European Copyright Law', op. cit., pp. 537-38.

141 See Commission of the European Communities, *First evaluation of Directive 96/9/EC on the legal protection of databases*, DG Internal Market and Services Working Paper, 12.12.2005, available at: http://ec.europa.eu/internal_market/copyright.

d'auteur jurisdictions, as they were the fruit of the author's own intellectual creation) and a new form of *sui generis* protection in favour of "non-original" databases (which resulted from substantial investment in either the obtaining, verification or presentation of their contents, and would easily meet the common law copyright standard).[142]

With the enactment of the Software and the Database Directives, in particular, it was evident that the Commission pursued the primary objective of eliminating distortions that the different basic requirements for protection in the laws of the different Member States would create on the European markets for computer programmes and databases.[143] By this kind of horizontal copyright legislation, the Commission sought to eliminate trade distortions at the level of *primary* exploitation of exclusive rights provided under national copyright laws. The subject-matter of the legal protection of computer programmes and databases was harmonised mainly in order to remove uncertainty with regard to the minimum requirements for the legal protection of these information goods, and to create higher economic incentives for investments on the related markets. The co-existing objective of removing the obstacles to the free movement of these particular goods and the operation of the exhaustion rule came into consideration only as a *subsequent* policy objective, which was that of facilitating the Community-wide exploitation of copyrighted goods after primary exploitation.

The change in the European Commission's copyright policy, subsequent to the publication of the 1989 Green Paper, which advocated a piecemeal approach to copyright harmonisation, and the subsequent proliferation of horizontal measures in the field of copyright, were mainly due to an institutional change in the EU decision-making process. The constitutional amendments that followed the entry into force of the 1988 Single European Act (SEA), allowed the Community's internal market legislation, including copyright measures, to be adopted by the European Council (*i.e.*, by the Member States) on the grounds of qualified-majority voting instead of unanimity.[144] As argued by Weatherill, the absence of any national veto

---

[142] See *First evaluation of Directive 96/9/EC*, p. 3.

[143] See Pardo, *Copyright and Multimedia*, Kluwer Law International, The Hague, 2003, p.148, who recalled the two primary *raisons d'être* of the Software Directive, according to its own preliminary recitals: (i) a financial reason ("based on the high financial investment of human and technical resources required for the creation of software"); and (ii) a legal reason ("based on the need to obtain an identical, uniform and complete protection of these works in all Member States of the Community").

[144] See Weatherill, *EC Consumer Law and Policy*, Longman, London and New York, 1997, p. 7; and de Witte, 'Non-market values in internal market legislation', in Shuibhne (ed), *Regulating the Internal Market*, Edward Elgar, Cheltenham, 2006, p. 61, at p. 67 ("By providing for qualified-majority voting in the new Article 100a (though not in the 'old' Article 100) and in most of the specific internal market legal bases, the authors of the SEA contributed indeed to the smooth legislative implementation of the internal market programme set out in the Commission's White Paper of 1985 [...]"). De Witte stresses even that, following the enactment of the 1992 Maastricht Treaty and the 1997 Amsterdam Treaty, the scope of "pure" internal market legislation, originally encompassed by the legal basis provided by Articles 94 (ex 100: unanimity) and 95 (ex 100a: qualified majority), was reduced by the creation of sector-specific policies such as envi-

under Article 100a (now Article 95) ensured the vitality of this provision as a basis for making a large number of measures associated with the process of completion of the internal market.[145] This change of legal basis for internal market legislation, together with the re-orientation of the Commission's Internal Market Directorate objectives around 1990,[146] contributed to the smooth implementation of harmonisation measures which ensured the free movement of copyrighted goods within the Community.

3.2.2. Legal basis and specific objectives of the InfoSoc Directive

Similar to other Community interventions in the field of copyright, the InfoSoc Directive based its legitimacy mainly on the grounds of Article 95 (formerly Article 100a) of the EC Treaty. This legal basis enabled the Community law-makers to enact measures which were designed to pursue the approximation of laws for the creation of a single market.

3.2.2.1. The legal basis of Article 95 of the EC Treaty

The wording of Article 95 refers to Article 14 in order to specify that such approximation must be intended to permit or favour the creation of a Community-wide "internal market".[147] Under Article 95, therefore, the Community is allowed to take harmonisation measures in so far as they either help to remove disparities between national provisions that hinder the free movement of goods, or help to remove disparities that cause distorted conditions of competition.[148]

The introductory recitals of the InfoSoc Directive show indisputably that the policy objective of removing disparities between national provisions in the field of digital copyright law was an indirect result of the pursuit of another, primary objective. The Preamble reveals that, when adopting this new regulation of copyright, Community institutions were motivated by the intent "to create a general

ronmental protection, health and safety of workers, social policy, migration, and civil law and procedure.

145 See Weatherill, *EC Consumer Law and Policy*, op. cit., p. 7.

146 See Cohen Jehoram, 'European Copyright Law', op. cit., p. 536, who emphasised that, "around 1990, the atmosphere in the copyright department of what is now Directorate XV, internal market, began to change. New personnel was appointed with other ambitions and orientation than those that went before [...]".

147 Article 14(2) of the EC Treaty states: "The internal market should comprise an area without internal frontiers in which the free movement of goods, persons, services and capital is ensured in accordance with the provisions of this Treaty [...]".

148 See de Witte, 'Non-market values in internal market legislation', op. cit., pp. 75-76, who argues that, for internal market legislation to be constitutionally valid, the approximation of laws allowed under Article 95 must pursue either the objective formulated in Article 3 (h) of the EC Treaty ("The approximation of the laws of Member States to the extent required for the proper functioning of the common market") or the objective formulated in Article 3 (f) (namely, "the institution of a system ensuring that competition in the common market is not distorted").

and flexible legal framework at Community level in order to foster the development of the information society in Europe [...]".[149] According to Recital 2, this achievement would have required the existence of an internal market for new products and services, whose creation, development and marketing were deemed to be both protected and stimulated by copyright and related rights. Thus, copyright harmonisation was viewed in the context of the Directive more as a precondition for the pursuit of the primary objective of fostering substantial investment in creativity and innovation than as a policy objective in itself. From its Preamble, the InfoSoc Directive determines copyright harmonisation to be a means to an end, with the aim of "growth and increased competitiveness of European industry".[150] To this end, the Preamble makes it clear that copyright and related rights should have been adapted and supplemented in order to respond adequately to new economic realities by promoting investment in new forms of exploitation of creative works and in the development of network infrastructure.[151] The wording of these recitals upholds the view that EU law-makers intended to use the form of copyright law for the digital environment as a form of industrial policy. Recital 6 of the Directive confirms that, in the intention of EU law-makers, only copyright harmonisation at Community level could prevent the Member States from responding to technological challenges in this field with isolated initiatives that might have resulted "in significant differences in protection and thereby in restrictions on the free movement of services and products incorporating, or based on, intellectual property [...]". The InfoSoc Directive moved from the assumption that, had the Member States been left with the freedom to create the fragmentation of the internal market and legislative inconsistency, such legislative differences would have had a negative impact upon the development of the information society and may have hindered economies of scale for new products and services containing copyright and related rights. As Ullrich has claimed, the Directive, as almost any other measure of intellectual property harmonisation in the EU, was motivated as much by concerns of strengthening the industrial development of European industry as by the objective of avoiding distortions of competition in internal trade.[152]

3.2.2.2. The objectives of the 1995 Green Paper

In its ambitious 1995 Green Paper on Copyright in the Information Society,[153] the European Commission originally identified several legislative adjustments that would have served the purpose of creating the legal framework described in the

[149] See Recital 2 of the InfoSoc Directive.

[150] See Recital 4 of the InfoSoc Directive.

[151] See Recital 5 of the InfoSoc Directive.

[152] See Ullrich, 'Legal Protection of Innovative Technologies: Property or Policy?', op. cit., p. 471.

[153] See Commission of the European Communities, *Green Paper. Copyright and Related Rights in the Information Society*, Brussels, 19.07.1995, COM (95) 382 final, 49.

Preamble of the 2001 Directive. In the Green Paper, the Commission argued that, for such a framework to be realised, Community law should have dealt with:

- international private law criteria to identify the law applicable to the contracts and copyright infringements taking place on the Internet;
- the re-definition at Community level of the subject matter and the extension of economic and moral rights on creative works; and
- an effective harmonisation of provisions regarding collective rights management and technological protection of digital works.

3.2.2.3. The objective to implement the 1996 WIPO Copyright Treaty

Less than half of the measures listed in the Green Paper were incorporated into the 2001 reforms. Such a result was due to the fact that, when the Commission made its proposal for the text of a copyright directive for the information society, another objective external to the EC Treaty took preference over the accomplishment of intra-Community purposes. As explicitly mentioned in Recital 15 of the Info-Soc Directive, this objective consisted of the implementation, by the European Union, of a number of international obligations set out in the 1996 WIPO Copyright Treaty and the WIPO Performances and Phonograms Treaty, which were negotiated directly by the Commission with third countries.[154] The two major reforms embodied in these treaties concerned, on the one hand, the explicit recognition in favour of copyright holders of the exclusive right of authorising any communication to the public, including the making available of copyrighted material to the public in such a way that members of the public may access these works from a place and at a time chosen by them.[155] On the other hand, the WIPO Treaties introduced into international copyright law the duty for Contracting Parties to provide adequate legal protection and effective legal remedies against the circumvention of effective technological measures that are used by rights-holders in connection with the exercise of their rights.[156]

While a simple operation of "copy and paste" of these relevant international provisions into Community law would probably have accomplished the task, it appeared that the European Commission, in drafting its proposal, was unable to resist the temptation of enhancing the level of copyright protection set out in the WIPO Treaties. Like its U.S. counterpart, the Commission gave the impression of being much more concerned with the drafting of broad "technological" property rights than with the careful assessment of how such a new kind of property had an

---

[154] See WIPO Copyright Treaty and WIPO Performances and Phonograms Treaty, adopted in Geneva in December 20, 1996, available at: http://www.wipo.int/treaties.

[155] See Article 8 of the WIPO Copyright Treaty; Articles 10 and 14 of the WIPO Performances and Phonograms Treaty. A more in-depth commentary on the enactment of these measures was provided in Mazziotti, 'Il diritto d'autore comunitario nel nuovo ambiente digitale', 7(1) *Ciberspazio e Diritto* 2006, p. 55, at pp. 61-63.

[156] See Article 11 of the WIPO Copyright Treaty and Article 18 of the WIPO Performances and Phonograms Treaty.

impact upon the balanced nature of the copyright system.[157] Ricolfi, in particular, while commenting on Article 6 of the draft of the InfoSoc Directive, stressed that Article 11 of the WIPO Copyright Treaty clearly stated that technological measures aimed at protecting copyright should *not* have restricted the exercise of copyright exceptions (*i.e.*, "acts permitted by law", under the phrasing of this provision). As explained below,[158] one of the most unfortunate drawbacks of the InfoSoc Directive was that so-called "anti-circumvention" law did not create a legal mechanism which permitted the users of copyrighted goods to engage in "acts permitted by law", notwithstanding the operation of technological protection measures that control both the access to and the use of digital works. This flaw in the architecture of the InfoSoc Directive may be seen as further evidence of the fact that the primary policy objective of the Directive was *not* that of avoiding distortions of competition in internal trade. In contrast, the implementation of the WIPO Treaties served as a vehicle for the policy objective of promoting and protecting European industrial investment in copyrighted digital works and in network infrastructure.

3.3. The re-definition of the copyright scope

The InfoSoc Directive required Member States to update and harmonise the scope of exclusive rights concerning digital works. In spite of its widely horizontal nature, the Directive failed to address the most important aspect of copyright protection, namely, the definition of its subject matter.

3.3.1. The national dimension of copyright's subject matter

In defining the objective and the scope of the InfoSoc Directive, Article 1(1) provides that the Directive "concerns the legal protection of copyright and related rights in the framework of internal market, with particular emphasis on the information society [...]". Article 1(2), then, makes it clear that the Directive leaves intact and in no way affects the existing Community provisions relating to the specific subject of the previous directives in the field of copyright, namely, computer programmes and databases. Significantly, the scope of the InfoSoc Directive, as shaped in Article 1, does not include the harmonisation of the basic requirements for copyright protection in the EU. Nor does it include the harmonisation of the transformative uses that are reserved to the copyright owner and require his or her authorisation to be undertaken lawfully (*i.e.*, acts of translation, adaptation or modification of the copyrighted work).[159]

[157] See Hugenholtz, 'Why the Copyright Directive is Unimportant, and Possibly Invalid', (22) *EIPR* 2000, p. 500; Ricolfi, 'Intellectual Property rights and legal order', *Il Diritto di Autore* 2001, p.132.

[158] See §4.5, see *infra*.

[159] See §1.3., see *supra*.

3.3.1.1. The absence of a single standard of originality

As stated above, two specific directives intervened to provide copyright protection for computer programmes and databases in order to avoid distortion in competition and obstacles in the intra-Community market for these new types of goods. Software and database protection are, therefore, the only frameworks within which Community law dealt with the definition of the copyright subject matter.

Although its scope was identified by reference to the protection of "computer programmes", the 1991 Software Directive failed to define the notion of such goods in explicit terms. Article 1(2) of the 1996 Database Directive, in contrast, did provide a definition of "databases".[160] No other harmonisation measures, not even the InfoSoc Directive, have, in general, dealt with this issue. This means that, outside the specific fields of the protection of computer programmes and databases, Member States are still free to decide upon their own regime with regard to the standards of originality which determine copyright protection.

Thus, EU law has a long way to go before it can establish Community copyright, which - in principle - would be the best way to establish a truly common (*i.e.*, unique) market for copyright-based goods. To date, the process of unification has regarded the creation of single, Community-wide intellectual property entitlements for trademarks and industrial design with the purpose of establishing central registration systems which cover all of the EU territories.[161] EU law is also far from establishing a uniform copyright standard to be adopted in national subsystems.

The twin objectives of creating a single (*i.e.*, Community-wide) copyright entitlement, and, to harmonise the copyright subject matter in its entirety seem to be highly unrealistic, especially if one takes the considerable differences between common law and *droit d'auteur* copyright systems into account. As Ullrich has observed, the unification of copyright entitlements at Community level would empty national copyright of all of its substance and relegate it to a default position.[162] As opposite to what happens in the area of industrial property, copyright protection is acquired by the act of creation, *i.e.*, without any requirements of registration, but simply by operation of the law. Due to the automatic operation of unified copyright protection, a hypothetical Community copyright would simply supersede national copyright, in a way that the two titles could never co-exist (as national and Community trademarks, for instance, do).[163]

---

160 See Article 1(2) of the 1996 Database Directive: "For the purpose of this Directive, 'database' shall mean a collection of independent works, data or other materials arranged in a systematic or methodical way and individually accessible by electronic or other means."

161 See, for trademarks, Regulation 40/1994/EC, OJ L 011, 14.01.1994; and, for industrial designs, Regulation 6/2002, OJ, L 3, 5.01.2002.

162 See Ullrich, 'Harmony and unity of European intellectual property protection', in: Bently and Vaver (eds), *Intellectual Property in the New Millenium: Essays in Honour of William R. Cornish*, Cambridge University Press, Cambridge, 2004, pp. 20-46, at p. 37.

163 *Ibidem*.

Clearly, national disparities might easily cause fragmentation and distortion of competition on the fast-developing markets for digital goods, where copyright protection is sought every day for new kinds of creations. Even if a minimum harmonisation of the copyright subject matter stems from the fact that all of the EU Member States are contracting parties of the Berne Convention, the identification of the classes of protected works provided under this Convention is of little guidance to national law when copyright protection is sought for new kinds of creations. For instance, potential disparities in the scope of copyright protection under national copyright laws may easily arise in respect of new types of works, such as Internet websites, which have emerged mainly after the last update of the Berne Convention in 1991, when the notion of "literary work" accepted under the Convention was extended in order to include computer programmes. Moreover, it must be noted that, in a trans-border scenario where the making of derivative works by end-users is even easier, cheaper and commercially relevant, an additional factor of distortion is created by the fact that the InfoSoc Directive does not harmonise the scope of the exclusive right of authorising the modification or the re-working of copyrighted works. In the absence of a clear, unique notion of "derivative work" in the EU, important cases of transformative uses undertaken by end-users are likely to be subject to very different legal regimes from one Member State to another. Eventually, the European Commission must decide whether to stretch the legal basis of copyright harmonisation (*i.e.*, Article 95 of the EC Treaty) in order to bypass the explicit prohibition laid down in Article 295, and ultimately, it must decide whether to harmonise the copyright standard of originality and the notion of "derivative work" under EU copyright law.

3.3.2. Territorial restrictions in copyright management

The increasing trans-border marketing of copyright-based goods on the Internet and in other digital settings has recently presented - once again - the basic tension that exists between the principle of the free movement of goods and undistorted competition and the strictly national dimension of copyright subject matter and management. It is worth noting that the European Commission's attention has been recently caught by the partitioning effect of copyright management on markets for online music services. As has been observed elsewhere, the emergence of online music services such as Apple's iTunes Music Store currently gives rise to business practices which partition the Internal Market because of the national dimension of copyright licensing.[164] In this respect, an antitrust investigation launched by the European Commission in April 2007 on the grounds of Article 81(1) of the EC Treaty demonstrates that the Commission is taking the partition-

164 See Mazziotti, 'Did Apple's Refusal to License Proprietary Information Enabling Interoperability with Its iPod Music Player Constitute an Abuse under Article 82 of the EC Treaty?', 28(2) *World Competition* 2005, p. 253, at p. 261.

ing effects of copyright management seriously.[165] A statement of objections sent by the Commission to Apple Inc. and to the major record companies operating in Europe alleged that distribution agreements between Apple and each record company contain territorial sales restrictions which violate Article 81 of the EC Treaty.[166] The Commission is seeking to ascertain whether agreements that impose on a platform operator such as Apple a condition restricting downloads distribution to consumers who reside in licensed countries may be deemed incompatible with the common market.[167] Pursuant to the Commission's approach, the outcome of these agreements is the restriction of the consumer choice of where to buy digital music, what music to buy and at what price. As a result, these agreements should be meant as restrictive business practices that Article 81 prohibits and declares void.[168]

Prior to opening the above-mentioned antitrust investigation, the Commission undertook policy measures that were aimed at preventing the partitioning of the European common market stemming from the national dimension of copyright licensing. In its 2004 Communication on "The Management of Copyright and Related Rights in the Internal Market",[169] the European Commission disclosed its policy objective of fostering the "Community-wide" licensing of certain rights concerning activities with a cross-border reach. The Commission displayed uncertainty concerning the most appropriate legal measure to be adopted to achieve this goal. In particular, there were discussions about whether the Community should have intervened by mandating collecting societies to issue Community-wide li-

---

165 See Commission of the European Communities, *Competition: European Commission confirms sending a Statement of Objections against alleged territorial restrictions in on-line music sales to major record companies and Apple*, Press releases, Brussels, 3 of April 2007, available at http://www.europa.eu/rapid/pressReleasesAction.do?reference=MEMO/07/126.

166 Article 81(1) of the EC Treaty states: "The following shall be prohibited as incompatible with the common market: all agreements between undertakings, decisions by associations of undertakings and concerted practices which may affect trade between Member States and which have as their object or effect the prevention, restriction or distortion of competition within the common market, and in particular those which: [...] (b) limit or control production, markets, technical development, or investment [...]".

167 It must be noted that the condition of the country of residence can be easily verified by iTunes thanks to the compulsory requirement that consumers' payments take place through either debit or credit cards linked to bank accounts based in their country of residence.

168 As provided by Article 81(2) of the EC Treaty: "Any agreements or decisions prohibited pursuant to this article shall be automatically void."

169 See Commission of the European Communities, Communication from the Commission to the Council, the European Parliament and the European Economic and Social Committee, *The Management of Copyright and Related Rights in the Internal Market*, COM/2004/0261 final.

censes, or, by simply focusing on "good governance rules" for the functioning of the same societies and their modalities of collective management, instead.[170]

A year later, the Commission decided to accelerate the pursuit of its objective with specific regard to the recently emerged market for online music services. Indeed, the release of a Commission Staff Working Document on the cross-border licensing of online copyrighted music in July 2005[171] preceded the adoption of the Commission Recommendation of 18 October 2005 on collective cross-border management of copyright and related rights for legitimate online music services.[172] By virtue of these interventions in the field of collective management of copyrights and related rights, the European Commission manifested its intention to cure market fragmentation by recourse to a radical modification of today's licensing structures in the online music sector.

As noted by the Commission in the Working Document which accompanied the 2005 Recommendation, reciprocal representation agreements among national collecting societies give rise to territorial restrictions in the administration of the rights involved in the online exploitation of copyrighted music.[173] Reciprocal representation agreements such as the Santiago and Barcelona Agreements (both of which expired at the end of 2004) had traditionally allowed national collecting societies to administer, along with its own national repertoire, the repertoire of the affiliated, foreign collecting societies that participated in the agreements.[174]

---

170 *Ibidem*, under Section 1.2.4 (labelled "The Call for Community-wide Licensing"), where the Commission questioned whether, in this context, "it should be left for the market to develop Community-wide licensing further, while respecting the basic rules of intellectual property protection, including its territorial nature, or whether the Community legislator should seek to facilitate greater Community wide licensing".

171 See Commission of the European Communities, Commission Staff Working Document, *Study on a Community Initiative on the Cross-Border Management of Copyright*, Brussels 7.07.2005, available at: http://www.europa.eu.int (hereinafter "Commission Working Document").

172 See Commission Recommendation of 18 October 2005, OJ L 276, 21.10.2005, pp. 54-57 (hereinafter "Commission Recommendation"). The objectives of the Recommendation are clarified by Recitals from 4 to 9, where it is stated that, in the era of online exploitation of musical works, new commercial users such as online music service providers need a licensing policy that corresponds to the ubiquity of the online environment and which is multi-territorial. Recital 7, in particular, emphasises that licensing of exclusive rights covering the process of online distribution is often restricted by territory, in such a way that commercial users are forced to negotiate in each Member State with each of the respective collective rights managers for each right that is included in the online exploitation (*i.e.*, the reproduction and communication to the public rights).

173 See Commission Staff Working Document, *Impact Assessment reforming cross-border collective management of copyright and related rights for legitimate online music services*, Brussels 11.10.2005, available at: http://www.europa.eu.int.

174 The function of such agreements is addressed by the July 2005 Commission Working Document, op. cit., p. 6: "[I]n the traditional system of managing copyright and related rights, if copyright works are accessible in another territory, the society active in that territory (the "affiliated society") normally enters into reciprocal representation agreement with the collective rights manager that holds the repertoire on behalf of the right-

The point that was raised by the criticism of the European Commission was that these contracts created restrictive clauses which prohibited collective rights managers from licensing their cross-licensed repertoire outside their (national) territory of activity. Generally speaking, the soft law of the Commission Recommendation urged Member States and collective rights managers:

"to take the steps necessary to facilitate the growth of legitimate online services in the Community by promoting a regulatory environment which is best suited to the management, at the Community level, of copyright and related rights for the provision of legitimate online music services."[175]

In particular, the Commission sets out this policy objective by recommending the liberalisation of the relationship between right-holders, collective rights managers and commercial users throughout the whole territory of the Community. The attainment of this liberalisation is being pursued by two types of legal measures:

- Member States are invited to screen their national legislation in order to prohibit all territorial restrictions created by reciprocal representation agreements and membership contracts that ultimately forbid each collecting society, wherever they be located in Europe, from managing online rights for the whole territory of the European Union, regardless of the residence of the authors and regardless of the economic location of the commercial users.
- A code of "recommended practice" has been created with a view to enhancing the degree of efficiency and transparency of collective rights managers and to enabling effective competition among these actors. To this end, the Recommendation provides that right-holders should have the right "to entrust the management of any of the online rights necessary to operate legitimate online music services, on a territorial scope of their choice, to a collective rights manager of their choice [...]".[176]

---

holder [...]". The same Document, at p. 9, footnote 16, reports that the Santiago and Barcelona agreements, referring respectively to the collective management of the communication to the public and reproduction rights, were not renewed by collecting societies of the European Economic Area on the assumption that the European Commission was highly critical of the so-called "economic residence" clause in them.

175 See the Commission Recommendation, paragraph 2. It is worth recalling that the above-mentioned Commission Working Document of 7.07.2005, pp. 28-31, when discussing the legal basis for the proposed Community's action, stated: "The EU's mandate to act results from the fact that collective rights management services are provided (1) cross-border; (2) to nationals of other Member States; (3) under reciprocal representation agreements which contain restrictions which limit the provision of these services, *inter alia*: (i) by territory; (ii) by nationality; (iii) by Member State of economic residence."

176 See Commission Recommendation, paragraph 3.

According to the Recommendation, therefore, contract or statutory membership rules which restrict the freedom of right-holders to withdraw any of their online rights and transfer their multi-territorial management to another collective rights manager should be strictly prohibited.[177]

3.3.3. The overstretched exclusive right of digital reproduction

The InfoSoc Directive provides for a complete re-definition of the scope of national property rights on traditional, creative works. To this end, it has taken as a model the form of protection previously afforded to information goods, such as software and databases. In proposing the re-definition of the copyright concept of "reproduction", the European Commission started from the notion of reproduction adopted with regard to computer programmes and re-stated for databases.[178]

Article 2 of the InfoSoc Directive defines the reproduction right as:

> "[...] the exclusive right to authorise or prohibit direct or indirect, temporary or permanent reproduction by any means and in any form, in whole or in part [...]"

of copyrighted works and of performances, phonograms, films and broadcasts protected by so-called neighbouring rights.

3.3.3.1. The notion of reproduction under the EC Software Directive

In 1991, copyright law dealt - for the first time - with the technical assumption that digital technology required *any* and *all* uses of computer programmes to create a temporary copy of it as a necessity. This new assumption was clearly described by the technical functioning of computer programmes. A computer programme (software) is formed by a set of instructions given to a machine (hardware) by means of a code (the so-called "source-code") written in a readable, programming language. The source code which constitutes a computer programme is usually expressed in several text files, but the same code may be either printed in a book or recorded on tape. Considering that the source code contains the instructions to be given to the machine each time a certain programme is performed, the end-user of the programme needs to make temporary reproductions of the source code into his or her hardware (normally through the intermediation of an operating system) in order to convert the code from the human-readable form to an equivalent computer-executable form. As pointed out by Hugenholtz, in the absence of patent or copyright protection, software producers and distributors developed a contractual business model, according to which copies of computer programmes were "licensed", instead of being "sold", to end-users.[179] Hugenholtz observed that these

---

[177] *Ibidem*, paragraphs 3-5.

[178] See Article 4(a) of the Software Directive and Articles 5(a) and 7(2)(a) of the 1996 Database Directive.

[179] See Hugenholtz, 'Caching and Copyright: The Right of Temporary Copying', (22) *EIPR* 2000, p. 482, at p. 486.

user licenses, which were "reminiscent more of patents than of copyright licences", aimed at stretching the reproduction right so as to include acts of end usage (which were left unprotected by copyright law) into an exclusive right of use.[180]

In taking such a trade practice as a model for a legislative solution, the 1991 EC Software Directive shaped the reproduction right in such a way as to reserve any and all temporary fixation of a computer programme (*i.e.*, "the permanent or temporary reproduction of a computer program by any means and in any form, in part or in whole") to the copyright owner.[181]

Article 4(a) of the Directive made it clear that:

> "Insofar as loading, displaying, running, transmission or storage of the computer program necessitate such reproduction, such acts shall be subject to authorization by the right-holder [...]".

By the inclusion of temporary copying within the scope of the reproduction right, copyright ended up by legally covering the mere use of the work.[182] Article 4(a) made it clear that, as a consequence of the general restriction created by copyright law on reproduction, certain acts are subject to authorisation by the copyright owner because they cannot be performed without carrying out an act of reproduction. Since the aftermath of the enactment of the Software Directive, the question of whether the acts of loading, displaying, running, transmission or storage have become restricted in and of themselves has been controversial. In particular, it is still unclear whether these acts are restricted by Article 4 of the Directive as specific types of reproduction or if they are implicitly permitted in so far as a right to use the programme is acquired.[183]

The most remarkable aspect of this definition of the notion of copyright reproduction for computer programmes is that the law started to regulate what had formerly been regulated through licence contracts with users, namely, the reproduc-

---

180 See Hugenholtz, 'Caching and Copyright', op. cit., p. 486.

181 See Article 4(a) of the Software Directive.

182 See Dusollier, 'Technology as an Imperative for Regulating Copyright: From the Public Exploitation to the Private Use of the Work', (27) *EIPR* 2005, p. 201 ("[W]hen copyright was chosen as the means to protect computer programs, the worm started eating the fruit. It was felt necessary to prevent uses of software by multiple users from one single copy hosted on a shared server."); and Romano, *L'opera e l'esemplare nel diritto della proprietà intellettuale*, Cedam, Padova, 2001, p. 193, who observed that the strict regulation of use through the provision of a very broad right of reproduction on software could be justified on the assumption that software is a means to use rather than a work to communicate.

183 See Czarnota and Hart, *Legal Protection of Computer Programs in Europe, A Guide to the EC Directive*, Butterworths, London, 1991, pp. 56-57, who argued that most licences controlled the use that could be made of the programme in terms of ability to store or transmit it. These authors concluded that, whatever interpretations can be made of the second part of Article 4(a), acts such as loading and running, although technically requiring reproduction, and therefore legally requiring authorisation, should be meant to be impliedly permitted if a right of ordinary use is acquired.

tion and consumption of copies. As pointed out by Dusollier, this new law inevitably altered the natural scope of copyright, which is designed as a right which protects intellectual property. By the inclusion of acts of consumption into the scope of copyright, this form of intellectual property on computer programmes started to be confused with the subsidiary role of contract and/or *real* property rules, which established the normal framework for the protection of the distribution of copies.[184] Moreover, by including the private copying of computer programmes into the scope of copyright protection, the Software Directive intended to protect the commercial exploitation of the work from copying for personal use, which, due to its cheap and perfect nature, could easily have been re-converted by users into a source of "viral" counterfeiting.[185]

3.3.3.2. Exemption of certain software reproductions from copyright protection

To avoid anti-competitive and other negative effects that such an overbroad notion of reproduction would imply, the Software Directive recurred to statutory exceptions to exempt certain software reproductions which serve purposes of consumption, study, research, and the creation of interoperable programmes by the person who has a right to use a copy of the computer programme (*i.e.*, the so-called "lawful acquirer") from the copyright scope.

According to Articles 5 and 6 of the 1991 Software Directive, the right of reproduction is delimited by the recognition to the lawful acquirer of the following rights:

- The right to use software "in accordance with its intended purpose, including for error correction";[186]
- The right to make a "back-up" copy of a computer programme;[187]
- The right to observe, study or test the functioning of the programme in order to determine the ideas and principles which underlie any element of the programme if the user does so while performing any of the acts of loading, displaying, running, transmitting or storing the programme which he is entitled to do;[188]
- The right to reproduce the programme code and to translate its form when these acts are indispensable to obtain the information necessary to achieve the interoperability of an independently created programme with other pro-

[184] See Dusollier, 'Technology as an Imperative for Regulating Copyright', op. cit., p. 201.

[185] See Ricolfi, 'Le nuove frontiere della proprietà intellettuale, da Chicago al cyberspazio', in: Clerico and Rizzello (eds), *Diritto ed economia della proprietà intellettuale*, Cedam, Padova, 1998, p. 83, at pp. 93-94.

[186] See Article 5(1) of the Software Directive.

[187] See Article 5(2) of the Software Directive.

[188] See Article 5(3) of the Software Directive.

grammes (the so-called "decompilation" or "reverse engineering" of computer programmes).[189]

It is worth noting here that the effectiveness of this regulation of software-related copyright is ensured by the explicit protection of all the exceptions to the reproduction right against contractual override provided under Article 9(1) of the Software Directive.[190] The sole exception that is not protected under this provision is the one which allows use of software in accordance with its intended purpose (including error correction: cf. Article 5(1)). However, the wording of the Preamble of the Directive makes it clear that even this exception, like the others, "may not be prohibited by contract [...]".[191] In contrast, what seems to be a negative aspect of this effective regulation is the inappropriate restriction of the pro-interoperability exception created under Article 6(1). As observed by Ricolfi, Article 6(1) restricted the field of application of technical operations such as decompilation and reverse analysis of the software source code, which might easily serve innovation purposes.[192] Such operations are banned if they are used for goals other than that of achieving the interoperability of an independently created computer programme.[193]

3.3.3.3. The exclusive right of reproduction under the InfoSoc Directive

While covering private use, the all-encompassing exclusive right of reproduction created under the Software Directive veers dangerously away from the legal notion of reproduction by wholly espousing its technical concept.[194] Several scholars pointed out that, as a result of the adoption of this technical notion, the basic func-

189 See Article 6(1) of the Software Directive.

190 Article 9(1) of the Software Directive states: "Any contractual provisions contrary to Article 6 or to the exceptions provided for in Articles 5(2) and (3) shall be null and void."

191 See the Preamble of the Software Directive, where it reads "Whereas the exclusive rights of the author to prevent the unauthorized reproduction of his work have to be subject to a limited exception in the case of a computer program to allow the reproduction technically necessary for the use of that program by the lawful acquirer; whereas this means that the acts of loading and running necessary for the use of a copy of a program which has been lawfully acquired, and the act of correction of its errors, *may not be prohibited by contract* [...]" (emphasis added).

192 Ricolfi, 'Proprietà intellettuale, antitrust e reti', in: Cambini and Valletti (eds), *I mercati della comunicazione nell'era digitale*, Il Mulino, Bologna, 2002, p. 66.

193 See Article 6(2)(a) of the Software Directive. In the U.S. literature, the same issue was examined by Reichman, 'Legal Hybrids Between the Patent and the Copyright Paradigms', (94) *Columbia Law Review* 1994, p. 2432; and Lemley, 'The Economics of Improvements in Intellectual Property Law', (75) *Texas Law Review* 1997, p. 997.

194 See Hugenholtz, 'Caching and Copyright', op. cit., p. 485.

tion of digital reproduction gave rise to an unprecedented condition of simultaneity among the different modalities of commercial exploitation of a work.[195]

Ten years after the Software Directive, the InfoSoc Directive extended this software-related approach to all copyrighted works. In particular, Article 2 drafted a very broad definition of the right of reproduction, while Article 5(1) restricted it by the only mandatory copyright limitation provided under the InfoSoc Directive.[196] Article 2 makes any form of permanent and temporary reproduction subject to the authorisation of the copyright owners, while Article 5(1) specifies that temporary acts of reproduction are to be exempted from the reproduction right when they are:

> "[T]ransient or incidental [and] an integral and essential part of a technological process and whose sole purpose is to enable: (a) a transmission in a network between third parties by an intermediary, or (b) a lawful use of a work or other subject-matter to be made, and which have no independent economic significance [...]".

This "convoluted text" enacted two distinct provisions.[197] On the one hand, Article 5(1)(a) exempts certain temporary acts, for example, caching,[198] and routing,[199] which enable intermediaries such as Internet service providers (ISPs) temporarily to store and reproduce digital packets of copyrighted works through their cables and network infrastructure. Hugenholtz contended that online digital transmission as such would not implicate the reproduction right if it was accepted that "tempo-

---

[195] See Ginsburg, 'Putting Cars on the "Information Superhighways": Authors, Exploiters and Copyrights in Cyberspace', (95) *Columbia Law Review* 1995, p. 1466; Ricolfi, *Comunicazione al pubblico e distribuzione*, Annali Italiani di Diritto d'Autore (AIDA) 2002, p. 48, at p. 75; Hugenholtz, 'Adapting Copyright to the Information Superhighway', in: Hugenholtz (ed), *The Future of Copyright in a Digital Environment*, op. cit., p. 80.

[196] See Recital 21 of the InfoSoc Directive, that warns that the Directive "should define the scope of the acts covered by the reproduction right with regard to the different beneficiaries. This should be done in conformity with the acquis communautaire. A broad definition of these acts is needed to ensure legal certainty within the internal market."

[197] It is an expression borrowed from Cohen Jehoram, 'European Copyright Law', op. cit., p. 540. For a detailed analysis of the provision of Article 5(1) of the InfoSoc Directive, see *Study on the implementation and effect in Member States' laws of Directive 2001/29/EC on the harmonization of certain aspects of copyright and related rights in the Information Society*, Final Report, Institute for Information Law, University of Amsterdam, February 2007, available at http://www.ivir.nl/index-english.html.

[198] As recalled by Hugenholtz, 'Caching and Copyright', op. cit., "[C]aching (etymologically related to the French "cacher": to hide) is the automatic creation of temporary copies of digital data (in a "cache") in order to make the data more available for subsequent use".

[199] The term "routing", instead, describes a modality of transmission by which each whole of digital data is fragmented into many "packets", each of which is sent electronically to the required destination through the shortest way.

rarily stored digital packets are usually far too small to qualify as 'reproductions' in a legal sense".[200]

On the other hand, Article 5(1)(b) allows end-users to engage in temporary acts (*e.g.*, browsing, caching) which have "no independent economic significance". The Explanatory Memorandum presented by the European Commission with the Proposal for the InfoSoc Directive clarified that the expression "no independent economic significance" is intended to enable the application of the exemption to the case of reproductions "made for the sole purpose of executing another act of exploitation of a work".[201] With regard to acts of temporary reproduction by end-users, this exemption indisputably applies to acts of browsing and caching.

However, the extent to which this exemption applies to acts of browsing remains uncertain. Despite the explicit statement of Recital 33 of the InfoSoc Directive on this issue, Article 5(1) made the browsing exemption dependent upon the interpretation of unclear conditions.[202] As effectively outlined by Hart, it is largely unclear what type of temporary copying may have "no independent economic significance".[203] Furthermore, as emphasised persuasively by the authors of a study on the implementation of the InfoSoc Directive, the circumstances in which Article 5(1)(b) requires the use enabled by the exempted temporary reproduction to be "lawful" increase considerably the uncertainty of a condition of application of the copyright limitation at issue.[204] These authors observed that the main, unsolved question created by this wording concerns the identification of the relevant criteria external to the scope of Article 5(1) that must be taken into account to determine lawfulness.[205] In principle, such criteria may be taken from the last section of Re-

---

200 See Hugenholtz, 'Caching and Copyright', op. cit., p. 487. The author elaborated this view by commenting sarcastically on the appropriateness of the above-mentioned exemption: see Hugenholtz, 'Why the Copyright Directive is Unimportant, and Possibly Invalid', op. cit., p. 501 ("Did we really need a European lawmaker to tell us that caching and browsing are allowed without authorisation? A common sense right would have done the job as well, if not much better [...]").

201 See Commission of the European Communities, Explanatory Memorandum, Proposal for a European Parliament and Council Directive on the harmonization of certain aspects of copyright and related rights in the Information Society, COM (97) 62, p. 30.

202 According to Recital 33, to the extent that the acts of temporary reproduction meet the conditions spelt out under Article 5(1) of the Directive, "this exception should include acts which enable browsing as well as caching to take place, including those which enable transmission systems to function efficiently, provided that the intermediary does not modify the information and does not interfere with the lawful use of technology, widely recognized and used by industry, to obtain data on the use of the information [...]".

203 See Hart, 'The Copyright in the Information Society Directive: an Overview', (24) *EIPR* 2002, p. 58, at p. 59. Recital 33 of the Directive attempted to clarify the above-mentioned concept by providing that the acts of reproduction concerned by this limitation "should have no separate economic value on their own."

204 See *Study on the implementation and effect in Member States' laws of Directive 2001/29/EC*, op. cit., p. 33.

205 *Ibidem*, pp. 34-35.

cital 33, which tried to clarify the notion of "lawful use" for the purposes of the InfoSoc Directive by providing that:

"A use should be considered lawful where it is authorised by the rightholder or not restricted by law."

According to the above-mentioned study, the application of this definition to the case of Article 5(1)(b) would not make the interpretation of this provision easier. Indeed, whereas it is not difficult to think of a practical case in which a copyright holder authorises a temporary reproduction (*e.g.*, the uploading of a protected work by its copyright owner on a publicly accessible webpage could be viewed as an implied authorisation to the transient reproductions allowing this work to be browsed on the Internet), it is much harder to conceive of an act "not restricted by law" (*e.g.*, an act permitted under a copyright exception) that would qualify as a temporary reproduction and, consequently, would be exempted under Article 5(1)(b).[206]

With particular regard to the transient reproductions made by information carriers and exempted under Article 5(1)(a), it was emphasised that this exemption serves the purpose of excluding carriers from indirect liability for copyright infringements carried out by their customers.[207] The technical functioning of the Internet – in the same way as a huge "copy-machine" - requires intermediaries to engage in temporary reproductions of small digital packets for digital content to be communicated over networks. Thus, the law was forced to make it clear that acts of transient reproduction do not fall within the legal notion of "copies" that are subject to the control of copyright holders. The complementary provisions of Article 5(1)(a) of the InfoSoc Directive and Articles 12 to 15 of the 2000 Electronic Commerce Directive restrict, under certain clear conditions, the liability of ISPs acting as mere conduits, caching and hosting service providers for the communication of infringing material.[208]

At the time of the negotiations for the 1996 WIPO Copyright Treaty, the issue of transient reproductions was far from being taken for granted. This question was highly debated in Geneva, where the U.S. delegation proposed the adoption of a notion of copyrighted reproduction that would have intentionally invoked the liability of information carriers for their acts of communication through networks. The intention was that of requiring such intermediaries to police unauthorised flows of copyrighted works through their infrastructure. The U.S. proposal, which

---

206 *Ibidem.*

207 See Ricolfi, 'Intellectual property rights and legal order', op. cit., p. 132.

208 See Directive 2000/31/EC of 8 June 2000, on electronic commerce, OJ L 178, 17.07.2000, 1 (hereinafter "E-Commerce Directive"), Articles 12 to 15. On the connection between the InfoSoc Directive and the Electronic Commerce Directive, see Hart, 'The Copyright in the Information Society Directive', op. cit., p. 59; Cohen Jehoram, 'European Copyright Law', op. cit., p. 544; and *Study on the implementation and effect in Member States' laws of Directive 2001/29/EC*, op. cit., pp. 36-37.

was eventually rejected, had previously been elaborated in the so-called 1995 White Paper.[209]

3.3.4. The exclusive right of communication to the public

Apart from the broadly defined right of reproduction, the InfoSoc Directive enacted a Community-wide adaptation of the classical rights of communication to the public and of distribution to the digital environment.[210] By implementing the wide definition laid down in Article 8 of the 1996 WIPO Copyright Treaty,[211] Article 3 provided authors, performers and the producers of copyrighted works with:

> "[T]he exclusive right to prohibit any communication to the public of their works, by wire or wireless means, including the making available to the public of their works in such a way that members of the public may access them from a place and at a time chosen by them."

Recital 23 of the Directive makes it clear that this right "should be understood in a broad sense covering all communication to the public not present at the place where the communication originates [...]" and it should include "any such transmission or re-transmission of a work to the public by wire or wireless means, including broadcasting [...]".

The InfoSoc Directive made two important points with regard to the right of digital communication. Firstly, the Directive restated the broad provision contained in Article 8 of the 1996 WIPO "Internet" Treaty, which shaped the right of communication to the public as an exclusive right of making copyrighted works available, which covers, in particular, the interactive on-demand transmission of copyrighted works over digital networks.[212]

Secondly, the Directive strictly delimits the right of distribution to the realm of physical (*i.e.*, tangible) media, in such a way that the above-mentioned principle of Community-wide exhaustion cannot apply to the dissemination of intangible copies over networks. As pointed out below, Article 4(2) of the Directive understands the dissemination of intangible works over digital networks as a provision of "services" rather than as a distribution of "goods".[213] This aspect provides further evi-

---

209 See U.S. Department of Commerce, Patent and Trademark Office, Information Infrastructure Task Force, *Intellectual Property and the National Information Infrastructure: The Report of the Working Group on Intellectual Property Rights*, available at: www.uspto.gov/web/offices/com/doc/ipnii/front.pdf.

210 See Articles 3 and 4 of the InfoSoc Directive.

211 Article 8 of the 1996 WIPO Copyright Treaty ("Right of Communication to the Public") provides as follows: "[...] authors of literary and artistic works shall enjoy the exclusive right of authorizing any communication to the public of their works, by wire or wireless means, including the making available to the public of their works in such a way that members of the public may access these works from a place and at the time chosen by them."

212 See Recital 25 of the InfoSoc Directive.

213 See §3.3.6., see *infra*.

dence of the fact that, by creating an exclusive right of making copyrighted works available to the public, the InfoSoc Directive, as dictated by Article 8 of the WIPO Copyright Treaty, mainly intended to pursue a commercial policy objective.

3.3.5. The right of distribution of tangible copyrighted goods

The Directive makes a careful distinction between the distribution right and the right of making the copyrighted work available to the public. Article 4 of the Directive speaks of "distribution" with exclusive regard to the sale of physical media which incorporate the protected work. This distinction is upheld by the wording of Recital 28, which clarifies that copyright protection covers "the exclusive right to control distribution of the work incorporated in a tangible article". The Directive then draws upon the basic distinction between tangible and intangible copies of the copyrighted work to clarify the scope and the application of the exhaustion principle.

According to Article 4(2), which draws from the *acquis communautaire* on exhaustion, the distribution right:

> "should not be exhausted within the Community in respect of the original or copies of the work, except where the first sale or other transfer of ownership in the Community of that object is made by the right-holder or with his consent."

Even in this respect, two Directive Recitals intervened to set aside possible uncertainties. Recital 28 made it clear that the first sale exhausting the right to control resale in the Community refers only to the work incorporated in a tangible form, while Recital 29 specified that the question of exhaustion did not arise in the case of services (on-line services, in particular) whose dissemination of copyrighted works fell, instead, within the scope of the right of making the works available to the public.

The applicability of the principle of exhaustion to the limited framework of tangible articles was recently relied on by the ECJ in the preliminary ruling on *Laserdisken ApS* v. *Kulturministeriet*.[214] The case was made by Laserdisken, a commercial company which sells *inter alia* copies of cinematographic works to individual purchasers through its sales outlets in Denmark. Until the end of 2002, the company imported these copies mainly from the other Member States of the European Union, but also from non-member countries. The core business of this company consisted of the distribution of cinematographic works that were not or would not be available in Europe. Laserdisken brought legal proceedings against the Kulturministeriet (the Ministry of Culture) before the Østre Landsret (Eastern Regional Court) after having registered a significant reduction in its operations following the coming into force of the Danish act that implemented the InfoSoc

---

[214] See *Laserdisken ApS* v. *Kulturministeriet*, C-479-04, Judgment of the Court (Grand Chamber), 12 September 2006, available at: http://www.curia.europa.eu (hereinafter *Laserdisken*).

Directive.[215] The claimant called into question the legitimacy of this Act in the context of the transposition of Article 4(2) of the InfoSoc Directive. By means of this Act, Danish law reformed, *inter alia*, the scope of the principle of exhaustion (or "first sale doctrine") by permitting the further distribution of a copy of a copyrighted work on condition that the copy was sold with the consent of the copyright holder, or transferred in some other manner to another party within the European Economic Area.[216]

In this case, the ECJ had the opportunity to clarify an important effect of the provision of Article 4(2) on the copyright laws of the Member States. Indeed, the Court strongly rejected Laserdisken's claim that this provision left the possibility of providing for a rule of "international exhaustion" (that is, a rule other than the Community-wide exhaustion) open to the Member States.[217] This judgment made it clear that, due to the harmonisation measure embodied in Article 4(2), Member States were legally prevented from providing for the exhaustion of the exclusive right of distribution on a tangible copyrighted object of which the first sale or transferral of the object had taken place *outside Community territory*. Thus, the ECJ found the reform of the Danish law to be fair with regard to the implementation of Article 4(2) of the Directive. According to the ECJ, this was the only interpretation consistent with the main purpose of the Directive, which was that of ensuring the functioning of the Internal Market.[218] The emphasis given by the ECJ to the goal of market integration in reviewing the harmonisation measure embodied in Article 4(2) corroborates the criticism that will be expressed below in respect of other horizontal measures of the Directive, which evidently failed to meet the objective of market integration.[219]

3.3.6. Intangible copyrighted goods as services

As outlined above, the InfoSoc Directive provides that the operation of the exhaustion principle should be limited to markets for physical media which incorporate the copyrighted work.[220] A hypothetical implementation of the exhaustion

---

[215] See Act N.1051 of 17 December 2002.

[216] To understand Laserdisken's claim better, it must be considered that, prior to transposition of Directive 2001/29, Section 19 of the Danish Law on copyright provided no territorial restrictions to the operation of the exhaustion principle. The former version of Section 19 provided that "[w]hen a copy of a work is, with the copyright holder's consent, sold or in some other manner transferred to another party, the copy may be distributed further." Following reform of that law, which intended to implement the provision of Article 4(2) of the InfoSoc Directive, Section 19(1) has since read as follows: "When a copy of a work is, with the copyright holder's consent, sold or in some other manner transferred to another party *within the European Economic Area*, the copy may be distributed further [...]" (emphasis added).

[217] See *Laserdisken*, paragraphs 23-24.

[218] See *Laserdisken*, paragraph 26.

[219] See §5.2.2., see *infra*.

[220] See §3.3.5., see *supra*.

principle to the case of intangible goods would be simply inconceivable, since the Directive understands intangible copyrighted goods as protected "services" to be exploited primarily on the grounds of the strict principle of territoriality of copyright protection. The exhaustion rule is designed to regulate the circulation of physical media which embody copyrighted works at the level of secondary exploitation, *i.e.*, when the copyright holder has already sold, or agreed upon transferring, ownership over these media within the EU territory. The purpose of this principle is to co-ordinate the principle of territoriality of copyright protection with that of the free movement of goods embodied in Articles 28 and 29 of the EC Treaty.

The problem raised by the InfoSoc Directive in respect of its institutional objective of market integration in the online environment relates to the absence, in the copyright regulation provided by the Directive, of harmonisation measures which seek to avoid territorial partitions in the cross-border dissemination of copyrighted works through the Internet. It was pointed out above that the InfoSoc Directive had not taken the appropriate measures to enable the Community-wide licensing of online services providing intangible copyrighted works.[221] This objective was pursued only in October 2005 by the action undertaken by the European Commission with its Recommendation on collective cross-border management of copyright and related rights for legitimate online music services.[222] The starting point of this action, which had completely been ignored (or, at best, underestimated) in the InfoSoc Directive, is that there would be no European Common Markets for copyrighted digital works in the borderless environment of digital networks such as the Internet unless the EU found a way to ensure the compatibility of national copyright protection and management with the constitutional principle of the free movement of goods and services.

It seems paradoxical that, in a legislative measure devoted to the Information Society, the only purpose of market integration was explicitly confined to the old framework of tangible goods. While providing no appropriate innovation on how to enforce the principle of the free movement of copyrighted goods and services on the Internet, notwithstanding the assumption of national copyright protection, the InfoSoc Directive displayed a questionable lack of commitment to an objective that it should have pursued in accordance with Article 95 of the EC Treaty, namely, the effective integration of online markets for copyrighted works.

The above-mentioned judgment of the ECJ in *Laserdisken* v. *Kulturministeriet* upholds this critical view. The ECJ explicitly based its final interpretation of Article 4(2) on the argument that the Directive must be applied in accordance with the objective that it pursued, to wit, the purpose of ensuring the functioning of the Internal Market. The ECJ's judgment stated that:

"A situation in which some Member States will be able to provide for international exhaustion of distribution rights whilst others will provide only for Community-wide exhaustion

[221] See §3.3.2, see *supra*.

[222] See the Commission Recommendation of 18 October 2005, cit., §1.2.2.

of those rights will inevitably give rise to barriers to the free movement of goods and the freedom to provide services."[223]

As argued in greater depth below,[224] the evident failure of the InfoSoc Directive in harmonising the legislative aspects of national laws which give rise to barriers on the fast-growing markets for online (*i.e.*, intangible) copyrighted works calls into question the constitutional validity of the Directive. It is still unclear, in my view, why, under this Directive, the purpose of ensuring the functioning of the Internal Market in the offline world took preference over the same objective in the online digital environment, which lies at the heart of the European Information Society.

3.4. Anti-circumvention law in defence of technological protection measures

One of the most important and controversial issues raised by the InfoSoc Directive was the implementation of the obligation set out in Article 11 of the 1996 WIPO Copyright Treaty.[225] In accordance with the purpose of this provision, Articles 6 and 7 of the Directive created a complex set of rules which required the law of the Member States to afford special legal protection to the technological protection measures used by copyright holders to restrict unauthorised access to and use of their works and to forbid third parties from altering and removing related right-management information.

3.4.1. The provisions of Articles 6 and 7 of the InfoSoc Directive

Under Articles 6 and 7 of the InfoSoc Directive, Member States are required to provide two kinds of prohibitions in order to protect and ultimately encourage the development of encryption and DRM technologies:

- Articles 6(1) and 7(1)(a) outlaw, respectively, acts of circumvention of any technological measure and the removal or alteration of any rights management information carried out knowingly by any person;
- Articles 6(2) and 7(1)(b) outlaw, respectively, so-called preparatory activities (that is, any act of manufacture and distribution of technologies which enable or facilitate circumvention of effective technological measures) and the making

223 See *Laserdisken*, paragraph 26.

224 See §5.2., see *infra*.

225 Article 11 of the 1996 WIPO Copyright Treaty ("Obligations concerning Technological Measures") provides as follows: "Contracting Parties shall provide adequate legal protection and effective legal remedies against the circumvention of effective technological measures that are used by authors in connection with the exercise of their rights under this Treaty or the Berne Convention and that restrict acts, in respect of their works, which are not authorized by the authors concerned or permitted by law."

available of copyrighted work whose electronic rights management information has been removed or altered without authority.[226]

Rights management technologies have developed at an impressive pace and have become even more sophisticated in the last years. In identifying which technologies deserved protection from acts of circumvention, Articles 6 and 7 of the InfoSoc Directive relied on a broad definition of "technological measures" and "rights management information".

As regards technological protection measures, Article 6(3) states that:

"For the purposes of this Directive, the expression 'technological measures' means any technology, device or component that, in the normal course of its operation, is designed to prevent or restrict acts, in respect of works or other subject-matter, which are not authorised by the rightholder of any copyright or any right related to copyright as provided for by law or the *sui generis* right provided for in Chapter III of Directive 96/9/EC. Technological measures shall be deemed to be 'effective' where the use of a protected work or other subject-matter is controlled by the rightholders through application of an access control or protection process, such as encryption, scrambling or other transformation of the work or other subject-matter or a copy control mechanism, which achieves the protection objective."

According to Article 7(2):

"For the purposes of this Directive, the expression 'rights management information' means any information provided by rightholders which identifies the work or other subject-matter referred to in this Directive or covered by the *sui generis* right provided for in Chapter III of Directive 96/9/EC, the author or any other rightholder, or information about the terms and conditions of use of the work or other subject-matter, and any numbers of codes that represent such information."

These broad definitions give rise to several concerns. Whereas, in principle, the wide scope of the definitions could allow legislation not to become obsolete as long as technology developed, the distinction between technological protection measures and rights management information became outdated very early on. The above-mentioned definitions failed to predict how control and rights management technologies would have developed in the years following the enactment of the Directive. The consequence of this failure is that the definition of technology protection from circumvention, today, is no longer compatible with the most impor-

---

[226] This type of regulation found a precedent in the European Union in the law of Directive 98/84/EC of the European Parliament and of the Council of 20 November 1998 on the legal protection of services based on, or consisting of, conditional access, OJ, L 320, 28.11.1998, 54 (hereinafter "Conditional Access Directive"). In a way fairly similar to that of prohibitions laid down in Articles 6(2) and 7(1)(b) of the InfoSoc Directive, Article 4 of the Conditional Access Directive required Member States to prohibit on their territories all activities regarding the manufacture, marketing, use, possession and communication of any equipment or software designed or adapted to give access to a protected service (*e.g.*, television and radio broadcasting) without the authorisation of the service provider.

tant systems of control and rights management of digital copyrighted works (that is to say, DRM systems), which today blend both functions of access- and copy-control with rights management information. Moreover, the adoption of vague terms to identify technological measures resulted in a non-homogeneous transposition of these definitions into the law of the Member States.[227]

3.4.2. What "access right" in the EU?

In the same way as their equivalents under U.S. law, the above-mentioned anti-circumvention provisions were the subject of an intense and ongoing debate in both academia and society.[228] Both in Europe and in the U.S., it was argued that the legal protection ensured by such circumvention bans went far beyond the traditional purpose of copyright by conferring to right-holders an unprecedented "access right" over their works.[229] Under Article 6 of the InfoSoc Directive, as well as under Section 1201 of the U.S. Copyright Act, prohibitions regarding the circumvention of exclusion tools, such as DRM systems, and the outlawing of any decryption technologies end up by treating circumvention which serves both legal and illegal purposes in the same way.[230] Adding a wholly separate tort of unauthorised circumvention, such provisions have the effect of forbidding users from circumventing technological protection by engaging in transformative or non-transformative acts permitted by law.[231] In conclusion, Article 6 mandates inde-

---

[227] See Gasser and Girsberger, 'Transposing the Copyright Directive: Legal Protection of Technological Measures in EU-Member States. A Genie Stuck in the Bottle?', The Berkman Center for Internet and Society at Harvard Law School, Berkman Publication Series No.2004-10, November 2004, available at: http://cyber.law.harvard.edu/publications, p. 16; see also *Study on the implementation and effect in Member States' laws of Directive 2001/29/EC*, op. cit., Part II.

[228] "Anti-circumvention" provisions were enacted in the U.S. by the Digital Millennium Copyright Act, which entered into force on 28 October 1998 by adding Sections 1201 to 1205 to the U.S. Copyright Act (U.S. Code, Title 17). Section 1201 ("Circumvention of copyright protection systems") contains two types of prohibitions very similar to the ones laid down in Article 6 of the InfoSoc Directive.

[229] In the U.S. literature, for instance, see Ginsburg, 'From Having Copies to Experiencing Works: the Development of an Access Right in U.S. Copyright Law', Columbia Law School, Public Law and Legal Theory Working Group, 2000, available at: http://papers.ssrn.com, who argued that the so-called "access right", as codified now under Section 1201 of the U.S. Copyright Act, was implicitly pre-supposed by the existence, under copyright law, of the exclusive rights of reproduction and distribution. *Contra*, see Heide, 'Copyright in the E.U. and United States: What "Access Right"?', (23) *EIPR* 2001, p. 469, who held that the recognition of the "power" to control access to creative works has nothing to do with traditional copyright protection.

[230] See U.S. Code, Title 17, Chapter 12, §1201.

[231] In commenting on the final version of the Directive, Vinje, 'Should We Begin Digging Copyright's Grave?', (22) *EIPR* 2000, p. 551, at p. 556, emphasised that "it is unfortunate that E.U legislators have chosen to adopt such a far-reaching prohibition on circumvention-related activities *with no link to infringement*." (emphasis added).

pendent protection for exclusion and management tools, under which the scope of copyright is shaped according to what copyright holders are able to protect through technology.[232]

To understand the scope of EU anti-circumvention law better, it is worth noting that the EU prohibition of circumvention is slightly different from its equivalent under U.S. law. Whereas Section 1201(a) of the U.S. Copyright Act, as amended by the 1998 DMCA, only forbids circumvention of access-control mechanisms, Article 6 of the EU Directive prohibits both the circumvention of mechanisms which ensure access- and copy-control.[233]

Consequently, the European prohibition is more extensive than the U.S. one. While, under U.S. law, the end-user is entitled to circumvent or hack copy-control technology in order to engage in a certain act covered by the fair use doctrine (for example, private copying), EU law, in contrast, requires Member States to prohibit end-users even from engaging in such kind of circumvention. What is prohibited under both legislations is the circumvention of technologies which control access to copyrighted works and the above-mentioned preparatory activities in respect of both access and copy-control technologies.[234]

A further difference arises with regard to the limitation of right-holder power to control access to copyrighted works. Whereas U.S. law clearly separated the protection of access-control technologies from copyright protection, the InfoSoc Directive took a more complex approach. U.S. law limited the anti-circumvention prohibition by the creation of a number of strict exemptions which are significantly unrelated (and opposed to) the philosophy of the fair use doctrine.[235] EU

[232] See Dusollier, 'Technology as an Imperative for Regulating Copyright', op. cit., p. 202 ("The anti-circumvention provisions are the most interesting battlefield between the traditional vision of the copyright law and the dictates of technology [...] The scope of copyright is no longer decided according to what the proper scope should be, but according to what technology can do.").

[233] See the final part of Article 6(3) of the InfoSoc Directive, which distinguishes analytically between *access*- and *copy*-control technologies ("[...] where the use of a protected work [...] is controlled by rightholders through application of an access control or protection process, such as encryption, scrambling [...]") and grants them equal treatment. See Gasser and Girsberger, 'Transposing the Copyright Directive', op. cit., pp. 9-10; Fallenboeck, 'On the Technical Protection of Copyright: The Digital Millennium Copyright Act, the European Community Copyright Directive and Their Anticircumvention Provisions', (7) *International Journal of Communication Law and Policy*, Winter 2002/2003, available in PDF at: http://www.ijclp.org, p. 40.

[234] See Article 6(2) of the InfoSoc Directive and Section 1201 of the U.S. Copyright Act, which prohibit the manufacture and distribution of technologies enabling or facilitating circumvention.

[235] Under Section 1201 of the U.S. DMCA, the separation between anti-circumvention protection (named even "paracopyright") and copyright protection is clearly demonstrated by the creation of strict exemptions to circumvention bans: see §1201, letters from (d) to (j). See Dusollier, *Droit d'auteur et protection des œuvres dans l'univers numérique. Droits et exceptions à la lumière des dispositifs de verrouillage des œuvres*, Larcier, Bruxelles, 2005, pp. 196-201; Nimmer, 'A Riff on Fair Use in the Digital Millennium

law, in Article 6(4) of the Directive, creates a legislative mechanism that provides that it is the ultimate responsibility of the copyright holders to accommodate certain exceptions.[236]

It is noteworthy that the EU solution was the fruit of a compromise reached by the European Commission and the Council after a difficult debate. In the initial proposal of the Commission, by virtue of a rather ambiguous provision, anti-circumvention rules were to protect technological measures as long as they restricted or prevented copyright infringements.[237]

In strict accordance with the purpose of copyright law, circumvention torts should, of necessity, have been linked to an objective violation of copyright or related rights. Having directly negotiated the 1996 WIPO Copyright Treaty on behalf of Member States, the Commission knew that, under Article 11 of the Treaty, entitled "Obligations Concerning Technological Measures", statutory copyright exceptions were given explicit immunity against the operation of technological measures. The Commission was conscious that, if copyright exceptions had not been safeguarded effectively under the Directive, the subsequent, technology-dictated re-definition of copyright protection could not be viewed as a straightforward implementation of Article 11.[238]

Nonetheless, the original link between anti-circumvention protection and copyright infringement was removed when the Commission and the European Council reached a Common Position in September 2000.[239] The Council was forced to find a compromise between the position initially expressed by the Commission, which intended to preserve the vitality of copyright exceptions, and several restrictive amendments proposed by the European Parliament, which attempted to make such exceptions wholly subject to the operation of technological measures.[240]

Copyright Act', (148) *University of Pennsylvania Law Review* 2000, p. 673, at pp. 701-702.

236 See Gasser and Girsberger, 'Transposing the Copyright Directive', op. cit., p. 17; and Braun, 'The Interface Between the Protection of Technological Measures and the Exercise of Exceptions to Copyright and Related Rights: Comparing the Situation in the United States and the European Community', (25) *EIPR* 2003, p. 496, at p. 499.

237 See Article 6(2) of the Proposal for a European Parliament and Council Directive on the harmonization of certain aspects of copyright and related rights in the Information Society, COM (97) of 10 December 1997, OJ, C 108, 7.04.1998, 6.

238 See Hugenholtz, 'Why the Copyright Directive is Unimportant', op. cit., p. 499.

239 See the Common Position (EC) 48/2000 of 28 September 2000, OJ C 344, 1.12.2000, 1.

240 See Dusollier, *Droit d'auteur et protection des oeuvres dans l'univers numérique*, op. cit., p. 161, who reminds us of the attempt of several amendments coming from the Parliament to extend the restrictive position adopted with regard to digital private copying to all other exceptions. As pointed out by the author, under Recital 27 of the Directive Proposal, it was established that exceptions such as private copying and remuneration schemes "should not inhibit the use of technological measures."

As a consequence of the Council's intervention, the original definition of "technological measure" embodied in Article 6(2) of the directive proposal [241] was replaced by a new definition providing that, for the purposes of the Directive:

"the expression 'technological measures' means any technology, device or component that, in the normal course of its operation, is designed to prevent or restrict acts, in respect of works or other subject-matter, *which are not authorised by the rightholder of any copyright or any right related to copyright* as provided for by law or the *sui generis* right provided for in Chapter III of Directive 96/9/EC [...]".[242]

As noted by Dusollier, the fact that the definition of protected technologies abandoned an objective criterion, though ambiguously formulated (namely, the violation of substantive copyright law) in favour of a subjective criterion (namely, right-holder willingness) removed the original link between the technical domain and the normative domain.[243] As a result, the scope of technological protection was expanded to cover all materials that right-holders are able to enclose into their digital boxes, regardless of what substantive copyright law provides.

To counterbalance such expansion, a fourth paragraph was added to Article 6 in order to safeguard the exercise of certain copyright exceptions notwithstanding the operation of technological measures.[244]

3.4.3. Discrepancies in the national implementation of anti-circumvention law

The transposition of the InfoSoc Directive into national laws was accomplished much later than the formal deadline of 22 December 2002.[245] As shown in the table provided in the Appendix II of this book, France and Spain were among the last Member States to implement this piece of legislation. This process of national implementation has already shown significant consequences with regard to the scope of the protection of technical measures and rights management information systems.[246]

The transposition of the Directive into domestic law has not resulted in the creation of uniform protection of technological measures which restrict the copying and use of copyrighted digital works. This was a predictable outcome of one

---

241 See Article 6(2) of the Directive Proposal, which referred to "any device, product or component incorporated into a process, device or product designed to prevent or inhibit the infringement of any copyright or any rights related to copyright".

242 See Article 6(3) in the final version of the InfoSoc Directive (emphasis added).

243 See Dusollier, *Droit d'auteur et protection des oeuvres*, op. cit., pp. 162-63.

244 See §4.5., see *infra*.

245 Only Greece and Denmark were able to comply with the deadline. Most Member States, instead, transposed the Directive with a considerable delay. In December 2003, the European Commission filed a case with the ECJ against 9 Member States, which had not been able yet to comply with their obligations.

246 See Gasser and Girsberger, 'Transposing the Copyright Directive', op. cit., p. 12.

of the chief drawbacks of the Directive, namely, that the broad and unclear terms of Article 6 allow Member States to define the scope of the protection of technological protection measures at their discretion. For instance, in Denmark (as opposed to Germany, United Kingdom and Italy) the protection of copy-control devices has been transposed in a manner which denies legal protection to access-control technologies, and thus acts of circumvention may be found to be legal or illegal depending on whether or not Danish law applies.[247] As reported by Gasser and Girsberger, in defining the term "effective technological measures", Section 75c(4) of the Danish Copyright Act neither expressly refers to copy-control nor to access-control technologies. Nonetheless, the explanatory text of the new Danish Copyright Law makes it clear that anti-circumvention provisions only protect technologies which aim to prevent copying. According to these authors, this view reflects the earlier position of Scandinavian countries on the exclusion from the scope of Article 6(3) of the InfoSoc Directive of access-control technology (since such technology does not necessarily prevent acts that would constitute copyright infringement).

Similarly, Hungarian anti-circumvention law seems to apply only to technologies designed to prevent or hinder the infringement of copyright, and not to acts which have not been authorised by right holders (as the Directive appears to require). This means that Hungarian end-users, unlike their German or British counterparts, might lawfully circumvent technical measures in order to engage in uses permitted under (Hungarian) law.[248] Like the Danish law, Article 95(2) of the Hungarian Copyright Act links the scope of anti-circumvention law to the use of technologies "designed to prevent or hinder the infringement of copyright [...]". Thus, contrary to the wording of Article 6(3) of the InfoSoc Directive, Hungarian law would seem to protect only technologies which aim to forbid acts which constitute copyright infringement.

These examples of discrepancy in Member States' laws show that the attempt by the InfoSoc Directive to provide a uniform notion of technological measures which qualify for anti-circumvention protection has been largely unsuccessful. Thus, such discrepancies could be brought to an end by an intervention of the ECJ, either upon the initiative of the Commission in pursuance of infringement procedures against the aforementioned Member States, or upon the initiative of national courts seeking clarification on the most correct interpretation of EU anti-circumvention law.

[247] *Ibidem*, p. 13.

[248] *Ibidem*, p. 15.

3.5. Summary

Chapter 3 has examined the copyright regulation created by the InfoSoc Directive. It has been shown that the Directive has not created a uniform notion of copyrightable work for the Community. Today's EU copyright law for the digital environment rests on the same notion of reproduction set out in the 1991 EC Software Directive. It has been stressed that, under Article 2 of the InfoSoc Directive, the re-definition of the concept of copyright reproduction now includes temporary copying and, with a few exceptions, digital reproduction for purposes of personal use. As a result, the scope of property rights on copyrighted digital works has been expanded by having in mind the digital nature of the media which embody the protected works. This expansion was undertaken with a view to reserving the exclusive right to authorise the mere use of the work (which is enabled by acts of temporary reproduction) and all forms of making such works available to the public to the copyright owner. Particular attention has been paid to the fact that the InfoSoc Directive understands the dissemination of intangible copyrighted works as a provision of *services*. Due to this qualification, the primary exploitation of online services which aim to supply intangible works has proven to be subject to a strict principle of territoriality which stems from the national character of copyright protection. It has been stressed that the dissemination of intangible works, which falls outside the field of application of the exhaustion principle, has resulted in territorial partitions of new markets for online copyrighted works, in sharp contrast to the purpose of market integration pursued by the Directive, at least on paper. The recent action undertaken by the European Commission to encourage the release of Community-wide licences for the exploitation of online music works has ultimately evidenced this failure of the Directive in the pursuit of its constitutional policy objective. Finally, it has been shown that the InfoSoc Directive afforded specific anti-circumvention protection to technologies which regulate access to and use of copyrighted works. Nonetheless, the adoption of vague and broad terms to indicate which technologies deserved protection has resulted in non-uniform provisions under national anti-circumvention laws.

4. The legal treatment of copyright exceptions under secondary EU law

4.1. Introduction: from vertical to horizontal exceptions

Before the enactment of the InfoSoc Directive in May 2001, EU law had addressed the issue of copyright exceptions in a purely "vertical" manner, *i.e.*, with regard to new and highly specific subject matters such as computer programmes and databases.[249] In 1992, another intervention in this field came with the harmonisation of particular types of rights: the rights of rental and lending and the so-called "neighbouring" rights.[250] A horizontal (*i.e.* general) regulation came into play only with the InfoSoc Directive, which was expected to define the "exceptions and limitations" set out by Member States "more harmoniously".[251]

From its earliest version (that is, the 1997 Commission's directive proposal), the Preamble of the InfoSoc Directive has embodied a strident contradiction with regard to the objectives that the harmonisation of copyright exceptions in the EU should pursue. As shown by a simple comparison of the phrasing of Recitals 31 and 32, this contradiction was maintained in the final text. According to Recital 31 of the Directive, the primary objective of harmonisation was the elimination of the negative effects that the existing differences in protection between Member States would have had on the internal market for copyrighted goods. The new electronic environment, in particular, was understood as making such differences "more pronounced in view of the further development of transborder exploitation of works and cross-border activities [...]."[252] Had the Directive been consistent with this objective, harmonisation measures could only have been taken when there was plain evidence that these discrepancies would affect intra-Community trade.[253] In this respect, the last part of Recital 31 provided that the degree of harmonisation should have been based upon the impact of exceptions on the smooth functioning of the internal market. Rather self-evidently, the first sentence of Recital 32 is at

---

[249] See Articles 5 and 6 of the 1991 Software Directive and Articles 6, 8 and 9 of the 1996 Database Directive.

[250] See Directive 92/100/EEC of 19 November 1992 on rental right and lending right and on certain rights related to copyright in the field of intellectual property, OJ L 346, 27.11.1992, p. 61.

[251] See Recital 31 of the InfoSoc Directive.

[252] *Ibidem.*

[253] See Cornish and Llewelyn, *Intellectual Property: Patents, Copyright, Trade Marks and Allied Rights*, op. cit., p. 441.

odds with this policy in so far as it states that the Directive provides "for an exhaustive enumeration of exceptions and limitations [...]".

In its Follow-up to the 1995 Green Paper on Copyright and Related Rights, the Commission disclosed its intention of setting out closely defined "fair use" exceptions to the exclusive right of reproduction designed to accommodate the interests of users or the public at large.[254] The Follow-up made it clear that such a list of exceptions should have been provided for cases where exceptions had not raised risks of unreasonable prejudice for the legitimate interests of the copyright holder or where they had not come into conflict with a normal exploitation of the intellectual property of the copyright holder.[255] In commenting on the Follow-up, the European Commission Legal Advisory Board was skeptical about the possibility of enacting an exhaustive list of copyright exceptions.[256] The Board argued that harmonisation of national exceptions did not necessarily mean that national systems were to be made uniform in this regard. Distinctive exceptions could be maintained in national systems as long as they did not hinder the attainment of a single market for copyrighted goods. The issue of the appropriateness of an exhaustive list was raised by Member States such as Italy, Spain and France, which believed that a closed number of exceptions would have ensured the attainment of a satisfactory degree of harmonisation with regard to the system of exceptions and remunerations.[257]

The contradictory purposes of the InfoSoc Directive on copyright exceptions framed the following questions: how could an exhaustive list, that is, a thorough list of the exceptions that Member States would be allowed to maintain or introduce into their systems, be compatible with the purpose of only harmonising exceptions which had an adverse impact upon trans-border trade? Moreover, how is it possible to combine exhaustiveness with the duty to take account of the different legal traditions that existed in the Member States, as provided under Recital 32?

The only viable solution in order to quickly achieve such an "ambitious" result was to satisfy the Member States by including all of the exceptions that they had requested in the list. Furthermore, from a political point of view, shaping the ex-

---

[254] See Communication from the Commission of 20.11.1996, *Follow-up to the Green Paper on Copyright and Related Rights in the Information Society*, COM(96) 586 final.

[255] As shown below (see §4.2.1.), the above-mentioned restrictive requirements mentioned by the Commission in the Follow-up for the enactment of harmonised copyright exceptions are drawn from the so-called "three-step test" embodied in Article 9(2) of the Berne Convention.

[256] See *Commentaires du Legal Advisory Board sur la Communication de la Commission du 20 Novembre 1996*, available (in French) at:
http://europa.eu.int/ISPO/legal/fr/proprint/labcomment.htm.
In May 1985, the European Commission established a Legal Advisory Board (LAB) with the task of increasing the awareness of the legal challenges related to the creation of a European information market. The main task of the LAB was that of submitting ideas and recommendations to the Commission on eliminating disparities and aligning national legal provisions in fields such as intellectual property and access to information. More information on the LAB can be found at:
http://europa.eu.int/ISPO/legal/en/lab/labdef.html.

[257] See Cohen Jehoram, 'European Copyright law', op. cit., p. 542.

ceptions as *non-mandatory* would have allowed the Member States to agree easily on the composition of the list. However, by making these concessions, the Directive completely missed its original purpose of integrating the Internal Market.

After much discussion, the final text of Article 5 made mandatory only the technical exception regarding temporary reproductions which served the purpose of transitory communication in a network between third parties.[258] All the other exceptions, including the most important expressions of public policy under copyright law, were conceived as *optional*, having been inserted into a list from which Member States were free to choose.[259] The list of exceptions grew significantly from the original seven to an incredible twenty items. Whereas the exceptions provided under Article 5(2) solely concern the right of reproduction, Article 5(3) lists optional exceptions to the rights of reproduction and communication to the public. Finally, Article 5(4) provides that, where the Member States may create or maintain an exception or limitation to the right of reproduction in accordance with Articles 5(2) and 5(3), they are entitled to enact an exception or limitation to the exclusive right of distribution "to the extent justified by the purpose of the authorised act of reproduction".

During the discussion between the Commission and the Member States, it was particularly significant that the most interesting and thoughtful proposal, which openly contradicted the argument of exhaustiveness, was rejected. Supported by Scandinavian countries, the Dutch government asked for the introduction of a general copyright exception carved out in the same manner as the open clause of "fair use" under U.S. law.[260] The most persuasive argument in support of this request was based upon the assumption that a closed and rigidly pre-determined list of exceptions would not be appropriate for the digital environment and the Internet, where new uses and business methods emerge at an impressive pace.[261] Luxembourg was also of the opinion that a closed list of exceptions would probably have prevented speedy adaptation to technological change.[262] Moreover, in presenting its project for the transposition of the Directive into national law, the

---

[258] See Article 5(1).

[259] See Cohen Jehoram, 'European Copyright Law', op. cit., p. 542; Hart, 'The Copyright in the Information Society Directive: an Overview', op. cit., pp. 59-61.

[260] See Cohen Jehoram, 'European Copyright Law', op. cit., p. 542; and Guibault, *Le tir manqué de la Directive européenne sur le droit d'auteur dans la société de l'information*, Institute for Information Law, University of Amsterdam, Publications, available at http://www.ivir.nl, at §3.1.

[261] Such critical remark to the approach taken by the Directive on exceptions was expressed by Hugenholtz, 'Why the Directive is Unimportant', op. cit., p. 501 ("How can a legislature in its right mind even contemplate an exhaustive list of exceptions [...] when the internet produces new business models and novel uses almost each day?"); and Vinje, 'Should We Begin Digging Copyright's Grave', op. cit., at 553-554 ("the best intellectual property is generally the most flexible legislation, in particular so it does not become obsolete as technology develops [...] contrary to the approach taken in the WIPO Copyright Treaty, the Directive goes so far as to prohibit Member States from adopting new exceptions that take account of technological change [...]").

[262] See Cohen Jehoram, 'European Copyright Law', op. cit., p. 542.

Dutch government persuasively remarked that Article 5 gave Member States the possibility of adopting elastic exceptions (for example, the case of use for the purpose of caricature, parody or pastiche)[263] which would be better understood and applied if courts were able to rely upon an open-ended formulation, such as the U.S. fair use clause.[264]

4.2. The introduction of the three-step test under EU law

In rejecting the above-mentioned proposal from the Dutch government, the European Commission contended that a general formulation would have come into conflict with the three-step test that Article 5(5) of the 2001 Directive had adopted from international agreements such as the Berne Convention, the TRIPS Agreement, the WIPO Copyright Treaty and the WIPO Performances and Phonograms Treaty.[265] The wording of Article 5(5) re-states the requirements embodied in Article 9(2) of the Berne Convention, Article 13 of the TRIPS Agreement, Article 10(2) of the WIPO Copyright Treaty, and Article 16(2) of the WIPO Performances and Phonograms Treaty. This provision of the InfoSoc Directive provides that:

"[T]he exceptions and limitations [...] shall only be applied in certain special cases which do not conflict with a normal exploitation of the work or other subject-matter and do not unreasonably prejudice the legitimate interests of the rightholder."

4.2.1. The three-step test under international law

The so-called "three-step test" instructed the Berne Convention Contracting Parties to comply with three requirements which restricted the scope of permissible copyright exceptions under national law. The test was created on the grounds of the study carried out in 1965 by the WIPO Committee of Experts in view of the revision of the same Convention at the 1967 Stockholm Conference. The creation of the test pursued the objective of enlarging the protection granted to authors by strengthening the reproduction right in the face of the threat of phonographic piracy.[266] This project was undertaken on the assumption that restrictions on repro-

---

263 See Article 5(3)(k) of the InfoSoc Directive.

264 See Guibault, *Le tir manqué de la Directive européenne*, op. cit., §3.1, who commented upon the explanatory memorandum of the project of transposition of the InfoSoc Directive into Dutch law.

265 See the Berne Convention for the Protection of Literary and Artistic Works; see also the Agreement on Trade-Related Aspects of Intellectual Property Rights (TRIPS), Annex 1C of the Marrakesh Agreement establishing the World Trade Organisation, Morocco on 15 April 1994, available at: http://www.wto.org; and the WIPO Copyright Treaty and WIPO Performances and Phonograms Treaty, adopted on 20 December 1996, available at: http://www.wipo.int/treaties.

266 See Senftleben, *Copyright, Limitations and the Three-Step Test*, op. cit., pp. 47-48.

duction rights varied considerably throughout the European Union.[267] Whereas the original version of the test provided by Article 9(2) of the Berne Convention, in its post-1967 version, referred to the sole exclusive right of reproduction, later versions of the test under international copyright law expanded its field of application to *all* authors' rights and neighbouring rights.[268]

The re-statement and extension of the three-step test under Article 13 of the 1994 TRIPS Agreement, in particular, considerably enhanced its degree of effectiveness. Unlike the Berne Convention, the law of the World Trade Organisation (WTO) has established an effective system of dispute settlement which enforces the TRIPS Agreement.[269]

Evidence of its effectiveness was reflected in the June 2000 decision of a WTO Dispute Resolution Panel, which held the United States liable for an infringement of Article 13, in a proceeding initiated by the European Union. Significantly, this was the first time that an international body had interpreted the test in question.[270] The decision found that Section 110(5) of the U.S. Copyright Act, as amended by the 1998 Digital Millennium Copyright Act, did not comply with the three-step test in exempting a wide range of retail businesses and restaurants from liability for the public performance of musical works by means of communication of radio and television transmissions. Such an exemption, in the Panel's view, did not come within the scope of Article 13 and was in conflict with authors' right to authorise any communication to the public regarding the performance of their work. This judgment resulted from an analysis of the U.S. exemption under the three requirements of the test, which are identical in all versions of the test, including the provision transposing the test into EU law.

The relevant literature makes it clear that, for national copyright exceptions to be allowed under the test, the three requirements are interpreted one after another and are applied cumulatively, on the understanding that there is an order of importance underpinning the structure of the test.[271] The first requirement provides the general criterion restricting copyright exceptions to uses that must serve specific purposes ("certain special cases"). Ricketson explains that this requirement aims to compel Contracting Parties to restrict the realm of copyright exceptions to narrow types of exceptions justified by clear reasons of public policy or some other

---

267 See Senftleben, *Copyright, Limitations and the Three-Step Test*, op. cit., p. 48; Cohen Jehoram, 'Restrictions on Copyright', op. cit., pp. 359-60.

268 See Article 13 of the 1994 TRIPS Agreement, Article 10 of the 1996 WIPO Copyright Treaty, and Article 16 of the WIPO Performances and Phonograms Treaty.

269 See Samuelson, 'Challenges for the World Intellectual Property Organization', (21) *EIPR* 1999, p. 581.

270 World Trade Organisation, United States – Section 110(5) of the U.S. Copyright Act, Report of the Panel, WT/DS160/R, 15 June 2000 (hereinafter "WTO's Panel decision"). For an in-depth analysis, see Ginsburg, 'Toward Supranational Copyright Law? The WTO Panel Decision and the "Three-Step Test" for Copyright Exceptions', (187) *RIDA* 2001, p. 17.

271 See Senftleben, *Copyright, Limitations and the Three-Step Test*, op. cit., pp. 126-27; Cohen Jehoram, 'Restrictions on Copyright', op. cit., p. 361.

exceptional circumstance.[272] The WTO Panel, however, rejected the argument that "special cases" should be equated with the existence of special public policy purposes.[273] The decision held that the first of condition of Article 13 of the TRIPS Agreement:

"[R]equires that an exception or limitation in national legislation should be clearly defined and should be narrow in its scope and reach [....] The wording of Article 13's first condition does not imply passing a judgment on the legitimacy of the exceptions in dispute. However, public policy purposes stated by law-makers when enacting an exception or limitation may be useful from a factual perspective for making inferences about the scope of an exception or limitation or the clarity of its definition."[274]

While veering away from the traditionally accepted interpretation, the WTO Panel seemed to uphold a merely *quantitative* test of the speciality criterion. Under this approach, the first (*i.e.,* "special cases") requirement is analysed by simply measuring the scope and reach of each exception, as shown by the assessment of the impact of each exception on the market to be exploited by the copyright holder. According to this kind of analysis, no exception should be applied if it significantly harms, in quantitative terms, the commercial exploitation of a copyrighted good. Thus, for an exception to be legitimate under the reasoning endorsed by the Panel, the impact of the exception on the market for the copyrighted good should prove to be confined to exceptional circumstances. In the case examined by the WTO Panel, the copyright exemption provided by Section 110(5) of the U.S. Copyright Act applied to around 70 per cent of American eating and drinking establishments and 45 per cent of retail businesses. Due to these statistics, the decision found that the U.S. exemption violated the three-step test because it constituted a rule, rather than an exception.

The Panel's merely quantitative analysis was criticised by scholars who upheld a *qualitative* (or normative) analysis of the speciality criterion.[275] Under this different approach, "special cases" for copyright exceptions should be scrutinised on the grounds of the function of uses that each statutory exception intends to enable. Supporters of the normative analysis warned that the WTO Panel's upholding of the quantitative test could set the stage for a purely economic-based enforcement of the three-step test. They argued that, if it were accepted that the room left for copyright exceptions could be progressively filled by the emergence of new markets to exploit, the survival of all exceptions would ultimately depend upon the extension of right-holder market practices.

Due to the structure of the test, this dichotomy is reflected even in the interpretation of the other two requirements, which specify the purpose of the first general

[272] See Ricketson, *The Berne Convention for the protection of literary and artistic works: 1886-1986*, London 1987, p. 535; Cohen Jehoram, 'Restrictions on Copyright', op. cit., p. 361.

[273] WTO Panel's decision, §6.111.

[274] WTO Panel's decision, §6.112.

[275] See Senftleben, *Copyright, Limitations and the Three-Step Test*, op. cit., 140; Dusollier, *Droit d'auteur et protection des oeuvres*, op. cit., p. 445.

criterion.[276] By prohibiting exceptions that permit uses that conflict with a normal exploitation of the copyrighted work, the second requirement aims to protect the actual and predictable sources of revenues of the copyright holder from the interference of copyright exceptions. The relevant literature points out that, if "normal exploitation" were understood to refer to all existent and potential (*i.e.,* future) markets for copyrighted works, the room for the implementation of the test would be negligible.[277] A similar assertion was enshrined in the interpretative analysis carried out by the WTO Panel.[278] Nonetheless, the decision emphasised that:

"in certain circumstances, current licensing practices may not provide a sufficient guideline for assessing the potential impact of an exception or limitation on normal exploitation [...]".[279]

The Panel made it clear that the fact that copyright holders may not exercise a particular exclusive right in a specific market, due to lack of effective or affordable means of enforcement, cannot be considered indicative of what constitutes normal exploitation.[280] This assertion pre-supposed more specifically the question of whether protection of normal exploitation may end up reserving to the copyright owner *all* types of commercial exploitation including those which, although not worthwhile or simply unviable at a given point in the market-place, should become available as a result of technological developments or changing consumer preferences.

In my view, the argument, advocated by the supporters of the normative interpretation, that such a notion of normal exploitation would result in the progressive erosion of exceptions, including exceptions which would serve the public interest by excluding certain socially-valuable uses from the subject matter of copyright, is persuasive. The best solution to avoid this undesirable conclusion is to endorse Ginsburg's argument that the conclusion reached by the WTO Panel should not be generalised and given too much importance as far as future enforcement of the test is concerned.[281] Ginsburg argued that the Panel's decision referred only to cases where no special public policy existed.[282] If exceptions to the pursuance of public policy objectives were at stake, Ginsburg concluded, more attention should be

---

276 See generally Senftleben, *Copyright, Limitations and the Three-Step Test*, op. cit., pp. 128-133.

277 See Dusollier, *Droit d'auteur et protection des oeuvres*, op. cit., p. 446; Marzano, *Diritto d'Autore e Digital Technologies, Il Digital Copyright nei trattati OMPI, nel DMCA e nella normativa comunitaria*, Giuffré, Milano, 2005, p. 261; Senftleben, *Copyright, Limitations and the Three-Step Test*, op. cit., p. 181.

278 See WTO Panel's decision, §6.167: "if 'normal' exploitation were equated with full use of all exclusive rights conferred by copyrights, the exception clause of Article 13 would be left devoid of meaning. Therefore, 'normal' exploitation clearly means something less than full use of an exclusive right."

279 WTO Panel's decision, §6.188.

280 *Ibidem.*

281 See Ginsburg, 'Toward Supranational Copyright Law?', op. cit., p. 29.

282 More explicitly, Cohen Jehoram, 'Restrictions on Copyright', op. cit., p. 362, spoke of "a pure case of pork barrel for the American restaurant owners".

paid to qualitative aspects.[283] At end of the day, the original purpose of the "normal exploitation" requirement was to prevent free users of the copyrighted work from entering into economic competition with the major sources of commercial exploitation of a copyrighted work. The records of preparatory works of the 1967 Stockholm Conference (which revised Article 9 of the Berne Convention) show that the Contracting Parties did not intend to reserve to the copyright owner all of the possible market segments; instead, they wished to preserve "all forms of exploiting a work which have, or are likely to acquire, *considerable* economic or practical importance" (emphasis added).[284]

The third and last requirement of the test seeks to protect the legitimate interests of authors from any unreasonable prejudices that copyright exceptions may cause. The fact that the wording of the test refers to *unreasonable* prejudice makes it clear, *a contrario*, that *reasonable* prejudice is permitted. At the end of the day, no exception has been created in order to pursue an economic interest of the copyright holders. Copyright exceptions encompass both the moral and economic rights of the author in so far as the prejudice that they raise is proportional to the objective that the exception pursues. In the case of prejudice against the economic rights of the author, in particular, this requirement compels legislators and interpreters to consider the impact of each exception on the right-holder's sources of revenues. This condition implies that unreasonable prejudice can be made reasonable either by financial compensation, in the form of compulsory licences, or by foreseeing strict quantitative restrictions to the permitted use.[285]

4.2.2. The transposition of the test into EU law

The introduction of the three-step test was the most remarkable attempt to harmonise national copyright exceptions undertaken by the InfoSoc Directive. At first sight, the transposition may seem a very limited contribution to the harmonisation purpose of the Directive, especially if one considers that most Member States that implemented the Directive did not incorporate the test into their legislation.[286] Member States such as Austria, Germany, Denmark, Spain, Finland, Netherlands, Portugal, and United Kingdom have not explicitly incorporated the three-step test into national law.[287] This decision was mainly based on the controversial assump-

[283] See Ginsburg, 'Toward a Supranational Copyright Law?', op. cit., p. 51; Dusollier, *Droit d'auteur et protection des oeuvres*, op. cit., p. 446.

[284] Indebted to Senftleben, *Copyright, Limitations and the Three-Step Test*, op. cit., p. 177. The Berne Convention for the Protection of Artistic and Literary Works was revised at Stockholm on 14 July 1967: see the website of the WIPO at http://www.wipo.int/treaties.

[285] See Cohen Jehoram, 'Restrictions on Copyright,' op. cit., p. 361; Marzano, *Diritto d'Autore e Digital Technologies*, op. cit., p. 264.

[286] See Guibault, *Le tir manqué*, op. cit., §3.1.

[287] See the comprehensive Report released by the Foundation for Information Policy Research (FIPR), *Implementing the EU Copyright Directive*, available at: http://www.fipr.org/, p. 22.

tion that Article 5(5) was directed at national legislators, and it was, therefore, up to national law to comply with the three-step test when formulating its own exceptions.

Hart argued that Article 5(5) appears to require Member States to apply the test when implementing exceptions into national law.[288] He reached this conclusion by comparing the text of Article 5(5) in the original directive proposal with its final version. The original provision, which followed Article 6(3) of the 1991 Software Directive, explicitly provided that:

"[E]xceptions and limitations [...] *shall not be interpreted* in such a way as to allow their application to be used in a manner which unreasonably prejudices the right-holders' legitimate interests or conflicts with the normal exploitation of their works or other subject matter."[289]

Whereas the original wording suggested that national courts would have been obliged to ensure that the interpretation of any exception did not conflict with the three-step test, Hart complained that, unfortunately, the final version refers to the *statutory* interpretation of the actual wording of each exception.

In my view, however, this cannot be the case. European law-makers would have had no reason to re-state - under Community law - a rule that Member States, as Contracting Parties of the Berne Convention and the TRIPS Agreement, were already bound to comply with.[290] Having provided for an *exhaustive* list, which did not leave any room for national initiatives on the creation of new exceptions, the Directive seemed to assess the compliance of its own detailed exceptions with the test. This interpretation seems to be supported by the wording of Recital 44 of the InfoSoc Directive:

"When applying the exceptions and limitations provided for in this Directive, they should be exercised in accordance with international obligations [...]".

This statement would be of little significance if the obligation provided under Article 5(5) was understood to address the Member States, which are already bound to comply with the three-step test under international obligations. In my view, the internalisation of the test into Community and national laws should serve, instead, as a common benchmark for judicial interpretation. If interpreted in this way, the incorporation of the test into EU law will, on the one hand, be likely to make the enforcement of the test more effective in the European Union than under the relevant international conventions. Indeed, the fact that the three-step test has become

---

288 See Hart, 'The Copyright in the Information Society Directive', op. cit., p. 61.

289 Emphasis added.

290 See Vinje, 'Should We Begin Digging Copyright's Grave?', op. cit., p. 553. *Contra* Hart, 'The Copyright in the Information Society Directive', op. cit., p. 61, who seems to view the re-statement of the three-step test under EU law as a measure ensuring the intra-Community enforcement of the test. Hart argued that any objection to whether Member States formulate their exceptions correctly "would have to be pursued by taking legal action against the Member State to seek the revision or removal of the exception".

European law has the important consequence that the test will be subject to interpretation by the ECJ, which, as argued by Cohen Jehoram, "is not bound by diplomatic reticence towards states, like a TRIPs Panel".[291] On the other hand, this incorporation may result in a process of *dynamic* harmonisation of the exceptions that Member States have *literally* taken from the list provided by the InfoSoc Directive. However, the Directive does nothing to prevent Member States from embarking on the further specification of the listed types of exceptions.[292] As shown by a few examples of national transpositions of the Directive, such negligence has resulted in further fragmentation of copyright law even in respect of the "first-class" exceptions that Article 6(4) intended to preserve from the operation of technological protection measures.

To conclude, the introduction of the three-step test under EU law should be interpreted as guiding national courts towards a uniform interpretation and application of the same types of exceptions throughout the Community.[293] In this context, of course, the final word on compliance with the test of national statutory provisions and judicial interpretations lies with the ECJ.

4.3. The new requirement of *legal access* at the expense of *lawful use*

Unlike the Software and the Database Directives, the exercise of copyright exceptions under the InfoSoc Directive does not rest upon the notion of "lawful use". This notion began to develop under the 1991 Software Directive, which referred to the beneficiary of copyright exceptions as the "licensee" or the "person having a right to use a copy of a computer program".[294] The fact that the exceptions are limited to the lawful acquirer of a copy must be viewed as a by-product of the specific copyright protection of software, which is conceived as a means of use by single licensees, rather than a work to be communicated to the public. Under this protection, copyright restricts any access to and use of the protected work, including temporary copying. Under Articles 6 and 9 of the 1996 Database Directive, a very similar notion stemmed from the expression "lawful users", which refers to a user who is authorised, by agreement with the right-holder, to access and use the database.[295]

The 2001 InfoSoc Directive, however, did not create a clear link between the notion of lawful use and the beneficiary of copyright exceptions. This result is at odds with the balanced notion of lawful use adopted by Recital 33 of the InfoSoc

[291] See Cohen Jehoram, 'Restrictions on Copyright', op. cit., p. 364.

[292] See Senftleben, *Copyright, Limitations and the Three-Step Test*, op. cit., p. 281.

[293] This view is shared by Dusollier, *Droit d'auteur et protection des oeuvres*, op. cit., pp. 439-441; Guibault, *Le tir manqué*, op. cit., §3.3; and Cohen Jehoram, 'Restrictions on Copyright and their Abuse', op. cit., p. 364. *Contra* Hart, 'The Copyright in the Information Society Directive', op. cit., p. 61.

[294] See Articles 5 and 6 of the Software Directive.

[295] See Recital 34 of the Database Directive.

Directive. According to this provision, a use should be considered lawful "where it is authorised by the right-holder or not restricted by law". This notion is more desirable than those adopted by the Software and the Database Directives because it draws on the idea that copyright exceptions are ultimately set out by the law and not merely by contractual conditions proposed by the copyright owner. The definitions of "lawful acquirer" and "lawful user" adopted, respectively, by the Software and the Database Directives, instead, diverge from the principles contained in Recital 33 of the InfoSoc Directive by making the exercise of exceptions subject either to the lawful acquisition of the medium embodying a protected computer programme (which is a requirement which creates confusion between the rules of intellectual property and the rules of real property) or to the acceptance of the licence terms accompanying the acquisition of a database.

Notwithstanding its suitability, the concrete enforceability of the balanced notion of lawful use adopted by the InfoSoc Directive is endangered by the circumstance that, in the absence of a contract interface protecting copyright exceptions from contractual overriding, the lawful uses listed in Article 5 can be restricted by technologies, such as DRM systems, which bar access to the protected work to all unauthorised users, regardless of their lawful or unlawful purposes. By providing that the beneficiary of an exception or limitation shall have legal access to the protected work, the wording of Article 6(4) of the InfoSoc Directive has conferred legitimacy to unlimited restrictions of lawful uses achieved through the user contractual consent and the operation of access-control technologies.[296]

The provision of Article 6(4), §1, makes it clear that, where technological measures protected under the Directive control the access to and use of the protected work, only users who have obtained *legal access* to the protected work are effectively entitled to exercise copyright exceptions. Under this unprecedented requirement, the combination of right-holder licences and technological measures may freely circumscribe acts that are not restricted by law. Given that access to the protected work can be easily controlled by technological measures, which now enjoy independent legal protection against circumvention, the end-user might end up obtaining legal access only after he or she has agreed upon the contractual terms set out by the copyright owner. If such terms, for example, aim to extract the binding promise from the end-user not to engage in uses permitted by law in exchange of access, then the user will have actually given up his or her statutory usage rights when accessing the work.

Here, a crucial issue becomes apparent. Unlike the Software and the Database Directives, the InfoSoc Directive does not provide expressly that contractual pro-

---

[296] Article 6(4), §1, states: "Notwithstanding the legal protection provided for in paragraph 1 [...] Member States shall take appropriate measures to ensure that rightholders make available to the beneficiary of an exception or limitation provided for in national law [...] the means of benefiting from that exception or limitation, to the extent necessary to benefit from that exception or limitation and *where that beneficiary has legal access to the protected work or subject-matter concerned.*"(emphasis added).

visions which restrict uses permitted by law should be deemed null or void.[297] For instance, Article 5(2) of the Software Directive states:

> "The making of a back-up copy by a person having a right to use the computer program may not be prevented by contract insofar as it is necessary for that use."

Article 9(1) of the same Directive provides that:

> "Any contractual provisions contrary to Article 6 or to the exceptions provided for in Article 5 (2) and (3) shall be null or void."

Article 15 of the Database Directive, which is entitled "Binding nature of certain provisions", reads:

> "Any contractual provision contrary to Article 6(1) and 8 shall be null and void".[298]

By contrast, the InfoSoc Directive does not oblige the Member States to create a contract interface in order to preserve the effectiveness of usage rights and to forbid the contractual overriding of copyright exceptions.[299] Instead, Recital 45 of the Directive practically encourages such contractual overriding in so far as it provides that:

> "The exceptions and limitations referred to in Article 5(2), (3), and (4) should not, however, prevent the definition of contractual relations designed to ensure fair compensation for the rightholders insofar as permitted by national law."

In my view, it is evident that the absence of a clear, explicit provision for the protection of lawful uses (*i.e.*, copyright exceptions) under the InfoSoc Directive has the potential to deprive the notion of *lawful use* of much of its substance, at least in the digital environment. The subjection of such uses to contractual clauses which set out the conditions of *legal access* to the protected work arises from the assumption that no copyright exception under the InfoSoc Directive is defined as mandatory (*i.e.*, non-waivable through contract). As pointed out by Heide, even the copyright limitation contained in Article 5(1), namely, the copyright exemption of digital temporary reproduction for mere purposes of digital communication, which is the only limitation that Member States are compelled to transpose

---

[297] The absence in the InfoSoc Directive of a "contract interface" dealing with the contractual overriding of copyright exceptions is examined by Heide, 'Copyright, Contract and the Legal Protection of Technological Measures', op. cit., p. 9; and Guibault, *Le tir manqué*, op. cit., §3.1 ("À quoi bon reconnaître des exceptions au droit d'auteur et aux droits voisins si celles-ci peuvent être écartées dans n'importe quelle circonstance, par n'importe quel contrat?").

[298] Article 6 of the Database Directive provides exceptions to restricted acts with regard to databases protected by copyright; Article 8, instead, sets out rights and obligations of lawful users in relation to databases protected by the so-called *sui generis* right.

[299] See Heide, 'Copyright, Contract and the Legal Protection of Technological Measures', op. cit., p. 10.

into national law, is not understood as enjoying an imperative nature.[300] Obviously, this situation of high uncertainty on the legal status of copyright exceptions at the level of EU law makes their effective enforcement in the digital environment wholly dependent on whether national law-makers and courts provide copyright exceptions with a mandatory force thereby shielding them from contractual overrides. Unfortunately, as is shown below, the regulation enacted by the InfoSoc Directive was not based on a credible doctrine of copyright exceptions and, as a result, it provides little guidance on what exceptions are declared mandatory and how to enforce them effectively.

4.4. The InfoSoc Directive's exhaustive list of copyright exceptions

Article 5 of the InfoSoc Directive identifies the exceptions that Member States are allowed to enact or maintain after the entry into force of the Directive. Besides "minor reservations" regarding reproductions and other uses made by categories of users other than individuals (such as libraries, educational establishments or museums, archives, broadcasting organisations, and social institutions such as hospitals and prisons)[301] the Directive deals with an exhaustive list of exceptions enabling both transformative and non-transformative use by the end-users of copyrighted works. Given the subject-matter of this book, the following analysis focuses solely on the private copying exception created under Article 5(2)(b) and on the transformative uses permitted under Articles 5(2) and (3) of the Directive.

4.4.1. Non-transformative use: private copying

As far as non-transformative use is concerned, Article 5(2)(b) provides that Member States are entitled to set out exceptions to the reproduction right in respect of copying:

> "[B]y a natural person and for ends that are neither directly nor indirectly commercial, on condition that the rightholders receive fair compensation which takes account of the application or non-application of technological measures referred to in Article 6 to the work or subject-matter concerned [...]".

Exceptions which allow the reproduction of the copyrighted work for personal use began to shrink with the advent of the digitisation of the subject-matter of copyright. Examples of this phenomenon can be found in both the Software and the

---

300 *Ibidem.*

301 See Article 5(2), letters (a), (c), (e). The term "minor reservation" is used in the *Study on the implementation and effect in Member States' laws of Directive 2001/29/EC*, op. cit., p. 45, to refer to copyright exceptions that clearly have a *de minimis* character.

Database Directives. Article 4(a) of the Software Directive restricts acts of personal use by making temporary reproduction of a protected computer programme subject to authorisation by the right-holder in so far as the loading, displaying, running, transmission or storage of the computer programme necessitate such reproduction. Articles 6(2)(a) and 9(a) of the 1996 Database Directive significantly restrict the exception of reproduction and extraction for private purposes to *non-electronic* databases.[302] This means that this exception does not apply to the case of electronic (*i.e.*, digital) databases covered by copyright or by the *sui generis* right provided under the same Directive. Following the same rationale, Article 5(3)(o) of the InfoSoc Directive provides Member States with the option of maintaining copyright exceptions in certain cases of minor importance provided that they only concern analogue (*i.e.*, non-digital) uses and do not affect the free circulation of goods and services within the Community.

Article 5(2)(b) of the InfoSoc Directive shows *a contrario* that digital reproduction for private use purposes is totally subject to the control of copyright holders. Nonetheless, this provision of the InfoSoc Directive gives Member States the option of freely estimating the desirability of declassifying the exclusive right to authorise private reproduction into a statutory licence, on condition that this declassification is accompanied by fair compensation in favour of right-holders, and that the level of such compensation takes account of the presence and operation of technological measures.[303]

The provision at issue has two important implications. On the one hand, it actually enables Member States to maintain or introduce so-called levy systems even in digital settings.[304] Member States are thereby given the option of determining the form, the detailed arrangement and the possible level of fair compensation, on condition that they carefully evaluate, among other circumstances, whether private copying causes minimal harm to right-holders or not.[305] On the other hand, the provision of Article 5(2)(b) provides that, if compensation schemes are *not* maintained or newly introduced, Member States must ensure the phasing-out of levies as long as technological measures such as DRM systems effectively control and enforce the private use and copying of protected materials.[306]

---

302 See Article 6(2) of the Database Directive ("Exceptions to restricted acts"): "Member States shall have the option of providing for limitations on the rights set out in Article 5 in the following cases: (a) in the case of reproduction for private purposes of a *non-electronic* database [...]"; see also Article 9 ("Exceptions to the sui generis right"): "Member States may stipulate that lawful users of a database which is made available to the public in whatever manner may, without the authorization of its maker, extract or re-utilize a substantial part of its contents: (a) in the case of extraction for private purposes of the contents of a *non-electronic* database [...]" (emphasis added).

303 See Recital 35, *in fine*.

304 It is worth noting that the U.K., Ireland, Luxembourg, Malta and Cyprus are the only Member States of the European Union where levy systems have never existed.

305 See Recital 35.

306 See Hugenholtz, Guibault, and van Geffen, *The Future of Levies in a Digital Environment*, Final Report, Institute for Information Law, Amsterdam 2003, available at: http://www.ivir.nl/staff/hugenholtz.html.

Thus, in relation to digital private copying, the Directive explicitly recognises that the market failure rationale behind this exception diminishes. By referring to the obligation to ensure "fair compensation which takes account of the application or non-application of technological measures", the Directive wished to create a strict interdependence between the effective availability and the use of rights management technologies which enable the control and the enforcement of the exclusive right of reproduction for personal use and fair compensation as ensured by national levy systems.

This policy objective lay in the progressive phasing-out of levy systems as DRM technologies become more widely available. Member States were required by the InfoSoc Directive to ensure that end-users do not pay levies "for private copying which cannot take place or which can only take place in return for direct compensation to the right-holder".[307] Recital 35 of the Directive provided limited guidance on the scope of what constitutes "fair compensation" by making it clear that no specific payment may be due "where right-holders have already received payment in some other form, for instance as part of a license fee [...]".[308] After almost five years from the enactment of the InfoSoc Directive, the Internal Market Directorate General of the European Commission disclosed its purpose of intervening in the complex interplay created by the increasing implementation of DRM technologies and the proliferation of national levies on digital copying equipment and digital media.[309]

After holding a consultation with EU Member States and all stakeholders in October 2004, the Internal Market Directorate General and its Commissioner, McCreevy, concluded that there was no common ground on how Member States were to implement the provision of Article 5(2)(b) of the Directive.[310] According to the Roadmap document regarding a possible copyright levy reform in the EU delivered by the Commission in 2006, the above consultation evidenced that levies were unequally applied in terms of equipment, media and amounts across EU Member States, and that there was a lack of transparency in relation to their collection and distribution. Most importantly, the Commission pointed out that, in contrast with the policy objective set out by Article 5(2)(b), the availability and use of DRM technologies had not yet had an impact upon the policy of the Member States regarding copyright levies. On the contrary, the Commission claimed that the unequal proliferation of national levies on digital equipment and media may have the intolerable consequence of charging consumers with double fees

---

307 See Hart, 'The Copyright in the Information Society Directive', op. cit., p. 60.

308 See the InfoSoc Directive, Recital 35.

309 See Commission of the European Communities, *Copyright levy reform, Commission's Work Programme for 2006 – Roadmap*, at: http://ec.europa.eu/internal_market/copyright/levy_reform/index_en.htm.

310 See the speech given by Charlie McCreevy (European Commissioner for Internal Market and Services), *Address to the European-American Business Council/Business Software Alliance Conference on Digital Rights Management*, High level Industry Seminar/Global Industry Roundtable on Levies and DRMs, Brussels, 12 October 2005, available at: http://ec.europa.eu/internal_market/copyright/copyright-infso/copyright-infso_en.htm.

when personal copying of the delivered copyrighted work is effectively entrenched and managed through DRM technologies.

The Commission also considered this situation of uncertainty to be affecting the producers of information and communication technologies in as much as the launching of a new digital device on the market might be discouraged or delayed if the sale or the importation of the device was deemed to attract a copyright levy in a given Member State. The Commission is therefore seeking to speed up the process of the phasing-out of national levies on digital copying devices and media by taking measures which may identify the conditions under which Member States are forced to take account of the availability and use of DRM technologies more precisely and thus refrain from imposing unjustifiable levies when private copying opportunities prove to be technically prevented.

It is still uncertain, though, whether these harmonisation measures will be transposed into a proposal for the amending of Article 5(2)(b) of the InfoSoc Directive, which would have a binding result, but would also imply a lengthy legislative process. The Commission seems to prefer the adoption of a Recommendation, which would provide all stakeholders (including Member States) with interpretative guidance on the relevant provisions of the InfoSoc Directive, including benchmarks on determining the availability and use of DRM technologies.

In my view, the policy objective set out by the Directive and pursued by the new initiative of the Commission is clear and reasonable. The phasing-out of copyright levies in a digital environment where the operation of DRM technologies is capable of managing the exclusive right of reproduction for personal use pursues the objective of enabling copyright holders to seek fair compensation while preventing the end-users of the copyrighted work from paying such compensation twice. This phasing-out is also beneficial to producers of digital copying devices and media players, which would otherwise be forced to charge a levy on the sale price of their technologies with a view to giving copyright owners a fee that they would be able to manage and collect through the functioning of DRM technology.

Notwithstanding the high desirability of the above-mentioned phasing-out of copyright levies, the InfoSoc Directive, as well as the new Commission's working document, failed to specify how the contraction of the private copying exception in the digital environment may be made compatible with the privacy-protecting rationale that has characterised the adoption of this statutory exception in most EU Member States. As emphasised above, the effective availability and use of DRM technologies have the potential of endangering the protection of the end-user's personal data by tracing consumption patterns and other uses of the protected work released in a DRM-protected format.[311] In accordance with the wording of Recital 57 of the InfoSoc Directive, both the European Commission and all of the addressees of Article 5(2)(b) of the Directive (*i.e.,* national law-makers and judicial authorities) should prompt the designers and users of DRM technologies to incorporate privacy safeguards into technologies which manage the exclusive right of reproduction for personal use.

---

[311] See §2.2.3., see *supra.*

This problem will be discussed more in depth when examining how the case law developed in Europe has dealt with the collision between DRM technologies and the enforcement of the private copying exception.[312]

4.4.2. Transformative uses

As far as transformative use is concerned, the InfoSoc Directive empowers Member States to provide copyright exceptions that have historically created safety-valves for the protection of competing values such as freedom of expression, speech and research, and the encouragement of incremental innovation. This is because exceptions which enable transformative uses have the effect of fostering the creation of competing works by leaving follow-on users free to share ideas or parts of pre-existing works.[313] To enable certain transformative uses, Article 5(3) restricts the exclusive rights of reproduction and communication of authors. It firstly lists an exception for the sole, non-commercial purpose of illustration for teaching or scientific research.[314] This is reinforced by the exception regarding use by communication or making copyrighted works available, for the purpose of research or private study, to individual members of the public by dedicated terminals on the premises of establishments such as publicly accessible libraries, educational establishments, museums, archives, *etc.*[315] The objective of enabling research and criticism is even addressed by exceptions regarding quotations[316] and the use of political speeches as well as extracts from public lectures or similar works or subject matter.[317] Whereas freedom of the press is taken into account by the exception for the use of works in connection with the reporting of current events,[318] the highest degree of productive use is potentially safeguarded by exceptions concerning the incidental inclusion of a work or other subject matter in other material[319] and, most importantly, use for the purpose of caricature, parody or pastiche.[320] The public policy nature of this group of exceptions is upheld by the inclusion under Article 5 of exceptions "in respect of uses, for the benefit of people with disability, which are directly related to the disability and of a non-commercial nature, to the extent required by the specific disability".[321]

Finally, it is noteworthy that Article 5(3)(o) provides a "catch-all" exception for use in certain cases of minor importance "provided that they are existing exceptions which only concern analogue uses and do not affect the free circulation of

---

312 See §7.5, see *infra*.
313 See Heide, 'Copyright, Contract and the Legal Protection of Technological Measures', op. cit., p. 2.
314 See Article 5(3)(a).
315 See Article 5(3)(n).
316 See Article 5(3)(d).
317 See Article 5(3)(f).
318 See Article 5(3)(c).
319 See Article 5(3)(i).
320 See Article 5(3)(k).
321 See Article 5(3)(b).

goods and services within the Community".[322] This "grand-father clause" is the only provision where the InfoSoc Directive makes a distinction between the uses of digital and analogue technology.[323] In my view, this residual clause evidences the intended purpose of the Directive, which was to deprive single Member States of the competence to enact new or particular exceptions in respect of digital settings, where each national copyright exception is expected to have, as such, a non-negligible impact on the circulation of goods and services within the EU Information Society. It is undeniable, in my view, that the policy choice of depriving the Member States of the competence to craft new exceptions in digital settings for the pursuit of market-integration purposes would have been credible only in so far as the InfoSoc Directive had enacted an effective and mandatory system of digital exceptions at the level of EU law. As shown below, this is not the kind of system enacted by the Directive.

4.5. Safety nets for copyright exceptions against DRM systems

This section focuses on the interface created by the InfoSoc Directive between copyright exceptions, and technological measures such as DRM systems. As mentioned above, Article 6(4) was a late addition to the main text of the InfoSoc Directive. It was issued when the European Commission and the Council reached a common position on the scope of anti-circumvention laws. The obligations introduced by this complex paragraph can be viewed as an attempt to counterbalance the expanded protection of digitally-protected works which result from the absolute (*i.e.*, unlimited) prohibition on circumventing encryption and DRM technologies. The original purpose of Article 6(4) was that of safeguarding the effective exercise of uses enabled by the copyright exceptions provided under Article 5.

After briefly examining the most unfortunate drawbacks of this legislation, it will become apparent that Article 6(4) turns out to apply only to a limited number of exceptions and does not create effective safety nets for the preservation of the most important public policy objectives which uphold certain restrictions on copyright. The unacceptable outcome of this legislation is that neither the European Commission nor the single Member States are given the legal tools to intervene quickly and effectively in defence of the public interest against the potentially unlimited restrictions enabled by DRM technologies.

---

322 See Hart, 'The Copyright in the Information Society Directive', op. cit., p. 61.

323 Dusollier, *Droit d'auteur*, op. cit., p. 431, who referred to the provision of Article 5(3)(o) as the "grand-father clause".

4.5.1. Obligations created by Article 6(4)

According to the first subparagraph of Article 6(4), notwithstanding the legal protection of technological measures:

> "Member States shall take appropriate measures to ensure that rightholders make available to the beneficiary of an exception or limitation provided for in national law [...] the means of benefiting from that exception or limitation [...]".[324]

Nonetheless, such intervention by Member States is expected only:

> "in the absence of voluntary measures taken by rightholders, including agreements between rightholders and other parties concerned [...]".[325]

Several obligations were incumbent upon Member States:

- An obligation to promote the adoption of (non-specified) "voluntary measures" by right-holders;
- A duty to monitor and diligently evaluate whether such measures are effectively taken and how they operate; and
- The subsidiary obligation to intervene with "appropriate measures" when right-holders fail to provide effective means enabling beneficiaries to engage in acts permitted by law.

At first sight, these safety nets for copyright exceptions suffered from several, intrinsic weaknesses. Vague and unusual expressions (*e.g.*, "voluntary measures", "appropriate measures", and "agreements between rightholders and other parties concerned") were left open to interpretation by Member States. While pointing out the absolute uncertainty with regard to the referred expressions, Hugenholtz provocatively questioned whether "voluntary measures" could be interpreted as including technical protection measures which automatically respond to eligible users or oblige, for instance, copyright holders to deposit analogue copies in national libraries for public inspection and reproduction.[326] He also asked whether the "appropriate measures" that Member States were expected to take could consist in prohibiting the use of certain technological protection schemes which impaired public access to works on a serious scale.[327] Unclear duties aside, it was predictable that the reactions of the Member States to the development and implementation of new technologies by right-holders could give shape to disparate, non-coordinated interventions, which would openly contradict the original harmonisation purpose of the Directive. If the drafters of this provision had only taken into account how new technologies are used to develop in digital settings, they could have expected encryption and rights management devices to emerge and operate

---

324 See Article 6(4), §1.

325 *Ibidem.*

326 See Hugenholtz, 'Why the Copyright Directive is Unimportant', op. cit., p. 500.

327 *Ibidem.*

as *de facto* standards. If this was the case, how could European law-makers seriously think of encouraging the adoption and the free circulation of such technologies within the European Common Market if Member States were entitled to evaluate the compliance of technology with the duty created by Article 6(4) separately? Would not the intervention of the police forces of the Member States risk creating national barriers to the development of a Community-wide market for these technologies?

4.5.2. The narrow scope of Member States' obligations

In creating an interface between the legal protection of technological measures and the effective exercise of copyright exceptions, Article 6(4) restricts its field of application to a closed number of exceptions. While four of them are of some relevance to end-users, the remaining exceptions target acts to be undertaken by other types of users.[328]

According to Article 6(4), §1, the only uses which benefit from the Article 6(4) set of remedies are, respectively:

- reprographic copying (*i.e.*, photocopying);
- quotations for teaching or scientific research purposes;[329]
- uses for the benefit of people with a disability;[330]

Whereas Member States are obliged to take safeguard measures in order to ensure the availability of these exceptions, they are given the mere option to take such measures for the sake of the private copying exception, where this exception proves to be entrenched by the operation of a technical measure. Article 6(4), §2, provides:

"A Member State may also take such measures in respect of a beneficiary of an exception or limitation provided for in accordance with Article 5(2)(b), unless reproduction for private use has already been made possible by rightholders to the extent necessary to benefit from the exception or limitation concerned and in accordance with the provisions of Article 5(2)(b) and (5), without preventing rightholders from adopting adequate measures regarding the number of reproductions in accordance with these provisions."[331]

---

328 Article 6(4), §1, includes: acts of copying by libraries, educational establishments or museums; ephemeral recordings made by broadcasters; and copying of broadcasts made by non-commercial social institutions.

329 See Article 5(3)(a): "use for the sole purpose of illustration for teaching or scientific research, as long as the source, including the author's name, is indicated, unless this turns out to be impossible and to the extent justified by the non-commercial purpose to be achieved."

330 See Article 5(3)(b): uses "which are directly related to the disability and of a non-commercial nature, to the extent required by the specific disability."

331 See Article 6(4), §2.

This provision replicates the hierarchical set of obligations contained in the preceding sub-paragraph on a smaller scale. Where an exception on private copying is available under the law of a given Member State, copyright owners are obliged to make feasible, from a technical point of view, the making of reproductions for personal use. In the logic of DRM systems, this obligation should result in a technological mandate for both the producer and the user of DRM technologies. Where a certain DRM system adopted by copyright owners cannot accommodate the feasibility of private copying exceptions, Member States would be entitled to intervene by compelling the modification of the design of the (illegal) technology. It is evident that the effective enforcement of the end-user's right to copy the protected work for personal use completely depends upon whether a given Member State adopts an exception for private copying for the digital environment and whether this Member State establishes a monitoring system to check whether copyright owners comply effectively with their obligation to make reproduction for private use possible. The scope of this obligation is, in any event, restricted by the last part of the reported provision, under which copyright owners should have the freedom to shape and use DRM and other similar technologies in a such a way as to enable only a small (*i.e.*, limited) number of reproductions. This restriction pursues the objective of making digital private copying compatible with the notion of strictly personal use set out in Article 5(2)(b) and specified under national copyright law.

The field of application of Article 6(4) is narrowed by two other restrictions of great relevance. Firstly, the operation of its copyright exceptions interface is made subject to the acquisition of *legal access* by the user, in such a way that no obligation exists to allow or to facilitate user access which aims at exercising one of the guaranteed exceptions. Instead, it is provided that users *who have already accessed* copyrighted works must be given the technical means to benefit from the mentioned exceptions. In summary, the Directive creates no publicly mandated access to copyrighted works protected by technological measures.[332] It only enables the lawful acquirers of copyrighted works, who have already accessed the work, to exercise the few exceptions that they are entitled to benefit from.

Secondly, the fact that Article 6(4) of the InfoSoc Directive actually empowers contracts to set out freely the conditions of access to and use of copyrighted works is ultimately upheld by the wording of its fourth sub-paragraph, which provides that Member State obligation to monitor and ensure the availability of technical means enabling the exercise of certain exceptions:

> "[S]hall not apply to works or other subject-matter made available to the public on agreed contractual terms in such a way that members of the public may access them from a place and at a time individually chosen by them."[333]

---

332 See Dusollier, *Droit d'auteur et protection des oeuvres dans l'univers numérique*, op. cit., p. 175, who outlined that the Directive does not compel copyright owners to facilitate access to the benefit of exceptions.

333 See Article 6(4), §4.

By generally addressing interactive on-demand services which take place on the Internet, this provision allows contracts freely to erase *all* exceptions regarding the online dissemination of copyrighted works. This conclusion is supported by the wording of Recital 53 of the InfoSoc Directive, which makes reference to a rather unclear or unexplained distinction between interactive and non-interactive services in order to exclude the former services from the field of application of the first and second sub-paragraph of Article 6(4).[334] Considering that most uses undertaken on the Internet are understood to be interactive and on-demand, the system contained in Article 6(4) does not apply to most online services. In this respect, it was observed in the relevant literature that, in so far as more and more material becomes available exclusively (or nearly exclusively) online, technical measures will become virtually untouchable, and certain copyright exceptions of great importance can, by and large, be abandoned.[335]

4.5.3. Consequences of the Article 6(4) system

The system of safety nets created by Article 6(4) has very important consequences. In the first place, it implies that exceptions that are not included in its catalogue of "guaranteed" exceptions can be freely overridden through contract (*e.g.*, "click-wrap" licences) and be practically prevented by the use of technological measures that end-users cannot legally circumvent. In the second place, Article 6(4) provides that Member States, when implementing or maintaining exceptions omitted by the safeguard mechanism of Article 6(4), are not entitled to take measures which preserve the vitality of such exceptions.

The exclusion of most of the exceptions which enable transformative uses from this interface raises the question as to whether this delineation might be supported by a rationale other than the inability to reach political consensus on the composition of a set of imperative (*i.e.*, non-overridable) copyright exceptions.

The Directive provides no convincing justification for its ranking of different exceptions. It is unclear why the Directive allows Member States to take measures which allow them to preserve the private copying exception while it does not permit the same thing in respect of equally (or probably more) important exceptions such as quotations for purposes of criticism or review, and use for the purpose of caricature, parody or pastiche.[336]

---

[334] See Recital 53 of the InfoSoc Directive: "The protection of technological measures should ensure a secure environment for the provision of interactive on-demand services, in such a way that members of the public may access works or other subject-matter from a place and at a time individually chosen by them. Where such services are governed by contractual arrangements, the first and second sub-paragraphs of Article 6(4) should not apply. Non-interactive forms of online use should remain subject to those provisions."

[335] See Vinje, 'Should We Begin Digging Copyright's Grave?', op. cit., p. 557; and Hart, 'The Copyright in the Information Society Directive', op. cit., p. 64.

[336] See Article 5(3)(d) and Article 5(3)(k) of the InfoSoc Directive.

According to some commentators, the choice made by Article 6(4) would be justified by the intent to identify and mandate the protection of "public policy exceptions".[337] If this were the case, however, the notion of public policy relied on by the Directive would be unreasonably narrow. It seems that the decision to safeguard only the few exceptions included in Article 6(4) has no plausible basis. At best, the inappropriate selection made by this provision might have been driven by the consideration of the *public nature* of most of the beneficiaries of the selected exceptions (*e.g.*, libraries, educational establishments or museums; broadcasters; non-commercial social institutions). Another factor may have been that such exceptions, among all uses permitted by law, were understood as the easiest ones to accommodate under the operation of technological measures. In the preamble of the Directive, Recital 51 advocated that the legal protection of technological measures applied "without prejudice to public policy, as reflected in Article 5, or public security [...]".[338] Nonetheless, the prejudice to public policy is apparent if one considers that the efficacy of core exceptions which enable freedom of expression and ultimately encourage the creation of new works is irreparably undermined.

It is clear that Article 6(4) views all exceptions, without distinction, as if they were less desirable with the advent of DRM technologies. However, a firm distinction should be made. As concluded above,[339] the availability and use of exclusion tools such as DRM systems and other rights management technologies reduce only the transaction costs which are usually associated with the exception of private copying. The implementation of effective DRM solutions would make the case for the repeal of the private copying exception in so far as this exception was justified from the mere perspective of market failure (or, more clearly, market *formation*), as it is in the most relevant U.S. legal scholarship on this issue.[340] In contrast, as pointed out earlier, the European understanding of the rationale behind the private copying exception has been considerably different until now.[341] German law and many other European legal systems have established remuneration systems based upon levies in order to protect the public policy objective of user privacy with regard to the enjoyment of copyrighted goods, while providing copyright owners with equitable compensation for unauthorised copies. The exception embodied in Article 5(2)(b) and the option given to Member States for the preservation of this exception under Article 6(4), §2, uphold the argument that the InfoSoc Directive understands private copying as an optional measure of public policy that national copyright laws may maintain or implement *ex novo* by means of statutory licences which establish levy systems on digital media.

---

[337] See Gasser and Girsberger, 'Transposing the Copyright Directive', op. cit., p. 10; and Braun, 'The Interface Between the Protection of Technological Measures and the Exercise of Exceptions to Copyright', op. cit., p. 500.

[338] See Recital 51 of the InfoSoc. Directive.

[339] See §2.2.2.4., see *supra*.

[340] See §2.2.2.2., see *supra*.

[341] See §2.2.3, see *supra*.

In the light of the above considerations, in my view, the argument that the case for exceptions that pursue public policy objectives, including the protection of user privacy, is convincing, remains valid and is not weakened by the availability and use of DRM technologies. The fact that the safety-net system created by Article 6(4) failed to oblige Member States to protect both private copying and legitimate transformative uses of copyrighted works from DRM-based usage restrictions seems to be very unfortunate.

This approach by the Directive ended up ignoring the wise opinion delivered by the Commission's Legal Advisory Board (LAB) on the legal treatment of copyright exceptions in the context of copyright harmonisation measures seeking to create the conditions for an effective integration of EU information markets.[342] As advocated by the Advisory Board in response to the Commission's Follow-up to the 1995 Green Paper, to achieve the objectives of the proposed legislative action, certain exceptions should, necessarily, have been harmonised.[343] Among these exceptions, the LAB included exceptions of unauthorised copying in relation to specific, socially-valuable purposes, such as private use, research, teaching, back-up and archiving. In the LAB's view, copyright exceptions aimed at protecting fundamental rights (privacy, constitutional freedoms, *etc*) needed to be recognised, harmonised and preserved from technical and contractual restrictions at Community level.[344] Moreover, as regards legal terminology, to reinforce the need of an effective limitation of exclusive rights of reproduction, the LAB's opinion advocated the use of the term "exemptions" instead of that of mere "exceptions".[345]

4.5.4. The model interface between copyright, contract and technical measures of the Software Directive

It was pointed out in the relevant literature that, in order to preserve the vitality of copyright exceptions within the new EU regulation of digital copyright, it would have been much wiser not to require Member States to intervene.[346] There was reason to doubt whether Member States would actually have taken the necessary actions "in terms of establishing mechanisms for meaningful negotiations, evaluating the efficacy of 'voluntary measures', and acting forcefully and quickly when technical measures fail to respect copyright limits and exceptions".[347] It was stressed that such actions were even more unlikely "in the light of the vast power and resources of the copyright industry, and the comparatively weak position of the beneficiaries of copyright limits and exceptions [...]".[348]As in the Commis-

[342] See *Commentaires du Legal Advisory Board sur la Communication de la Commission du 20 Novembre 1996*, paragraph 9A, available (in French) at: http://europa.eu.int/ISPO/legal/fr/proprint/labcomment.htm.

[343] See *Commentaires du Legal Advisory Board*, paragraph 9A.

[344] See *Commentaires du Legal Advisory Board*, paragraph 7B.

[345] See *Commentaires du Legal Advisory Board*, paragraph 7A.

[346] See Vinje, 'Should We Begin Digging Copyright's Grave?', op. cit., p. 557.

[347] *Ibidem.*

[348] *Ibidem.*

sion's original proposal, legal protection could have been granted to technological measures in so far as these measures were designed to restrict acts which constituted copyright infringement, and nothing else. If so, there would have been no reason to require Member States to monitor the implementation of such measures and intervene when acts permitted by law (*i.e.,* copyright exceptions) proved to be frustrated. Heide persuasively suggested that a "model interface" between technological protection and copyright exceptions was just round the corner.[349]

Article 7(1) of the Software Directive ("Special measures of protection") explicitly provides that technical devices which may apply to protect a computer programme should leave the rights and exceptions provided by Article 4, 5 and 6 intact:

> "Without prejudice to the provisions of Articles 4, 5 and 6, Member States shall provide, in accordance with their national legislation, appropriate remedies against a person committing any of the acts listed in subparagraphs (a), (b) and (c) below: [...]
>
> (c) any act of putting into circulation, or the possession for commercial purposes of, any means the sole intended purpose of which is to facilitate the unauthorized removal or circumvention of any technical device which may have been applied to protect a computer program."

According to the wording of sub-paragraph (c), Article 7 only targets technologies "the sole intended purpose of which is to facilitate the unauthorized removal or circumvention" of right-holders' technological measures. Considering that the Software Directive defines most of the copyright exceptions as imperative (that is, acts which must be understood to be "authorised" anyway) the putting into circulation of technical means which enable users to exercise one of these exceptions (*e.g.*, the making of a back-up copy of a computer programme) will never fall within the field of application of Article 7.

In conjunction with the wording of its sub-paragraph (c), the interface created by Article 7 implies that both acts of circumventing technological protection measures and developing devices necessary to engage in such circumvention are lawful in so far as they are carried out in order to apply any of the mandatory exceptions.[350] For instance, under the provision of Article 7, the user is entitled to circumvent technical measures which protect a computer programme for the purpose of engaging in acts of reverse-engineering of the source code of the programme where the reproduction of the code is necessary to achieve interoperability with an independently created computer programme.[351] The same circumvention would be unlawful, however, if the user of the computer programme sought to exercise exceptions that had been restricted through contract. For instance, Article 5 of the Software Directive provides copyright exceptions with regard to acts of permanent and temporary reproduction, adaptation, arrangement and any other alteration of a computer programme, where these acts are necessary

[349] See Heide, 'Copyright, Contract and the Legal Protection of Technological Measures', op. cit., 16.

[350] *Ibidem.*

[351] See Article 6 of the Software Directive.

for the use of the computer programme by the lawful acquirer in accordance with its intended purpose, including that of error correction.[352]

It is worth recalling here that the legal interface between copyright, technical measures and contract under the Software Directive is completed by means of the civil sanctions embodied in Article 9(1).[353] In contrast, in the InfoSoc Directive, the legal protection of technological measures is not linked to copyright infringement, whereas the "catch-all" provision of Article 6(2), while impairing research on cryptography, considerably restricts the development and the putting into circulation of standard devices which enable circumvention for the sole exercise of copyright exceptions. It is worth noting that the very broad prohibition provided by Article 6(2) with regard to the manufacture, design and distribution of circumvention technologies runs contrary to the good intent expressed in the last part of Recital 48 of the same Directive. According to the laconic expression of this Recital, the legal protection in respect of technological measures "should not hinder research into cryptography". Unlike the 1998 U.S. DMCA, the text of the Directive does not say, however, whether technologists engaging in cryptography research are exempted from copyright liability under Article 6.

By comparison, to enable research on cryptography, the 1998 DMCA introduced into the U.S. Copyright Act an exemption from the anti-circumvention provisions created under Section 1201.[354] This exemption lists several factors under which acts of circumvention of a technological measure, as applied to a copy, phonorecord, performance, or display of a published work, are permitted as acts of good faith encryption research. In this respect, the only relevant provision of the InfoSoc Directive is Recital 50, which makes it clear that the (overbroad) legal protection of technological measures provided under Article 6 should neither inhibit nor prevent the development or use of any means of circumventing a technological measure that is necessary to enable acts to be undertaken in accordance with the terms of Article 5(3) and 6 of the Software Directive.[355]

4.5.5. Monitoring systems on the effective enforcement of exceptions

The purpose of Article 12 shows that the drafters of the InfoSoc Directive were fully aware of the risk that unrestricted power in the hands of designers and users of rights management technologies could *de facto* eliminate copyright exceptions. Under the procedure created by the first paragraph of Article 12, the European

---

352 See Article 5(1) of the Software Directive.

353 See §4.3, see *supra*.

354 See U.S. Code, Title 17, §1201(g).

355 These provisions of the Software Directive establish copyright exceptions to the benefit of the "person having a right to use a copy of a computer program", who shall be entitled, without the authorisation of the right holder, (i) to perform acts of loading, displaying, running, transmitting or storing the program in order to observe, study or test its functioning in order to determine the ideas and principles which underlie any element of the program (cf. Article 5(3)); (ii) to reproduce the program code and translate its form in order to obtain interoperability information (cf. Article 6(1)).

Commission is bound to examine "whether acts which are permitted by law are being adversely affected by the use of effective technological measures" every three years.[356] The third paragraph of this provision established a contact committee, which should act as an advisor to the Commission for the monitoring of the impact of the Directive on the functioning of the Internal Market and, more generally, with regard to the exchange of information "on relevant developments in legislation and case-law, as well as economic, social, cultural and technological developments".[357]

With specific regard to the fate of copyright exceptions, the monitoring system envisaged by Article 12 reveals a rather constructive approach. By leaving the door open for a revision of the Directive, it entrusts a committee of specialists the task of periodically observing how digital markets for copyright goods develop, and whether, in the context of these markets, users are allowed to engage effectively in acts permitted by law. It is worthwhile noting that the monitoring system is established with regard to *all* of the exceptions listed in Article 5, and not just with regard to the few exceptions listed under the safety-net system of Article 6(4).

Nonetheless, Article 12 does not create special and faster procedures for the Commission to submit proposals for amendments to the Directive. Under the ordinary co-decision procedure,[358] any initiative to amend the Directive may take several years to be enacted and enter into force. A more appropriate strategy to deal with the fast-developing nature of technological measures was adopted by Section 1201 of the 1998 DMCA, which amended the U.S. Copyright Act.[359] As opposed to the InfoSoc Directive, U.S. copyright law attempted to safeguard fair use by the recourse to an administrative procedure which ensured a constant evaluation and a prompt adaptation of anti-circumvention law. Section 1201 empowers the Librarian of Congress, upon recommendation of the Register of Copyrights, to evaluate the adverse effect that the application of anti-circumvention provisions might have on fair use every three years.[360] In particular, Section 1201 confers to this administrative body the power to enact temporary liability exemptions for acts of circumvention which enable users to make non-infringing uses of particular classes of copyrighted works. Three rule-making proceedings have already allowed the Librarian of Congress to create, in 2000, 2003 and 2006, exemptions which enable the circumvention of access-control technologies used to protect six classes of works.[361] It must be noted that, unlike the InfoSoc Directive, Section 1201 of the DMCA also applies to copyrighted computer programmes. Accordingly, the ex-

---

356 See Article 12(1) of the InfoSoc Directive.

357 See Article 12(3) of the InfoSoc Directive.

358 See Article 251 of the EC Treaty.

359 See U.S. Code, Title 17, Chapter 12, §1201(a).

360 See U.S. Code, Title 17, §1201(a)(1)(C).

361 See Library of Congress, U.S. Copyright Office, Federal Register, *Exemption to Prohibition on Circumvention of Copyright Protection Systems for Access Control Technologies*, vol. 65, 31 October 2000, Rules and regulations, p. 64556; vol. 68, 31 October 2003, Rules and regulations, p. 62011; vol. 71, 27 November 2006, Rules and regulations, p. 68472, available at: http://www.copyright.gov/1201/index.html.

emptions created under the previously described rule-making proceedings also cover computer programmes.[362] Until now, the exemptions unrelated to software concern:

- Audiovisual works included in the educational library of a college or university's film or media studies department, when circumvention is accomplished for the purpose of making compilations of portions of those works for educational use in the classroom by media studies or film professors.
- Literary works distributed in e-book format when all existing e-book editions of the work (including digital text editions made available by authorised entities) contain access control that prevents the enabling of the e-book's read-aloud function and prevents the enabling of screen readers to render the text into a specialised format.
- Sound recordings, and audiovisual works associated with those sound recordings, distributed in compact disc format and protected by technological protection measures that control access to lawfully purchased works and create or exploit security flaws or vulnerabilities that compromise the security of personal computers, when circumvention is accomplished solely for the purpose of good faith testing, investigating, or correcting such security flaws or vulnerabilities.[363]

Notwithstanding its specific purpose and the interesting technique, which ensures a timely update of legislation, this mechanism has turned out to have had very little impact on the power of copyright owners to control access of their works. At the end of the day, it was easy to predict that exemptions driven by the identification of *particular* classes of works could not seriously accommodate the open-ended and flexible range of uses covered by the U.S. fair use doctrine.

4.6. National exceptions after the InfoSoc Directive: a brief overview

4.6.1. Preliminary remarks

There is no doubt that the many uncertainties regarding the merits and the viability of the system of safety nets created by Article 6(4) for the sake of copyright exceptions in the digital environment have made the transposition of the InfoSoc Directive more demanding and time-consuming for Member States. This held true, in particular, in certain countries where national parliaments were forced to face a very strong opposition and lobbying by groups of consumers and users. In France and Belgium, for instance, consumer unions took remarkable initiatives in public

[362] See *Exemption to Prohibition on Circumvention of Copyright Protection Systems for Access Control Technologies*, cit.

[363] *Ibidem.*

debates and in court in order to ask for a higher consideration and protection of consumer and end-user interests under digital copyright law.[364] In France, in particular, these initiatives resulted in case law that will be examined below.[365]

It was suggested above that the InfoSoc Directive leaves Member States with no guidance in the interpretation of crucial issues.[366] The definition and the scope of the protection of technological measures were addressed with ambiguous and vague terms that could not guarantee uniformity in the transposition of anti-circumvention rules under national law. Moreover, the Directive failed to specify what kind of legal tools and enforcement proceedings should have preserved, under national jurisdictions, the effective implementation of the obligation upon copyright owners to take voluntary measures in favour of certain copyright exceptions entrenched by the use of technological protection measures. Nor does it enumerate how Member States should monitor compliance with these duties, and when they should have taken appropriate action in respect of their violation.

As a result of these grey areas of the Directive, respective national legislation has not resulted in a harmonised legal framework creating an effective and balanced interface between copyright exceptions and technological protection measures. It is clear that such differences in national interpretation of the Directive reinforce the main dividing effect of the optional nature of copyright exceptions under Article 5.

In strident contrast with the harmonisation objectives of the Directive, the legal treatment of copyright exceptions is expected to vary considerably from one jurisdiction to another, with the creation of subsequent distortions in the EU Internal Market.

4.6.2. What national exceptions, in the concrete?

4.6.2.1. Private copying

Even if Member States have maintained or created exceptions for private copying when implementing the InfoSoc Directive, these exceptions are expected to operate mainly in the analogue world, where copying is still subject to old-fashioned limits (*e.g.*, reduction in quality; limited possibilities of dissemination, *etc*) and cannot be obstructed by the operation of technical measures. As shown by the table provided under Appendix II, Member States did not make broad use of the option to include private copying in the small circle of privileged exceptions which benefit from the specific enforcement procedures created under Article 6(4) of the Directive.[367] Among the few Member States included in the mentioned table, the ones that created a specific exception for private copying in respect of digital settings are Italy, Spain and France and, to some extent, the United Kingdom. The

364 See Helberger and Groenenboom, 'Digital Rights Management and Consumer Acceptability, Legal Aspect', p. 17, downloaded at: http://www.indicare.org.

365 See §7.5.2. and §7.5.3., see *infra*.

366 See §3.4.1., see *supra*.

367 See Appendix II, see *infra*.

majority of the Member States listed in the table preferred either to leave the concrete enforcement of this exception to the parties' freedom of contract,[368] or to adopt provisional solutions under which administrative authorities are entitled to add private copying to the list of preserved exceptions in so far as this exception proves to be compatible with copy-control measures, and, ultimately, with the restrictive criteria of the three-step test.[369]

According to Article 71-sexies, §4, of the Italian Copyright Act, users who have legal access to the copyrighted work have the right to make one copy for personal use (which can be also an analogue copy) notwithstanding the protection of technological measures.[370] However, neither a special enforcement procedure for the exercise of this right, nor an exemption from the prohibition to circumvent copy-control technologies is provided.

The French law that recently transposed the InfoSoc Directive is by far the most brave among the national versions of the private copying regulations. This law established a specific administrative authority which was given the power to settle disputes arising between copyright owners and users in respect of technical restrictions of the private copying exception.[371] This authority is also given the power to determine, in consideration of each specific type of protected work and of the ways by which the work is made available to the public, what threshold number of digital copies can be deemed to be compatible with the (strict) notion of personal use adopted under French law.[372] To this end, the authority is required to monitor whether the use of copy-control mechanisms aimed at restricting and/or regulating the number of feasible reproductions ends up frustrating the threshold number of copies allowed for strictly personal use.[373] New French copyright law also preserves the making of copies for personal use in the face of technical measures used by providers and distributors of digital TV services, which are thereby bound not to impair personal reproductions of their broadcasts.[374] Moreover, the licensor and the distributor of copy-protected materials bear a duty to inform the user about the restrictions that the application of a certain technical measure may imply in respect of private copying.[375]

---

368 See Denmark, Greece, Germany: cf. Appendix II, see *infra*.

369 See Netherlands and Belgium.

370 See the Italian Copyright Act, N. 641/1933, as amended by Law (*i.e.*, "Decreto legislativo") N. 68/2003 of 9 April 2003.

371 See Law 2006-961 of 1 August 2006 on copyright and related rights in the information society, adopted text N.596, Official Journal of the French Republic, 3 August 2006, available at: http://www.assembleenationale.fr/12/ta/ta0596.asp. Article 17 of this new law established an independent administrative body (*Autorité de régulation des mesures techniques*) which is required to ensure the effective enforcement of copyright exceptions notwithstanding the operation of technological protection measures.

372 See Art. L.331-8, §2, of the French Intellectual Property Code, as amended by Law 2006-961.

373 See new Art. L.331-9.

374 See Art. L.331-11.

375 See Art. L 331-12.

The copyright law of July 2006 which amended the Spanish Intellectual Property Act, although it includes the making of personal copies within the circle of exceptions to be preserved from copy-control measures, leaves the Government with the power to modify the regime of this exception in so far as the evolution of technical measures allows the management of the exclusive right of private copying while making copyright levies unjustified.[376] In this respect, the new provision of Article 25(7)(d) of the Spanish Intellectual Property Code gives the Government the power to create exceptions to the payment of copyright levies in respect of equipment, hardware and media that prove not to serve the purposes of private copying.[377] The adoption of this rule clearly demonstrates that the Spanish law-makers conceived this exception for the digital environment more as a remedy for a situation of market failure than as a legal tool that seeks to protect user privacy from external control while ensuring fair compensation for right-holders.

Finally, it is worth outlining that, when transposing the Directive's Article 6(4) system into the Copyright, Designs and Patent Act of 1988, the UK legislator included highly specific exceptions of private copying into the circle of exceptions preserved under the system of administrative complaints governed by the UK Secretary of State.[378] These cases of preserved private copying are, respectively, copying made by the visually impaired person wishing to have access to a single personal copy of the protected work, multiple copies for visually impaired persons, and recordings for purposes of time-shifting in respect of broadcasts.[379]

4.6.2.2. Transformative use

An important distinction must be made as far as transformative use is concerned. Whereas exceptions that were not included into the safety-net system of Article 6(4) can be freely overridden by contract (at least in those EU jurisdictions where national law-makers have not taken steps to shape copyright exceptions as *mandatory* provisions), the other few public policy exceptions covered by this system benefit from several types of enforcement proceedings created under Member States law. Such proceedings consist of systems ranging from mediation-based models and administrative complaints to direct recourse to courts.[380] By far, the most remarkable transposition of this safeguard mechanism has occurred in France, which has created an independent administrative body for the purpose of enforcing copyright exceptions and enacted specific complaint and appeal proceedings.

---

376 See the First Additional Provision (*Disposiciòn adicional primera*) of Law N.23/2006 of 7 July 2006, which amended the Intellectual Property Act enacted by Royal Legislative Decree N.1/1996, of 12 April 1996. The text of the new law is available at: http://www.boe.es (*Boletìn Oficial del Estado*).

377 See §4 of the Single Article (*Articolo único*) of Law N.23/2006, which amended Article 25 of the 1996 Spanish Intellectual Property Act.

378 See §296ZE of the UK Copyright, Designs and Patent Act 1998 (see the table provided in Appendix II, under "Remedies", see *infra*).

379 See §31A, §31B and §70 of the UK Copyright, Designs and Patent Act 1998.

380 See Gasser and Girsberger, 'Transposing the Copyright Directive', op. cit., p. 25.

As regards the scope of the application of the Article 6(4) system, the vast majority of Member States implemented *verbatim* the restriction concerning the non-applicability of the safeguard system in respect of interactive, on-demand delivery of copyrighted works.[381] As a result, the aforementioned enforcement proceedings do not apply to online deliveries, so that electronic contracts concluded online are also entitled to restrict the few public policy exceptions preserved by Article 6(4) in an unlimited manner.[382] The only exception to this trend is French copyright law. Under new Article L.331-10 of the French Intellectual Property Code, it is provided that the non-applicability of the Article 6(4) safeguard system in cases of on-demand deliveries refers exclusively to the exception of private copying, and not to the other exceptions that the same provision attempts to preserve.[383] Clearly, this attempt by French law to preserve several public policy exceptions in the Internet world veers away from the clear wording of Article 6(4) and might, as a possible consequence, have the undertaking of infringement proceedings against France by the European Commission.

4.6.2.3. A few examples of extension of the statutory protection of copyright exceptions

It is noteworthy that, along with the implementation of the safeguard mechanism provided by Article 6(4), and acting independently from the dictate of the Directive, the German, Belgian and French legislators seem to have expanded the statutory protection of copyright exceptions against the usage restrictions enabled by technical measures.[384] In this respect, Article 23-bis of the Belgian Copyright Act confers an imperative character to all of its exceptions. The final clause of Section 95(b)(1) of the German Copyright Act recognises the imperative nature of the sole exceptions preserved against technical measures under Article 6(4) of the Directive by providing that contractual agreements excluding right-holder obligations in respect of such exceptions are null and void.[385] By contrast, the French Intellectual Property Code does not adopt a contract law provision to protect exceptions; instead, under its new Article L.335-1, §6, it provides that:

> "The technical measures cannot oppose the free use of the protected work within the exceptions set out under this Code, as well as of the rights conferred by the right holders."[386]

This wording clearly mirrors the clause provided by Article 11 of the WIPO Copyright Treaty, under which copyright exceptions are given explicit immunity from anti-circumvention protection. Article L.335-1, §6, seems to provide that no copyright exception under the French Intellectual Property Code should be impaired by the operation of an effective technical measure. This means that, if the

[381] See Article 6(4), §4, of the InfoSoc Directive.
[382] See Gasser and Girsberger, 'Transposing the Copyright Directive', op. cit., pp. 17-25.
[383] See Article L.331-10 of the French Intellectual Property Code.
[384] See the table provided in Appendix II.
[385] See, in this regard, the example of German law in Appendix II, see *infra*.
[386] See French Law N.2006-961.

provision is to be understood as restricting stakeholders' freedom of contract, the contractual agreements by which the user of a protected work agrees upon giving up his or her statutory usage rights should be considered null or void.

4.7. Summary

This chapter has focused on the legal treatment of copyright exceptions under the InfoSoc Directive. It has been pointed out that the Directive does not provide a mandatory and uniform regulation of copyright exceptions, as its objective of market integration required. In particular, it has been explained that the Directive ambiguously addressed the intersection between copyright, technological measures and contract, in such a way that copyright exceptions may easily prove to be ineffective because of the contractual override enabled by the interplay of electronic contracts setting out the conditions of legal access to the copyrighted work and access- and copy-control technologies (such as DRM systems).

Indeed, the system of safety nets foreseen by Article 6(4) of the InfoSoc Directive in order to preserve the effective implementation of copyright exceptions was found to be unconvincing. Not only does this system use ambiguous language to define crucial obligations that should ensure the feasibility of certain uses that are free from copyright exclusivity, Article 6(4) also fails to make a distinction between mandatory and non-mandatory (*i.e.*, overridable) exceptions, leaving out of its safeguard net uses which protect constitutional values such as freedom of expression and communication under copyright law. It has been pointed out that this failure of Article 6(4) occurred because the EU legislators failed to follow the model of the interface for copyright exceptions and technical measures provided by Article 7 of the 1991 Software Directive. If, in the same way as the Software Directive, the InfoSoc Directive had provided that no circumvention prohibition should have inhibited the exercise of certain uses permitted by law, end-user acts of circumvention would have been lawful if carried out with the purpose of benefiting from one of the mandatory exceptions.

Finally, it has been concluded that, in the light of considerable discrepancies in the transposition of Article 6(4) of the InfoSoc Directive into Member State law, the effective enforcement and the breadth of statutory copyright exceptions vary greatly from one EU jurisdiction to another, in direct contrast to the harmonisation objectives of the Directive.

5. Digital copyright law: general policy issues under the EC Treaty

5.1. Introduction

This chapter outlines certain inconsistencies that exist between the legal treatment of copyright exceptions created by the InfoSoc Directive and constitutional clauses set out in the EC Treaty. It will be argued that the Directive must be deemed to have missed the objective of market integration, which it should have pursued in order to comply with the legal basis of Article 95 of the Treaty. This failure mainly results from the lack of harmonisation between the laws governing national legal treatment of certain copyright exceptions, which has the potential to distort competition and to have an adverse impact upon the smooth, cross-border dissemination of copyrighted digital works in the European Union.

Another point of contrast with the EC Treaty, which arises from the InfoSoc Directive, is given by the exhaustive nature of the list of optional exceptions. The chapter suggests that this factor is likely to disrupt (or, at best, hinder) national cultural policies which seek to pursue the achievement of certain public policy goals whose pursuit is ultimately preserved by the relevant clause of Article 151 of the Treaty. It is also suggested that the InfoSoc Directive failed to comply with Article 153(2) of the EC Treaty, which compels the Community to take consumer protection law and policy into account when defining and implementing other policies and legislative activities. This chapter will therefore seek to explain, in spite of the Directive's silence, what the consequences of applying EU consumer contract law to business-to-consumer transactions accompanying DRM technologies bundled with copyrighted goods are.

Not only does this kind of investigation have theoretical implications, it also explains that the new digital copyright law enacted by the InfoSoc Directive must co-exist with other important bodies of law considered under the EC Treaty. The results of this investigation are ideally addressed to the European Commission, which bears a general duty to monitor the impact of the Directive on the functioning of the Internal Market and to highlight any difficulties under Article 12 of the InfoSoc Directive.[387]

---

[387] See §4.5.5., see *supra*.

The Commission has already commenced its review and revision of the Directive. As mentioned earlier, the Commission has recently undertaken a couple of initiatives in the field of online copyright management and in respect of a possible copyright levy reform.[388] Both initiatives stemmed from the assumption that the Commission was, by and large, dissatisfied with the results evidenced by the early implementation of the Directive. The Commission observed that the implementation of the Directive did not ensure market integration. In particular, by taking measures in the field of online copyright management of music works, the Commission implicitly recognised that, while omitting to consider the strictly national dimension of copyright collective management, the Directive failed to unite the rapidly developing online markets for digital copyrighted music. From a market integration perspective, the Commission admitted that the Directive did not provide the commercial exploiters of digital copyrighted goods with the legal tools for the smooth marketing of these goods on a Community basis (instead of on a national basis).

In respect of its objective of phasing-out copyright levies on the availability and use of DRM technologies, the Commission acknowledged that the ambiguous wording of Article 5(2) of the Directive increased fragmentation within the Internal Market. This is a paradoxical outcome for a directive whose purpose was to strengthen the integration of national markets. As noted above,[389] the lack of clarity of this provision in specifying the technical conditions (*i.e.*, the standard of "availability" and "use" of DRM technologies entrenching private copying opportunities) under which Member States should compel the phasing-out of levies on digital devices and media has resulted in an unequal proliferation of national levies on copying equipment which supports and implements DRM technologies.

The Commission concluded that not only was such unequal proliferation of levies contrary to the objective of ensuring the free circulation of digital media devices within the common market, it was also detrimental to consumers, who may be impaired in their personal copying of DRM-protected goods despite having paid a levy on the sale price of their copying devices and recordable media.

Finally, there is another circumstance which suggests that an amendment or repeal of the InfoSoc Directive, in the light of its large drawbacks and its inconsistencies with the EC Treaty, is not that unrealistic. This circumstance is given by the approach shown by the Commission in its first evaluation of the Database Directive in December 2005.[390] In its evaluation of the Database Directive, ten years after its coming into force, the Commission considered the policy options of either repealing the whole Directive, by withdrawing the so-called *sui generis* right on "non-original" databases (that is, the mere aggregation of data) or amending the definition of the scope of protection of this controversial right.[391] This rather nega-

[388] See the European Commission's Recommendation on collective cross-border licensing of online copyright and related rights for legitimate online music services (see §3.3.2., see *supra*) and the *Copyright levy reform – Work Programme for 2006* (see §4.4.1., see *supra*).

[389] See §4.4.1., see *supra.*

[390] See the Commission's *First evaluation of Directive 96/9/EC*: see §3.2.1.3., see *supra.*

[391] See *First evaluation of Directive 96/9/EC*, cit., pp. 23-25.

tive conclusion was reached on the basis that the creation of the unprecedented *sui generis* right did not achieve the main policy goals foreseen by the Commission at the time of the adoption of the Directive. These goals were the growth of industrial investment on databases in the European market and the creation of uniform standards for the copyright protection of these products. This failure was evidenced by the unproven impact of the *sui generis* right on the rates of database production in Europe and by the lack of understanding and legal certainty of the protection scope of this new right, which resulted in an increasing recourse to litigation before national courts.[392]

In my view, it is not unrealistic that, after careful monitoring and evaluation, the Commission might continue to propose amendments to the InfoSoc Directive by targeting its most obvious gaps, such as the much needed harmonisation of (certain) copyright exceptions and the creation of an effective system to safeguard exceptions from the operation of DRM technologies.

5.2. The failure of the InfoSoc Directive in the pursuit of market integration

For the InfoSoc Directive to comply with the legal basis created by Article 95 of the EC Treaty, its harmonisation measures should facilitate the removal of disparities between national provisions which hinder the free movement of copyrighted goods in the so-called Information Society. Despite the clear intents shown by its initial recitals, the Directive clearly fails to achieve this objective.

It has been stressed earlier that two factors of paramount importance for market integration were left out of the scope of the Directive. On the one hand, the InfoSoc Directive provided no harmonisation measures with regard to the national subject matter of copyright and the notion of "derivative work".[393] On the other, it neglected the impact of national copyright management on the development of certain kinds of commercial exploitation with a cross-border reach.[394] While it seems highly unrealistic that Community law might cope with the former factor by the creation of a uniform notion of copyrightable work, the latter may be reformed very soon, as shown by the above-mentioned Commission's Recommendation on collective copyright management for legitimate online music services.

As far as the scope of the InfoSoc Directive is concerned, it must be outlined that the unclear terms which characterise the legal protection of technological measures and, most importantly, the non-harmonisation of copyright exceptions are likely to create significant distortions of competition and obstacles to the free movement of copyrighted digital goods and services. As noted below, such distortions might easily address markets for both tangible and intangible formats.

---

[392] *Ibidem.*

[393] See §3.3.1., see *supra.*

[394] See §3.3.2., see *supra.*

5.2.1. Fragmentation on markets for tangible and intangible goods

With regard to tangible goods, the different ranges of exceptions that technological measures should be forced to comply with might hinder the development and diffusion of standard DRM technologies throughout the Community. If guaranteed exceptions vary according to the applicable national law, copyright owners would be forced to shape and programme these technologies for each Member State in order to comply with the different sets of uses permitted and preserved by the relevant domestic law. If so, the operation of certain access- or copy-control devices or national (or regional) access codes implemented on the medium embodying a copyrighted work would be legal or illegal depending on the jurisdiction where the medium was physically marketed.

Similarly, with regard to intangible goods, national disparities in the legal treatment of copyright exceptions and a different understanding of anti-circumvention law may discourage the creation of trans-border delivery services on the Internet. The strictly national dimension of successful online music services that have emerged and developed over the last few years supports this scenario. In the European Union, the partition of online markets along national borders is mainly due to the fragmented dimension of copyright collective management. In this context, the limited harmonisation of copyright exceptions, as well as the unclear and ineffective interface between copyright and contract law, raise a further obstacle to the enforcement of the user acts which are permitted by law. If suppliers of digital copyrighted goods should find the research of national statutes and the implementation of services tailored to each Member State's particular exceptions too costly, they may eventually find it more desirable to create single platforms and provide consumers with standardised terms of use.[395]

At this point, due to the exemption of online delivery services from the safeguard mechanism envisaged by Article 6(4) of the InfoSoc Directive, these contractual terms could validly override and replace national exceptions, in a way in which purely market-driven forces could create a *de facto* harmonisation of usage conditions. Nonetheless, this harmonisation would have the effect of stifling the role of national *public* law and vesting copyright holders and content suppliers with the *private* power to authorise only uses that best suit their business. The "Terms of Service" of Apple's iTunes music store provides an example. While Apple's DRM system allows purchasers of music downloads to engage in inoffensive non-transformative uses (for example, making a certain number of private copies from the original; transferring downloads on a limited number of listening devices), it does not permit any significant transformative use (such as extracting a

[395] See *iTunes – How Copyright, Contract, and Technology Shape the Business of Digital Media – A Case Study*, Digital Media Project, Berkman Center for Internet and Society at Harvard Law School, 15 June 2004, downloaded at: http://cyber.law.harvard.edu, p. 24.

part of a downloaded song, or making an excerpt of a film clip for an educational presentation).[396]

5.2.2. Inconsistency with Article 95 of the EC Treaty

It can be concluded that the legal basis upon which the InfoSoc Directive's compliance with the EC Treaty is grounded is highly questionable. As noted above, Article 95 of the Treaty does not vest the Community with general powers in the enactment of legislative harmonisation measures. Authors such as Weatherill and de Witte maintain that the Community is entitled to take measures of approximation of national laws only on the grounds that their objective is market integration.[397]

In principle, the constitutional validity of the InfoSoc Directive may be questioned because, contrary to the requirements provided by Article 95 of the EC Treaty, this secondary legislation failed to harmonise - to their full extent - different aspects of national copyright laws (*i.e.*, exceptions, anti-circumvention laws) that, as they stand, create barriers to the free movement of copyrighted goods and distort the conditions of competition in the tangible and intangible dissemination of the self-same works. In reviewing the validity of the Directive, however, it must be considered whether, and to what extent, the Directive might have a function of "model law" which meets the threshold requirements of Article 95. In this respect, the fact that, while providing for a list of copyright exceptions which has an *exhaustive* character, the InfoSoc Directive pursues pure harmonisation objectives by forbidding Member States to create *new* copyrighted exceptions, cannot be neglected.

To see whether the InfoSoc Directive can be found to be consistent with the legal basis of Article 95 of the Treaty, it is insufficient to show that the Directive, while reforming copyright law for the Information Society, pursued a public policy objective other than that of the harmonisation of national laws and market integration. The observation that internal market legislation invariably and legitimately pursues other public policy objectives, which may, in fact, be the main reason why a certain harmonisation measure is ultimately adopted, is persuasive.[398] In this respect, it was emphasised above that the InfoSoc Directive was intended to pursue industrial policy objectives for which harmonisation measures in the field of copyright law were deemed to be a pre-condition.[399] The objectives of industrial policy pursued by the Directive do not necessarily come into conflict

---

396 See *iTunes – How Copyright, Contract, and Technology Shape the Business of Digital Media* , op. cit., p. 69, which reported that Section13(a) of the iTunes Terms of Service requires consumers not to use "proprietary information or materials in any way whatsoever except for use of the Service in compliance with the terms of this Agreement".

397 See Weatherill, 'Harmonisation: How Much, How Little?', 16(3) *European Business Law Review* 2005, p. 533, at pp. 534-535; de Witte, 'Non-market values in internal market legislation', op. cit., pp.75-76.

398 See de Witte, 'Non-market values in internal market legislation', op. cit., p. 76.

399 See §3.2.2., see *supra*.

with the policy objectives required for internal market legislation by Article 95 of the Treaty. Nevertheless, Articles 95 requires secondary legislation, such as the InfoSoc Directive, to make a plausible case that the adopted legislation either helps to remove barriers to the free movement of goods and services, or seeks to remove distortions of competition.

In the case of the InfoSoc Directive, it must be ascertained as to whether this piece of legislation, beyond its evident purposes of industrial/trade policy, was intended to embody effective harmonisation measures that would satisfy the requirements of Article 95. For this purpose, it is worth looking very briefly at how the ECJ has dealt with similar cases of supposed lack of a proper legal basis of internal market legislation. A first example is provided by the well-known case of the so-called 1998 Tobacco Advertising Directive.[400] Notwithstanding the remarkably broad nature of the harmonisation programme envisaged by Article 95, in October 2000, the ECJ annulled this piece of legislation, for the first time on the assumption that it was not validly based upon the Treaty provisions governing legislative harmonisation.[401] As pointed out by Weatherill, in the case of the Tobacco Advertising Directive, the ECJ found that this Directive had gone far beyond the permitted limits by enacting a measure of public health policy for which the Community was not competent.[402] In a later case, by dismissing an action for annulment brought by the Netherlands with regard to the compliance of the 1998 Directive on the Legal Protection of Biotechnological Inventions[403] with the legal basis of Article 100a (now Article 95), the ECJ confirmed that harmonisation measures can be validly based on Article 95 as long as their main objective is either the removal of legal obstacles to the free circulation of goods and services, or the creation/maintenance of conditions of undistorted competition within the Community.[404] Specifically, the main objective of harmonisation in the Biotech-

---

[400] See Directive 98/43/EC of the European Parliament and of the Council of 6 July 1998 on the approximation of the laws, regulations and administrative provisions of the Member States relating to the advertising and sponsorship of tobacco products, OJ L 213, 30.07.1998, at 9 (hereinafter "Tobacco Advertising Directive"). In terms of lack of a proper legal basis, a parallelism between the InfoSoc Directive and the 1998 Tobacco Advertising Directive was proposed firstly by Hugenholtz, 'Why the Copyright Directive is Unimportant', op. cit., pp. 501-502.

[401] See *Federal Republic of Germany* v. *European Parliament and Council of the European Union*, Judgment of 5 October 2000, Case C-376-98 [2000] ECR I-8419.

[402] See Weatherill, 'Harmonisation: How Much, How Little', op. cit., p. 537.

[403] See Directive 98/44/EC of the European Parliament and of the Council of 6 July 1998 on the legal protection of biotechnological inventions, OJ L 213, 1998, 13 (hereinafter "Biotechnology Directive").

[404] See *Kingdom of the Netherlands* v. *European Parliament and Council of the European Union*, Judgment of 9 October 2001, Case C-377/98 [2001] ECR I-07079, in particular paragraph 18. In the specific case of the Biotechnology Directive, the Court held that the harmonisation of national laws regarding the patentability of biotechnological inventions was validly enacted on the basis of Article 95, even if it resulted in promoting research and development in the field of genetic engineering. The ECJ confirmed that the Community had the competence to harmonise national laws in a field where it was

nology Directive was the removal of legal obstacles that would probably have emerged if national laws, case law and practices had developed in disparate ways in the process of granting patents on biotechnological inventions.[405]

In the light of the above-mentioned understanding of the requirements of Article 95 by the ECJ, it seems reasonable to conclude that the InfoSoc Directive evidently overstretched the legal basis of Article 95.[406] The Community acted as a pure copyright legislator and limited its action to the ratification of the external obligations taken by the European Commission on behalf of EU Member States when negotiating the 1996 WIPO Copyright Treaty and the Performances and Phonograms Treaty. This legislative action resulted in a horizontal regulation that did not seek to create a single market for the exploitation of copyrighted goods in the Information Society. The fact that the Community intended to superimpose a new form of copyright protection on national copyright systems by introducing an unrestricted anti-circumvention law under Article 6 of the InfoSoc Directive could have persuaded the European legislator that Article 95 could not serve as a correct legal basis.

In the recent judgment on the case *Laserdisken* v. *Kulturministeriet*, the ECJ held that the InfoSoc Directive was validly based on the grounds of Article 95 of the Treaty.[407] However, it seems evident to me that this conclusion was achieved with specific regard to the provision of Article 4(2) of the Directive. This Article provides for the exhaustion of the distribution right after the first sale or transfer within the European Union of a tangible object which embodies a copyrighted work. As concluded by the ECJ, by means of this provision, the Directive forbids Member States from taking legislative initiatives with regard to the international exhaustion of the distribution right in order to avoid significant differences in protection and thereby in restrictions on the free movement of services and products which incorporate, or are based upon, intellectual property.[408] Given that the ECJ's judgment limited the scope of its analysis of the legitimacy of the Directive to the

not given law-making powers by the Treaty (that is, patent law) insofar as such approximation aimed to create or maintain the unity of the European economic space.

405 See *Kingdom of the Netherlands* v. *European Parliament and Council of the European Union*, cit., paragraphs 26 and 27. In the Court's view, the fact that such measures spilled over into other policy areas falling within the scope of different clauses of the EC Treaty or pertaining to Member States' competences (*i.e.*, public health and public order) did not impede the Community from validly using the legal basis of Article 95. The Court rejected the plea according to which the Biotechnology Directive should have been adopted on the basis of Articles 157 and 163, and not Article 95 of the Treaty, on the assumption that its main object was that of supporting the industrial development of the Community and scientific research in the genetic engineering sector.

406 See, in a similar way, Bonofacio, 'The Information society and the harmonisation of copyright and related rights: (over)stretching the legal basis of Article 95(100A)?', *Legal Issues of European Integration* 1999, p. 1, at pp. 64-75, who argued that, due to the evident overstretching of Article 95 to achieve the main object of the InfoSoc Directive, it could be wise to treat Information Society legislation (as digital copyright law) as a mature Community policy separated from internal market legislation.

407 See §3.3.5 and §3.3.6, see *supra*.

408 See *Laserdisken* v. *Kulturministeriet*, cit., paragraph 34.

sole harmonisation purpose of Article 4(2), it is persuasive to conclude that the judgment on *Laserdisken* does not run contrary to the opinion expressed here with regard to the questionable constitutional validity of the InfoSoc Directive.

Given that the main objective of this Directive was that of tailoring a new model of copyright protection for the digital environment, the Directive would have been adopted better on the grounds of the so-called "implied powers" of Article 308.[409] The ECJ made it clear that the Community is competent, in the field of intellectual property, either to harmonise national laws on the grounds of Article 95, or to unify the terms of protection by the creation of Community titles on the basis of Article 308 (as it did for Council Regulation 40/94/EC on the Community trademark).[410]

The point advocated here is that, while creating a new form of stronger copyright protection under the law of the EU Member States, the InfoSoc Directive sought neither to remove national disparities which hinder the free circulation of copyrighted works and copyright-based services, nor to remove disparities which cause distortions of competition on related markets. Instead, the EU legislator developed a trade policy for the Information Society as if the EC Treaty had entrusted the Community with direct law-making powers in the copyright field.

5.3. The clash with Member States' cultural policies

In enacting a widely horizontal measure of harmonisation with regard to national copyright laws, the Community inevitably touched upon the cultural values that copyright has traditionally internalised. Considering the high degree of protection afforded to copyright owners and rights management technologies, and given the very weak consideration shown by the InfoSoc Directive with regard to exceptions, it is evident that the objective of preserving the reward/incentive function of copyright took priority over the competing goal of disseminating new works to the public.

---

409 See Article 308 of the EC Treaty, which allows the European Council, by acting *unanimously* and not by the qualified majority required by Article 95, to take legislative measures that prove necessary to attain, in the course of the operation of the common market, one of the objectives of the Community, even if the Treaty does not provide the necessary powers.

410 See Opinion 1/94 of 15 November 1994, Competence of the Community to conclude international agreements concerning services and the protection of intellectual property - Article 228(6) of the EC Treaty [1994] ECR I-5267, at point 59; *Kingdom of the Netherlands* v. *European Parliament and Council of the European Union*, op. cit., paragraphs 24-25.

5.3.1. The deadlock of national copyright exceptions

As outlined above, copyright exceptions ensure that, notwithstanding the temporary monopoly granted over the commercial exploitation of protected works, users are provided with the opportunity to access these works and engage in certain uses that ultimately enable freedom of expression and follow-on creativity.[411] In this respect, the main problem that arises with the InfoSoc Directive concerns the *exhaustive* nature of the copyright exceptions established by Article 5, which compels the Member States to adopt or maintain a closed number of (optional) exceptions. In restricting the freedom of the Member States to regulate, monitor and re-adjust the publicly mandated conditions of access to and use of copyrighted works through the exceptions, the Directive has substantively blocked a fundamental aspect of the cultural policy of the Member States. A question arises here as to whether this "blocking" effect is compatible with the cross-sectional clause of Article 151 of the Treaty. On the one hand, Article 151(5) forbids the Community from taking harmonisation measures in the area of cultural laws and policies. On the other, Article 151(4) compels the Community to take cultural aspects into account when legislating under the other provisions of the Treaty.[412]

5.3.2. Article 151(4) of the EC Treaty and national copyright exceptions

To appreciate the ambit of Article 151(4), it must be noted that this provision has not prevented the occasional use of European law-making powers from harmonising national cultural policy rules "through the backdoor", on condition that the adoption of cultural policy measures appeared necessary for the smooth functioning of the internal market.[413]

---

411 See §§ 1.3. and 2.2.1., see *supra*.

412 Article 151(4) of the EC Treaty provides as follows: "The Community shall take cultural aspects into account in its action under other provisions of this Treaty, in particular in order to respect and to promote the diversity of its cultures."
Article 151(5) states: "In order to contribute to the achievement of the objectives referred to in this Article, the Council: [A]cting in accordance with the procedure referred to in Article 251 and after consulting the Committee of the Regions, shall adopt incentive measures, *excluding any harmonisation of the laws and regulation of the Member States*. The Council shall act unanimously throughout the procedure referred to in Article 251 […]" (emphasis added).

413 See de Witte, 'Non-market values in internal market legislation', op. cit., p. 11, who argued that on each of these occasions "a question arises whether the European legislator has given adequate (or exaggerated) consideration to cultural diversity concerns when adopting a measure which, legally speaking, is primarily aimed at achieving economic (internal market) goals. A major object of controversy, in this respect, was, and still is, the Directive on Television without Frontiers. Whereas some observers have criticised it for privileging market efficiency over cultural policy concerns, others have argued that its provisions reserving a quota of television programming for works of European

Nonetheless, it was argued that, in order to be completely in line with Article 151 and the principles of subsidiarity and proportionality set out in Article 5 of the EC Treaty, the InfoSoc Directive should have covered copyright exceptions only in so far as their harmonisation facilitated the increasing cross-border exploitation of copyrighted works via the Internet and other digital modes.[414] This means that, in the absence of the political will to achieve effective harmonisation of the relevant exceptions, the legal constraints posed by Article 151 compelled the Community to abstain from restricting and interfering with the sovereignty of the Member States in the accommodation of old and new cultural concerns within their copyright systems. In contrast, the duty posed by Article 151 was completely ignored in the InfoSoc Directive and in its far-reaching preamble. As seen above, the exhaustive list of Article 5 has *sine die* prevented Member States from both enacting new exceptions tailored for the digital environment and from effectively tackling the systematic restriction of national exceptions through the combination of electronic contracts and technological measures.

It is my opinion that, in a legislative act which mainly targets the fast-changing settings of the Information Society, the optional nature of exceptions affords little deference to Member State sovereignty in this field. Ironically, the fact that Article 5(3)(o) of the Directive entrusts the Member States with the possibility of maintaining existing copyright exceptions in cases of minor importance with regard to analogue or non-digital uses that do not affect the free circulation of goods and services within the Community (*e.g*, national schemes providing authors with fair remuneration in the face of photocopying) is even more negligible.

5.4. End-use licences and EU consumer contract law: a neglected intersection

In defining its copyright policy for the Information Society, the Community should take consumer protection into account. This duty is created by the combined provision of paragraphs 1 and 2 of Article 153 of the EC Treaty with regard to all areas covered by Community action, including the harmonisation of copyright law.[415]

origin are an undue element of protectionism that artificially obstructs the functioning of the internal market for television programmes".

414 See §2.3., see *supra*.

415 Article 153(1) of the EC Treaty states: "In order to promote the interests of consumers and to ensure a high level of consumer protection, the Community shall contribute to protecting the health, safety and economic interests of consumers, as well as to promoting their right to information, education, and to organise themselves in order to protect their interests." Article 153(2) provides a cross-sectional clause, which binds the Community to take into account consumer protection requirements when legislating in other fields of the law ("Consumer protection requirements shall be taken into account in defining and implementing other Community policies or activities").

5.4.1. The absence of consumer protection measures under digital copyright law

Notwithstanding the crucial relevance of the interplay between copyright and contracts in the digital environment, no consumer protection safeguards were explicitly included in the text of the InfoSoc Directive. If, as mandated by Article 153, this Directive had really intended to take consumer interests into account, it should have provided a general clause that forbade copyright holders from validly overriding all exceptions in pursuance of public policy goals through the combined use of "click-wrap" licences and technological measures. In contrast, the InfoSoc Directive did not create an effective interface between copyright exceptions and contracts, as Article 9(1) of the Software Directive and Article 15 of the Database Directive did by requiring national law to declare all contractual clauses aimed at prohibiting the exercise of software- and database-specific exceptions null and void. Under Article 6 of the InfoSoc Directive, copyright holders (and, more generally, content suppliers) are free to shape consumer contracts and technical measures as they wish, regardless of whether these contractual and technical means end up by restricting the exercise of copyright exceptions. As argued above,[416] the clause of Article 6(4) has very limited scope, which only covers few typologies of use in the off-line world and excludes most forms of on-line content delivery from its field of application.

5.4.2. Consumer protection under EU private international law

Notwithstanding the unfortunate lack of coordination of the InfoSoc Directive with consumer protection policies, under EU law copyright holder freedom of contract in the setting out of the conditions of access to and use of copyrighted works is not as unlimited as the wording of the InfoSoc Directive might suggest.[417] On the one hand, the application of the relevant consumer contract law will make purchasers of digitally protected works aware of the statutory usage rights that they might be asked to give up when accessing and using copyrighted works. Consumer contract law provides a right of information that is expected to facilitate the consumer's acceptance of certain usage restrictions enabled by DRM technologies. On the other, special rules protect transactional decisions by consumers under Article 5 of the 1980 Rome Convention on the law applicable to contractual obligations[418] and Section 4 of the Council Regulation 44/2001 on international

416 See §4.5.2., see *supra*.

417 See Guibault and Helberger, *Copyright Law and Consumer Protection, Policy conclusions of the European Consumer Law Group (ECLG)*, Institute for Information Law, University of Amsterdam, downloaded at: http://www.ivir.nl/staff/guibault.html; *iTunes – How Copyright, Contract, and Technology Shape the Business of Digital Media*, op. cit., pp. 96-103.

418 See Convention on the law applicable to contractual obligations, opened for signature in Rome on 19 June 1980 (80/934/EEC), OJ L 266, 09.10.1980, 1 (hereinafter "Rome Convention"), Article 5 ("Certain consumer contracts").

civil procedure law.[419] These provisions entrust single consumers and consumer associations with the privilege of being able to make a claim against the violation of mandatory contract requirements by facilitating the effective fruition of consumer rights before courts and under the law of their country of residence. A brief overview of applicable private international law will help to make this point clearer.

Due to the mandatory provisions created by Article 16 of the EU Regulation 44/2001 and Article 5 of the Rome Convention, the law and the jurisdiction of the country of habitual domicile of the consumer cannot be validly derogated through contract by professional suppliers of goods and services, regardless of where the supplier's business is located. Both the Rome Convention and the Regulation 44/2001 define "consumer contracts" as contracts the object of which is the supply of goods or services to a person ("the consumer") for a purpose which can be regarded as being outside his trade or profession.[420]

With particular regard to the licensing of copyrighted digital works, the mandatory jurisdiction of courts in their country of residence may allow consumers to know better what copyright exceptions and remedies they can rely upon in order to engage effectively in consumptive and productive uses which national laws guarantee in accordance with Article 6(4) of the InfoSoc Directive.[421] It can reasonably be assumed that the consumer recourse to these judicial or administrative remedies will prove to be easier, cheaper, and faster before the home country's courts than within a foreign jurisdiction.

As far as the applicable law is concerned, Article 5(2) of the Rome Convention provides that, regardless of the law regulating a particular contract, consumers are, in any event, entitled to benefit from the *mandatory* provisions that would apply if the contract were subject to the law of their country of residence.[422] In the specific field of copyright exceptions, this provision might play an important function if the law of the Member States, even by resorting to its exclusive competence in the field of cultural policy, unilaterally defined certain exceptions as mandatory. A good example might be given by a provision created by a Member State in order

---

[419] See Council Regulation (EC) N. 44/2001 of 22 December 2000 on jurisdiction and the recognition and enforcement of judgments in civil and commercial matters, OJ L12, 16.01.2001, 1, Section 4 ("Jurisdiction over consumer contracts"), Articles 15 to 17.

[420] See Article 5(1) of the Rome Convention and Article 15(1) of the Regulation 44/2001.

[421] It must be reminded that, according to Article 16(1) of the Regulation N.44/2001, the jurisdiction of the Country where the consumer is domiciled can be validly derogated only by the consumer: " A consumer may bring proceedings against the other party to a contract either in the courts of the Member State in which that party is domiciled or in the place for the courts where the consumer is domiciled."

[422] Article 5(2) of the Rome Convention states: "Notwithstanding the provisions of Article 3, a choice of law made by the parties shall not have the result of depriving the consumer of the protection afforded to him by the mandatory rules of the law of the country in which he has his habitual residence [...]". Pursuant to Article 3(1) of the same Convention, the principal criterion that determines the law applicable to a contractual obligation is the law chosen by the parties. Article 4(1) of the Convention provides that, in the absence of choice, the contract shall be governed by the law of the country with which it is most closely connected.

to prohibit content traders from extracting from the consumer the contractual promise not to engage in uses permitted by copyright exceptions.[423] If the consumer who has his or her habitual residence within *that* Member State should nonetheless enter into such an agreement by agreeing upon the choice of an applicable foreign law, the contract would not have the effect of depriving the consumer of the privilege of use that he or she relinquished. If, for instance, a consumer's right to make one private copy of a digital copyrighted work under the Italian Copyright Act could not be validly overridden by contract, the consumer would continue to enjoy that right (and the right to invoke judicial and administrative remedies aimed at making such copying available), even if the end-use licence was explicitly made subject to another law that did not guarantee the selfsame exception.

5.4.3. Consumer contract law

Academic debate on the troubled interplay between end-user freedom of use and the contractual restrictions which accompany DRM technologies has focused mainly on U.S. law. An in-depth analysis of EU law shows that copyright owner freedom of contract in the drafting of end-user licences to be implemented into DRM systems is more restricted in the EU than in the U.S. This difference may play a key role in Europe by ensuring contractual fairness and transparency in the use of DRM technologies.

5.4.3.1. A brief comparison between U.S. and EU contract laws

In the specific body of consumer protection law, European contract laws have been designed to protect consumers in consideration of various aspects of their transactions with merchants. Whereas certain European contract laws have been adopted to regulate commercial activities such as door-to-door sales, insurance, travel, and credit, others regulate the use of standard form contracts. In this last case, European courts are often given the power to review and actively control the fairness of the terms presented in standard form contracts, including contracts which deal with information products.[424] In contrast with European law, the United States have never adopted specific regulation concerning the use of standard form contracts. Instead, U.S. courts developed an equitable concept of "unconscionability" to invalidate standard forms that could be regarded as "very unfair terms".[425]

---

423 This type of provision was enacted by Belgian law when implementing the InfoSoc Directive. Article 23-bis of the Belgian Copyright Act states explicitly the mandatory character of copyright exceptions: see the table provided in Appendix II, see *infra*.

424 See Guibault, *Copyright Limitations and Contracts*, op. cit., p. 147.

425 This judicial standard was finally codified by Section 2-302 of the U.S. Uniform Commercial Code, which is intended to make it possible for the courts to review the terms of a contract that they find unfair or unconscionable. However, the U.S. doctrine of unconscionability has been applied more restrictively than the European concept of objec-

The gap between the EU and the U.S. systems would have been even greater if the so-called 1999 Uniform Computer Information Transaction Act (UCITA) had been adopted.[426] The UCITA was originally designed to reform Article 2 of the U.S. Uniform Commercial Code (UCC) by the addition of Article 2B, which aimed at enacting new contract law provisions that would have conferred upon copyright holders and information suppliers an unrestricted power over the licensing of information protected through "automatic restraints".[427] Under the UCITA, information suppliers would have been empowered to restrict the use of copyrighted materials at their own discretion through contract, regardless of whether a certain use fell within the range of copyright exceptions.

The inclusion of Article 2B in the UCC was originally proposed by the National Conference of Commissioners on Uniform State Law (NCCUSL) and the American Law Institute (ALI). In response to criticism of the proposal, the ALI withdrew from the project. Only the NCCUSL continued to promote it under the title of UCITA. Only two states in the U.S. eventually adopted the Act (Virginia and Maryland); while other states enacted "bomb-shelter statutes" prohibiting their own courts from applying it.

The drafters of this proposal drew on the pre-emption analysis provided by the U.S. Court of Appeal in the *ProCD* v. *Zeidenberg* case.[428] In this decision, Judge Easterbrook addressed the issue of whether a shrink-wrap licence which placed a "home use" restriction on a non-copyrightable CD-Rom compilation of telephone data was or was not pre-empted under Section 301 of the U.S. Copyright Act.[429] This provision, enacted when the U.S. Congress amended the Copyright Act in 1976, provides for the pre-emption of state law claims encroaching upon copyright claims in certain ways.[430] In this case, the dispute centred upon whether the contractual restriction placed by the plaintiff on the use of its marketed CD-Rom could be enforceable under state law, notwithstanding the pre-emption clause of Section 301. In interpreting the pre-emption clause when referring to the require-

tive good faith. As pointed out by Guibault, *Copyright Limitations and Contracts*, op. cit., pp. 150-151, U.S. courts generally accepted that "parties must often conclude their contract quickly, that their bargaining power will rarely be equal and that courts are ill-equipped to deal with problems of unequal distribution of wealth in society [...]".

426 See, generally, Lemley, 'Beyond Pre-emption: The Law and Policy of Intellectual Property Licensing', (87) *California Law Review* 1999, p. 111; Caso, *Digital rights management. Il commercio delle informazioni digitali tra contratto e diritto d'autore*, Cedam, Padova, 2004, p. 145.

427 Section 605(a) of the UCITA defined "automatic restraint" as "[...] a program, code, device, or similar electronic or physical limitation the intended purpose of which is to prevent use of information contrary to the contract or applicable law".

428 See *ProCD v. Zeidenberg*, 86 F.3d 1447 (7th Circuit 1996).

429 See U.S. Code, Title17, §301 ("Preemption with respect to other laws").

430 Under the federal structure of the U.S. Constitution, copyright law falls under the power of Congress while contract law falls under state power. As pointed out by Guibault, *Copyright Limitations and Contracts*, op. cit., p. 230, "[...] a contractual clause of action that is otherwise enforceable under state contract law can be pre-empted by federal copyright policy either under section 301 of the U.S. Copyright Act or under the general Supremacy Clause of the U.S. Constitution [...]".

ment of the equivalence between state-created rights (either contractual or legal) and exclusive rights granted under federal copyright law,[431] U.S. Courts have generally considered that a state right is equivalent to copyright (and, consequently, is pre-empted) if it is infringed by the mere act of reproduction, performance, distribution or display of the work.[432] In *ProCD* v. *Zeidenberg*, Judge Easterbrook found that the shrink-wrap licence containing the use restriction created rights that were *not* equivalent to copyright. The contractual restriction was thereby held to be enforceable on the assumption that the rights created by the contract were distinct from the rights granted under the Copyright Act. Pursuant to the decision, contract terms could not be pre-empted under Section 301, given that contracts are not equivalent to copyrights.

It is interesting to note that, if the same facts of the *ProCD* v. *Zeidenberg* case had been reviewed by a court in a EU jurisdiction, the court, like the U.S. court, would likely have found the shrink-wrap licence containing the "home use" restriction valid, from a formal perspective, under Article 9(1) of the 2000 Directive on Electronic Commerce.[433] The main purpose of this provision concerning the formation of contracts was to ensure that the legal systems of the Member States allowed contracts to be validly concluded even by electronic means.[434] Nonetheless, the merits of the case would have been understood in a very different way since EU law, unlike U.S. law,[435] would protect a compilation of telephone data by either the copyright or the *sui generis* right created by the EU Database Directive in relation to original and non-original databases.[436] Thus, a European court would have reviewed the extent to which contracts (such a valid shrink-wrap licence) could interfere with the copyright law that automatically creates property rights on more or less creative databases. In the presence of such property rights (which are enforceable *erga omnes* by definition), the analysis of European judges on the

---

[431] See U.S. Code, Title 17, §301, which refers to "[...] all legal or equitable rights that are equivalent to any of the exclusive rights within the general scope of copyright as specified by section 106 [...]"(emphasis added).

[432] As explained by Guibault, *Copyright Limitations and Contracts*, op. cit., p. 231, "[...] the courts generally consider that a right is not 'equivalent' to any of the rights specified in Section 106 if it incorporates an 'extra element' beyond those necessary to prove copyright infringement [...]".

[433] See Directive 2000/31/EC of the European Parliament and of the Council of 8 June 2000 on certain legal aspects of information society services, in particular electronic commerce, in the Internal Market, OJ L 178, 17.07.2000, 1 (hereinafter "E-Commerce Directive").

[434] See Article 9 ("Treatment of contracts") of the E-Commerce Directive.

[435] In the U.S., the Supreme Court addressed the question of database protection through copyright in *Feist Publications v. Rural Telephone Co.*, 499 U.S. 340 (1991), in which the Court clarified that an "entirely obvious" compilation of data could not qualify for copyright protection since it lacked the minimum standard of creativity required under the Copyright Act of 1976. In its opinion, the Court noted that the Intellectual Property Clause of the U.S. Constitution (see Article 1, Sect. 8, Clause 8) was intended to reward originality and not effort.

[436] See Articles 3 and 7 of the Database Directive. The case for harmonisation of the copyright protection of databases in the EU was discussed at § 3.2.1.3., see *supra*.

merits of a case identical to *ProCD v. Zeidenberg* would have been limited to the evaluation of whether contractual terms could legally create additional usage restrictions (such as a "home use" restriction) that would add to the uses of the database that the Directive requires to be reserved to the copyright owner. Under Article 6 of the EU Database Directive, a "home use" restriction would have qualified as an act covered by the private use exception to the right of reproduction, which is delimited by the Directive to the realm of *non-electronic* databases and is overridable by contract.[437] Therefore, a contract-based usage restriction placed on an *electronic* database embodied in a CD-Rom would probably be valid and enforceable within a EU jurisdiction, on condition that the end-use licence had complied with the EU imperative laws that aim at providing the consumer with certain information before the completion of whatever business-to-consumer transaction (*i.e.*, regardless of its electronic or non-electronic form).

The following sections of this chapter aim at shedding light on these imperative provisions on the assumption that they apply to the distribution and the making available of DRM-protected works to the public.

5.4.3.2. Duties of transparency in the EU Distance Contract Directive

EU law applicable to consumer contracts in the new electronic environment includes the 1997 Distance Contract Directive[438] and the 2000 E-Commerce Directive. Transactions accompanying the distribution of copyrighted content protected by DRM technologies are thereby subject to these regulations.[439] Transparency provisions set out in the Distance Contract Directive compel content traders to disclose certain information to consumers before the completion of each transaction.[440] According to Article 2, the Distance Contract Directive applies to:

> "[A]ny contract concerning goods or services concluded between a supplier and a consumer under an organized distance sales or service-provision scheme run by the supplier, who, for the purpose of the contract, makes exclusive use of one or more means of distance communication up to and including the moment at which the contract is concluded."

From the specific perspective of copyright contract law, it is remarkable that Article 4 of the Distance Contract Directive eventually imposes upon copyright own-

---

[437] See § 4.4.1, see *supra*.

[438] Directive 97/7/EC of the European Parliament and of the Council of 20 May 1997 on the protection of consumers in respect of distance contracts, OJ L 144, 4.06.1997, 19 (hereinafter "Distance Contract Directive").

[439] Guibault, *Copyright Limitations and Contracts*, op. cit., p. 206, shares this view.

[440] In this respect, see also Article 10 of the E-Commerce Directive. Article 10(1) requires Member States to create an obligation upon service providers to provide certain information (*i.e.*, the different technical steps to follow to conclude the contract; the languages offered for the conclusion of the contract, *etc*) "clearly, comprehensibly and unambiguously", and "prior to the order being placed by the recipient of the service". Article 10(3) states: "Contract terms and general conditions provided to the recipient must be made available in a way that allows him to store and reproduce them."

ers and content suppliers (in the same way as any other kinds of business suppliers) a duty to disclose relevant information regarding "the main characteristics of goods and services".[441] If this duty was understood and enforced correctly on markets for copyrighted digital works (for example, CDs, DVDs, music downloads, *etc*) content traders making use of DRM systems would be forced to inform consumers of the characteristics of the technological measures that would be applied in order to restrict statutory usage rights *before* the completion of each transaction. For most of these goods, moreover, Article 6 of the same Directive provides consumers with the right to withdraw from the transaction without penalty or justification.[442] Even if Article 6(3) expressly removes this right with regard to contracts for the supply of audio or video recordings or items of computer software "which were unsealed by the consumer",[443] the possibility of withdrawing should empower consumers to return all copyrighted goods that are not covered by this exemption.

A question arises here with regard to intangible goods such as music downloads. Indeed, it is still unclear whether courts will look at on-line content deliveries as a form of distribution of *goods* or as a provision of *services*. In principle, the return of digital intangible copies is technically feasible and some online store operators have eventually provided customers with this opportunity (*e.g.*, Tiscali's UK online music store).[444] When discussing the non-applicability of the principle of exhaustion (or first sale doctrine) to the exploitation of copyrighted works through intangible copies, it was pointed out that Article 4(2) of the InfoSoc Directive explicitly excludes on-line content dissemination from the scope of the distribution right and, consequently, from the operation of the exhaustion principle.[445] The InfoSoc Directive shapes intangible dissemination as falling under the scope of the sole right of communication to the public, regardless of whether content is delivered by downloading or streaming technologies.[446] If digital dissemination of copyrighted materials were understood as a *service* (notwithstanding the fact that copies are purchased and stored permanently on the hard-

441 See Article 4(1)(b) of the Distance Contract Directive. For the identification and discussion of this issue I am indebted to Guibault and Helberger, *Copyright Law and Consumer Protection*, op. cit., p. 12.

442 See Article 6(1) of the Distance Contract Directive.

443 See Article 6(3), which states: "Unless the parties have agreed otherwise, the consumer may not exercise the right of withdrawal provided for in paragraph 1 in respect of contracts: [...] for the supply of audio or video recordings or computer software which were unsealed by the consumer [...]".

444 See http://www.tiscali.co.uk/music/.

445 See §3.3.6., see *supra*.

446 As each Internet user knows, the difference between *streaming* and *downloading* technology lies in that the former, as opposite to the latter, does not enable the recipient to store permanently the content delivered through the Internet. In the same way as other traditional media (TV, radio, *etc*), streaming technology enables the recipient to watch and/or listen to a certain piece of content only at the time of the delivery. In my view, while the functioning of streaming technology may be correctly understood as a provision of service, downloading technology creates new copies that are permanently acquired by the consumer and that, to some extent, could be defined as *goods*.

ware of consumers) the return of intangible copies and media under the Distance Contract Directive would inevitably be restricted. Indeed, the right of withdrawal is removed in respect of contracts for the provision of services "if performance has begun, with the consumer's agreement, before the end of the seven working days period referred to in paragraph 1 [...]".[447] Given that, in contracts which regulate on-line deliveries, performance normally begins by enabling consumers to download and promptly access marketed information, the qualification of downloads as on-line *services* would exclude such fast-growing markets and related contracts from the application of the right to withdraw. Instead, if downloads were more appropriately viewed as *goods* under consumer contract law, the right of withdrawal would apply and allow consumers the option of returning "unsealed" (*i.e.*, non-accessed) copyrighted materials within the time provided by law. This "cooling off" period would reduce inequalities between contracting parties by allowing consumers to evaluate mandatory information that content suppliers are required to disclose at the time of the conclusion of standard form contracts. As argued earlier in this section, suppliers of copyrighted content, when providing this information, should include a description of technical measures that restrict statutory usage rights. The presence of technical restrictions may, indeed, be understood as one of the "main characteristics of goods and services" that Article 4 of the Distance Contract Directive requires be disclosed.

The most successful on-line content providers, namely on-line music stores, have incorporated rather ambiguous "no-return" policies into their terms of service. Apple's iTunes Music Store, for instance, delivers downloads on the grounds of contractual conditions that, on the one hand, define sales as "final" and, as a result, do not permit the return of downloads.[448] On the other hand, iTunes Music Store does not specify whether download ownership is effectively transferred to consumers, that is, whether they are "sold" or merely "licensed" to consumers.[449] In my view, regardless of the partisan qualification given by content suppliers to the subject matter of contracts accompanying on-line content deliveries, judges facing this problem may make a useful distinction between digital *goods* and *services* for the purpose of enforcement of consumer contract law. In the absence of a specific provision on this point, courts may interpret all Internet-based transfers of intangible copyrighted works which are stored *permanently* into users' hardware to be sales of goods, and consequently apply the consumer's right of withdrawal embodied in the Distance Contract Directive. In contrast, all forms of copyrighted content delivery which do not give consumers the opportunity to store digital works in their hardware on a permanent basis (*e.g.*, non-interactive radio or TV webcasting; on-line music services which offer monthly subscriptions for the ac-

[447] See Article 6(3) of the Distance Contract Directive.

[448] See Guibault and Helberger, *Copyright Law and Consumer Protection*, op. cit., p. 12.

[449] See *iTunes*, op. cit., pp. 56-57, where it is reported that Apple has evaded clarifying whether iTunes Music Store songs are sold or licensed. Even if users have generally perceived relevant transactions as sales of products, Apple refers to its business model as a service: see iTunes Terms of Service, Section 13(a).

cess to their collections, *etc*) should be understood as *services* and be subject to the EU consumer protection regulations which apply to end-use licence terms.[450]

5.4.3.3. Overriding copyright exceptions as an unfair commercial practice?

Despite the existence of guarantees of transparency, consumers of copyrighted digital works would not ultimately be able to preserve their usage privileges if they could not rely on a general clause ensuring contractual fairness in the setting out of end-use licence terms. EU consumer law does provide such a general clause in Article 3 of Directive 93/13/EEC.[451]

With the enactment of the 1993 Directive on Unfair Contract Terms, EU law has required Member States to prohibit contract terms which are contrary to the requirement of good faith with regard to general conditions included in non-negotiated contracts (*i.e.*, mass-market licences).[452] The scope of application of the 1993 Directive is specifically restricted to contractual conditions and it covers neither the definition of the subject matter of the contract nor the pricing of the goods or services provided pursuant to it.[453] Nonetheless, it is still unclear as to whether a licence term which restricts statutory usage privileges under copyright law would fall within the aforementioned notion of "unfair" (and, consequently, prohibited) general condition.

The non-exhaustive list of presumptively "unfair" terms annexed to the 1993 Directive fails to shed light on this issue, considering that none of the expressions used could reasonably encompass the contractual override of copyright exceptions.[454] Nor has any relevant case law developed to put such uncertainty to rest.[455]

The opportunity to resolve this problem with the inclusion of contractual override of copyright exceptions on the blacklist of unfair commercial practices arose

---

450 See §5.4.3.3. and §5.4.3.4, see *infra.*

451 See Directive 93/13/EEC of 5 April 1993 on unfair terms in consumer contracts, OJ L 95, 21.04.1993, 29 (hereinafter "Unfair Terms Directive"). See Article 3(1): "A contractual term which has not been individually negotiated shall be regarded as unfair if, contrary to the requirement of good faith, it causes a significant imbalance in the parties' rights and obligations arising under the contract, to the detriment of the consumer." The definition of "consumer" is provided by Article 2(b): "[…] any natural person who, in contracts covered by this Directive, is acting for purposes which are outside his trade, business or profession […]".

452 See Article 3(2) of the 1993 Unfair Terms Directive ("[A] term shall always be regarded as not individually negotiated where it has been drafted in advance and the consumer has therefore not been able to influence the substance of the term, particularly in the context of a pre-formulated standard contract.").

453 See the Unfair Terms Directive, Article 4(2).

454 As pointed out by Guibault and Helberger, *Copyright Law and Consumer Protection*, op. cit., p. 14, the only clause listed in the annex to the Unfair Terms Directive that might apply to the contractual override of copyright exceptions is the one "irrevocably binding the consumer to terms with which he had no real opportunity of becoming acquainted before the conclusion of the contract." (See Annex, paragraph (i)).

455 See Guibault and Helberger, *Copyright Law and Consumer Protection*, op. cit., p. 14.

with the enactment of Directive 2005/29/EC concerning business-to-consumer commercial practices in the Internal Market.[456] Unfortunately, in the same way as the 1993 Unfair Terms Directive, the Annex to the new Unfair Commercial Practices Directive does not explicitly include the contractual override of copyright exceptions on the blacklist of commercial practices that "shall in all circumstances be regarded as unfair".[457] However, it is noteworthy that paragraph 10 of the Annex to this Directive lists the act of "presenting rights given to consumers in law as a distinctive feature of the trader's offer" as a presumptively unfair commercial practice. By referring to "rights given to consumers", this provision pursues the objective of making consumers aware of the existence of (imperative) consumer protection measures (*e.g.*, the right of withdrawal), which cannot be confused in any way with permissions created by traders in order to increase the appeal of their products. It is highly uncertain whether this paragraph might provide guidance to courts in cases where copyright exceptions are presented as a "distinctive feature" of the trader's product. This conclusion would be hindered by the fact that copyright exceptions are often deemed neither to enjoy an imperative nature nor to attribute a "right" to the consumer. Nonetheless, courts may reach the conclusion that presenting a copyright exception as a trader's concession constitutes an unfair (and consequently prohibited) commercial practice by invoking the general prohibition on misleading actions by traders under the Directive.[458]

5.4.3.4. The end-user's information right against technical restrictions

While creating a Community-wide set of common rules to regulate business-to-consumer practices (mainly advertising and marketing), the Unfair Commercial Practices Directive supplements a general prohibition on unfair commercial practices by the elaboration of two kinds of unfairness: misleading practice, and aggressive practice. In my view, by prohibiting misleading actions and omissions by the trader, Section 1 of this Directive proves to be of some relevance for the object of preserving copyright exceptions in the commercial exploitation of copyrighted works protected by DRM and other similar technologies. On the one hand, Article 6 prohibits the disclosure of false, untruthful or deceptive information by the trader in relation to the "main characteristics of the product", such as usage specification or the results to be expected from its use.[459] On the other hand, Article 7(1) specifies that the prohibition of misleading information extends to the omission of:

---

[456] Directive 2005/29/EC of the European Parliament and of the Council of 11 May 2005 concerning unfair business-to-consumer commercial practices in the internal market and amending Council Directive 84/450/EEC, Directives 97/7/EC and 2002/65/EC of the European Parliament and of the Council and Regulation (EC) No 2006/2004 of the European Parliament and of the Council, OJ L 149, 11.06.2005, 22 (hereinafter "Unfair Commercial Practices Directive").

[457] See Article 5(5) of the Unfair Commercial Practices Directive.

[458] See §5.4.3.4., see *infra*.

[459] See Article 6(b) of the Unfair Commercial Practices Directive.

"[M]aterial information that the average consumer needs, according to the context, to take an informed transactional decision, and thereby causes or is likely to cause the average consumer to take a transactional decision that he would not have taken otherwise."

Article 7(2) goes further by specifying that it should also be regarded as a misleading omission when a trader:

"[H]ides or provides in an unclear, unintelligible, ambiguous or untimely manner such material information as referred to in paragraph 1 [...] or fails to identify the commercial intent of the commercial practice if not already apparent from the content and where, in either case, this causes or is likely to cause the average consumer to take a transactional decision that he would not have taken otherwise."

The transposition and enforcement of these provisions under national jurisdictions is likely to provide consumers (either on a single or on a collective basis) with the opportunity to ask courts to block misleading actions and omissions in the marketing of copyrighted goods whose use is restricted by DRM systems. If this were so, national (and ultimately European) courts would be able to clarify whether an unclear presentation or an omission of information about the characteristics and consequences of DRM protection constitute unfair (*i.e.*, misleading) practices pushing the consumer towards a transactional decision that he or she would not take if he or she was aware of usage restrictions enabled by DRM technology.

The enforcement of this information duty, which refers to the implementation and consequences of DRM protection, can be viewed as a re-statement of well known principles of civil law.[460] Evidence of the lack of novelty of this duty is provided by two French decisions which, prior to the adoption of the Unfair Commercial Practices Directive, found the omission of information about technical restrictions implemented onto copyrighted music CDs unlawful under civil law governing the contract of sale.

In the first case, the Nanterre *Tribunal de Grande Instance* held that the implementation of technological protection measures which disable the correct functioning of a music CD on most types of car radios was a *vice caché* ("hidden vice") which thereby enabled the purchaser to seek cancellation of the contract of sale.[461] In the second decision, upholding a decision of the Paris *Court de Grande Instance,* the Versailles Appeal Court found it misleading that a music CD which contained a warning about the implementation of an anti-copy device did not specify that the CD would not work on certain portable music players and car radios.[462] The court found this practice unlawful under the French civil law notion of tort and under French consumer protection law. Consequently, the Appeal Court af-

---

460 See Guibault and Helberger, *Copyright Law and Consumer Protection*, op. cit.

461 See *Francoise M.* c. *EMI France, Auchan France*, Tribunal de Grande Instance de Nanterre, 6ème Chambre, Judgment of 2 September 2003, available at: http://www.legalis.net.

462 See, respectively, *EMI Music France* c. *CLCV*, Cour d'Appel Versailles, 1ère Chambre, Judgment of 30 September 2004, and *Association CLCV* c. *EMI Music France*, Tribunal de Grande Instance de Nanterre, 6ème Chambre, Judgment of 24 June 2003, both available at: http://www.legalis.net.

firmed the lower court's order that the record producer should have clearly printed on the back of the contested CD a warning advising consumers that the CD was unreadable on certain portable players and car radios.

Despite the overlap between newly enacted prohibitions on misleading practices and well-established principles of civil law and consumer contract law, the prohibition - under EU law - of specific conduct as unfair commercial practices may be useful for national courts when reviewing the contractual fairness of informing end-users about DRM-based usage restrictions. The new EU legislation has the potential to provide national courts with common criteria for the review of violation of a consumer's right of information which could lead to the harmonisation of the case law on practices which hamper the disclosure of the operation and the effects of DRM-based restrictions. Moreover, after the transposition of this information duty in all Member States of the EU, DRM technology makers and the copyright industry will have a greater incentive to act transparently when designing and implementing technical usage restrictions onto media embodying copyrighted works.

5.4.3.5. Conclusive remarks on consumer protection

It seems persuasive to conclude that the InfoSoc Directive, as EU secondary legislation, should be enforced in accordance with the constitutional clause of Article 153 of the EC Treaty. This clause binds the Community to pursue the goals of promoting the interests of consumers and of ensuring a high level of consumer protection by protecting, *inter alia*, the economic interests of consumers and promoting their right to information and education. Article 153(2) provides that consumer protection requirements should be taken into account in defining and implementing other Community policies and activities. It was shown that the development of a Community copyright policy for the Information Society has become an important policy objective pursued by means of internal market legislation. Despite the absence of consumer protection measures under digital copyright law, EU consumer law regulates the formation process and the merits of contractual terms transposed into the copyright end-user licences which accompany the operation of DRM technologies. The enforcement of consumer law in this field gives the user an important right of information on the implementation of usage restrictions in markets where copyrighted works are made available to individuals, rather than to the public as a whole. In a legal framework such as EU law, where the law does nothing to refrain copyright owners and DRM technology devisers from overriding copyright exceptions through contract, the enforcement of the duties of information created by consumer protection law upon content traders is expected to have an important function. Indeed, the product-related information disclosed in advance by content suppliers may greatly enhance the awareness of consumers with regard to the conclusion of "click-on", "shrink-wrap" and other non-negotiated transactions associated with DRM technologies. In other words, consumer information rights have the potential to guarantee a certain degree of acceptability and a high level of transparency in respect of the implementation and effects of DRM-related usage restrictions.

5.5. Summary

This chapter has elaborated upon several inconsistencies that exist between the InfoSoc Directive and the EC Treaty. The analysis has found that the Directive did not comply with constitutional clauses governing the adoption of internal market legislative measures and their encroachment upon the areas of national cultural policy and consumer protection. Firstly, it has been analysed how the InfoSoc Directive failed to achieve the objective for which it was specifically enacted: market integration. By referring to both markets for tangible and intangible goods, it has been shown that the non-harmonisation of the copyright scope at EU level has increased the degree of partition of both the traditional and the newly emerged markets along national borders.

Secondly, it has been explained how the exhaustive pool of optional copyright exceptions listed under Article 5 of the InfoSoc Directive has the potential to block national cultural policies which aim to restrict copyright exclusivity for the pursuit of certain public policy goals. It has been pointed out that national sovereignty, in this respect, is preserved by both the subsidiarity principle set out in Article 5 of the EC Treaty, and the mainstream clause contained in Article 151. In a supranational legal framework characterised by a high degree of fragmentation, it has been argued, the fact that national policy-makers and law-makers are not allowed to enact their own re-adjustments of the statutory conditions of access to and use of copyrighted digital works reveals a dramatic lack of attention with regard to the public interest.

Thirdly, it has been emphasised that, in welcoming and conferring legitimacy to the advent of electronic licences which override copyright exceptions in the digital dissemination of creative works, the InfoSoc Directive ignores the cross-sectional clause of Article 153(2) of the EC Treaty. It has been concluded that, in spite of the lack of connection between these two bodies of law, EU digital copyright law needs to be coordinated and implemented in strict accordance with EU consumer protection law. It has been shown that consumers, when entering into business-to-consumer transactions concerning end-user licences for the access to and the use of DRM-protected copyrighted goods, are assisted by certain non-derogable measures created under EU international private law and consumer contract law. It has been concluded that such measures, even if not prohibiting the contractual override of copyright exceptions expressly, are likely to enhance the awareness of consumers about both the presence and the effects of technological restrictions. In particular, it has been demonstrated that the objective of a transparent presentation and implementation of contractual restrictions enforced by DRM technologies is strongly encouraged by specific information rights which ensure commercial fairness to the benefit of the end-user.

PART III
UNSETTLED ISSUES

6. Implications of sharing copyrighted works on the Internet

6.1. Introduction

The decentralised structure of the Internet has increasingly empowered end-users to disseminate creative works to an unprecedented extent. Since EU copyright law reserves all acts of digital reproduction and communication to the public of their works to the copyright holders, it is necessary to define what modes of lawful dissemination remain for the end-user. While it is indisputable that Internet users are free to communicate and share the public domain and any and all authorised materials, it is questionable whether and under what conditions end-users are entitled to share - or at least download - unauthorised copyrighted works pursuant to the U.S. fair use doctrine, or under the European copyright exception of private copying. Considering that the scope of the distribution right set out by Article 4(2) of the InfoSoc Directive is confined to the distribution of *tangible* copies of copyrighted works,[463] it is worth pointing out from now that the sole exclusive rights called into question by Internet users "sharing" intangible copies are the right of reproduction and the right of communication to the public.[464]

This chapter considers the legal implications of user-to-user transfer of copyrighted works enabled by peer-to-peer software and networks. Peer-to-peer software enables computers to communicate directly with each other. The term generally refers to software which enables a computer to locate a content file on another networked computer and to copy the encoded data onto its own hardware. Since its emergence on the Internet, people have used peer-to-peer technology in order to reproduce and disseminate copyrighted music and other protected works without right-holder authorisation. In recent years in the United States, extensive jurisprudence has emerged on both direct and indirect liability concerning file-sharing of copyrighted works on peer-to-peer networks. In contrast, this area was mainly ignored in Europe until 2004, when there was a series of cases in the Netherlands and France. At the same time, the French Parliament deliberated a legislative proposal to introduce a "global licence" scheme which sought to legalise unauthorised file-sharing of copyrighted works on peer-to-peer platforms by the use of a complex mechanism of financial compensation.[465] Consequently, these events

---

463 See §3.3.5., see *supra*.

464 See §3.3.3. and §3.3.4., see *supra*.

465 The French proposal of a "global licence" is discussed under §8.3.3.1, see *infra*.

have vigorously reawakened the debate in Europe about the most suitable legal treatment of file-sharing.

A comparison of the European and U.S. case law shows that any attempt to enforce on-line exclusive rights of reproduction and communication to the public might easily end up outlawing the very architecture of peer-to-peer technology, independently of whether the technology is being used to infringe copyright or not. This technology is a prime example of dual-use technology, that is to say, it is capable of both infringing and non-infringing uses.

The decisions analysed in this chapter clearly illustrate that peer-to-peer networking gives rise to two distinct types of possible copyright liability. On the one hand, we have the *direct* copyright liability of end-users who engage in unauthorised reproduction and dissemination of copyrighted works. On the other, there is the *indirect* liability of the technology providers who supply the tools - software - which enable infringement to be performed. Both types of liability may suggest that legal restriction of design, supply and use of this technology can eliminate or reduce the disruptive effects of infringement on the markets for copyrighted digital works.

However, it is my contention that this objective should not be achieved by depriving Internet users of the technology to exchange and share materials that are not covered by copyright protection.

6.2. End-user liability: the United States

The issue of the direct liability of users has been examined and settled by two U.S. appellate decisions. In both cases, the courts considered whether user-to-user dissemination of copyrighted works could be excused under the U.S. fair use doctrine.

6.2.1. The birth of file-sharing technologies

The birth of peer-to-peer networking followed the emergence and diffusion of proprietary software which was distributed free of charge on the Internet by the Californian start-up Napster, in 1999. After having downloaded this software from Napster's website, users could log-on to the system and share MP3 music files with other users who were logged-on to the system. This integrated system gave members of the network the unprecedented ability to locate music by their favourite artists in MP3 format. This technology resulted in a network which enabled single users to carry out two distinct operations. Technically speaking, each user could request and download (*i.e.*, reproduce) a file from the hard disk of another network user while, at the same time, allowing others to copy files stored on his or her own hard drive's archive. In this way, users automatically became both copiers and suppliers of the materials requested by other users. Napster claimed to be taking the frustration out of locating servers with MP3 files, by providing a file-sharing system that permitted account holders to conduct sophisticated searches for music files on the hard drives of millions of other anonymous users.

Even though it was created by a college student who wished to make swapping music with his roommate easier, Napster was not simply a distribution for friends and family. It was estimated that, by the end of the year 2000, there were 75 million computers using the Napster network. Given that thousands of copyrighted works were disseminated without authorisation on the Napster file-sharing network, a number of U.S. record companies and music publishers brought a lawsuit against the newly established enterprise for contributory copyright infringement. However, to hold the provider of file-sharing technology liable, it was indispensable to ascertain that the activities carried out by the people using file-sharing technology were directly infringing copyright.

6.2.2. File-sharing under the U.S. fair use doctrine

The first and leading case, *A&M Records* v. *Napster*, was brought before the U.S. Court of Appeals for the Ninth Circuit in 2001, on appeal from the District Court for Northern California.[466] The second case was reviewed much more recently by the U.S. Court of Appeals for the Seventh Circuit in the case *BMG Music* v. *Gonzales*, an action brought by a large music company against a single unauthorised downloader.[467]

The facts of these cases can be summarised as follows. In *Napster*, it was disputed whether file-sharer activities, described by Napster as serving legitimate purposes such as sampling and space-shifting, could be excused under the doctrine of fair use pursuant to Section 107 of the U.S. Copyright Act. Pursuant to Napster jargon, "sampling" referred to the user's (hypothetical) practice of copying protected works from the network for the purpose of deciding which work to purchase. "Space-shifting", instead, is an expression which, in the *Napster* case, was used to show that file-sharing technology enabled users to gain access to sound recordings that they already owned in audio CD format by means of the system.

In the *BMG* v. *Gonzales* case, a single user of the Kazaa peer-to-peer network was caught after downloading 1,370 copyrighted songs without authorisation. The user contended that her activity was fair use because she was just sampling music in order to determine which songs to buy at retail. The Seventh Circuit's decision focused on whether the downloading of 30 songs that the user admitted not to have bought after sampling constituted copyright infringement. The Court found that the defendant had not deleted the downloads but had retained them on her computer.

---

[466] See *A&M Records* v. *Napster*, 114 Federal Supp.2d (N.D. Cal. 2000), p. 901; *A&M Records* v. *Napster*, 239 F.3d 1004 (9th Circuit), hereinafter *Napster*.

[467] See *BMG Music* v. *Gonzales*, N. 05-1314 (argued October 27 – decided December 9, 2005), 7th Circuit, on appeal from U.S. District Court for the Northern District of Illinois, Eastern Division, N. 03 C 6276, hereinafter *BMG Music* v. *Gonzales.*

Following reform of the U.S. Copyright Act in 1976, any analysis of fair use rests upon the examination of a non-exhaustive list of factors.[468] This list was the result of a legislative codification which drew upon an equitable rule of reason elaborated within a case law that shaped fair use as an essentially judge-made doctrine. The list includes:

- the purpose and character of the use, including whether such use is of a commercial nature or is for non-profit educational purposes;
- the nature of copyrighted work;
- the amount and substantiality of the portion used in relation to the copyrighted work as a whole; and
- the effect of the use upon the potential market for or value of the copyrighted work.

The U.S. Supreme Court made it clear, in *Sony Corp. of America* v. *Universal City Studios*, that Congress had not provided definitive rules when it codified the fair use doctrine in the 1976 Act.[469] It had simply incorporated a list of factors to be considered by the courts.

6.2.2.1. Purpose and character of file-sharing

Pursuant to the first factor, the judges in the *Napster* case found that the purpose and character of the use of its file-sharing network militated against a finding of fair use. Both the District Court and the Court of Appeal were persuaded by the copyright holders' argument that downloading MP3 files did not transform the copyrighted music, as had also been found in *UMG Recordings, Inc.* v. *MP3.Com*.[470] They concluded that repackaging copyrighted recordings in MP3 format suitable for downloading added no new aesthetics, new insights and/or understandings to the original. As a result, downloads were found not to be fair use even if the downloader already owned a purchased copy.

Also relevant under the first factor, taken together with the fourth, was the necessity for the court to determine whether the use of copyrighted material was commercial or not. Indeed, a finding of commercial use would have weighed against (but not precluded) a determination of fairness. Even though the court recognised that the downloading and uploading of MP3 music files did not amount to a commercial activity, the file-sharing of copyrighted works was found to fall outside of the category of personal use, in the traditional sense. The court found that the fact that Napster users did not engage in downloading music in order to sell it for profit did not mean that the sharing of files with a large number of anonymous requesters necessarily amounted to private use. Napster users reaped economic

[468] See U.S. Code, Title 17, §107.

[469] See *Sony Corp. of America* v. *Universal City Studios, Inc.*, 104 Supreme Court 774, 78 L. Ed. 2d, p. 442 (1984) - hereinafter *Sony* – at pp. 475-476.

[470] See *UMG Recordings, Inc.* v. *MP3.Com*, 92 Federal Supplement 2d 349, p. 351 (S.D.N.Y. 2000).

advantages from the use of the Internet service, while they downloaded for free what they would otherwise have had to buy.

This position was upheld by the U.S. Seventh Circuit in the review of *BMG Music* v. *Gonzales*, where the user was found not to engage in a non-profit use on the assumption that she downloaded and kept whole copyrighted songs on her hard disk.[471] In the Court's view, a copy downloaded, played, and retained on one's hard disk for future use was a direct substitute for a purchased copy and could not be excused as sample. As the decision pointed out, "downloading on a try-before-you-buy basis is good advertising for copyright proprietors, expanding the value of their inventory".[472] The Court considered that the single user could not invoke fair use while downloading for the purpose of sampling, because sampling copyrighted music downloads constituted a profitable market practice. Evidence of this was provided by licensed Internet music sellers such as the iTunes Music Store, which were offering samples on the market by paying copyright owners a fee for the right to do so.[473]

In support of the argument of fair use by its users, Napster claimed that the purpose and character of downloading unauthorised copyrighted from its network could be compared, in terms of fairness, to use of Sony's Betamax technology in the 1980s. The so-called *Sony* case had been reviewed in the 1984 by the U.S. Supreme Court.[474] On that occasion, an association of copyright owners (Universal City Studios) claimed that the invention, production and marketing of the Sony home-taping system had seriously damaged the motion picture industry in its commercial exploitation of movies. The Court found that the Betamax technology could have served substantial non-infringing use purposes, namely, the "time-shifting" of TV programmes and movies, and that, as a consequence, it could not be banned in order to eliminate threats to copyright enforcement policy. In order to establish a clearer link with this judgment, Napster argued that users of its new technology engaged in a fair use when converting a CD they already owned into MP3 format and then using Napster technology to transfer the music to a different computer (for example, from home to office). As an expression of this function, Napster employed the expression "space-shifting". Nonetheless, the argument that the space-shifting use referred to by Napster could be sufficiently analogous to the notion of time-shifting recognised in *Sony* was rejected outright. Space-shifting, it was said, did not mean a non-commercial personal use in the same way as "time-shifting" did, the effects of which remained within the viewer's household. Moreover, the courts found no evidence that space-shifting purposes constituted a significant use of the Napster system, whereas the most credible explanation for the exponential growth of traffic on Napster's website was the vast array of free MP3 files offered by other users.

---

471 See *BMG Music* v. *Gonzales*, pp. 2-3.

472 *Ibidem*, p. 3.

473 *Ibidem*, p. 4.

474 See *Sony*, p. 442.

6.2.2.2. Nature and portion of the work used

Under the second factor of the U.S. fair use doctrine (*i.e.*, the nature of copyrighted work), both the Ninth and the Seventh Circuit acknowledged that music songs, as pure entertainment, were creative in nature, and that, consequently, the argument concerning the nature of the work could not give rise to a fair use claim. In reviewing the Section 107 second factor, the U.S. Supreme Court reasoned that "the law generally recognizes a greater need to disseminate factual works than works of fiction or fantasy", thereby emphasising that the nature of the work should be taken into account when assessing the extent to which one must permit expressive language to be copied.[475] According to this reasoning, the more a work is intrinsically creative, the less the proportion of use permitted by the rule of reason of fair use becomes. As argued by the Seventh Circuit in *BMG Music* v. *Gonzales*, copyrighted music is as creative as poetry, for which "copying more than a couplet or two is deemed excessive". This argument explained why both the *Napster* and the *BMG Music* v. *Gonzales* decisions found that the third factor of the doctrine (*i.e.*, the portion of the work used) could not be taken into consideration. In both cases, it was undisputed that music songs under copyright were reproduced on users' computers in their entirety.

6.2.2.3. Effect of file-sharing on the market for copyrighted works

The analysis of the fourth factor (*i.e.*, the effect of file-sharing on the market for the copyrighted work) proved to be crucial in the determination that Napster users were not engaging in a fair use. In the judges' view, there was convincing evidence that the use of Napster, to some extent, harmed the market for copyrighted musical compositions and sound recordings. File-sharing of copyrighted works was deemed to have the effect of reducing CD sales, even if the results shown by the economic expertise in the case were unclear. More importantly, the courts were persuaded that unauthorised file-sharing was creating barriers to the plaintiffs' entry into the market for on-line music.

The Seventh Circuit in *BMG Music* v. *Gonzales* upheld this view at a time when the market for copyrighted music downloads was more developed than in the period covering the *Napster* decision. The Court found that the fact that sales of recorded music had decreased by approximately 30% in four years was likely to be related to the increase of file-sharing in the same period.[476] Finding that music downloaded for free on the Internet was a substitute for purchased music, the decision concluded that unauthorised downloads had the effect of harming both markets for tangible and intangible formats which embodied copyrighted music.[477]

This conclusion shows deference to the market-centred justification of fair use under the U.S. copyright system. In the United States, an exemption from copyright is inconceivable where a supposedly *fair* use harms a market which already

---

475 See *Harper & Row Publishers* v. *Nation Enterprises*, 105 S. Ct. 2218 (1985), p. 563.

476 See *BMG Music* v. *Gonzales*, p. 3.

477 *Ibidem*.

exists or, where non-existent, is likely to develop.[478] This rationalisation of the theory of fair use was developed in the early 1980s in response to the impact of uncontrolled home-taping on the market for copyrighted movies and TV programmes. In the article "Fair Use as Market Failure" of 1982, Gordon explained that, when no functioning market for a certain use of copyrighted works existed, the pursuit of the public interest, which was the main objective of copyright under the intellectual property clause of the U.S. Constitution, was best served by exempting users from seeking unenforceable or impractical permission.[479] Merges, elaborating upon this, stated that a situation of market failure occurred when "the transaction costs of a voluntary transfer are so high that a consensual transfer is unlikely to take place spontaneously".[480] This situation was exemplified by the inability of copyright holders to exert control over the home-taping activities enabled by Sony's Betamax Video Cassette Recorder. Under Gordon's rationale, home-taping for time-shifting purposes was deemed to be fair because users could not purchase the desired use on the market, transferring control of the use served the public interest, and the use did not impair the incentives of the copyright owners.[481]

In contrast, in the case of file-sharing on the Napster network, the U.S. Ninth Circuit considered that the original market failure in the on-line distribution of copyrighted music by legitimate right-holders was not permanent. If the *Napster* Court had applied the market failure rationale without ascertaining whether the market for music downloads had a chance to develop, the subsequent implementation of the fair use defence would have stifled the development of on-line music services, such as Apple's and Sony's music stores,[482] which were enabled by the new technologies of management and control.

6.3. End-user liability: the European Union

6.3.1. Peer-to-peer downloads under the exception of private copying

Recent European case law on end-user liability illustrates that file-sharing of unauthorised copyrighted works touches upon two distinct types of exclusive rights created by copyright law. Where unauthorised downloading of copyrighted works from a peer-to-peer network involves the right of digital reproduction, the symmetrical uploading which occurs when file-sharers agree to make materials stored in their hard disks available to each other encroaches upon the right of making these materials available to the public. While these decisions concerning end-user liability concluded that uploading acts infringed the exclusive right of making

478 See §2.2.2.2., see *supra*.

479 See Gordon, 'Fair Use as Market Failure: A Structural and Economic Analysis of the Betamax Case and Its Predecessors', (82) *Columbia Law Review* 1982, p. 1600.

480 See Merges, 'The End of Friction', op. cit., p. 130.

481 Gordon, 'Fair Use as Market Failure', op. cit., p. 1601.

482 See, respectively, http://www.apple.com/itunes and http://www.connect.com.

copyrighted material available to the public, there has been much uncertainty about the infringing nature of mere downloading acts. The latter expression is intended to refer to reproductions from peer-to-peer networks, which are not shared with anyone else and are simply stored in the user's hard disk.

Under the legal framework created by the EU InfoSoc Directive, the first issue that courts had to resolve was whether unauthorised peer-to-peer downloads could be described as permissible personal copies. The non-mandatory exception provided by Article 5(2)(b) of the Directive gives a definition of private copying which refers to copying "by a natural person and for ends that are neither directly nor indirectly commercial".[483] The legality of the use is therefore based upon the absence of direct or indirect commercial ends by the copier, regardless of whether he or she uses the copy personally or shares the copy with someone else. This wording implies that no single notion of personal copy was defined by the Directive. As a result, national courts are free to continue to apply different notions stemming from statutes which shape the exception with a focus on the strictly personal nature of unauthorised use. For instance, both French and Italian statutes explicitly make lawful private copying subject to a strict condition of non-public destination of the copy, in such a way that no person beyond the original user is protected by the exception.[484]

Apparently, the first decision in Europe which addressed the question of whether mere downloads could be exempted from copyright infringement as personal copies was delivered in the Netherlands by the Court of Harlem in May 2004.[485] The court held that unauthorised file-sharers were not exempted from copyright liability when making copyrighted materials that they owned or had downloaded from the Internet available to other users. The decision admitted, though, that the mere download of an unauthorised MP3-file could be excused under the private copying exception if the user of the download did not reproduce or make it available to others.[486] This judgment, in the same way as a very similar decision issued by the Canadian Federal Court in March 2004,[487] considered that certain peer-to-peer software enables users not to share what they download from the network.

In France, the subtle distinction between infringing acts of uploading and possibly non-infringing acts of downloading was raised for the first time by a decision

483 See §4.4.1., see *supra*.

484 See Article 122-5 of the French Intellectual Property Code, which outlaws the "collective" use of personal reproductions; and Article 71-sexies of the Italian Copyright Act, which forbids third parties from making lawful reproductions of someone else's copy.

485 The case was mentioned by Bernault and Lebois, *Peer-to-peer et propriété littéraire et artistique. Etude de faisabilité sur un système de compensation pour l'échange des oeuvres sur internet*, Institut de Recherche en Droit Privé de l'Université de Nantes, June 2005, available at: http://alliance.bugiweb.com/usr/Documents/RapportUniversite Nantes-juin2005.pdf, at p. 34. However, no proper reference to the source of this case was made available by these authors.

486 *Ibidem.*

487 See Bernault and Lebois, *Peer-to-peer et propriété littéraire et artistique*, op. cit., p. 35.

from the Court of Rodez in October 2004,[488] which was fully upheld by the Court of Montpellier in March 2005.[489] The facts of this case are particularly interesting for the discussion of how the exception at issue might be implemented in cases of peer-to-peer downloads. A user (Mr. D. Aurelien) was found with five hundreds unauthorised copyrighted movies reproduced on CD-Roms. The user acknowledged that these copies had, in part, been downloaded from the Internet onto his hard disk as a result of file-sharing activities. Given that these materials were no longer stored on the user's hard drive and, as a result, were not shared with anyone else, the decision could focus specifically on the legal understanding of mere acts of reproduction from the Internet. It was unclear from the circumstances of the case whether the sole downloading and subsequent shift to the CD-Rom format of these copyrighted works infringed the author's exclusive right of reproduction. The Court's decision held that the user's movie reproductions on CD-Rom format met the requirements of the private copying exception provided by Article L. 122-5 of the French Intellectual Property Code, because there was evidence that these reproductions were used exclusively for personal (*i.e.*, non-collective) purposes, such as home viewing.[490] The fact that neither commercial nor sharing ends were demonstrated by the user implied that the only restriction of the user's freedom of personal use could have been found under the so-called three-step test.[491] As pointed out below,[492] the restrictive criteria of the test, which binds national courts after the implementation of the InfoSoc Directive, seem to prohibit the judiciary from excusing acts of mere downloading under the private copying exception.

In the later decision issued by the *Tribunal de Grande Instance de Pontoise* in February 2005,[493] the issue of mere personal copying was not addressed properly because the case concerned a file sharer (Mr. Alexis B.) who was using peer-to-peer software (so-called *DC++*) that did not enable the user to disactivate the uploading function in a way that restricted the use of the programme to mere reproduction ends. Given that the user engaged in both downloading and uploading ac-

---

488 See *Ministère Public, Fédération nationale de distributeurs de film, Syndicat de l'édition vidéo et autres, Twentieth Century Fox et a.* c. *D. Aurélien*, Tribunal correctionnel de Rodez, 13 October 2004, commented by Sirinelli, 'Monopole d'exploitation-Exception de copie privée – Copie privée ou ayant droit privés du droit de copie?', (14) *Propriétés intellectuelles*, January 2005, p. 56.

489 See *Ministère Public, Fédération nationale des distributeurs de film, Syndicat de l'édition vidéo et autres* c. *Aurélien D.*, Court d'Appel Montpellier, commented by Sirinelli, 'Exceptions au monopole – Copie privée – Statuts des reproductions effectuées par l'intermediaire d'échanges de pair à pair à l'issue de ces derniers – La copie privée de *peer* en pire', (15) *Propriétés intellectuelles*, April 2005, p. 168.

490 Art. L. 122-5 of the French Intellectual Property Code provides as follows: "Lorsque l'oeuvre a été divulguée, l'auteur ne peut interdire: […] 2° Les copies ou reproductions strictement réservées à l'usage privé du copiste et non destinées à une utilisation collective […]".

491 See §4.2.2., see *supra*.

492 See §6.3.3., see *infra*.

493 See *Ministère Public, SACEM, SDRM, SPPF, SCCP* c. *Alexis B.*, Tribunal de Grande Instance de Pontoise, 10 March 2005, commented by Sirinelli, 'Exceptions au monopole – Copie privée', op. cit., p. 169.

tivities with regard to approximately ten thousand unauthorised works of music, the judges found that the user had infringed both the exclusive rights of reproduction and the right of making the transmitted works available to the public. However, the decision did not specify whether the infringement referred only to the user's uploads, without covering the activities of mere reproduction.

In my view, neither the Dutch nor the French above-mentioned judgments properly addressed the question of whether mere downloads could be legally treated as personal reproductions, thereby avoiding copyright exclusivity. In France, until the advent of the InfoSoc Directive, this exception was defined very strictly, as being bound by the requirement of non-public destination of the copy. Nonetheless, neither the Rodez/Montpellier judgment nor the Pontoise decision considered how this requirement could be located in the context of file-sharing activities. This distinction could hardly apply to the inextricable cross-exchange of data occurring on peer-to-peer networks, where it might prove to be unfeasible to determine who plays the role of the copier and who is simply a follow-on user.[494] It must be considered that, in the working of file-sharing technologies, both the uploader and the downloader engage in reproductions when sharing the protected work. Transmissions on the Internet require the information to be divided into a number of "packages" which are subject to intermediate storage and copying during transmission, until the information is assembled on the receiving computer. Nonetheless, it seems to me that decisions such as those of the courts in Rodez and Montpellier erred in not addressing the argument of the non-collective destination of works shared on the Internet, given that this is the only requirement which French copyright law sets out for unauthorised reproduction to be excused as personal copying.

Instead, these judgments held the peer-to-peer user not liable on the mere assumption that he stopped sharing his collection of unauthorised copyrighted movies and shifted them from his hard disks to CD-Roms, without clarifying the legal status of subsequent reproductions. As observed by Sirinelli, it was as if the judges excusing the unauthorised copier found that the shift of unauthorised downloads onto recordable formats upon which levies were charged had the effect of making these reproductions legal and the source of copyrighted materials irrelevant.[495]

---

494 See Sirinelli, 'Exceptions au monopole', op. cit., pp. 170-171.

495 See Sirinelli, 'Monopole d'exploitation', op. cit., p. 59 ("A bien comprendre le raisonnement du tribunal, il conviendrait de ne pas appréhender l'opération dans son ensemble et de ne considérer que le dernier maillon de la chaîne des reproductions. Il serait même possible au copiste d'étancher sa soif d'oeuvres à des sources illégales pourvu que l'acte final de reproduction blanchisse tout [...]).

6.3.2. Peer-to-peer networks as a lawful source of unauthorised copyrighted works?

Earlier in this book,[496] it was pointed out that Article 6(4) of the InfoSoc Directive requires lawful access to the copyrighted work to empower users to take advantage of safeguard measures which enable certain copyright exceptions which are obstructed by technological measures. It was explained that the Article 6(4) requirement of "legal access" is satisfied with the lawful acquisition of a copy of the protected work by the user. Considering that this requirement does not fit the case of peer-to-peer networking, where no technical measure normally forbids personal copying, a question arises as to whether the InfoSoc Directive makes the exception of personal copying subject to the acquisition of the protected work from a lawful or authorised source. When examining this notion under Recital 33 of the Directive, it was emphasised that this Recital understands both uses "authorised by the rightholder" and uses "not restricted by law" to be lawful.[497] By providing this definition, Recital 33 transposed the same notion accepted under Article 11 of the 1996 WIPO Copyright Treaty into the InfoSoc Directive. This notion implies that, beyond the uses which are explicitly reserved to the copyright owner as a consequence of the exercise of her exclusive rights, other uses shall be meant to be free unless they are explicitly restricted by law.[498] According to this notion, it is ultimately incumbent upon national copyright statutes to define whether the making of personal copying should be subject to the condition of the lawful source that the protected work is taken from. Most of the national copyright statutes implementing the InfoSoc Directive do not explicitly provide for this condition. Only the German Copyright Act, under Article 53, outlaws reproduction for private use where the copy is made from an "apparently unlawful source".[499] In France, the relevant statute provides for a requirement of non-public destination of the copy, in such a way that lawful personal copying is limited to the sole original user, without excusing subsequent unauthorised reproductions. Nonetheless, the Rodez and Montpellier courts reached the opposite conclusion, while failing to consider that unauthorised downloads were obtained from a source, that is, other users' hard disks, where copies of copyrighted materials were unlawfully given a collective destination, in violation of Article L. 122-5 of the French Intellectual Property Code.[500]

Caron and Gaubiac argued that the lawful source requirement may be deemed to be mandated by the general principle under which original illegality irreparably invalidates subsequent or dependent acts (*fraud omnia corrumpit*).[501] To uphold

---

[496] See §4.3., see *supra*.
[497] *Ibidem*.
[498] See Dusollier, *Droit d'auteur et protection des oeuvres*, op. cit., p. 452.
[499] The original version of Article 53 of the German Copyright Act is available at: http://bundesrecht.juris.de/urhg/__53.html.
[500] See §6.3.1., see *supra*.
[501] Caron and Gaubiac, 'L'échange d'oeuvres sur l'Internet ou le P2P', in: *Mélanges Victor Nabhan – Hors série Les Cahiers de Propriété Intellectuelle*, Edition Yvon Blais, Montréal 2005, p. 32.

the implementation of this principle in the case of unauthorised downloads, the authors drew on a recent judgment of the French *Court de Cassation* which held that counterfeiting copies should be considered as "out-of-commerce" goods.[502] This view suggests that what is the fruit of an infringement or what is counterfeit inevitably makes subsequent copying of infringing goods unlawful. As a result, unauthorised downloads certainly fall outside the exception of private copying in as far as downloaders are unable to argue the lawful acquisition of the copy of the works stored on their hard disks. In my view, under French law, the requirement of non-collective destination indirectly codifies this general principle. There is no room for a different conclusion under a system that shapes the notion of personal use in such a strict way. In France, "non-collective destination" means that the making a copy from someone else's copy constitutes a copyright infringement, regardless of whether the unauthorised (*i.e.*, follow-on) copier is able to prove purposes of personal use.

Unlike the Software and the Databases Directives, which seem to provide no exception for digital private copying except for the right of making back-up copies of computer programmes,[503] the InfoSoc Directive left Member States with the option of carving out an exception on copying for personal use on condition that certain requirements were met. The fact that Article 5(2)(b) of the Directive does not include lawful acquisition of the work among these requirements means that, when implementing the private copying exception, the law of the Member States is free to create this further restriction in order to ensure a higher degree of copyright protection and legal certainty in the on-line environment.[504] As demonstrated by the case of German copyright law, this policy decision may arise because the InfoSoc Directive does not specifically address the problematical situation of copying from peer-to-peer networks.

German law provides the most rigorous solution to the problem of unauthorised file-sharing by specifically outlawing private copying from a clearly unlawful source. Member States willing to ensure stronger copyright protection in the face of peer-to-peer networking may well follow the example of the German Copyright Act when implementing (or re-adjusting the implementation of) the InfoSoc Directive. However, it remains to be seen how this solution will work in practice and "hether the notion of "apparently unlawful source' will be understood in a consistent and reliable way in the German case law.

Until now, the lack of guidance for the provision of Article 5(2)(b) has resulted in different interpretation of the status of unauthorised downloads in other Member States. Where courts in the Netherlands and France have found that, under certain conditions, unauthorised downloaders could be excused under the shield of

[502] *Ibidem.*

[503] As pointed out above, it is still controversial whether, under Article 4(a) of the Software Directive, an implicit exception of private copying exists with regard to acts of reproductions that are indispensable for the mere use of the computer programme: see §3.3.3.1.

[504] Dusollier, 'L'utilisation légitime de l'oeuvre: un nouveau sésame pour le bénefice des exceptions en droit d'auteur?', *Communications - Commerce Electronique*, November 2005, p.17.

personal use, regardless of where they take their materials from, Italian law punishes copying from peer-to-peer networks through administrative sanctions. Following amendments to the Copyright Act in 2004 and 2005,[505] Italian law now distinguishes the conduct of sharing or uploading unauthorised copyrighted work from acts of mere downloading. Where the former is punished by criminal sanctions,[506] the latter exposes downloaders to administrative fines.[507] Nonetheless, both acts are meant to constitute copyright infringement and to oblige unauthorised users to pay damages to copyright holders.

6.3.3. Unauthorised downloads under the three-step test

Existing case law does not consider in detail the fact that Article 5(5) of the InfoSoc Directive requires any decisions regarding private copying in the digital environment to comply with the three-step test. As already explained, the test aims to make sure that, even when a copyright exception is provided for in a special case (first step), the exception does not conflict with the normal exploitation of the work (second step), and does not unreasonably prejudice the legitimate interests of the right-holder (third step).[508]

The examined national case law which excuses unauthorised downloads under the shield of personal copying ignores the test under all three requirements. As far as the "special case" requirement is concerned, it was emphasised earlier that the personal copying exception in the civil law tradition of copyright was traditionally justified by the public policy objective of preserving the privacy of users when the copyright work is used in their own private sphere.[509] In the digital environment, and especially in cyberspace, the need to preserve user privacy increases because new management and control technologies enable the tracking of consumption patterns and on-line use.

However, privacy concerns were absent from these file-sharing cases. The only rationale that may have supported the implementation of the personal copying exception was the defence of the user's right to use the copyrighted work privately, that is, without intrusion into the user's private sphere by the copyright holder. However, having acquired their copies from a presumptively unlawful or non-personal source, hardly would unauthorised downloaders have been able to invoke the right to privacy without showing that they owned a lawful original copy of the downloaded works.[510]

---

505 See Law 128/2004 and Law 43/2005, which amended the Italian Copyright Act (*i.e.*, Law 633/1941) and are known cumulatively as "Decreto Urbani", from the name of the Italian minister proposing the adoption of the new Act.

506 See Article 171-ter of the Italian Copyright Act (L. 633/1941).

507 See Article 174-ter of the Italian Copyright Act (L. 633/1941).

508 The structure and the interpretation of the test are discussed at §4.2.1., see *supra*.

509 See §2.2.3., see *supra*.

510 It is worth noting that the protection of user privacy may come into play in the context of copyright infringement suits based on peer-to-peer transfers of copyrighted works in relation to the processing, retention and disclosure of users' personal data that right-

With regard to the normal exploitation of the work in question, the case law omitted to consider that this requirement bars the implementation of personal copying when the user enters into economic competition with the right-holders' actual and predictable sources of revenues. If the judgments had correctly considered the "normal exploitation" requirement, they should have declined to uphold that unauthorised downloads could constitute lawful personal copying. Indeed, downloading activities enabled these users to reproduce hundreds (or thousands) of copyrighted works without permission. Such use engages in fierce, direct competition with on-line markets for copyrighted goods.

In today's on-line environment, there are plenty of commercial services selling these works under fully licensed schemes. If the users had been willing to acquire these works lawfully, they could have bought them on the market. The consequence of this conduct was that copyright holders were deprived of revenues for each unauthorised item that was downloaded from the Internet without authorisation. Here, the conflict with the normal exploitation of the protected work was evident, especially if it is considered that no market failure existed in the purchase of the desired use of the protected works.

As far as the "unreasonable prejudice" of right-holders' legitimate interests is concerned, the reported case law veered decidedly away from the constraints of Article 5(2)(b) of the InfoSoc Directive, which permits the implementation of the personal copying exception "on condition that the rightholders receive fair compensation which takes account of the application or non-application of technological measures [...]". It is evident that this provision was designed to internalise the restriction posed by the third step of the test into the specific field of private copying. As noted above,[511] Article 5(2)(b) leaves Member States with the option of keeping or establishing this exception *ex novo*. Notwithstanding its optional na-

---

holders need to identify individual infringers in order to sue them. As argued recently before the Rome District Court in respect of a request for disclosure of user identity made to an ISP by two copyright owners on music files and videogames, user personal data (such as Internet Protocol addresses, user identity and other personal information) can be lawfully retained, processed and disclosed only under the exceptional circumstances embodied in Article 15 of Directive 2002/58/EC on privacy and electronic communications, OJ L 201, 31 July 2002, 37. These exceptional circumstances include State security, defence, public security, and the prevention, investigation, detection and prosecution of criminal offences or of unauthorised use of electronic communication systems. In rejecting the copyright owners' claim, the Rome Court found that, under the Italian and EU laws regarding the interplay between privacy protection and digital copyright enforcement regulations, the user right to confidentiality in electronic communications takes preference, in civil proceedings, over the competing goal of disclosing identity and other personal data related to file-sharers who commit on-line copyright infringement: see *Techland and Peppermint Jam Records* v. *Wind Telecomunicazioni*, Tribunale Ordinario di Roma, Order at interim proceedings. N. 26125/2007, 16 July 2007, available at
http://www.altroconsumo.it/images/17/173003_Attach.pdf.
Judicial remedies available in the EU for purposes of digital copyright enforcement targeted at individuals are analysed at §8.3.1.2., see *infra*.

511 See §4.4.1., see *supra*.

ture, this provision makes it clear that, where the exception is granted, national law must ensure a system of fair compensation. In the literature regarding the interpretation of the three-step test, financial compensation is unanimously understood to ensure that statutory licences authorising personal copying do not result in an unreasonable prejudice to the author's legitimate interest in obtaining remuneration for the use of his or her works.[512]

In France, the fact that personal computers were not included on the list of copying devices exempted from liability under the levy regime provided by Article L. 311-4 of the French Intellectual Property Code did not dissuade certain courts from excusing unauthorised downloaders under the guise of personal use. The above-mentioned decisions by the Rodez and Montpellier courts, in particular, seemed to accept that the fact that unauthorised materials were shifted onto tangible media upon which levies were charged could make original acts of downloading lawful under the private copying regime.[513] In doing so, however, the judges confused the legal status of unauthorised downloads with that of subsequent reproductions that might have been exempted because of the levy system.

In most countries of the European Union, fair compensation is ensured by national levy systems which charge fees on the sale price of certain types of recording devices and blank/recordable media identified by law.[514] The problem that arises with unauthorised downloads is that, in no EU jurisdiction where a levy system exists, does the sale price of personal computers - which could be understood as copying equipment - include a levy charge. Furthermore, it must be taken into consideration that, in the case of file-sharing, personal computers (or hard disks) serve both reproduction and storage purposes.

This issue was raised and rejected in the U.S. *Napster* case, where the statutory exemption created by the 1992 Audio Home Recording Act (AHRA) to protect non-commercial reproductions of digital music recordings made by consumers of "digital audio recording devices" from infringement actions was found not to apply to cases of unauthorised file-sharing, given that, under the exemption, personal computers were deemed not to fall within the definition of digital audio recording device.[515] In Europe, a copyright levy reform which seeks to include personal computers in the realm of copying devices that are subject to the payment of copyright levies has recently been proposed in Germany, also in consideration of a de-

---

512 See Senftleben, *Copyright, Limitations and the Three-step Test*, op. cit., p. 129, who argued that the payment of equitable remuneration has a mitigating effect on the finding of an unreasonable prejudice; Cohen Jehoram, 'Restrictions on Copyright and their Abuse', op. cit., p. 361.

513 See Code de la Propriété Intellectuelle, Article L. 311-4.: "La rémunération prévue à l'article L. 311-3 est versée par le fabricant, l'importateur ou la personne qui réalise des acquisitions intracommunautaires, au sens du 3° du 1 de l'article 256 bis du code général des impôts, de supports d'enregistrement utilisables pour la reproduction à usage privé d'oeuvres, lors de la mise en circulation en France de ces supports."

514 See Marzano, *Diritto d'Autore e Digital Technologies*, op. cit., p. 264.

515 See 17 U.S. Code §1008 (enacted by the 1992 Audio Home Recording Act).

cision taken by the District Court of Munich in December 2004.[516] This decision settled a dispute initiated by a German collecting society representing all private German TV and radio broadcasters (*i.e.*, VG Media) against Germany's largest personal computers maker (*i.e.*, Fujitsu Siemens). The Munich District Court found that the Fujitsu Siemens owed to VG Media a copyright levy (*i.e.*, 12 Euro) for every computer sold on the German market.[517] In recognising the personal computer maker as debtor of a copyright levy, the decision of the Munich Court was based on the assumption that VG Media was barred from the collection and distribution of copyright levies as a consequence of the exclusion of broadcasting rights, managed by VG Media, from the German statutory levy system.

The proposals of Germany and of other Member States concerning the legislative implementation of copyright levies on different kinds of hardware, including personal computers, are now being carefully monitored by the European Commission under the above-mentioned work programme for a copyright levy reform.[518]

In my view, the third requirement of the three-step test, contained in the definition of Article 5(2)(b) of the InfoSoc Directive, clearly outlaws any uncompensated reproduction of copyrighted works, regardless of whether these reproductions are kept within the downloader's private sphere. The resulting policy is clear: in the absence of compensation systems which make right-holders' economic losses a *reasonable* prejudice, the exception of private reproduction cannot excuse unauthorised copying from peer-to-peer networks. It will be explained below that the establishment of statutory compensation systems is one of the possible remedies to reduce the disruptive effects of unauthorised file-sharing on the markets for copyrighted digital works.[519]

6.4. Peer-to-peer software providers' liability: the United States

Owing to the fact that suing millions of direct infringers engaging in unauthorised file-sharing of copyrighted works would have been too costly and practically unfeasible, the relevant U.S. case law focused almost exclusively on whether peer-to-peer technology providers were indirectly liable for the direct infringement of its users. There were three possible forms of copyright liability under U.S law:

---

516 See *VG Media* v. *Fujitsu Siemens*, District Court of Munich, Az: 7 O 18484/03, 23 December 2004, available at http://www.juris.de.

517 See 'German court sets copyright levy on new PCs', *IT World*, 24.12.2004, available at http://www.itworld.com; 'Fujitsu Siemens loses German PC levy case', *The Register*, 3.01.2005, at http://www.theregister.co.uk; 'Tech industry condemns German PC levy', *Out Law News*, 21.01.2005, at http://www.out-law.com.

518 See §4.4.1., see *supra*.

519 See §8.3.2., see *infra*.

contributory infringement, vicarious liability or the theory of inducement.[520] The notion of contributory infringement refers to the conduct of one who, fully aware of his or her infringing activity, induces, causes or materially contributes to the infringing activity of another. Vicarious liability stems from the legal principle that one who has the right and the ability to supervise the direct infringer and also has a financial interest in the infringer's activity may be held liable for the conduct of the people under their supervision. Finally, the theory of inducement provides that one who takes active steps with the intent of promoting an infringement is liable for the resulting acts of infringement by third parties.

6.4.1. The U.S. case law

In the U.S. case law, the issue of the copyright liability of peer-to-peer providers was addressed from several perspectives. At a early stage of the case law, when peer-to-peer networks still worked through the functioning of a central server listing directories of materials that users wished to share with their peers, the first issue to be considered was whether a peer-to-peer service could benefit from the same liability exemptions granted to Internet Service Providers (ISPs) under the 1998 DMCA. This statute exempts ISPs engaging in "transitory network communication", which is said to occur if the service does not initiate the transmission, if it routes or provides the connections automatically, and if it does not select the recipients of the material, from copyright liability.[521] The early ruling of the District Court for Northern California in *Napster* found that Napster could not invoke this liability exemption because, in contrast to this provision's requirements, transmitted materials did not pass through Napster's private network.[522] This file-sharing system merely located music files on the hard drives of users connected to the network.

As soon as peer-to-peer technology enabled connection of each user's hardware to each other, with no central server providing information on the location of the infringing materials, the assimilation of peer-to-peer providers to ISPs lost its substance. The case law on the liability of peer-to-peer providers focused on two crucial issues regarding indirect liability.

Firstly, U.S. courts considered whether providers of new peer-to-peer software, which enabled completely decentralised file-sharing among software users, could be held indirectly (that is, "vicariously", under the meaning of Anglo-American law) liable for maintaining the ability to supervise and control their subscribers'

---

520 See von Lohmann, *IAAL (I Am A Lawyer): What Peer-to-Peer Developers Need to Know about Copyright Law*, Electronic Frontier Foundation, January 2006, downloaded at: www.eff.org, p. 3.

521 See U.S. Code, Title 17, §512(a), introduced by the 1998 DMCA, under which a service provider is largely exempted from liability for providing "transitory digital network communications".

522 See von Lohmann, *IAAL: What Peer-to-Peer Developers Need to Know*, p. 11.

activities, and whether or not they derived a financial benefit from those activities.[523]

Secondly, when considering whether software providers could be found liable for inducing users to infringe because of the very architecture of peer-to-peer technologies, U.S. courts concentrated on non-infringing uses enabled by this technology and which effectively occurred over the resulting networks. In the resultant case law, an interesting comparison was established between the case of peer-to-peer technology and Sony's Betamax Video Cassette Recorder (VCR) in the 1980s with regard to a suitable exemption of dual-use technology makers from copyright liability.

6.4.1.1. The Napster case

Since the review by the U.S. Court of Appeals for the Ninth Circuit in *Napster*, it became clear that, from its infancy, peer-to-peer software was a product that could easily escape the provider's control. The court's analysis emphasised that the Napster system's architecture had not been developed in such a way as to permit the system-creator to read the actual content of the indexed files. Music files remained in the users' hard drives and only the file names were listed on the Napster directory. The users designated file names and the service software only verified that the available files were properly formatted. The first decision taken by the District Court of Northern California ordered Napster to make sure that no unauthorised work owned by the plaintiffs was uploaded or downloaded on the Napster network. Thus, this order compelled Napster to bear the burden of developing the technical means to change its system's architecture, given that Napster's technology, as it stood, had no control over the effective content of user file-sharing. The subsequent decision by the U.S. Court of Appeal for the Ninth Circuit reformed the scope of the lower court's injunction by holding Napster indirectly liable on the grounds of its knowledge that specific infringing material was being disseminated on Napster's system. The precedent relied on by the Court of Appeals in its reasoning was *Religious Technology Center* v. *Netcom On-Line Communication Services*,[524] wherein the Northern District of California held that an on-line service provider's contributory liability depended upon demonstrating that the service had actual knowledge of *specific* infringing acts. This judgment further stated that if the service, after having been notified of the alleged infringements, failed to purge the infringing material from its system, the service could be held indirectly liable. As pointed out by Ginsburg,[525] this analysis of Napster's secondary liability led to a generalisation of the so-called "notice and take down" approach, which was implemented by the U.S. Congress with respect to the liability of the ISPs under Sec-

523 See Ginsburg, 'Copyright Use and Excuse on the Internet', The Center for Law and Economic Studies, Working Paper n.178, Columbia Law School, 2001, p. 29.

524 See *Religious Technology Center* v. *Netcom On-Line Communication Services, Inc.*, 907 F. Supp. 1361 (N.D. Cal. 1995).

525 See Ginsburg, 'Copyright Use and Excuse on the Internet', op. cit., p. 36.

tion 512(d) of the U.S. Copyright Act, as modified by the 1998 DMCA.[526] While treating Napster as an ISP, the Ninth Circuit held that the burden both to police and to notify the system lay with the copyright owner and with the system-creator to respond, in such a way that the more notices Napster received, the more vulnerable its system became, unless it could devise a means to separate non-infringing from infringing uses. This conclusion amounted to the *de facto* condemnation of Napster's peer-to-peer system as being illegal, considering that the system deviser, especially if notified on a continuous basis about specific infringements, would have been forced to redesign the system so as to prevent systematic infringement.

This situation became much more complex when new peer-to-peer technology started enabling the creation of networks that could not be effectively supervised by their system devisers. When the *Napster* dispute was about to be settled in favour of the entertainment industry, other file-sharing software started being equipped with technology designed to enable *pure* peer-to-peer networking. Even if new technology worked in a way that was conceptually analogous to Napster, its operation had no central servers involved in the transmission of file-related information, in such a way that the resulting networks functioned as totally decentralised communication tools connecting Internet users to one another. For example, unlike the Napster system, when users searched for and initiated transfers of files using the Grokster system, they did so without any information being transmitted to or through any computers owned or controlled by Grokster or StreamCast.[527] The consequence of this system architecture was that software producers and distributors were not able to supervise the conduct of their users. As a result, U.S. decisions on provider liability started focusing on whether technology designers could be found liable for the mere fact that the architecture of their technology did not enable user supervision over direct infringement; not surprisingly, this technology was referred to as being "wilfully blind".

6.4.1.2. The Aimster case

The decision of the Court of Appeals for the Seventh Circuit in *In re Aimster Copyright Litigation*[528] signalled the post-Napster review of peer-to-peer providers' copyright liability. The incriminated "blindness" of the Aimster system, which was analogous to Napster in terms of technology architecture, was created by a technical feature which encrypted, or hide, the content of the information exchanged by users when locating and transmitting desired files from the host server to the recipient. In doing so, the Aimster system did not allow the deviser of the

---

526 See U.S. Code, Title 17, §512(d), which grants immunity from "infringement of copyright by reason of the provider referring or linking users to an online location containing infringing material or infringing activity, by using information location tools, including a directory [...]".

527 See §6.4.1.3., see *infra*.

528 See *In re Aimster Copyright Litigation*, U.S. Court of Appeals 334 F.3d 643 (7th Circuit 2003), cert. denied, 124 S. Ct. 1069 (2004), reported by Merges, Menell and Lemley, *Intellectual Property in the New Technological Age, 2004 Case and Statutory Supplement*, Aspen Publishers, New York 2004, pp. 47-57.

central server to release file-related information to check effectively whether its users engaged in the unauthorised distribution of copyrighted works via the network. In Justice Posner's view, the fact that Aimster was using encryption to shield itself from actual knowledge of the unlawful purposes for which its service was being used could not ensure immunity from liability. This circumstance, united to the fact that, in explaining how to use its software, Aimster provided a tutorial which gave - as its *only* examples of file-sharing - the sharing of copyrighted music (which the recording industry had notified to Aimster was being infringed by its users) proved that users were encouraged to use the service to infringe copyright.[529]

In addition, the encouragement of copyright infringement by Aimster was demonstrated by the fact that the peer-to-peer system, by means of membership agreements, enabled members to download the music most often shared by Aimster users, which turned out to be music copyrighted by the plaintiffs (*i.e.*, the recording industry), with a single click for a monthly fee of only $4.95. As a consequence, judge Posner upheld and affirmed the preliminary injunction issued against Aimster by the Illinois District Court.[530]

6.4.1.3. The Grokster case

In *Metro-Goldwin-Mayer Studios, Inc.* v. *Grokster*, the U.S. District Court of Central California[531] and, later on, the Court of Appeals for the Ninth Circuit,[532] respectively, issued and affirmed an order refusing to grant a motion filed by organisations in the motion picture and music recording industries against peer-to-peer software designers and providers for contributory and vicarious copyright infringement. As in the former cases, the dispute arose from the free exchange of copyrighted material over the Internet. The defendants, Grokster and Streamcast, were distributors of free software that users could download free of charge over the Internet.[533] All of them used the Fast Track technology, which exemplified and created what previously had been referred to as *pure* peer-to-peer architecture and networking. This technology operated by means of "nodes" that worked as "super nodes". A "node" is an end-point on the Internet (typically, a user's computer);

---

529 See *In re Aimster Copyright Litigation*, cit., p. 54.

530 See *In re Aimster Copyright Litigation*, 252 F.Supp. 2d 634, 653 (N.D. Illinois 2002).

531 See *Metro-Goldwyn-Mayer Studios, Inc.* v. *Grokster*, 259 F.Supp.2d 1029 (C.D. Cal. 2003), hereinafter *Grokster*.

532 See *Metro-Goldwyn-Mayer Studios, Inc.* v. *Grokster*, 380 F. 3d 1154 (Court of Appeals 9th Circuit 2004), hereinafter *MGM* v. *Grokster*.

533 Despite formal independence, defendants' differently branded and marketed computer programs were initially powered by the same network technology, namely "Fast Track". This new technology was developed by Niklas Zennström and Janus Friis, who had already launched another system on the Internet: Kazaa. The original defendants (Kazaa, Grokster and StreamCast) were licensees of the Fast Track technology and they used it in their own company's file-sharing software. Thus, Fast Track worked on all three platforms and it allowed users of these platforms to connect substantially to the same seamless peer-to-peer network and to exchange files.

and a "super-node" is a node that has a heightened function, accumulating information from numerous other nodes. In short, *pure* peer-to-peer networks are structured in a way that "an individual node [...] automatically self-selects its own super-node status; a user's node may be a super-node one day and not on the following day, depending on resource needs and the availability of the network [...]".[534] The District Court and the Court of Appeals acknowledged that, from a technical point of view, the defendants no longer operated as super-nodes, whereas Napster used a single super-node owned and operated by the same system-creator. Grokster's software was preset with a list of "root super-nodes", each of which principally functioned to connect users to the network by directing them to active super-nodes. Nonetheless, while Grokster may briefly have had some control over a root super-node, it was made clear that the technical process of locating and connecting to a super-node and the Fast Track network "occurred essentially independently of defendant Grokster [...]".[535] Moreover, the courts noted that, after the adoption of an open-source peer-to-peer platform called Gnutella, which worked by passing search requests from user to user until a match was found or the search request expired, the operating of StreamCast was actually more decentralised than that of Grokster.[536] The fact that the technical process of locating and connecting to the dispensers of file-related information occurred independently of defendants meant that the "notice and take down" approach developed in *Napster* could not apply to the Fast Track technology. Indeed, the plaintiffs' hypothetical notices of specific infringing conduct would have been irrelevant if issued when the defendants did nothing to facilitate, and could not do anything to stop, the alleged infringement.[537]

Considering the conflicting decisions on Aimster's and Grokster's liability, the U.S. Supreme Court granted the plaintiffs' petition to appeal *MGM* v. *Grokster* on writ of *certiorari* to the U.S. Court of Appeals for the Ninth Circuit. Interestingly, the resultant 2005 judgment by the Supreme Court did not address the issue of contributory copyright infringement.[538] The Supreme Court vacated the judgment of the Ninth Circuit on the grounds of the so-called theory of inducement, rather than on the basis of contributory copyright infringement, as the Courts of Appeal for the Seventh and the Ninth Circuits ultimately did with opposite results. Grokster was held liable on the assumption that there was convincing evidence that it had taken "active steps" to foster copyright infringement by the users of its software. The Supreme Court found that there was no need to revisit the precedent of the 1984 *Sony* decision in order to evaluate Grokster's indirect liability. In *Sony*, the U.S. Supreme Court considered the potential copyright liability of Sony, the defendant company, that sold a machine (*i.e.*, the VCR) that could be illegally

---

534 See *Grokster*, op. cit., p. 1040.

535 *Ibidem.*

536 See *Grokster*, p. 1041.

537 See *Grokster*, p. 1037.

538 See *Metro-Goldwyn-Mayer Studios Inc.* v. *Grokster, Ltd.*, 545 U.S. Supreme Court, decided June 27, 2005. The text of the decision is available at: http://www.eff.org (§Cases). For a commentary upon this decision, see Ganley, 'Surviving Grokster: Innovation and the Future of Peer-to-Peer', (28) *EIPR*, 2006, p. 15.

used to copy protected material. On that occasion, the Supreme Court had held that the sale of copying equipment, in the same way as the sale of other articles of commerce, could not give rise to contributory liability "if the product is widely used for legitimate, unobjectionable purposes. Indeed, it needs merely be capable of substantial noninfringing uses".[539]

The Supreme Court found that, in *MGM* v. *Grokster*, the Ninth Circuit had erred in giving an unreasonably broad interpretation of this doctrine, under which the distributor of dual-use technology, such as Grokster's, could not be held indirectly liable for third party infringement, even when an actual purpose to cause infringing use was demonstrated. The Supreme Court pointed out that the *Sony* decision provided a theory of liability *only* for the case of the distribution of a product capable of both lawful and unlawful uses without displacing other secondary liability theories. In particular, it did not permit the ignoring of evidence of culpable intent if there was such evidence. Thus, in the Supreme Court's view, *Sony* could not be interpreted as if it had foreclosed rules of fault-based liability derived from the common law.[540] Under the classic inducement theory (which applies when one induces another to commit an infringement, or persuades another to infringe), direct evidence of Grokster's unlawful purpose did not permit it to escape liability.[541] The Court stressed that several factors provided evidence of such intent by Grokster. Not only did Grokster's efforts to supply services to former Napster users demonstrated an intent to capture Napster's unlawful market for the unauthorised use of copyrighted works. In the Court's view, the defendant's culpable intent was shown indisputably by the very fact that, instead of developing filtering tools or other mechanisms to reduce the infringing activity, as it had repeatedly been asked to, Grokster sold advertising space by directing advertisements to the screens of computers employing its software.

6.4.2. How consideration of non-infringing uses has an impact on indirect liability

The fact that peer-to-peer software is dual-use technology was given increasing consideration in the review of the indirect liability of the software providers. The potential of peer-to-peer software as a tool that enables socially valuable, non-infringing uses was recognised by the U.S. Court of Appeals for the Ninth Circuit in the *Napster* case. The Ninth Circuit held that the District Court for Northern California had improperly confined the use analysis of the Napster system to current uses, thus ignoring the system's capabilities and disregarding the binding precedent of *Sony*.[542] When rejecting the claim that the Napster system was pro-

539 See *Sony*, p. 442.

540 See the Opinion of the Court, in *Metro-Goldwyn-Mayer Studios Inc.* v. *Grokster, Ltd.*, 545 U.S. Supreme Court, p. 17.

541 *Ibidem*.

542 See *Napster*, 239 F. 3d 1004, pp. 1020-1021 ("We are bound to follow *Sony*, and will not impute the requisite level of knowledge to Napster merely because peer-to-peer file sharing technology may be used to infringe plaintiffs' copyrights").

tected from liability by the standard set out in *Sony*, the early District Court's injunction had relied upon the minimal importance of the alleged non-infringing uses of the system (*e.g.*, chat rooms, a so-called "New Artist Programme" that, at least on paper, intended to disseminate authorised copyrighted works by unknown artists, *etc*). The fact that Napster had not been able to show that its technology was effectively capable of significant non-infringing uses persuaded the District Court that the *Sony* standard was inapplicable. When reviewing the case, the Court of Appeals, in line with *Sony*, held that Napster could not be held liable for contributory infringement "[M]erely because the structure of the system allows for the exchange of copyrighted material [...] To enjoin simply because a computer network allows for infringing uses would, in our opinion, violate *Sony* and potentially restrict activity unrelated to infringing use."[543]

While decidedly moving away from the *Sony* decision on dual-use technology, the *Aimster* decision by judge Posner found that the Aimster system, although merely capable of substantial non-infringing uses, could not be exempted from contributory copyright liability because it was used *mainly* for infringing purposes. What was remarkable was that Posner's reasoning relied upon an unprecedented cost-benefit analysis of peer-to-peer networking in relation to the magnitude of the infringing and non-infringing uses carried out by networked users. As opposed to the *Sony* standard, which requires the mere capability of non-infringing uses for a product to be exempted from indirect liability, Posner found that, when a supplier is offering a product or service that has non-infringing as well as infringing uses, an estimate of the respective magnitudes of these uses was necessary for a finding of contributory infringement. However, Posner made it clear that the balancing of costs and benefits was necessary only in so far as substantial non-infringing uses, present or prospective, were demonstrated.[544] Considering that there was no demonstration of *actual* non-infringing uses, and it was plainly evident that most of the material exchanged on Aimster's network was under copyright, the U.S. Court of Appeals for the Seventh Circuit held that Aimster's technology could not be exempted from liability under the *Sony* standard.

As persuasively pointed out by Yen, judge Posner's reasoning missed the point of *Sony* from a twofold perspective.[545] First, it allowed liability against a defendant whose technology was merely capable of a substantial non-infringing use. Second, it imposed a further cost-benefit analysis by making the exemption from liability subject to a criterion that was contrary to the *Sony* logic. Indeed, Posner argued that even if there were non-infringing uses of an Internet file-sharing service, if the infringing uses had been substantial, then, to avoid liability as a contributory infringer, the provider of the service should have demonstrated that it would have

543 See *Napster*, 239 F.3d 1004 (9th Circuit), p. 1021.

544 See *In re Aimster Copyright Litigation*, op. cit., p. 52.

545 See Yen, 'Sony, Tort Doctrines, and the Puzzle of Peer-to-Peer', (55) *Case Western Reserve Law Review* 2005, Symposium Issue, available at: http://ssrn.com/abstract=661168, p. 25.

been *disproportionately costly* for him to eliminate or at least reduce the infringing use substantially.[546]

In contrast to the cost-benefit analysis proposed and relied upon by judge Posner in the *Aimster* case, the *Grokster* courts did not seek to check and balance the magnitudes of infringing and non-infringing uses of the Fast Track technology. Instead, having ascertained that there were substantial non-infringing uses for the defendants' software, the District Court for Northern California and the Court of Appeals for the Ninth Circuit upheld and further developed the reasoning relied upon by the same Ninth Circuit in the revision of the first injunction issued against Napster.[547] On that occasion, the Court of Appeals had refused to impute the requisite level of knowledge to Napster "merely because peer-to-peer file-sharing technology might be used to infringe plaintiffs' copyrights".[548] However, by compelling Napster to remove all the material identified by the plaintiffs as being copyrighted, the Ninth Circuit's order had subordinated the "substantial non-infringing use" requirement to the "knowledge" requirement, thus undermining the objective of the doctrine laid down in *Sony*.

Similarly to the Ninth Circuit in *Napster*, the Court of Appeals deciding on *Grokster* analysed the Fast Track capability of substantial non-infringing use as part of knowledge of infringement. However, unlike the Ninth Circuit in *Napster,* the inquiry on substantial non-infringing uses was separated from the knowledge enquiry. The enquiry on the existence of non-infringing uses was rapidly given a persuasive answer. Not only was the Fast Track technology capable of *future* non-infringing uses, it was already offering *current* uses that served the public interest by allowing Internet users to benefit from sharing and copying non-protected information, works in the public domain, government documents, media content for which distribution was authorised, media to which the rightful owners did not object to distribution, and computer software for which the distribution was permitted.

In my view, it is noteworthy that, whereas the above-mentioned opinion by the U.S. Supreme Court was unanimous with regard to Grokster's liability under the inducement theory, the Court split into two camps on whether the *Sony* standard could apply to Grokster's technology as far as contributory copyright infringement was concerned. Significantly, the justices did not find a common position on whether the *Sony* doctrine should have been revised in the light of the impact of new copying equipment such as Grokster's technology on the markets for copyrighted works.

While Justice Ginsburg's opinion (joined by the Chief Justice Rehnquist and Justice Kennedy) substantially affirmed Posner's reasoning in the *Aimster* case, by arguing that dual-use technology cannot be exempted from liability when it is used

---

546 *Ibidem.*

547 The defendants showed several non-infringing uses of their technology: distributing movie trailers, free songs or other non-copyrighted works; using the software in countries where it is legal; and "sharing the works of Shakespeare": see *Grokster*, p. 1035.

548 See *Grokster*, p. 1036.

mainly to infringe copyright,[549] Justice Breyer (joined by Justices Stevens and O'Connor) delivered a dissenting opinion which held that Grokster's technology met the *Sony* liability theory requirement.[550] Ginsburg's opinion emphasised that the *Grokster* case was markedly different from the *Sony/Betamax* case. Justice Ginsburg argued that the present dispute was not about the use of peer-to-peer technology generally; instead, it was about whether the specific use of Grokster's technology could exempt the software provider from liability, in the light of the evidence of actual and substantial non-infringing uses. In particular, Ginsburg stressed that the difference between *Sony* and *M.G.M.* v. *Grokster* was marked by the fact that, whereas the vast majority of Betamax users engaged in a use that was deemed fair, such as the home-taping of TV programmes for time-shifting purposes, Grokster users mainly engaged in unlawful uses such as copying and exchanging copyrighted works without authorisation. Ginsburg's analysis concluded that Grokster could not escape copyright liability simply because evidence of *actual* (and not future) and *substantial* non-infringing uses of its technology was lacking.

In contrast, Justice Breyer argued with this substantive revision of the *Sony* standard. He advocated that limiting the analysis of the capability of substantial non-infringing uses of technology to actual (*i.e.*, current) uses, and comparing such uses to infringing uses in terms of magnitude would have unduly stifled *Sony*'s technology-protecting rationale. Breyer pointed out that, under a liability standard "which seeks to protect not the Groksters of this world (which in any event may well be liable under today's holding) but the development of technology more generally [...]",[551] Grokster was required to show that its technology was *merely* capable of substantial non-infringing uses, including uses which are not actual, but are very likely to develop.

Due to these two contrasting approaches, there was clear divergence between Ginsburg and Breyer on the evidence of *substantial* non-infringing uses shown by Grokster. Whereas Justice Ginsburg found that - in the face of "overwhelming" infringing uses[552] - there was "little beyond anecdotal evidence" of non-infringing uses, whose substantial and commercially significant development was unclear, Justice Breyer emphasised that the records of the case revealed a significant future market for non-infringing uses of Grokster-type peer-to-peer software, which was a good reason for not revising the liability standard of *Sony*.[553] Among significant and fast-developing non-infringing uses, Breyer mentioned the file-sharing of both copyrighted and public domain works and information, which all together were estimated to represent around the 10% of the materials that were already exchanged on the Grokster and Streamcast networks. Breyer explicitly referred to initiatives

---

549 See Ginsburg, *Concurring Opinion*, in *Metro-Goldwyn-Mayer Studios Inc.* v. *Grokster, Ltd.*, 545 U.S. Supreme Court (2005), cit.

550 See Breyer, *Concurring Opinion*, in *Metro-Goldwyn-Mayer Studios Inc.* v. *Grokster, Ltd.*. cit.

551 See Breyer, *Concurring Opinion*, p. 8.

552 See Ginsburg, *Concurring Opinion*, p. 7.

553 See Breyer, *Concurring Opinion*, p. 6.

such as the Internet Archive (which welcomes the redistribution of authorised films by peer-to-peer users), the Prelinger Archive (which allows the file-sharing of public domain films), Our Pictures (a peer-to-peer photo-swapping service), the BBC Creative Archive (which lets users rip, mix and share the BBC content), Intent MediaWorks (which protects licensed content sent through peer-to-peer networks) and the open content collected and licensed under Creative Commons licences.[554] This percentage of non-infringing uses was very similar, Breyer argued, to the 9% or so of authorised time-shifting uses of the Betamax technology that the Supreme Court had faced in *Sony*.

6.4.3. Findings from the U.S. case law

In my view, it is possible to conclude that the U.S. Supreme Court's decision of June 2005, while finding Grokster liable for having induced copyright infringement by its users, did not touch upon the *Sony* doctrine as far as the intersection between contributory copyright infringement and dual-use copying technology was concerned. In the digital environment, this doctrine provides U.S. courts with firm guidance when addressing copyright infringement claims against peer-to-peer developers and suppliers. This means that the peer-to-peer software provider cannot be held liable for indirect copyright infringement unless it is shown that the provider was vicariously liable for exerting control, or had the possibility to exert control, of the exchange of data and had a financial interest in the infringing activity, or was indirectly liable under the theory of inducement for taking active steps to induce the users of its technology to infringe copyright. Moreover, it must be noted that evidence of increasing and even more important non-infringing uses of peer-to-peer technology makes the *Sony* test easier to meet for peer-to-peer technology providers. A different solution to the problem of on-line copyright infringement may only arise from a policy decision of the U.S. Congress, which may create new law with the objective either of replacing the *Sony* doctrine with the adoption of the cost-benefit analysis proposed by judges Posner and Ginsburg, or by imposing technological mandates on peer-to-peer technology's architecture.

6.5. Peer-to-peer software providers' liability: the European Union

The question of whether the design and supply of peer-to-peer software may be a cause of liability for indirect copyright infringement under EU law may be addressed from a number of perspectives. Firstly, it will be ascertained whether and how the specific exemptions of certain categories of on-line intermediaries from copyright liability apply to the activity of peer-to-peer software providers. In this respect, it must be noted that today's most successful peer-to-peer platforms en-

---

[554] See Breyer, *Concurring Opinion*, p. 7.

able perfectly decentralised communication in a way that software suppliers provide no material contribution to the user's direct infringement. This means that, when reviewing indirect liability, whether direct infringements occur independently of the software provider's activity or not must be carefully considered. Secondly, the fact that civil and criminal proceedings which aim to ensure the effective enforcement of intellectual property rights in the EU may be meant to create indirect liability upon peer-to-peer software providers must also be taken into account. Under this body of law, indirect liability may stem from the mere fact of developing technology which makes copyright infringements more difficult (or even impossible) to detect. Thirdly, it will be pointed out that, even if the technology's decentralised architecture may not enable the provider to have actual knowledge of a specific infringement at a time when it can take action to prevent it, indirect copyright liability may occur for the breach of duties of care under tort law if the provider is found either to support direct infringement actively by allowing parties to use its technology or for failing to exercise due care when giving shape to the technology itself.

6.5.1. Copyright liability in the *Kazaa* and *BitTorrent* cases

The first and most important case where indirect copyright liability by the provider of peer-to-peer software was examined in Europe was the so-called *Kazaa* case in the Netherlands.[555] In December 2003, the Dutch Supreme Court upheld a decision of the Amsterdam Court of Appeal, which found that the producer and supplier of peer-to-peer software identical to that of Grokster (Kazaa B.V.) was not indirectly liable for the copyright infringement of third parties using its technology.[556] Due to a matter of procedure (*i.e.*, preliminary injunction proceedings) the Supreme Court's review did not address the merits of the case in their entirety. The Court simply upheld the Appellate Court's decision in so far as it rejected the claim that Kazaa should have been compelled to adapt its software in order to reduce the infringing files. The Dutch Supreme Court's decision left unanswered the most important claim that had been submitted by the Dutch copyright collecting society Buma/Stemra, namely, whether Kazaa could be found liable of contributory infringement merely by having provided people using the same file-sharing network with the tool to copy and disseminate copyrighted works on the Internet.

None of the forms of direct and indirect liability specifically foreseen by EU directives dealing with copyright in the electronic environment fitted the case of Kazaa's software. The records of the case showed that copyright infringement by us-

---

[555] See *BUMA & STEMRA* v. *Kazaa*, Supreme Court of the Netherlands, The Hague, First Chamber, Order of 19 December 2003, Nr. C02/186HR JMH/AT, available at: http://www.muddlawoffices.com (§Cases). The decision was commented upon by Vollebregt, 'An analysis of the Kazaa case', *E-commerce Law and Policy*, 14 December 2003; and Strachan, 'The Internet of Tomorrow: The New-Old Communications Tool of Control', (26) *EIPR* 2004, p. 123, at p. 135.

[556] See *BUMA & STEMRA* v. *Kazaa*, Amsterdam Court of Appeal, 4th Three-judge Section, 28 March 2002, available at: http://www.eff.org, §Cases.

ers of this technology occurred independently of the provider's activity. In the same way as the Grokster system, Kazaa's completely decentralised architecture did not enable supervision possibilities on the users' exchange of materials. Consequently, there was no activity by Kazaa which could be found to infringe copyright either directly or indirectly.

6.5.1.1. Direct liability

Direct infringement would stem from carrying out on-line activities such as hosting, caching and mere conduit of unauthorised copyrighted materials. Articles 13 and 14 of the E-Commerce Directive provide that ISPs engaging in caching and hosting activities are liable only if, while having actual knowledge of transmission of unlawful information over their networks, fail to remove expeditiously or disable access to the unlawful information. In the specific field of EU digital copyright law, Article 5(1) of the InfoSoc Directive exempts temporary acts of reproduction by an intermediary whose sole purpose is to enable mere transmission of copyrighted materials between third parties from copyright liability.[557] In the *Kazaa* case, the Dutch copyright collecting society claimed that Kazaa's software distribution involved a form of transmission which could be compared to the transmission of TV pirate channels. The Advocate General of the Dutch Supreme Court disagreed with this contention by emphasising that, whereas pirate channels transmitted infringing materials by distributing the signal carrying the infringing content over its network and by deciding what precisely was to be distributed over its network, the Kazaa system only provided the means to exchange files without engaging in any act of file exchange or transmission.[558] Hence, there was no direct infringement by Kazaa.

6.5.1.2. Indirect liability

As far as indirect infringement is concerned, Kazaa might have been held liable if its file-sharing system had been found to disclose information on the location of infringing materials. This would have created indirect liability by evidencing that the software provider had actual knowledge of specific infringements and could thereby have intervened to stop infringing activities. Article 8(3) of the InfoSoc Directive provides that EU Member States

> "shall ensure that rightholders are in a position to apply for an injunction against intermediaries whose services are used by a third party to infringe a copyright or related right".

This means that copyright owners have the right to obtain an injunction against file-sharing services which are found to provide copyright infringers with the means of infringing copyright. Even if this was not the case of Kazaa, against which this provision could do nothing, it is noteworthy that Article 8(3) has re-

---

557 See §3.3.3.3., see *supra*.

558 See Vollebregt, 'An analysis of the Kazaa case', op. cit., p. 15.

cently been used throughout the European Union as a legal basis to stop the supply of information location tools which disclosed where unauthorised copyrighted materials could be found on other file-sharing platforms, such as Bit Torrent and e-Donkey, to direct infringers.[559] From December 2004 onwards, national courts in Finland, Germany, the United Kingdom, Slovenia, Sweden, Belgium and the Netherlands took precautionary measures on the grounds of Article 8(3) against web servers publishing links to unauthorised materials made available on the BitTorrent file-sharing systems.[560] In the specific case of BitTorrent's technology, implementation of enforcement measures based on Article 8(3) was feasible because of technical features of this peer-to-peer protocol, which implied some degree of accountability that other protocols (such as Kazaa) lacked.

To understand why it was possible to attack on-line intermediaries in the case of BitTorrent, it must be noted that this software does not offer a search facility to find files by name. This stems from the fact that, to make data transmission faster and enable transmission of very large files (*e.g.*, movies, computer programmes, *etc*), the BitTorrent file-sharing technology is designed to choose the peer with the best network connections for the fragments that it is requesting. To distribute a particular file (or a collection of files) BitTorrent's technology requires users to create temporarily *ad hoc* peer-to-peer networks (the so-called "swarms"). This is a mechanism that increases the overall efficiency of file exchange because clients request the fragments that are available from the fewest peers, making most fragments widely available to many machines and thereby avoiding bottlenecks. As a result, file fragments are not usually downloaded in sequential order and need to be re-assembled by the receiving machine. To create temporary networks and to start sharing information in such a complex way, a BitTorrent user needs to know which users own the desired content on their hard disks and have made such content available through the system. Uploading and search facilities are provided by user-run web servers (the so-called "trackers") that keep track of which users are sharing a given file on a specific host (or hosts) and distribute the tracker address(es) in the shared file. In this way, BitTorrent's technology makes no attempt to conceal the host ultimately responsible for the availability of a given file. Consequently, websites which function as trackers for the exchange of unauthorised copyrighted works may be easily attacked and shut down on the grounds of Article 8(3) of the InfoSoc Directive.

As noted above, very popular BitTorrent tracker websites (such as supernova.org, thepiratebay.org, razorback.com, dutchnova.com, *etc*) which distributed millions of unauthorised files through the BitTorrent file-sharing system were closed as a result of shut-down injunctions based on Article 8(3).[561] This remedy, however, could not work with regard to pure peer-to-peer networks such as Ka-

---

559 For a detailed description of how the BitTorrent and e-Donkey file-sharing systems operate, see the Wikipedia entries available, respectively, at: http://en.wikipedia.org/wiki/Bit_torrent and: http://en.wikipedia.org/wiki/EDonkey_network.

560 A constantly updated report of decisions implementing enforcement measures against BitTorrent user-run websites is provided at: http://en.wikipedia.org/wiki/Bit_torrent, §4.2 (Copyright enforcement); and http://www.dirittodautore.it (§News Archive).

561 See http://www.dirittodautore.it, § News Archive, "P2P" Section.

zaa's, where no middleman could be legally attacked for finding and identifying the users who shared the unauthorised files.

6.5.2. Possible technology's restrictions under Article 8 of the EU Intellectual Property Rights Enforcement Directive

Whereas Article 8(3) of the InfoSoc Directive proves to be worthless in its attempt to reduce copyright infringement occurring on completely decentralised peer-to-peer networks, restrictions on the design and supply of file-sharing software such as Kazaa and Grokster may stem from implementation of Article 3 of Directive 2004/48/EC, which requires Member States to provide for effective, proportionate and dissuasive measures, and the procedures and remedies necessary for the enforcement of intellectual property rights (IPRs) in the EU Internal Market.[562] Articles 9 to 12 of this Directive specify which types of provisional and precautionary measures (*i.e.*, interlocutory injunctions, seizure or confiscation of infringing materials, pecuniary compensation) and which corrective measures (*i.e.*, recall and removal from the channels of commerce or destruction) Member States are bound to provide to comply with the general obligation posed by Article 3.

To allow and facilitate the disclosure of infringements in the context of the proceedings for the enforcement of IPRs, Article 8 of the Directive (which is labelled "Right of information") provides that Member States shall ensure that:

> "[T]he competent judicial authorities may order that information on the origin and distribution networks of the goods or services which infringe an intellectual property right be provided by the infringer and/or any other person who [...] was found to be providing on a commercial scale services used in infringing activities or was indicated [...] as being involved in the production, manufacture or distribution of the goods or the provision of the services."

This provision aims to ensure that national judicial authorities enforcing IPRs are empowered to discover where infringing materials come from and which networks distribute such materials. When identifying the addressees of such information disclosure obligation, Article 8 refers both to the infringer and to any other person who provides services used in infringing activities or is indicated as being involved in the distribution of infringing goods.

In my view, due to its wording and rationale, this provision is capable of creating a legal basis for the discovery of indirect copyright liability by designers and suppliers of peer-to-peer software. Even if Article 8 of the IPRs Enforcement Directive was designed to facilitate enforcement proceedings against counterfeiting activities occurring in the real (*i.e.*, physical) world, it seems not unrealistic to argue that this provision might be used in the near future as an enforcement measure against peer-to-peer software providers. In theory, providers of this technology

---

562 See Directive 2004/48/EC of the European Parliament and of the Council of 29 April 2004 on the enforcement of intellectual property rights, OJ L 157, 40.4.2004 (hereinafter "IPRs Enforcement Directive").

could be seen as supplying the means of committing digital piracy on a commercial scale and of materially contributing to the on-line distribution of infringing goods under the wording of Article 8. As will be explored in greater depth below, in the light of the enforcement of the tort law principle of due care in the on-line environment in national jurisdictions, peer-to-peer software providers are in a position in which they may incur indirect copyright liability should they prove to be technically unable or simply reluctant to disclose information on the origin and distribution networks of infringing goods. In addition to this, the legislative proposal submitted by the European Commission at the end of April 2006, which aims to enact criminal sanctions against those who counterfeit goods protected by IPRs (including copyright) on a commercial scale,[563] may create liability for peer-to-peer software providers on the grounds of merely having designed and distributed file-sharing technology which is unable to prevent copyright infringement and/or track the behaviour of counterfeiters. The April 2006 version of the directive proposal amended the proposal approved by the Commission on 12 July 2005. By means of this amendment, the Commission intended to respond to the ECJ's ruling of 13 September 2005 in the *Commission of the European Communities* v. *Council of the European Union* case, according to which only the criminal law provisions necessary for the effective implementation of Community policies are a matter for Community law.[564] In the directive proposal, all intentional infringements of an intellectual property right made on a commercial scale, including attempting, aiding and abetting such infringements, are treated as criminal offences. Hence, the adoption of this directive would easily criminalise the mere conduct of encouraging or intentionally aiding (or with mere awareness) the file-sharing of unauthorised materials.

Having said this, it is possible to conclude that, in the light of civil and criminal procedures which are designed to ensure copyright enforcement in the EU, peer-to-peer technology providers might soon be mandated (or at least have a great incentive) to re-design the architecture of their software with the following twofold object:

- to be able to comply with judicial orders compelling disclosure of information on the origin and distribution networks of infringing materials; and

---

563 See European Commission Press Office, *Counterfeiting and piracy: Commission proposes criminal law provisions to combat intellectual property offences*, IP/06/532, Brussels, 26 April 2006. The Commission's directive proposal concerning the Community-wide implementation of criminal penalties for the infringement of intellectual property rights is discussed below: see §8.3.1.2, see *infra*.

564 See *Commission of the European Communities* v. *Council of the European Union*, C-176/03, Judgment of 13 September 2005, available at: http://curia.europa.eu. This judgment annulled the Council Framework Decision 2003/80/JHA of 27 January 2003 on the protection of the environment through criminal law, OJ 2003, L 29, p. 55. By this decision, the ECJ upheld the European Commission's claim that the legislature is competent to require the Member States to prescribe criminal penalties for infringements of Community environmental protection legislation if the Commission takes the view that this is a necessary means to ensure that the legislation is effective.

- to avoid the possibility of criminal liability.

As the next section reveals, the existence of an "alternative design" obligation is supported by the argument that peer-to-peer software providers may be deemed to be bound to embed copyright-protecting devices into the architecture of their technology under an obligation to exercise due care derived from national tort law.

6.5.3. Indirect liability under the principle of due care

The purpose of this section is to ascertain whether the tort law principle of due care applies to peer-to-peer software providers and what technical measures this duty may require them to implement.

6.5.3.1. Duties of care on the Internet after the E-Commerce Directive

As shown in this section by reference to the purpose of the E-Commerce Directive, EU law implicitly relies on the principle of "due care" in the on-line environment. The E-Commerce Directive has a horizontal scope which refers to any kind of illegal activity; not only copyright infringement, but also defamation, misleading advertising, trade marks infringement and so forth. After careful analysis, the contradictory wording of this Directive upholds the view that its codified ISPs liability exemptions should be viewed as narrow exemptions to a general liability principle of due care. As pointed out by Strachan, this Directive imposes no obligation to seek facts or circumstances that indicate illegal activity on the part of ISPs.[565] The Directive provides that caching and hosting providers are not liable for damages unless they have actual knowledge or become aware of facts and circumstances pertaining to illegal activities. Upon obtaining knowledge or awareness, Article 14 requires hosting providers to remove or to disable access to illegal information expeditiously.

Despite this obligation, the E-Commerce Directive fails to identify the circumstances and requirements which detail how caching and hosting providers might come to have actual knowledge or become aware of facts and circumstances regarding illegal conduct. Strachan emphasised that this failure creates uncertainty about the duties of ISPs to police illegal on-line activities, and thus ISPs and developers of infrastructure technology have a great incentive to implement monitoring mechanisms that may shield them from indirect liability claims.

In the absence of further specification by the E-Commerce Directive on acts of on-line policing to be performed in order to benefit from indirect liability exemptions, the need to accommodate varying national laws and values throughout the EU gives ISPs and the developers of infrastructure technology a high incentive to adopt strict monitoring measures on a voluntary basis.

[565] See Strachan, 'The Internet of Tomorrow', op. cit., p. 132; see Article 15 of the E-Commerce Directive.

The fact that the legal treatment of ISPs activities mainly depends on national law is upheld by the wording of Recital 48 of the E-Commerce Directive. This Recital provides that the Directive:

"[D]oes not affect the possibility for Member States of requiring service providers, who host information provided by recipients of their service, to apply duties of care, which can reasonably be expected from them and which are specified by national law, in order to detect and prevent certain types of illegal activities."

This provision makes it clear that, beyond the scope of the specific liability exemptions created by the E-Commerce Directive with the objective of harmonising and identifying certain duties for the providers of hosting and caching activities, it is incumbent upon national law to implement other duties of due care for the Internet.

Another factor which shows that the specification of such duties is still a matter of national law is given by the transposition of the Directive's liability exemptions into the law of the Member States, which resulted in country-specific law. For instance, whereas the E-Commerce Act in Spain, in contrast to the E-Commerce Directive, protects information location tools (such as search engines, content aggregators, *etc*) from liability, French law protects hosting intermediaries without exempting caching or access providers.[566] Hence, to escape indirect liability, ISPs have a strong incentive to develop technologies which implement monitoring measures and ensure compliance with the various national laws of the EU.

6.5.3.2. Duties of care upon ISPs and network operators

Recent decisions by national courts have enforced duties of care in the digitally networked environment by requiring ISPs to carry out their activities while preserving certain cultural and economic values, and while trying to prevent infringement of rights of third parties wherever possible.

Out of the field of copyright, the most publicised decisions concerned the case brought by the Union of Jewish Students of France ("UEJF") and the League Against Racism and Anti-Semitism ("LICRA") against Yahoo! Inc.[567]

Yahoo established an auction website where Internet users could purchase Nazi memorabilia, the sale of which was deemed to be illegal under the French Penal Code. Relying on expert reports, the Paris *Tribunal de Grande Instance* ascertained that Yahoo was able to screen the vast majority of its users as well as the illegal content by using technology that identified the geographical origin of users (disclosed by users' Internet Protocol addresses) and by soliciting the good faith declarations of their nationality. On this assumption, the Paris Court compelled Yahoo to take all possible measures to dissuade and block French access to web pages stored on Yahoo's US-based servers. Another decision delivered in June

[566] See Strachan, 'The Internet of Tomorrow', op. cit., p. 130.

[567] See *UEJF et Licra c/ Yahoo! Inc. et Yahoo France*, Tribunal de Grande Instance de Paris, Ordonnance de référé, 22 May 2000, available at: http://www.juriscom.net.

2005 again by the Paris *Tribunal de Grande Instance*,[568] ordered several Internet access providers, including AOL France, France Télécom, Tiscali Accès, to block access from the French territory to a website which published materials on Holocaust revisionism.[569]

In the specific field of on-line copyright liability, recent decisions in Belgium and Denmark have enforced the principle of due care against, respectively, an Internet access provider (Tiscali Accès) and a network operator (TDC Solutions) both of which provide file transfer protocol (FTP) servers.[570] In the former case, upon the initiative of the Belgian copyright collecting society (SABAM), the Bruxelles *Tribunal de Première Instance* ordered Tiscali Accès to take appropriate measures against copyright infringements which occurred on its network by means of peer-to-peer programmes.[571] Even if Tiscali was a mere network provider and did not have knowledge of what materials were exchanged by its subscribers using file-sharing technologies, the Bruxelles Court found that Tiscali held the position of an intermediary whose services were used to infringe copyright. As a result, the court held that Tiscali could be compelled, on the grounds of Article 8(3) of the InfoSoc Directive, to implement technical measures, in other words, filtering systems, to forbid its subscribers from exchanging unauthorised files on its network.

In the latter case, the Danish Supreme Court upheld an injunction by the Danish Eastern High Court against the network provider TDC Solutions, which was ordered to monitor and censor transmissions to and from two FTP servers with a view to preventing the transmission of unauthorised copyrighted works.[572] The Danish Supreme Court acknowledged that the owners of the two FTP servers committed extensive copyright infringements by making copyrighted works available to the general public on the servers without the permission of the rightholders.[573] The Supreme Court's order considered that TDC transmission through its FTP servers implied an unlawful temporary reproduction of copyrighted materials that constituted copyright infringement even if the reproduction came to TDC attention through the copyright owners enquiry. The Court found that FTP-enabled reproduction of copyrighted materials on the TDC network was unlawful even if such reproduction was transient and incidental, in a way that its sole pur-

---

568 See *UEJF, SOS Racisme, J'Accuse, MRAP* c. *OLM, Planet.com, France Télécom, Free, AOL France*, Tribunal de Grande Instance de Paris, Ordonnance de référé, 13 June 2005, http://www.juriscom.net.

569 See Association des Anciens Amateurs de Récits de Guerre et d'Holocauste, at: http//www.vho.org/aaargh.

570 An FTP server is a piece of software installed on the user's computer which makes a user-defined selection of data stored on the computer available to other Internet users, who can thus download and upload files from and to the FTP server.

571 See Tribunal Première Instance Bruxelles, 26 November 2004, *SABAM* c. *Tiscali*, http://www.juriscom.net, 26 November 2004.

572 See Danish Supreme Court, Order of Friday, 10 February, 2006, *TDC Totallsninger A/S* v. *IFPI Danmark, KODA, Nordisk Copyright Bureau, Danish Musicians' Union, Danish Artists' Union*, Case no. 49/2005 (2nd division), Transcript of the Court Register of the Appeals and Objections Committee.

573 See *TDC Totallsninger A/S* v. *IFPI Danmark*, p. 10.

pose was to enable the transmission of information on the network. In the Danish Supreme Court's view, the exemption of temporary copying from the copyright exclusivity provided by Section 11(a) of the Danish Copyright Act and Article 5(1) of the InfoSoc Directive did not apply because the unauthorised reproduction was not made on the basis of a legal original of the copyrighted work, as required by Section 11(3) of the Act.[574] The Supreme Court concluded that it was possible for TDC to comply with the preliminary injunction by either shutting down the Internet connection to the FTP servers, or to the subscribers in question, as provided in TDC's subscription terms for the case of infringement of third party copyright by the subscriber.

This case law shows that some national courts have found that on-line intermediaries and network operators hold a special responsibility, which stems from the assumption that ISPs and network providers are best placed to police unlawful activities on the Internet. In the above-mentioned cases, this responsibility was deemed to create a broad and positive obligation to exercise due care even in cases where the ISP or the network provider did not run a service or had not devised a technology infrastructure which was capable, as such, of monitoring and stopping unlawful conduct. The creation of this duty was also a consequence of the non-applicability of the liability exemptions created by the E-Commerce Directive and by the InfoSoc Directive, which benefited providers of hosting, caching and transitory communication services. Unlike the safe harbours provisions of Section 512 of the U.S. Copyright Act, which requires the copyright owner to notify the ISP about activities which infringe copyright, the corresponding EU exemptions do not specify who bears the duty to monitor and report infringements, or what elements this notification must contain. This circumstance implies that, under EU law, the service or network provider that wishes to avoid copyright liability must locate itself and expeditiously remove infringing materials.[575] In both non-copyright and copyright cases, the referred decisions compelled service and network operators to take structural remedies which altered the way in which their technologies worked. At the same time, these remedies did not guarantee the effective enforcement of the decisions. Indeed, it was highly unclear to what extent, and by what technical measures, network providers could effectively put unlawful behaviour to an end. From a technical point of view, it was uncertain whether the administrator of the Yahoo auction website or the France-based Internet access providers could effectively develop a means of blocking access to webpages publishing and offering illegal information from computers located in France. It was also unclear whether Tiscali Accès' and TDC Solutions' networks could be capable of developing filtering tools to forbid the users of their networks and of their FTP servers from exchanging unauthorised copyrighted materials. These decisions resulted in orders which had the consequence of compelling technology providers

574 In other words, the Danish Supreme Court concluded that the transient reproduction at issue would not qualify for the exemption created under Article 5(1)(b) of the InfoSoc Directive since the FTP-enabled reproduction did not allow lawful use of the copyrighted works: see §3.3.3.3., *see supra*.

575 See Strachan, 'The Internet of Tomorrow', op. cit., p. 132.

to modify their services and products under the courts' guidance in order to render communication technologies incapable of unlawful uses. This conclusion shows that, in the national case law, the objective of protecting copyright on the Internet seems to take priority over the possible liability exemption of information carriers, such as service and network providers, which are increasingly required to redesign or modify their communication technologies in the light of copyright enforcement measures.

6.5.3.3. Duties of care upon peer-to-peer software providers

Considering that the duty to exercise due care in respect of copyrighted digital works on the Internet has the potential to condition the design of communication technology, this duty may place pervasive restrictions upon the architecture of peer-to-peer software, regardless of whether this software operates in a completely decentralised way (that is, with no material contribution from the software deviser to the direct infringer). The conclusion that indirect liability may arise from the mere supplying of the tools by which one may infringe copyright is upheld by the wording of the InfoSoc Directive.

Recital 59 of this Directive makes it clear that the right-holder's possibility of applying for an injunction against an intermediary who transmits a third party infringement of a protected work

"[S]hould be available even where the acts carried out by the intermediary are exempted under Article 5."

This provision makes it clear that, even if an intermediary engages in acts of transitory communication which are exempted from copyright liability under Article 5(1) of the InfoSoc Directive, the intermediary may very well be subject to an injunction based on Article 8(3) of the same Directive in so far as its services are used to infringe copyright. Not only does this specification uphold the above-mentioned national courts' findings that ISPs and network providers bear a positive duty of due care even when they have no knowledge of infringing activities and should thereby seek such knowledge by themselves. It also proves that provider liability and its subjection to requests of injunctive relief by copyright owners does not stem solely from the material contribution to infringements under EU law. This subjection also depends on the factual assumption that the provider is best placed to bring such infringements to an end, as acknowledged by the wording of Recital 59.[576]

In my view, national courts in the European Union have no reason for not applying this conclusion to the case of peer-to-peer software design and supply. Even if the devisers of such technology do not transmit infringing materials and do not materially contribute to direct infringements (for instance, by disclosing in-

576 Recital 59 of the InfoSoc Directive states: "In the digital environment, in particular, the services of intermediaries may increasingly be used by third parties for infringing activities. *In many cases such intermediaries are best placed to bring such infringing activities to an end* [...]" (emphasis added).

formation about the location of such materials), they are, nevertheless, in the best position to protect third parties' copyright from infringement when designing file-sharing technology. This means that copyright owners may successfully seek to compel the file-sharing technology deviser to modify its software in order to reduce or eliminate infringements.

In the above-mentioned *Kazaa* case in the Netherlands, the Dutch Supreme Court left the question of whether the fact of providing users with a means of infringing copyright could be held unlawful in ways other than as copyright infringement unanswered. This conclusion would probably have been different if the plaintiffs of the *Kazaa* case had provided evidence of wilful or culpable intent by the software provider.[577] At the end of the day, while doing nothing to stop copyright infringements occurring by means of its technology, Kazaa was profiting from advertising income in the same way as Grokster, which was found liable under the U.S. theory of inducement. The Advocate General of the Dutch Supreme Court, in the absence of guidance on contributory infringement under the 1912 Dutch Copyright Act, raised the question of whether Kazaa's indirect liability could arise from a breach of an unwritten rule of tort law which required the maker and the supplier of file-sharing technology to exercise due care in order to prevent copyright infringement wherever possible.[578] In line with the position expressed above, the Advocate General's opinion concluded that such an unwritten duty of care in the digitally networked environment had already been found in a line of Dutch case law which showed that an ISP acts unlawfully if it is aware of infringing or otherwise illegal content made available to the public through its servers, but does nothing to intervene.[579]

With regard to the enforcement of an "alternative design" obligation upon peer-to-peer software providers, an injunctive relief to compel Kazaa to modify its software was sought as a less restrictive alternative to an order to refrain from offering and distributing software which enabled copyright infringement. According to the Dutch Supreme Court, upholding this contention would have meant that future versions of the Kazaa software could be modified under the copyright owners' guidance in order to render the software incapable of infringing use.[580]

Without resulting in such an unrealistic (and undesirable) obligation, the judicial implementation of the above duty of care may, in my view, be probably understood as compelling the software deviser to shape peer-to-peer technology in a way which makes it feasible for the file-sharing network to filter unauthorised copyrighted works from authorised and other out-of-copyright materials. This technological mandate was implemented in a decision taken in September 2005 by the Federal Court of Australia against the supplier of the Kazaa software (Sharman

---

577 The possibility of implementing the notions of wilful or culpable intent to the case of peer-to-peer software providers in civil law jurisdictions was emphasised by Strowel, 'Le P2P: un problème pressant en attente d'une réponse législative?', (17) *Propriétés intellectuelles*, October 2005, p. 428, at p. 431.

578 See Vollebregt, 'An analysis of the Kazaa case', op. cit., p. 16.

579 *Ibidem*.

580 Vollebregt, 'An analysis of the Kazaa case', op. cit., p. 14.

Networks).[581] On the grounds of Section 101 of the 1968 Australian Copyright Act, which outlaws the conduct of authorising any act comprised in the copyright (*i.e.*, including on-line dissemination of copyrighted files),[582] the Australian court ordered Sharman Networks to refrain from authorising (*i.e.*, enabling) unlawful dissemination by installing filtering systems that were agreed upon by the plaintiffs and by the court onto the Kazaa software. This measure was somehow suggested by the circumstance that the Kazaa system had already developed two different types of file-sharing models. While the first system was the common file-sharing system which enabled the dissemination of all files, regardless of whether they were copyright-protected or not, the second system was based on the so-called Altnet technology, which was capable of detecting authorised and digitally-rights-managed files identified by a golden icon, which was used in contrast to the blue icon of indiscriminate files. On the aforementioned grounds, it seems persuasive to conclude that courts enforcing EU copyright law are entitled to impose this kind of technological restriction on peer-to-peer software providers in so far as this technology develops, and a duty to prevent copyright infringement is internalised by the technology.

6.5.4. Findings from EU law and from the national case law

After analysing the relevant EU legal framework and having briefly reviewed some national case law on indirect liability of communication technology providers, which included peer-to-peer software providers, it is worth drawing the following conclusions.

Using the example provided by the *Kazaa* case in Netherlands, it has been emphasised that the operation of completely decentralised peer-to-peer software neither implies direct nor indirect copyright infringement from the software provider. In a few European jurisdictions, a question of indirect liability arose with regard to the functioning of specific peer-to-peer software (BitTorrent) which required users to run web-servers in order to provide uploading information and search facilities for the transmitted materials. It was against certain user-run websites which communicated unauthorised copyrighted materials (and not against the software provider itself) that national courts issued shut-down injunctions based upon Article 8(3) of the InfoSoc Directive. Instead, with regard to software providers, it has been found that the existence of an obligation which compels alternative designs

581 See *Universal Music Australia Pty Ltd* v. *Sharman License Holdings Ltd*, [2005] Federal Court of Australia 1242 (5 September 2005). For a review of this decision, see Lucas, 'Responsabilité des éditeurs de logiciels permettant des échanges de pair à pair', (17) *Propriétés intellectuelles*, October 2005, p. 444.

582 The 1968 Australian Copyright Act - Sect 101 (*Infringement by doing acts comprised in copyright*) provides as follows: "(1) Subject to this Act, a copyright subsisting by virtue of this Part is infringed by a person who, not being the owner of the copyright, and without the licence of the owner of the copyright, does in Australia, or authorizes the doing in Australia of, any act comprised in the copyright."

of the peer-to-peer technology used to infringe copyright stems from two legal bases.

On the one hand, it has been highlighted that an obligation to make peer-to-peer technology more accountable may come from the implementation of judicial measures which enable the disclosure of the identities of counterfeiters and infringers under civil and criminal proceedings aimed at enforcing copyright on the Internet.

Also, it must be pointed out that, despite the copyright liability exemptions provided by the E-Commerce Directive, the most relevant case law before national courts has relied upon a general principle of due care to require providers of communication technology to modify the architecture of their services and devices in order to monitor and detect copyright infringement. As a result, notwithstanding the opposite conclusion of the Dutch Supreme Court in the *Kazaa* case, peer-to-peer software providers are likely to become subject to technological mandates which ensure that this technology can filter and exclude unauthorised copyrighted works from file-sharing activities.

6.6. Summary

The first section of this chapter has drawn upon U.S. and European case law to see whether the U.S. fair use defence and the private copying exception envisaged by the EU InfoSoc Directive could be implemented to cover and excuse the file-sharing of unauthorised copyrighted works by users of peer-to-peer software. The analysis has shown that both the U.S. fair use defence and the European-continental private use exception were found not to be applicable to this new legal situation. It has been emphasised that, under both the U.S. and the EU copyright systems, the factor that counted most in preventing file-sharing from being exempted from the exclusivity of copyright was the economic impact of this practice on the markets for copyrighted works.

In the United States, the potentially disruptive effects of unauthorised file-sharing on the emerging markets for copyrighted works on the Internet were understood to outlaw this practice under the fourth factor of the fair use doctrine, which required courts to consider the effect of unauthorised file-sharing upon the market in the determination of fair use. In the European Union, instead, the relevant case law was developed mainly in France, where the courts have mainly failed to review file-sharing cases in the light of the transposition of the so-called three-step test under EU law.

In particular, when maintaining that acts of mere downloading could be excused under the shield of private use - as opposite to acts of uploading, which were deemed unlawful in any form – the reviewed French judgments erred in enforcing the second and third steps of the test transposed into EU law by Article 5(5) of the InfoSoc Directive. It has been considered that the same courts failed to consider carefully that the practice of downloading unauthorised works from peer-to-peer networks was clearly in conflict with the normal exploitation of the work and implied an unreasonable prejudice to the interest of the right-holder on the assumption that, in contrast with the prescription of Article 5(2)(b) of the InfoSoc Directive, no fair compensation was provided under the form of levies on the technical equipment which is normally used by file-sharers to download and store copyrighted works (*i.e.*, personal computers).

The second section of this chapter has commented upon U.S. and European decisions in reviewing cases of liability of peer-to-peer software providers with the view to making it clear whether such prominent dual-use communication technology could - to the great detriment of Internet users - be the subject of restrictions due to on-line copyright enforcement policies. Unlike the conclusion reached on the issue of end-user liability, the conclusion regarding software provider liability has turned out to vary from the U.S. to the EU in terms of liability requirements.

In the U.S. copyright system, the settlement of the *Grokster* case by the U.S. Supreme Court on the grounds of the so-called inducement theory has left the so-called *Sony* doctrine as it stood. Under this doctrine, the supplier of dual-use copying equipment cannot be held liable for an indirect copyright infringement if it is shown that the technology is capable of substantial non-infringing uses and is effectively used in that way, as in the case of Grokster. According to the relevant U.S. case law, indirect liability by the peer-to-peer software provider can be sought only if the provider is shown to monitor (or having the possibility of monitoring) the exchange of the infringing materials occurring on the network created by its software, or if the provider's activity shows a culpable intent by actively inducing direct infringement and/or by benefiting commercially from the infringing activities.

With regard to the EU copyright system, it has been concluded that the enforcement of the general principle of due care in the digital environment creates a duty to make peer-to-peer technology more accountable in order to enable the detection of on-line copyright infringements. The fact that peer-to-peer technology may prove not to infringe copyright - either directly or indirectly - does not necessarily exempt the technology provider from liability. Two arguments suggest that the operation of peer-to-peer technology is likely to be restricted in the EU by injunctions which may compel the adoption of copyright-protecting architecture. The first is given by the disclosure obligation created under Article 8 of the IPRs Enforcement Directive upon any person who is found to provide services used in infringing activities on a commercial scale. It has been emphasised that peer-to-peer software providers are very likely to fall within this category of persons under civil and criminal proceedings and investigations aimed at shedding light on the origin and distribution networks of infringing goods. The second relies upon the above-mentioned duty of care in the digital environment, which was recently interpreted and implemented by a few national courts in cases of indirect liability regarding ISPs and network providers.

In the conclusion of this chapter, it is worth highlighting why on-line copyright enforcement raises an unsolved issue from the Internet user's perspective. In the U.S., it seems clear that peer-to-peer software, as such, cannot be subject to technological restrictions if it enables non-infringing uses, and it is effectively used in that way (as demonstrated by the *Grokster* case). In the European Union, instead, in the absence of a single copyright liability criterion comparable to the U.S. *Sony* doctrine for the case of dual-use technology, peer-to-peer software may be legally restricted regardless of whether this technology is increasingly used to disseminate out-of-copyright works, copyrighted works published under licences such as Creative Commons and free information on the Internet. This conclusion shows that, in the law of the European Union and in the national case law, the objective of copyright protection in the digital environment seems to take preference over that of preserving user-to-user communication of free-to-disseminate materials. Chapter 8 of this book will point out that this preference for copyright protection needs to be reconciled, both at national and at Community levels, with the constitutional protection of freedom of speech and communication on the Internet.

7. Freedom of use *vs.* DRM Technology

7.1. Introduction

The case study analysed in the last chapter showed that the digital environment established by the Internet and, in particular, by peer-to-peer networks represents a significant threat to providers of copyrighted information. This chapter will analyse an opposite, new case study in which digital technologies such as DRM systems and "Trusted Computing" (hereinafter "TC") platforms promise to eliminate threats to all unauthorised copying and infringing uses of digital works.

An Appendix to this book provides an overview of the type of protection that these technologies of control and management enable in respect of digital media.[583] The overview also shows the current state of the art concerning today's markets for these technologies and their effective implementation on media, software and hardware. Here, it is sufficient to recall that DRM is an advanced compound of technologies that is capable of controlling access to and use of digital works, and whose logic of perfect control over digitally-protected content may soon be extended to and implemented into end-user personal computers by means of "trusted" systems.

The chapter points out that, while affording unlimited legal protection to DRM technology, EU law risks irreparably undermining the survival of the rights of use of digital works provided under national copyright laws. The first part of the chapter locates DRM technology into the legal framework created by the InfoSoc Directive and examines the European Commission's views and objectives in respect of this technology. The second part analyses the specific problems that DRM technology raises in respect of free uses: the possible lack of interoperability between different DRM systems, which hinders the portability of digitally works from one medium to another, the restriction of private copying, and, finally, the technical frustration of lawful transformative uses.

---

583 See Appendix I, see *infra*.

7.2. DRM technology under EU law

7.2.1. Legal basis for the protection of DRM technology

As pointed out when analysing Articles 6 and 7 of the InfoSoc Directive,[584] the rationale of so-called anti-circumvention law is to protect technological tools that are capable of re-establishing the excludability of copyrighted digital works and making electronic publishing safer and economically viable.

DRM technology components fall either under the definition of "effective technological measures" provided by Article 6(3) of the Directive, or under the notion of "rights management information" of Article 7(2).

The definition contained in Article 6(3) covers DRM technology in so far as it refers to:

> "any technology, device or component that, in the normal course of its operation, is designed to prevent or restrict acts, in respect of works or other subject-matter, which are not authorised by the rightholder of any copyright or any right related to copyright[…]".

This provision makes it clear that a technological measure must be deemed "effective" where the use of a protected work is controlled:

> "through application of an access control or protection process, such as encryption, scrambling or other transformation of the work or other subject-matter or a copy control mechanism, which achieves the protection objective."

Article 7(2) defines rights management information as:

> "any information provided by rightholders which identifies the work […] the author or any other rightholder, or information about the terms and conditions of use of the work or other subject-matter, and any numbers or codes that represent such information."

The distinct targets of these two provisions indicate that the compound of technologies that give shape to today's DRM systems is not eligible for protection as such (*i.e.*, as a single technology). Instead, anti-circumvention protection is afforded to each DRM component or device in accordance with the task that the component or device is intended to perform within the architecture of a certain system. For instance, components such as encryption technologies, audio and video encoding standards and communication protocols are protected under Article 6(3), given that they comprise measures which enable access control or the protection process by virtue of the encryption or transformation of the protected work, usage restrictions and codification of pieces of digital content by securing its transfer between trusted repositories. Technologies such as Rights Expression Languages (RELs), in contrast, consist of rights management information under the meaning of Article 7(2) because they provide a universal method of translating usage conditions of digital content into machine-readable languages that can de-

[584] See §3.4.1., see *supra*.

clare rights and permissions by the use of metadata attached to each protected object.[585]

7.2.2. From an *ex post* to an *ex ante* determination of fairness

The distinct targets of Articles 6 and 7 of the InfoSoc Directive do not change the substance of the (almost identical) circumvention prohibitions that these provisions created. Regardless of whether acts of circumvention turn out to affect technological measures rather than systems of rights management information, the referred prohibitions created an independent tort of unauthorised circumvention to which, paraphrasing the words that David Nimmer used in respect of §1201(a) of the U.S. Copyright Act, the *ex post* logic and review of copyright exceptions is simply inapplicable.[586]

Articles 6 and 7 imply that the circumvention of a DRM device is unlawful, irrespectively of whether it is carried out for the purpose of infringing copyright. In open violation of Article 11 of the 1996 WIPO Copyright Treaty, these provisions failed to immunise copyright exceptions (*i.e.*, "acts permitted by law") from the operation of access- and copy-control mechanisms.[587] Consequently, the InfoSoc Directive established an unprecedented access right in respect of copyrighted works protected and administered by virtue of DRM systems. The subsequent *ex ante* foreclosure of access to copyrighted information enabled by these technologies outlaws both the conduct of the single user who circumvents the technology for the purpose of engaging in a free use, and the technology provider who offers tools that enable decryption, circumvention, alteration or the removal of DRM components and related information.

It is thereby evident that, thanks to this *per se* protection granted to technical measures such as DRM systems, EU law inevitably inverts the way in which the lawful character of a certain use of a DRM-protected work is reviewed and ascertained. As argued elsewhere, this inversion implies a necessary privatisation of the process of reviewing usage fairness.[588] Whereas in a DRM-free environment, this process takes place *after* the supposedly lawful use, the appreciation of which is left to the judge, in a world characterised by DRM and "trusted platform" protection, the determination of fairness foregoes the use of the work, with the consequence that the *ex ante* identification of usage rights is left in the private hands of DRM technology designers and users. For statutory usage rights to be effectively enforced in spite of DRM technologies, the only effective solution would be that

---

585 An overview of the concept and function of Rights Expression Languages (RELs) is provided in Appendix I, §B, see *infra*.

586 See Nimmer, 'A Riff on Fair Use in the Digital Millennium Copyright Act', (148) University of Pennsylvania Law Review 2000, p. 673, at p. 731.

587 See §3.4., see *supra*.

588 See Mazziotti,'Utilisations libres des oeuvres protégées dans le contexte numérique européen: d'une regulation publique à une regulation privée', (54) *Petites Affiches* 2005, Numéro Spécial (*Le clivage acteurs publics/acteurs privés à la lumière du droit européen* – Université Paris X-Nanterre, 29 June 2004), p. 12.

of compelling the technical restriction of access- and copy- control mechanisms by law, so that these measures may accommodate uses that copyright law wishes to remain free from copyright holder control.

7.2.3. DRM and the EU ambiguous system of copyright exceptions

Given that the functioning of DRM and other technological measures relies on the *ex ante* foreclosure of access to the digitally-protected work, a basic problem arises with regard to the accommodation of free uses that should be technically enabled irrespectively of access foreclosure and without copyright owner consent. Effective freedom of use should not tolerate any form of technical or legal control of access to and use of the work.

In the context of the InfoSoc Directive, the technical accommodation of free uses is hindered by the ambiguous model of copyright exceptions set out by the Directive. The Directive sought a trade-off between the strict approach to copyright exceptions typical of the French and other *droit d'auteur* systems and the open-ended formulation of common law systems. Whereas systems of narrow exceptions give shape to each exception at the legislative layer by means of an *ex ante* exemption of a certain class of uses from the copyright scope, under systems such as the U.S. fair use doctrine and the UK fair dealing doctrine, the determination of fairness of unauthorised uses essentially consists of an *ex post* appreciation of the judge.[589]

---

[589] Both the U.S. fair use and the UK fair dealing doctrines rest mainly upon a case-by-case analysis. Under U.S. law, even if the review of fair use is firmly guided now by Section 107 of the Copyright Act, as amended by the codification of 1976, it still falls to judges to recognise that the exemption from the copyright scope of certain valuable uses can be understood as "stimulating productive thought and public instruction without excessively diminishing the incentives for creativity [...]": see Leval, 'Toward a Fair Use Standard', in Merges and Ginsburg (eds), *Foundations of Intellectual Property*, Foundation Press, New York 2004, p. 387, at p. 388. The key role of the judge in the determination of fairness, notwithstanding the legislative codification, was pointed out by the U.S. Supreme Court in *Sony Corporation of America v. Universal City Studios*, Inc., cit., at pp. 475-476 ('Although courts have constructed lists of factors to be considered in determining whether a particular use is fair, no fixed criteria have emerged by which determination can be made. Nor did Congress provide definitive rules when it codified the fair use doctrine in the 1976 Act; it simply incorporated a list of factors "to be considered" [...]'). The UK concept of fair dealing is premised upon statutory provisions which confer certain performing rights to classes of users for purposes of research or private study, reporting current events and criticism or review: see the UK Copyright Designs and Patents Act 1988, Sections 29, and 30 (1) and (2). Such concept, thus, is not general and central as the U.S. fair use; it is rather limited to the very definition of the various forms of rights that it confers. Nonetheless, fair dealing looks like fair use in that it is understood in the case law as leaving to judges' fairness a wide room for an *ex post* qualitative assessment of all the circumstances characterising a certain use, which makes such analysis mainly "a matter of degree": see Cornish and

In the InfoSoc Directive, these two models are somehow blurred. At first sight, while looking at the catalogue of exceptions listed in the first part of Article 5, one may be persuaded that the Directive opted for the *droit d'auteur* model of narrow, pre-defined copyright exceptions. However, this conclusion is contradicted by the introduction of the three-step test into EU law by virtue of Article 5(5). As argued above,[590] the enforcement of this test, in the same way as the application of the U.S. fair use doctrine and the UK fair dealing doctrine, is based upon an open-ended formulation of principles that inevitably strengthens the role of the judge in the *ex post* review of cases that may fall within the catalogue of uses provided under Article 5.

In principle, a system of pre-defined narrow exceptions would better accommodate the *ex ante* logic of DRM technology protection. To accommodate free uses, the scope of the protection enabled by this technology needs to be restricted at the time of programming the technology, when several usage rights that are pre-identified (and eventually compelled by law) can be translated into the specific digital rights language by a certain DRM programme. Unfortunately, the wording of the InfoSoc Directive does not allow (or even facilitate) this balanced solution, in consideration of the fact that DRM technology turns out not to be bound to comply with or to accommodate the specific uses that Article 5 spells out. Moreover, with regard to the *ex post* enforcement of the three-step test, the unlimited anti-circumvention protection granted under Articles 6 and 7 of the Directive to DRM-enabled restrictions of access to and use of copyrighted information has the consequence of eliminating or dramatically reducing the opportunities of *ex post* judicial review anyway. Under today's EU anti-circumvention laws, the user defeating a DRM measure in order to engage in acts permitted by law (or even preserved by law) would incur copyright liability anyway. Indeed, whereas the intervention of the judge after an act of circumvention may recognise the lawful character of the user's conduct on its merits under Article 5 of the InfoSoc Directive, it may *not* exempt the user from circumvention liability under Article 6(1) because this provision conceives circumvention as a totally independent tort.[591]

7.2.4. Consequences of the condition of *legal access* to DRM-protected works

Under both the InfoSoc Directive and Section 1201 of the U.S. Copyright Act, the acts of circumvention of DRM technology measures are to be considered *per se* unlawful. Consequently, each act of circumvention inevitably draws liability regardless of whether the character of the use - following access to the protected work - is lawful or not. This situation occurs because today's anti-circumvention law is unrelated to copyright infringement, so that only *ex ante* exemptions can ef-

Llewelyn, *Intellectual Property: Patents, Copyright, Trade Marks and Allied Rights*, op. cit., pp. 440-44.

590 See §4.2., see *supra*.

591 See §3.4.1. and §3.4.2., see *supra*.

fectively immunise certain classes of uses from access restrictions. This technique was adopted by Section 1201 of the U.S. Copyright Act (as amended by the 1998 DMCA), which abandoned the open-ended logic of the fair use doctrine while exempting a number of very specific categories of acts from circumvention bans. These exemptions concern certain acts performed by non-profit libraries, archives and educational institutions and other acts of circumvention performed for purposes of law enforcement, intelligence and other government activities, reverse engineering, encryption research, exceptions regarding minors, and security testing.[592]

In contrast, the InfoSoc Directive shaped its circumvention bans as virtually unlimited, considering that unauthorised access turns out to be foreclosed even in respect of the few end-user acts whose exercise is ultimately preserved by national administrative and judicial enforcement proceedings under which the user is entitled to claim the compulsory disclosure and supply of the technical means to carry out those acts effectively.[593] The unlimited character of EU anti-circumvention laws has the unfortunate consequence that the copyright owner who controls access over his or her works by means of effective technical measures (such as those that are commonly integrated into DRM systems) is *de facto* given the power to authorise access in exchange for the user's binding promise not to undertake acts that the first part of Article 6(4) intends to guarantee notwithstanding the legal protection of technical measures.[594]

As far as the suitability of this kind of DRM protection is concerned, Dusollier persuasively argued that the requirement of legal (*i.e.*, authorised) access to the protected work may be a reasonable, supplementary condition in respect of the sole exception of private copying, and not of other exceptions such as quotation and parody.[595] According to this author, the supplementary condition of legal access to the work may be justified in respect of copying for personal use where this condition of exercise is intended to restrict the scope of this exception in accordance with the restrictive criteria of the three-step test.[596] Under the test, unauthorised copying is to be allowed in so far as this use does not conflict with a normal exploitation of the work (*i.e.*, the second step) and does not deprive the copyright

---

592 See U.S. Code, Title 17, §1201, letters from (d) to (k). For an overview of these exemptions see Dusollier, *Droit d'auteur et protection des oeuvres*, op. cit., pp. 196-201.

593 See §4.5.2., see *supra*. It is useful to remind that the copyright exceptions that Article 6(4) of the InfoSoc Directive wishes to be preserved to the benefit of the end-user are: reprographic copying, quotation for teaching or scientific research purposes, uses for the benefit of people with a disability and, optionally, private copying. Pursuant to the Article 6(4) provision, the administrative and judicial proceedings mentioned in the text can be undertaken on condition that copyright owners do not make available the technical means of benefiting from the "guaranteed" exceptions spontaneously or as a result of agreements with consumer associations: see §4.5.2., see *supra*.

594 See §4.3., see *supra*.

595 See Dusollier, 'L'utilisation légitime de l'œuvre:un nouveau sésame pour le bénéfice des exceptions en droit d'auteur?', *Communications – Commerce Electronique*, Nov. 2005, p. 17, at pp. 19-20.

596 *Ibidem*.

holder of considerable sources of revenues (*i.e.*, the third step). To meet these requirements, copyright legislators may consider it appropriate to allow copying on condition that the user makes his or her personal copy after having lawfully acquired a medium which embodies the protected work (*e.g.*, fully licensed Compact Discs, CD-Roms, music downloads, *etc*). While outlawing unauthorised copying undertaken by users other than the original (and authorised) copier, the condition at issue may assure that this use does not end up depriving the copyright owner of the opportunity of selling or licensing additional copies of the work.

It is noteworthy that Article 6(4) of the InfoSoc Directive, which establishes the requirement of legal access in respect of the few end-user acts to be preserved from the restrictive power of technical measures, does not extend this requirement to the private copying exception. When leaving Member States with the option to estimate freely as to whether to preserve private copying in the digital environment or not, the Directive posed no condition of exercise other than the absence of commercial ends by the copier (who must be a "natural person") and the payment of fair compensation in favour of the right-holder.[597] Consequently, Member States are free to restrict the scope of this exception by requiring the user to copy the work from a medium that he or she has legitimately accessed or acquired. The German Copyright Act addresses the problem of the legal treatment of peer-to-peer downloads under the private copying exception. It was pointed out above that Section 53 of this Act expressly outlaws the making of copies for personal use where copying derives from an "apparently unlawful" source.[598] In this way, from a theoretical perspective, German law has clearly restricted the application of this exception so that unauthorised downloads cannot be excused under the shield of personal use.

Instead, in respect of the few end-user acts preserved from technical restrictions, the requirement of legal access created by Article 6(4) proves to be overly restrictive and devoid of any plausible justification. The undesirability of this requirement stems mainly from the assumption that today's DRM technology has the potential to foreclose *de facto* unauthorised access to copyrighted information. It is unclear why the end-user wishing to carry out uses that Article 6(4) defines as "first-class", privileged acts (*e.g.*, quotation for teaching or scientific research purposes, uses for the benefit of a disabled person) should obtain the copyright owner's permission prior to accessing the work. In the Directive architecture, this unreasonable restriction risks frustrating irreparably the objective of the protection of the constitutional values which uphold the exemption of these uses from the copyright holder's power of control.

Along with the unfortunate circumstance that the InfoSoc Directive shaped copyright exceptions as freely overridable through contract, the restriction of legal access, which has become fully enforceable by means of access-control technology, has had the consequence of leaving DRM system devisers and copyright owners with a virtually unlimited power of control over the most important follow-on uses of copyrighted works. The judge may not be able to review *ex post*

---

[597] See Article 5(2)(b) of the InfoSoc Directive.
[598] See §6.3.2., see *supra*.

the legality of unauthorised uses because these uses could prove to be *a priori* entrenched. Consequently, judges are deprived of the possibility of applying the newly introduced three-step test analysis, and eventually excusing the user, every time that access to the work is effectively restricted by a DRM measure and the user is forced to circumvent this measure in order to carry out one of the abovementioned privileged uses.

7.3. The European Commission's view of DRM technology

7.3.1. The 2004 Communication on copyright management

Today's technological and legal settings regarding DRM and TC technologies openly seem to challenge the goals set out by the European Commission in its Communication to the Council and to the European Parliament of April 2004, concerning the complex issue of the management of copyright and related rights in the Internal Market.[599] On that occasion, the European Commission referred to DRM technologies by means of a comprehensive definition which addressed all the purposes enabled by these technologies:

"In the context of the discussions on the management of copyright and related rights in the new digital environment, digital rights management (DRM) has become a key issue [...] DRM systems can be used to clear rights, to secure payment, to trace behaviour and to enforce rights. DRM systems are, therefore, crucial for the development of new high volume, low transactional value business models, which include the pricing of access, usage, and the service itself, subscription models, reliance on advertising revenue, credit sales or billing schemes. DRM systems are a means to an end, and as such, clearly are an important, if not the most important, tool for rights management in the Internal Market of the new digital services [...]".

The Commission acknowledged that DRM technologies had become crucial for today's copyright management because they enable the translation of digital property rights into the technical languages of encryption and other algorithm-based techniques (*i.e.*, the so-called RELs). Nonetheless, the Communication testified its full awareness of the risk that DRM systems and trusted platforms might end up replacing copyright law by dictating the supremacy of what Lessig called "code", *i.e.*, a system of private governance in which the code of computer programmes (not the law) regulates which acts users are entitled to perform or not.[600] This risk was pointed out very clearly in the Commission's Communication:

[599] See Commission of the European Communities, Communication from the Commission to the Council, the European Parliament and the European Economic and Social Committee, *The Management of Copyright and Related Rights in the Internal Market*, COM/2004/0261 final, §1.2.5.

[600] See generally Lessig, *Code and Other Laws of Cyberspace*, op. cit.

"DRM systems are not in themselves an alternative to copyright policy in setting the parameters either in respect of copyright protection or the exceptions and limitations that are traditionally applied by the legislature."[601]

This statement shows that the European Commission correctly understands that DRM technologies are a mere means to pursue a certain end. Under this approch, the above-examined DRM technologies and trusted platforms cannot have the consequence of superseding the law, on the consideration that they are not, themselves, capable of ensuring the appropriate balance among the complex interests involved in copyright protection, be they the interests of authors, other rightholders, users, consumers, *etc*. By endorsing this view of DRM technologies, the Commission expressed the concern that, if DRM and trusted platform technologies were permitted to operate irrespectively of copyright law, they would have the potential of systematically disabling access to and use of any kind of data, including out-of-copyright and public domain materials that anyone is free to use and build upon. The Commission is thereby of the opinion that, even if DRM technologies provide tools of crucial importance for enforcing digital copyright law, it is still dependent upon the law to create access and usage rights and to guarantee their enforcement. Thus, from the Commission's perspective, DRM technologies should merely serve the purpose of clearing and enforcing state-backed rights by securing payment and protecting digital works in strict accordance with the property rights and the exceptions provided by copyright law.

7.3.2. The main Commission's objectives

To preserve the copyright balance, the Commission's Communication identified a number of policy goals that DRM technology should pursue in order to bring additional value to both sides of copyright owners and users of digital works. The main goals set out by the Commission are, respectively, the establishment of a global and interoperable DRM infrastructure which supports open standards of communication and encoding, and the enforcement of copyright exceptions.[602]

With regard to interoperability, today's increasing trend of propertisation of DRM foundational technologies threatens the achievement of this objective. The Commission's goal to foster consumer freedom of choice by allowing the unrestricted delivery and use of copyrighted works by means of various equipment, networks and services is likely to be foreclosed by the lack of interoperability that affects today's digital media, applications and hardware which support different DRM systems. The particular situation of Microsoft's DRM technology and of its future TC platform shows that the objective of a single DRM infrastructure might be achieved by letting Microsoft leverage its power of quasi-monopolist in the upstream market for personal computer operating systems into the downstream mar-

601 See Commission of the European Communities, *The Management of Copyright and Related Rights in the Internal Market*, cit., §1.2.5.

602 *Ibidem*.

ket for DRM solutions.[603] If Microsoft should successfully bundle its DRM technology with its operating systems and trusted platform, this technology may become almost ubiquitous and all media and hardware providers would have a strong incentive to make their products available only for Microsoft's technology. As a result, Microsoft would take all of the market for DRM technology and its Windows Rights Manager would become a (proprietary) *de facto* standard.

Notwithstanding the feasibility of this solution, it is my opinion that the Commission would find it unacceptable. Not only would this solution eliminate or greatly reduce competition among technology designers on the markets for DRM technologies, it would also restrict the choice of the best interoperable DRM infrastructure. Indeed, it is likely that the supremacy of Microsoft's DRM technologies will stem from Microsoft's integration of these technologies into its dominant complementary products (*i.e.*, operating systems, media players) and not from the market's choice of the best DRM system.

The subsequent, extraordinary concentration of power in the hands of one firm that owns property rights on this standard communication technology making digital media, software and hardware interoperable may also undermine other Commission's goals regarding DRM technology. It is worth recalling that one of these goals is the achievement of a wider user acceptance and trust in respect of DRM systems. It is reasonable to assume that this goal can be achieved only by ensuring the protection of end-user privacy and anonymity through a careful monitoring of the DRM technology components which have the potential to track end-user behaviour. In my view, the pervasive implementation of control and rights management technologies belonging to a single private company is likely to make the goal of fostering a culture of licensing copyrighted digital content (and counteracting the perception that the content that is available on the Internet is necessarily for free) more difficult to achieve. Indeed, the hypothesis of a possibly ubiquitous Microsoft-produced rights-management platform which allows either the platform deviser (*i.e.*, Microsoft) or the copyright owners to forbid unauthorised acts and to implement forms of remote (*i.e.*, on-line) control may have the consequence of convincing computer users to abandon Microsoft's platform and shift to a radically alternative, open platform (such as that based on the Linux open-source operating system).[604] More drastically, a non-negligible number of end-users may

---

603 An overview of the Microsoft case is provided in Appendix I, §D2, see *infra*. According to the investigation and economic analysis of the European Commission that led to the Decision of 24 March 2004, relating to a procedure under Article 82 of the EC Treaty, Case COMP/C-3/37.792 (Microsoft), available at: http://europa.eu.int/comm/competition/antitrust/cases/decisions/37792/en.pdf, Microsoft held a market share of 92.8% in the market for personal computer operating systems.

604 This scenario seems to have come true with the release of "Windows Vista" (*i.e.*, the most recent personal computer operating system marketed by Microsoft). Windows Vista includes a set of technologies (so-called "Protected Media Path") which creates a "trusted" platform that automatically recognises and enforces DRM-based protection applied to content. An overview of the case of Microsoft's integration between DRM and TC technologies is provided in Appendix I, §D2, see *infra*.

also decide to boycott the idea of having their content and data under the control of Microsoft's TC technology and use trusted machines, as it seems technically feasible, to create "blacknets" for sharing unauthorised materials with other users and to immunise their machines from external (and remote) interference and control. As Anderson warns, an increase of on-line copyright infringement might derive from the fact that trusted machines can be easily used by the other side of the content industry to establish peer-to-peer networks which are much more resistant to external attacks, since only genuine clients will be able to participate.[605]

With regard to the enforcement of copyright exceptions, the above-mentioned Communication by the Commission addressed this issue in respect of both the scope of protection of the copyrighted work and its time-limited duration.[606] The Commission seemed to take seriously the duty created by Article 12 of the InfoSoc Directive, which requires the Commission constantly to monitor whether free uses of the work are being adversely affected by DRM technology. As a result of this monitoring activity, the Commission may soon propose the adoption of legislative reforms which compel the providers and users of DRM technology to design and apply this technology in conformity with copyright exceptions. In the absence of such technological mandates, the enforcement of the virtually unlimited anti-circumvention protection granted to DRM technology under the InfoSoc Directive would uphold Samuelson's claim that "Digital *Rights* Management" is a pure misnomer for the acronym DRM, which would be better understood as "Digital *Restrictions* Management".[607]

7.4. Specific issues raised by DRM technology: Interoperability

The increasing implementation of DRM solutions on the fast-growing markets for copyrighted digital works has challenged the practical enforcement of statutory usage rights. This situation is reflected in a number of factors. The first of such factors is the possible lack of interoperability which occurs where digitally-protected content cannot interoperate with media players and hardware that do not support the same DRM system. The absence of interoperability obstructs the portability of digital content, with a subsequent, unfair restriction of the user's opportunities of access and personal use of lawfully acquired works.

---

605 See Anderson, ''Trusted Computing' and Competition Policy – Issues for Computing Professionals', 4(3) *Upgrade, The European Journal for the Informatics Professional* 2003, http://www.upgrade-cepis.org, p. 35, at p. 37.

606 See *The Management of Copyright and Related Rights in the Internal Market*, COM/2004/0261 final, §1.2.5.

607 See Samuelson, 'DRM {and, or, vs.} the Law', (46) *Communication of the ACM*, April 2003, No.4.

7.4.1. DRM systems as copyright-protected computer programmes

To introduce the problem of interoperability, it is indispensable to start from the assumption that DRM systems are, as such, computer programmes (*i.e.*, software) eligible for copyright protection when the standard of originality set out for this particular type of work is met. Due to the peculiar nature of software copyright protection, under which the so-called "source code" (*i.e.*, the human-readable code) of the computer programme remains undisclosed, the copyright holder over a certain DRM system is entitled to keep the programme code secret and, thus, to retain essential information enabling interoperability between products (such as content, media players, hardware, *etc*) which support that particular DRM system.[608] This technology is not only a tool that aims at regulating access to and management of copyrighted information, it is also a technical factor that can often restrict usage rights where the lawful acquirer of DRM-protected content wishes to use this content in conjunction with hardware and software that are *not* designed to interoperate with the specific DRM programme embedding the content. As a result, it may occur that a copyrighted digital work for which the user has lawfully obtained a bundle of usage rights is not capable of functioning on the user's machine or it cannot be read by the media player that the machine is equipped with. The DRM programme of iTunes Music Store is a useful example.

7.4.2. Copyright *vs.* interoperability: the case of Apple's DRM system

Both in the United States and in the European Union, competitors on the markets for music downloads have recently warned that Apple's proprietary DRM system (called "Fairplay") disabled interoperability between their music downloads and Apple's iPod portable player. In both jurisdictions where these claims arose (namely, the United States and France), Apple was given the opportunity to rely on its copyright on the mentioned DRM in order to deny legally the disclosure of secret interface information and specifications that were necessary to obtain interoperability between the competitors' downloaded music and the iPod portable music player.[609] In the U.S. dispute between Real Networks and Apple, the former company sought to obtain this interoperability information by reverse engineering the source code of the Fairplay computer programme.[610] In France, in contrast, the Virgin Mega on-line music provider claimed - before the French Competition Authority (*i.e.*, *Conseil de la Concurrence*) - that Apple's refusal to license its DRM

[608] A computer programme's source code is the collection of files that can be converted from human-readable (*i.e.*, "literary") form to an equivalent computer-executable form. The source code is either used to produce object code, or to be run by an interpreter. In the distribution of copyrighted computer programmes, as opposite to the distribution of free software, the human-readable (*i.e.*, source) code is kept secret by the proprietor, who makes available merely the computer-executable form.

[609] See Mazziotti, 'Did Apple's refusal to license [...]', op. cit., pp. 253-254.

[610] For more information, see 'Apple brings discord to Hymn', *The Register*, 13.01.2005, available at http://www.theregister.co.uk/2005/01/13/apple_breaks_hymn/.

system and other interoperability information constituted an abuse of Apple's dominant position on the market for music downloads.[611] This claim was based on the grounds that Apple's technology could be viewed as a so-called "essential facility" for the purpose of entering the market for iPod-compatible digital music.

In both the aforementioned cases the copyright of the Fairplay DRM system provided Apple with strong legal protection against the initiatives of its competitors. In the United States, Apple had the opportunity to warn Real Networks about the possibly infringing nature of the attempt to reverse engineer the source code of the copyright-protected DRM system under the anti-circumvention provisions of Section 1201(a) of the U.S. Copyright Act. This case showed that a claim of copyright infringement over secret DRM information has the potential to foreclose the downstream market for music downloads. Regardless of whether Real Networks originally violated Apple's copyright by "hacking" the code of its DRM programme, the dispute at issue was brought to an end when Apple upgraded the iTunes software in order to have the possibility of re-designing the architecture of Fairplay in such a way as to ensure that any interoperability attempts would give rise to liability under the circumvention prohibitions created by the DMCA in 1998. The ability to adopt this strategy successfully demonstrates very clearly that, even if the reverse engineering of DRM platform software is allowed for interoperability purposes (such as under Article 6 of the EC Software Directive or under Section 1201(F) of the U.S. Copyright Act), proprietary inputs of access technologies confer upon their holders the power to make such pro-competitive activity, which is often very costly and time-consuming, ineffective.

In France, the copyright over the Fairplay DRM programme provided Apple with an objective justification for legitimately refusing to licence its secret DRM information without incurring the costs of a compulsory licence for the protected programme.[612] The French Competition Authority rejected the claim that, while refusing to license information related to its DRM technology, Apple had abused its dominant position within the meaning of Article 82 of the EC Treaty.[613] The case analysis showed that Apple was dominant neither on the market for portable music players (the definition of which was found very difficult given the fast development of such devices) nor in the market for DRM technologies. Furthermore, the decision of the French Authority clarified that, even if Apple had been found to hold a dominant position on one of these markets, the situation of Apple's

---

611 See Conseil de la Concurrence, Décision N° 04-D-54 du 9 Novembre 2004 relative à des pratiques mises en œuvre par la société Apple Computer, Inc. dans les secteurs du téléchargement de musique sur Internet et des baladeurs numériques, available at: http://www.conseil-concurrence.fr/pdf/avis/04d54.pdf.

612 See Mazziotti, 'Did Apple's refusal to license [...]', op. cit., pp. 269-271.

613 Article 82 of the EC Treaty states: "Any abuse by one or more undertakings of a dominant position within the common market or in a substantial part of it shall be prohibited as incompatible with the common market in so far as it may affect trade between Member States. Such abuse may, in particular, consist in: [...] (b) limiting production, markets or technical development to the prejudice of consumers [...]".

DRM technology did not meet the so-called "indispensability test".[614] Under this test, the case law of the ECJ has allowed the compulsory licensing of intellectual property rights in so far as the exclusive right has the effect of eliminating competition from an *upstream* to a *downstream* market.[615] Hence, in the case of Apple, it was found that the refusal to license the copyright of the Fairplay DRM technology did not have the consequence of eliminating competition from the market for portable hardware to the market for music downloads. Moreover, the refusal to

---

614 The so-called "indispensability test" was relied on by the ECJ for the first time in *Radio Telefis Eireann (RTE) and Independent Television Publications Ltd (ITP)* v. *Commission*, Joined cases C-241/91 and C-242/91 P, 1995, ECR I-743 (hereinafter *Magill*) and recently re-stated in *IMS Health GmbH & Co. OHG* v. *NDC Health GmbH & Co. KG*, Case C-418/01(hereinafter *IMS Health*). The requirements of the test, as spelt out by the ECJ for the case of refusal to license an intellectual property right by an undertaking holding a dominant position, are the following ones: (i) the undertaking which requests the licence intends to offer a new product or service not offered by the owner of the exclusive right and for which there is a potential consumer demand; (ii) the refusal is not justified by objective considerations; (iii) the refusal is such as to eliminate competition on a market other than the one where the right owner holds the dominant position. The first case in which the ECJ case law considered specifically whether the simple refusal to license an intellectual property right could be abusive under Article 82 was *AB Volvo* v. *Erik Veng (UK) Ltd.*, C – 238/87, 1988 ECR-6211. In this case, the ECJ held that the mere unilateral refusal by a dominant firm to license its registered design right did not in itself constitute an abuse under Article 82. However, it added (see paragraph 9) that "the exercise of an exclusive right by the proprietor of a registered design in respect of car body panels may be prohibited by [Article 82] if it involves, on the part of an undertaking holding a dominant position, certain abusive conduct such as the arbitrary refusal to supply spare parts to independent repairers, the fixing of prices for spare parts at an unfair level or a decision no longer to produce spare parts for a particular model even though many cars of that model are still in circulation." This judgment thus laid the foundation for the above-mentioned indispensability test, which played a central role in the subsequent case law including *Magill* and *IMS Health*.

615 Although *Magill* did not hold that compulsory licensing of intellectual property rights in "exceptional circumstances" must be limited to "two-market" situations, eminent legal scholars have explained that extending the application of the essential facility doctrine to "one market" cases would discourage competition. See, for instance, Temple Lang, 'Anti-competitive abuses under Article 82 involving intellectual property rights', paper presented in the Eight Annual EU Competition Law and Policy Workshop, European University Institute, RSCAS (6-7 June 2003), *What is an Abuse of a Dominant Position?*, downloaded at: http://www.iue.it/RSCAS/Research/Competition/2003/200306COMP-TempleLangsIII.pdf, p. 18. "The essential facility principle applies in two-market situations because a competitor in the downstream market that gains control of a necessary input is not offering a better or a cheaper product in the downstream market, but only getting power to harm consumers in that market by shutting out its competitors. It is inherently pro-competitive, on the other hand, to allow competitors to develop or invent their own competitive advantages on the markets in which they are operating. If competitors were required to share competitive advantages that are important enough, competition would be discouraged, not promoted."

disclose information which enables interoperability was found to be justified by the objective consideration that such information was protected by copyright.[616]

The outcome of the French case shows that the implementation of compulsory licensing measures which ensure the effective disclosure of DRM interoperability information protected by copyright and trade secrets is given very little room under EU competition law and, in particular, under the indispensability test created by the case law of the ECJ. This means that the main objective of interoperability in respect of DRM technology can hardly be achieved by means of the exceptional remedy of compulsory licensing.

Therefore, the correct solution to achieve the European Commission's objective of full interoperability between digital content and DRM technology must be found elsewhere. New French copyright law - commented on in the following paragraph - shows that an alternative solution may be provided by the creation of an interoperability clause under the copyright system. In this respect, France established a statutory disclosure obligation upon DRM technology providers in respect of essential information that may avoid technical incompatibility between different DRM technologies.

7.4.3. The example of new pro-interoperability legislation in France

In consideration of situations of technical incompatibility such as that raised by Apple's DRM-protected hardware and media player in respect of a competitor's digital music, the French legislature took the issue of interoperability seriously when implementing the InfoSoc Directive in June 2006.[617] French law transposing the Directive introduced pro-interoperability legislation, which has no equivalents in other copyright legislation of EU Member States, into the Intellectual Property Code. Although the Directive dealt with interoperability merely in terms of encouragement,[618] the French Parliament found it convenient to develop - under the new Article L.331-5 of the Intellectual Property Code - a general disclosure obligation in respect of essential information which enables interoperability to the benefit of providers of technological protection measures such as DRM systems. Under this legislation, "essential information" for the purpose of interoperability is constituted by the technical documentation and the programming interfaces that are necessary to allow a measure of technological protection to have access to a work that is protected by another technical measure and to the joint information in electronic form, on condition that the originally established conditions of use of the work are respected by the party requesting the information.[619]

---

616 See Conseil de la Concurrence, Décision N° 04-D-54 du 9 Novembre 2004, cit., paragraphs 96-102.

617 See Law 2006-961 of 1 August 2006 on copyright and related rights in the information society, adopted text N.596, available at: http://www.assembleenationale.fr/12/ta/ta0596.asp.

618 See Recital 54 of the InfoSoc Directive.

619 See Article L.331-7, §2, of the French Intellectual Property Code, as amended by Article 14 of Law 2006-961 of 1 August 2006.

Under the French legislative framework, the objective of ensuring the free availability of essential information enabling interoperability is closely linked to the purpose of making the means from which to benefit from copyright exceptions effectively available. This provision may thereby be viewed as a broadened implementation of the safeguard mechanism that Article 6(4) of the InfoSoc Directive applies to an unreasonably narrow set of privileged exceptions and which, in contrast, the new French statute seems to apply to *most* exceptions.[620]

Although the imperative nature of the exceptions is not clearly stated in this law, two provisions of the new statute seem to provide for the immunisation of copyright exceptions from technical incapability to interoperate which affects digitally protected content, software and hardware. Firstly, Article L.331-5 provides that technical measures cannot oppose the free uses of the copyrighted work set out by both the copyright holder's usage licence and the statutory exceptions established under the Intellectual Property Code. Secondly, Article L.331-8 requires the new regulatory authority created by the same act (*Autorité de Régulation des Mesures Techniques*) to monitor the implementation of technical measures with the aim of ensuring that this implementation does not have the effect of impairing a group of exceptions that is much broader than the list of preserved acts established by Article 6(4) of the InfoSoc Directive.[621]

The new Article L.331-6 makes it clear that the disclosure obligation placed upon the providers of technological measures aims to ensure that these measures do not have - in consideration of their mutual incompatibility or incapability to interoperate - the technical frustration of acts covered by copyright exceptions as a consequence. This provision makes it clear that these preserved acts are constituted by the exceptions provided by copyright law, which supplement and are independent of the exceptions expressly set out by the copyright owner through contract.[622] By referring to exceptions that are *supplementary to and independent from* those created by the copyright owner by means of DRM technology, this provision evidences that the objective of interoperability is perceived as instrumental to the immunisation of copyright exceptions from DRM-enabled restrictions.[623] This means that, in so far as the technical impairment of the free uses that Article L.331-8 wishes to technically ensure stems from the incapability of technical measures to interoperate, the French regulatory authority should be entitled to or-

---

620 See Article L.331-8, §1.

621 See Article L.331-8, §1. This group of exceptions includes private copying, quotation for purposes of review, critic and teaching, performance and reproduction of excerpts from protected works for teaching and research ends, *etc*: see Appendix II, see *infra*.

622 The provision was added to the French Intellectual Property Code by Article 14 of Law 2006-961 of 1 August 2006.

623 New Article L.331-6 provides as follows: "L'Autorité de régulation des mesures techniques [...] vieille à ce que les measures techniques [...] n'aient pas pour conséquence, du fait de leur incompatibilité ou de leur incapacité d'interopérer, d'entrainer dans l'utilisation d'une oeuvre des *exceptions supplémentaires et indépendentes de celles expressément décidées par le titulaire d'un droit d'auteur* sur une oeuvre autre qu'un logiciel ou par le titulaire d'un droit voisin sur une interprétation, un phonogramme, un vidéogramme ou un programme"(Emphasis added).

der the disclosure of essential information enabling media to interoperate upon the request of the interested parties. However, Article L.331-7 runs contrary to this purpose while, at the same time, restricting access to the administrative proceedings before the regulatory authority considerably. It provides that the authority may hear requests for interoperability information that can *only* come from software developers, providers of technical measures and the users of these services (*i.e.*, copyright owners, content suppliers) who seek compatibility of digitally-protected works for their products (*e.g.*, media players, hardware devices, *etc*).[624]

It is unfortunate, in my view, that this legislation does not give end-users, consumers or their advocates the opportunity to commence administrative proceedings for the purpose of directly fostering the publication of technical documentation which enables their contents and media to interoperate. As pointed out above, the problem of interoperability arose firstly in the context of consumer-driven initiatives which had targeted cases of "hidden" implementation of anti-copy devices on CDs.[625] Given that such devices disabled the correct functioning of music CDs on certain types of portable players and car radios, French courts settled these disputes in favour of consumers on the grounds of civil and consumer protection law. The courts found that the consumer had a right to be informed about the implementation of such anti-copy devices. They found that, in the absence of a proper warning, these were "hidden vices" which affected the validity of the sale of the good in question.[626]

In spite of the emphasis placed upon the preservation of free uses by the new French statute, neither end-users nor consumer associations are allowed to request interoperability information from the regulatory authority. This position indicates that this law was not adopted to safeguard the interests of end-users. As claimed by Rosenblatt, the French Parliament's original intent with this legislation was probably that of breaking the Apple iTunes monopoly over on-line music deliveries.[627] Even in this respect, however, the resulting legislation is actually counterproductive, considering that the obligation to disclose interoperability information is ultimately restricted by requirements which allow the owner of the protected information to refuse its disclosure legitimately. Article L.331-7 provides that requests of interoperability information can be addressed to the authority whenever access to essential information is refused by the provider of a technological pro-

624 See Article L.331-7, §1: "Tout éditeur de logiciel, tout fabricant de système technique et tout exploitant de service peut, en case de refus d'accès aux informations essentielles à l'interopérabilité, demander à l'Autorité de régulation des mesures techniques de garantir l'interopérabilité des systèmes et des services existants, dans le respect des droits des parties, et d'obtenir du titulaire des droits sur la mesure technique les informations essentielles à cette interopérabilité […]".

625 See §5.4.3.4., see *supra*.

626 This information right is codified now under Article L.331-12 of the French Intellectual Property Code with regard to the exception of private copying. It is expressly provided by law that the user shall be informed about restrictions of this exception enabled by anti-copy devices.

627 See Rosenblatt, 'France Approves Modified Copyright Bill', *DRM Watch*, 22.06.2006, available at: http:// drmwatch.com/legal/article.php/3615596.

tection measure and the disclosure of such information can be ordered while still respecting the (exclusive) rights of the parties concerned.[628] Under these circumstances, ownership of intellectual property rights (*i.e.*, copyrights) and trade secrets on information such as application programming interfaces (APIs) and the source code of DRM programmes may justify the refusal of the information disclosure by the requested party. This conclusion is upheld *a contrario* by the provision of Article L.331-7, under which the right-holder of the requested technical measure is allowed to prevent the beneficiary of the disclosed information from publishing the source code and the technical documentation of an independently created and interoperable software in so far as there is evidence that such publication would considerably prejudice the security and effectiveness of the technical measure.[629] In other words, if the essential interoperability information is a proprietary item of computer code, the beneficiary of this information may be forbidden from publishing its own code which includes the disclosed proprietary item.

While preserving the information owner's freedom of contract, the French statute provides that, before adopting a decision on the request of essential information, the Authority may consider the parties' commitment to enter into agreements that are capable of bringing practices contrary to the purpose of interoperability to an end.[630] In this situation, both the parties holding and seeking the essential information are thereby given an incentive to settle the issue of technical incompatibility between their products privately. Given that such technical features can be negotiated during content licensing discussions, the French statute effectively enables a clear market leader (*e.g.*, Apple) using proprietary DRM technology (*e.g.*, Apple's Fairplay) to extract the contractual promise not to ask the authority for interoperability documentation from content owners. It must be also considered that, under Article L.331-7, the party seeking interoperability information and having access to a DRM-protected work is obliged to shape its own DRM programme in such a way as to respect the conditions of use originally attached to the accessed work. This further restriction implies that essential information cannot be requested for interoperability with services that will offer more liberal conditions of use for the work.

7.4.4. Copyright protection and EU interoperability policy

It seems clear to me that French pro-interoperability legislation will prove to be largely ineffective in the pursuit of the objective of interoperability regarding different DRM technology. Considering that most of the technical information capable of enabling interoperability between different DRM systems (*e.g.*, programming interfaces, RELs, software specifications, *etc*) is covered by strong intellectual property rights, the legislation adds little to the pre-existing indispen-

[628] See the above-mentioned text of Article L.331-7 of the French Intellectual Property Code.

[629] See Article L.331-7, §3.

[630] See Article L.331-7, §4, of the French Intellectual Property Code.

sability test developed by the ECJ in respect of the compulsory licensing of essential information. Under French copyright law, the conditions under which the disclosure obligation applies to the holder of essential information are even more restrictive than the "exceptional circumstances" spelt out under the ECJ case law. If located in the technological and legal settings described above, the French legislature's choice of compelling disclosure of interoperability information on condition that the rights of the interested parties are respected (*i.e.*, untouched by the information disclosure) makes little sense. This condition, combined with the fact that the information holder is given great incentive to settle interoperability disputes through licensing agreements, has the negative consequence of practically foreclosing the enforcement of the obligation each time that the supply of this information encroaches upon the subject-matter of an exclusive right. The situation would have been slightly different if, as provided under the Assembly's initial draft of the statute (which was subsequently modified by the Senate), the requests of interoperability information could have come from any and all interested parties, including consumers and end-users, and not just from content owners and the providers of competing DRM solutions.[631] As argued above, these parties are actually subject to the licensing power of the information owner, in such a way that interoperability information may never be publicly disclosed to end-users.

It is worth emphasising here that the definitive version of the copyright statute approved in France, which actually strengthened the position of property rightholders over interoperability information, runs contrary to the decision on interoperability adopted by the European Commission in March 2004 and substantially affirmed by the Court of First Instance in September 2007, following an appeal brought by Microsoft.[632] While ordering the disclosure of complete and accurate software specifications which enable interoperability on the market for "Work Group Server" (WGS) operating systems, the Microsoft decision demonstrated that the protection of intellectual property rights which obstruct the purpose of interoperability between different operating systems may be subject to restrictions under Article 82 of the Treaty (*i.e.*, abuse of dominant position), beyond the boundaries of the interoperability exception provided in respect of copyright protection under Article 6 of the EC Software Directive.[633] In the case of Microsoft's

---

[631] See Standeford, 'France Forges Ahead With Copyright Law', *Intellectual Property Watch*, 16.05.2006, available at: http://www.ip-watch.org.

[632] See Commission Decision of 24 March 2004, relating to a procedure under Article 82 of the EC Treaty, Case COMP/C-3/37.792, (hereinafter "Microsoft decision"), available at: http://europa.eu.int/comm/competition/antitrust/cases/decisions/37792/en.pdf. See also *Microsoft Corp* v. *Commission of the European Communities*, T-201/04, Judgment of 17 September 2007, available at: http://www.curia.europa.eu.

[633] See Hart, 'Interoperability Information and the Microsoft Decision', (28) *EIPR* 2006, p. 361, at p. 365. Article 5(a) of the Microsoft decision required Microsoft to make "Interoperability Information available to any undertaking having an interest in developing and distributing work group operating system products." According to Article 1(1) of the same decision, interoperability information was defined as "the complete and accurate software specifications for all the Protocols implemented in Windows Work Group

software information, the Commission found that all information which made WGS operating systems supplied by Microsoft's competitors technically interoperable with the Microsoft Windows PC operating system was considered *essential* in spite of the copyrights, patents and trade secrets owned by Microsoft on this information. Under the ECJ indispensability test, the ownership of these exclusive rights could provide an objective justification for a legitimate refusal to issue a licence. As explained by Leveque, instead of discussing openly whether Microsoft's non-disclosure of information impeded new products being placed on the market (as the indispensability test would have required), the Commission introduced an assessment on incentives to innovate.[634] In assessing such incentives, the Commission emphasised that the non-disclosure of interoperability information impeded Microsoft's competitors from capturing the benefits of their own innovations upon the market for WSG operating systems.[635] As a result, the Commission concluded that, on balance, the possible negative impact of an order of disclosing information on Microsoft's incentives to innovate was outweighed by its positive impact on the level of the innovation of the whole industry (including Microsoft).[636]

A similar assessment on incentives to innovate might be developed by the European Commission, either at the level of legislative proposals or under antitrust enforcement proceedings, in consideration of the objective of enabling interoperability between DRM technologies implemented on copyrighted digital content on the one hand, and on media players and hardware on the other. To achieve the objective of the establishment of a global interoperable platform, which would foster innovation and free competition on both markets for copyrighted content and information goods, the Commission may consider the pursuit of the policy option of pre-empting the acquisition of property rights over DRM technology in order to promote the adoption of open standards.[637]

The economist Varian claims that open standardisation would be the most suitable solution in respect of DRM technology because this technology holds an exceptionally important position in the light of its function of "bottleneck" between two types of industry (*i.e.*, the digital media industry on the one hand, and the information technology industry on the other) that are inevitably complementary and whose technologies need to interoperate.[638] Nonetheless, Varian admitted that this policy objective is actually hindered by the fact that big companies in the high-tech sector have already invested considerable amounts of money in the research and development of privately owned DRM systems and have acquired strong in-

Operating Systems and that are used by Windows Work Group Servers to deliver file and print services and group and user administration services."

634 See Leveque, 'Innovation, leveraging and essential facilities: Interoperability licensing in the EU Microsoft case', available at: http://www.cerna.ensmp.fr/Documents/FL-Ms-WorldCompetition.pdf, pp. 1-25.

635 See Leveque, 'Innovation, leveraging and essential facilities', op. cit., p. 11.

636 See the Microsoft decision, paragraph 783.

637 This policy option is discussed more in depth at §9.3.3, see *infra*.

638 See Varian, 'Economics of DRM', Presentation made at the 3rd DRM Conference, Berlin, 13-14 January 2005; Mazziotti, 'Did Apple's refusal to license [...]', op. cit., p. 273.

tellectual property rights on foundational DRM components. In this respect, the case of the patent portfolio of crucial technology owned by ContentGuard, which is embedded into the standard of the "MPEG-21" rights expression language, shows that open standardisation would pose the problem of the relevant switching costs that all firms already using proprietary DRM solutions should bear in order to opt for open standards.[639] Varian puts forward that the acquisition of a monopoly power on DRM technology would pave the way for a "nightmare scenario", in which a middleman provides DRM technology that offers buyers and sellers of content a seemingly open platform, but retains enough proprietary pieces to exercise control over the platform development.[640]

The recent acquisition of ContentGuard by a joint venture including Microsoft has enormously strengthened the position of Microsoft on the market for DRM solutions.[641] In my view, this situation has the potential to give shape to the scenario figured out by Varian in real terms. Notwithstanding the conclusion that, due to the acquisition of an equity stake in ContentGuard by other two stakeholders (*i.e.*, Time Warner and Thomson), Microsoft is not in a position to shape ContentGuard's licensing policy to the detriment of Microsoft's competitors, the Commission acknowledged that the dominant position acquired by Microsoft in the DRM sector needs to be closely monitored under EU antitrust law.[642] The risk that Microsoft's key role in the administration and design of DRM proprietary technologies may lead to a vertical, inextricable integration of dominant DRM systems (such as Windows Rights Manager) with Microsoft's dominant applications (including the new, trusted version of the Windows PC operating system, the Windows Media Player, Microsoft's Office, *etc*) is very high.

In this respect, Anderson and Stallman persuasively warned that Microsoft's proprietary, highly integrated software applications have the potential of locking-in end-user computers with data which supports Microsoft's DRM systems and trusted specifications to the detriment of software and digital works which support other (*i.e.* non-compatible) DRM technologies (*e.g.*, Apple's Fairplay) or technology disseminated under open source and open content licences.[643] In these situa-

639 An overview of the development of the MPEG-21 standard and of ContentGuard's patent portfolio on the foundational components of this standard is provided in Appendix I, §B, see *infra*.

640 See Mazziotti, 'Did Apple's refusal to license [...]', op. cit., p. 273.

641 The dominant position of Microsoft on the market for DRM technologies is briefly discussed in Appendix I, §D.2, see *infra*.

642 See Commission of the European Communities, *Mergers: Microsoft and Time Warner abandon acquisition of control in ContentGuard as Thomson purchases a one third stake*, Press Release, IP/05/295, 15 March 2005, available at: http://europa.eu.int/rapid/searchAction.do.

643 In the language of Stallman, 'Can you trust your computer?', available at: http://www.gnu.org/philosophy/can-you-trust.html, the risk of content lock-in by what he defines as "treacherous" (*i.e.*, trusted) computing is explained in the following terms: "Word processors such as Microsoft Word could use treacherous computing when they save your documents, to make sure no competing word processors can read them. Today we must figure out the secrets of Word format by laborious experiments in order to

tions, the problem of interoperability is very likely to remain unsettled, at least it will be for all end-users who do not opt for Microsoft's vertically integrated (and DRM-protected or, worse, trusted) platform. The same problem will affect users who find themselves locked-in by the Microsoft DRM platform and are not able to use digital media which support incompatible DRM technology on their computers.

7.5. Restriction of private copying

7.5.1. The policy option of preserving private copying notwithstanding DRM

It was pointed out earlier that the InfoSoc Directive does not oblige Member States to introduce or maintain the exception of private copying.[644] Nor does the Directive compel them to take appropriate measures of enforcement to ensure copying for personal use against anti-copy devices. Article 6(4), §2, clearly conceives the effective enforcement of this exception in the digital environment as a mere policy option.[645]

Furthermore, Article 5(2)(b) requires national legislators to take account of the presence of technological measures when determining the form and the possible level of fair compensation (*i.e.*, copyright levies). According to this principle, levies should be phased-out as long as anti-copy devices incorporated into DRM technology effectively control the private use and copying of protected materials.

The European Commission is currently trying to speed up the process of phasing out of copyright levies by taking legislative measures which, unlike the generic wording of Article 5(2)(b), identify more precisely the technical conditions under which, due to the right-holders' effective control of private copying, Member States should be forced to refrain from imposing an unjustifiable levy.[646]

make free word processors read Word documents. If Word encrypts documents using treacherous computing when saving them, the free software community won't have a chance of developing software to read them – and if we could, such programs might even be forbidden by the Digital Millennium Copyright Act." See, also, Anderson, ''Trusted Computing' and Competition Policy', op. cit., p. 38 ("If the TC/Windows becomes the dominant platform, most developers will make their products available for it first, and for others later (if at all) [...]").

644 See §4.4.1., see *supra*.

645 This provision allows a Member State to take appropriate measures "[...] in respect of a beneficiary of an exception or limitation provided for in accordance with Article 5(2)(b), unless reproduction for private use has already been made possible by rightholders to the extent necessary to benefit from the exception or limitation concerned and in accordance with the provisions of Article 5(2)(b) and (5), without preventing rightholders from adopting adequate measures regarding the number of reproductions in accordance with these provisions".

646 See Commission of the European Communities, *Copyright levy reform, Commission's Work Programme*, available at:

Nonetheless, copyright levies may not disappear from the digital environment under those jurisdictions where the exception of private copying and its enforcement are specifically preserved against technical restrictions.

In accordance with Article 5(2)(b), levies may not be phased-out where legislators should exercise the policy option of maintaining and enforcing the statutory licence of private copying, notwithstanding the potential of DRM technology to eliminate and enforce unauthorised copying. Under the system created by the InfoSoc Directive, the fact that this technology may enable perfect protection against unauthorised copying does not necessarily mean that Member States should repeal statutory licences which allow the reproduction of the protected work for purposes such as personal use, study, research, and so on.

Quite to the contrary, as argued below,[647] new levies may be created under national law, in accordance with Article 6(4), §2, of the Directive, where the law should create exceptions that allow certain types of digital reproduction with the objective of preserving user privacy from the control of DRM technology. The only requirement for these exceptions to comply with Article 5(2)(b) is that of providing copyright holders with fair compensation by an extension of levies to copy-machines and media facilitating digital copying.

A few national statutes overviewed in the table provided in Appendix II to this book have exercised this option by drawing on the public policy dimension of this exception and, in particular, on its privacy-enhancing rationale to provide for its imperative application against anti-copy devices. This is certainly the case of Italy, the United Kingdom (but only for certain special cases, such as the copying made by visually impaired persons), Spain and, more explicitly, France.

7.5.2. The *Mulholland Drive* case in France: does a *right* of private copying exist?

The most important and interesting case in which French courts had the opportunity to discuss the legal nature of the private copying exception and its possible enforcement against the restrictive power of digital anti-copy devices is the so-called *Mulholland Drive* case.[648] This litigation stemmed from a film by film-maker David Lynch, which was distributed in France in copy-protected DVD format and was brought by a French user who wished to make a private analogue copy. The user's purpose was that of copying the film from the DVD to a VHS format, so that he could be able to watch the film at his parents' home, where no

http://ec.europa.eu/internal_market/copyright/levy_reform/index_en.htm.

647 See §7.5.4., see *infra*.

648 Three are the judgments concerning the so-called *Mulholland Drive* case: *Stéphane P., UFC Que Choisir* c. *Société Films Alain Sarde*, Tribunal de Grande Instance de Paris (3ème ch.), Judgment of 30 April 2004; *Stéphane P., UFC Que Choisir* c. *Universal Pictures Video France and others*, Cour d'Appel de Paris (4ème Chambre), Judgment of 22 April 2005; *Société Studio Canal et autres* c. *Perquin et UFC Que Choisir*, Cour de Cassation, Judgment of 28 February 2006. All of these judgments are available at: http://www.legalis.net.

DVD player was available. The copy-protection device installed on the digital medium frustrated this purpose. Hence, the user and the French consumer union *UFC-Que Choisir* jointly sued the producer of the DVD (*i.e.*, Alain Sarde) before the Paris *Tribunal de Grande Instance*, claiming that the copy-protection device violated the user's "right" of private copying. According to the plaintiffs, this right was clearly provided by Articles L.122-5 and L.211-3 of the French Intellectual Property Code, under which holders of copyright and related rights:

"[…] cannot prohibit copies or reproductions that are strictly reserved to a private use by the copier and are not used collectively."[649]

After two conflicting judgments by the *Tribunal de Grande Instance* and the Paris Appeal Court, the French Supreme Court resolved the dispute at end of February 2006.[650] The dispute focused basically on two issues. The first issue concerned the question of whether a subjective right of making a private copy of a protected work could be deemed to exist under French copyright law, or, in turn, whether this copyright exception could be viewed as a mere defence against infringement claims. The latter issue focused on whether this right (or mere exception) prevailed over the protection measure applied by the right-holder to protect his copyright in the DVD film.

With regard to the intrinsic qualification of private copying, none of the three above-mentioned judgments found that this exception established a subjective right that the user could enforce against the copyright owner. However, it is worth emphasising that the decision of the Paris Court of Appeal, subsequently invalidated by the Supreme Court, enforced the private copying exception as if it were a positive, subjective *right* of the user. Indeed, the Court of Appeal found that, in so far as the anti-copy device frustrated the user's legitimate purpose of copying for strictly personal use, as defined under Article L.122-5, §2, the technical device which harmed the user's statutory "benefit" should have been removed from *all* of the DVD formats embodying the copyrighted film in question.[651] Clearly, if this judgment had not been overturned by the Supreme Court, it had the potential of sending shockwaves through the French home video entertainment market.

In contrast with the decision of January 2006 by the Paris *Tribunal de Grande Instance* in a similar case between a consumer and a music CD producer,[652] in *Mulholland Drive* the Court of Appeal did not specify whether the enforceability of the private copying exception stemmed from its "public order" (*i.e.*, imperative) nature. Notwithstanding the absence of an explicit statement on the nature of the

---

649 Author's own translation.

650 The judgment by the *Cour de Cassation* was commented upon by Lucas, 'Mesures techniques de protection – Copie privée – Triple test', (19) *Propriétés intellectuelles*, April 2006, p. 179.

651 See Lucas and Sirinelli, 'Exceptions de copie privée et mesures techniques de protection', (16) *Propriétés intellectuelles*, July 2005, p. 340, at p. 342.

652 See *Christophe R. et UFC Que Choisir* c. *Warner Music France et FNAC*, Tribunal de Grande Instance de Paris (5ème Chambre), Judgment of 10 January 2006, available at: http://www.legalis.net.

exception by the Court, its decision ended up treating the private copying exception as if it gave rise to a subjective, totally enforceable right against the adopter of technical restrictions.[653] In summary, the Paris Appeal Court held that the exception forbade the copyright owner from technically entrenching the making of copies for personal use in the same way as, symmetrically, the exception immunised the private copier from the copyright owner's infringement claims.

Thus, the Paris Court of Appeal found that the exception of private copying could be positively enforced against restrictions coming from the copyright holder, and could justify the condemnation of the copyright owner to the payment of damages and to the removal of the anti-copy device from all marketed copies of the DVD. The Court rejected the widely-shared view that the social justification upholding the exception of private copying would be that of mere tolerance in respect of acts which, although falling within the copyright scope, were not enforceable by the right-holder until the advent of anti-copy devices and, now, DRM technology.[654] As emphasised earlier,[655] in the presence of technical measures which enable perfect control over unauthorised uses of digital works, the market failure argument behind the exception of private copying is unanimously deemed to shrink.

Following the market failure argument, Lucas and Sirinelli strongly criticised the decision of the Paris Court of Appeal by arguing that, from an historical perspective, a user right of private copying has never existed under French law.[656] These authors pointed out that the exception carved out in 1957 under Article L.122-5 of the Intellectual Property Code was introduced mainly in consideration of the practical impossibility of enforcing the reproduction right in the user's private sphere, and not as a result of the political will to create a consumer right of private copying.[657] In their view, the advent of technical measures enables copyright owners to enforce their exclusive right of reproduction even within the user's private sphere. They further emphasised that the social justification for upholding the private copying exception is weaker than the social justifications for other copyright exceptions.[658] In support of their position, they note that private copying was not included in the small range of exceptions that the safeguard system of Article 6(4) of the InfoSoc Directive preserves from technological protection measures.

As argued above,[659] the argument that Article 6(4) provides an unreasonably narrow selection of "first-class" exceptions is persuasive. In my view, these exceptions have no stronger social justification that those which are excluded from the list of privileged uses. For this reason, it was emphasised earlier that Article

653 See Lucas and Sirinelli, 'Exceptions de copie privée et mesures techniques de protection', op. cit., p. 342.

654 *Ibidem*, pp. 343-344.

655 See §2.2.2.2., see *supra*.

656 See Lucas and Sirinelli, 'Exceptions de copie privée et mesures techniques de protection', op. cit , p. 343.

657 *Ibidem*.

658 *Ibidem*.

659 See §4.5.3., see *supra*.

6(4) has the very bad consequence of leaving most of the productive (and, as a result, most valuable) uses that copyright law allows with no protection from DRM and other similar technologies.

The argument raised by Lucas and Sirinelli is also contradicted by the fact that Article 6(4), §2, gives Member States the policy option to take measures which allow the enforcement of the private copying exception despite the implementation of anti-copy devices. In my view, this highlights that the Directive does not have as low a consideration of this exception as that claimed by Lucas and Sirinelli. Under Article 6(4), Member States are given the opportunity to ground their own exceptions of private copying on a social justification other than that of the market failure rationale.

It was maintained above that an alternative, powerful justification for making digital private reproductions subject to a statutory licence scheme, with a subsequent exclusion of private copying from the exclusive right of the author, may be found by national legislators in the privacy-enhancing rationale.[660] In contrast to the contraction of the market failure rationale, the protection of user privacy is an argument that is immensely strengthened by the increasing implementation of technology, such as DRM, which is capable of monitoring and tracing end-user consumption patterns.

At the time of the *Mulholland Drive* dispute, the French legislator had not yet transposed the regulation of private copying created by the InfoSoc Directive into national law. Thus, French law did not explicitly outline its policy option in respect of the possible frustration of attempts of private copying by anti-copy technology. The dispute was finally settled in favour of the copyright owner on the grounds of the (still unsettled) conflict between the statutory recognition of the private copying exception under Article L.122-5 of the French Intellectual Property Code and the anti-copy restriction installed on the DVD film.

The (rather unclear) judgment by the French Supreme Court found the decision of the Paris Appeal Court erroneous on the assumption that the lower court, although admitting that the law created a mere exception to the exclusive right of reproduction and not an enforceable user right, veered away from this statement when concluding that the exception could not be validly stifled by an anti-copy device in the absence of a statutory clause which expressly allowed this possibility.[661]

The setting aside of the Appeal Court's decision by the Supreme Court, conversely, held that, given that no provision under French law specifically preserved the making of digital copies for personal use from the potential override enabled by anti-copy measures, the implementation of these measures could ultimately be found to prevail on the enforcement of the (unprotected) exception. The Supreme Court considered that French law had not exercised the option left by Article 6(4), §2, for the preservation of private copying in the digital environment. As a result, and in the light of the new anti-circumvention law created by the InfoSoc Direc-

[660] See §2.2.3., see *supra*.

[661] See *Société Studio Canal et autres* c. *Perquin et UFC Que Choisir*, Cour de Cassation, Judgment of 28 February 2006.

tive, the exception of private copying could be lawfully overcome by technical measures. Lucas and Sirinelli endorsed this reasoning by arguing that the conclusion was upheld by the last part of the Directive Recital 39, where it is provided that

> "[...] exceptions and limitations should not inhibit the use of technological measures or their enforcement against circumvention."[662]

After the coming into force of the act transposing the Directive into the French Intellectual Property Code, the statutory interface created by this law for the preservation of the private copying exception would impede the Supreme Court from holding what it held in February 2006. The new Article L.331-8, Sections 1 and 2, of the Intellectual Property Code explicitly protects the beneficiary of the exception of private copying from technical restrictions. Moreover, Article L.331-8, §3, gives the authority which regulates these technical measures the power to determine the threshold number of copies that can be deemed compatible with the notion of strictly personal use adopted under Article L.122-5, §2. To this end, the authority is constantly required to assess whether copy-control devices monitor this threshold number of copies effectively. Finally, the private copying exception, as all of the other exceptions preserved from technically-enabled restrictions under Article L.331-8, can be enforced by any interested party that commences proceedings before the authority. The authority can either dismiss the claim or compel the copyright owner to make available the means enabling the beneficiary of the exception to carry out the guaranteed use.[663]

7.5.3. May private copying of copy-protected works be compatible with the three-step test?

It is remarkable that new French copyright law allows the exception of private copying to be enforced by the user of the protected work before a special administrative authority. The fact that enforcement proceedings must be commenced before an administrative (and not a judicial) authority may leave doubt about whether this exception is given the status of a subjective right or that of an enforceable "legitimate interest" (from the French *intérêt légitime*) of the user. This qualification may have important consequences with regard to the opportunity for the user to seek damages before judicial courts as a consequence of the technical frustration of the permitted use. Regardless of this uncertain classification, what is relevant to point out of this law is that private copying was finally defined as an enforceable use against technical devices. In conformity with Article 5(5) of the InfoSoc Directive, the enforceability of the private copying exception was made subject to the specific requirements of the three-step test.

---

662 See Lucas and Sirinelli, 'Exceptions de copie privée et mesures techniques de protection', op. cit., pp. 342-343.

663 See Articles L.331-12 to L.331-16 of the French Intellectual Property Code, as amended by Law 2006-961 of 1 August 2006.

The new provision of Article L.122-5, §9, of the Intellectual Property Code states:

"The exceptions listed by this article can neither conflict with the normal exploitation of the work nor cause an unjustified prejudice to the legitimate interests of the author."[664]

The incompatibility of private copying with the test, and especially with its second step (*i.e.*, the normal exploitation of the work), was the main legal basis on which the French Supreme Court overturned the judgment of the Paris Court of Appeal, which required the producer of the *Mulholland Drive* DVD to pay damages to the user and remove anti-copy devices from the DVD. The Supreme Court's final decision found that the mere copying of the film, even if carried out by means of an analogue medium (such as a VHS cassette), was in conflict with the requirement of "normal exploitation" in consideration of:

"[…] the risks related to the new digital environment as well as the safeguard of copyrights and the economic importance that the exploitation of the work in the DVD format may have for the coverage of the costs of cinematographic production […]".[665]

The Supreme Court ultimately found that the private copying exception:

"[…] cannot hinder the insertion onto media on which a protected work is embodied of technological protection measures aimed at forbidding the copy, where this copy would have the effect of conflicting with the normal exploitation of the work […]".[666]

While drawing on the statement of Recital 39 of the InfoSoc Directive, which is at odds with the wording of Article 6(4), §2, of the same Directive, the Supreme Court's decision lawfully permitted technical measures to eliminate private copying opportunities in so far as technical protection aimed to ensure the normal exploitation of the protected work.[667]

The Supreme Court made the crucial point that technical measures, where implemented for the exercise of the exclusive right of reproduction, should *always* be understood as prevailing upon private copying exceptions, even if the enforcement of such exceptions takes preference over the protection of technical measures, as in the case of the new statutory interface created by French law. As Dusollier pointed out, the contradiction of the Court's statement with the Directive's policy option of enabling private copies in the face of technical restrictions results from the fact that the Court treated two separate issues as a single one.[668] The first of these issues was the evaluation *in concreto* of the compliance of a specific case of

---

664 Author's own translation.

665 See *Société Studio Canal et autres* c. *Perquin et UFC Que Choisir*, Cour de Cassation, Judgment of 28 February 2006 (author's own translation).

666 *Ibidem.*

667 See Dusollier, 'Le dernier tournant de l'affaire Mulholland Drive, note of Cass. fr., 28 Feb. 2006', (2) *Auteurs & Médias*, 2006, p. 177, at p. 180.

668 See Dusollier, 'Le dernier tournant de l'affaire Mulholland Drive', op. cit., p. 180.

private copying (*i.e.*, the copy of a DVD film transferred onto a VHS cassette) with the statutory exception which allowed this use. In *Mulholland Drive*, the evaluation of the courts should merely have addressed and ascertained the user respect of the statutory conditions of exercise established by law for the making of a private copy to be lawful. The second issue concerned the co-existence *in abstracto* of the private copying exception with technical measures such as anti-copy devices. For the sake of legal certainty, this evaluation should, preferably, be carried out by the law, with a careful assessment of the conformity of the statutory exception which allows private copying with the three-step test and, in particular, with the requirement of the "normal exploitation" of the work.

Instead, the French Supreme Court seemed to confuse these two issues by failing to consider that the concrete user purpose was completely in line with the French statutory licence which allowed private reproductions. The user, in fact, wished to copy the DVD film on a blank medium, over which he would have paid a copyright levy. Moreover, the user's intent was that of making an analogue copy of the film in order to use it personally at a place where no DVD player was available.

An interesting question would arise if the *Mulholland Drive* DVD were copied onto a digital medium such as a blank DVD. Would this digital copy be allowed under the private copying exception? Would this copy be admissible under the three-step test?

At the time of the dispute, French copyright law provided no distinction between analogue and digital reproductions for personal use. Consequently, French courts should have reviewed this hypothetical case of digital private copying by applying both the statutory exception and, in the absence of a legislative adaptation of the exception to the three-step test, the same test. In the light of the private copying regime created by the InfoSoc Directive, the courts should have considered that Article 6(4), §2, explicitly provided for the enforcement of the exception of *digital* private copying against the operation of technological protection measures. This provision seeks to combine the enforcement of digital copying with the right-holders' use of technical measures. After restating the primary right-holder's duty to make technical means available to the extent necessary for the user to benefit from the exception of reproduction for private use (clearly, only where this exception is provided), this provision confers on the Member States the power to take appropriate measures to compel the supply of such technical means.[669]

Notwithstanding these obligations, Article 6(4), §2 makes it clear that a mechanism which safeguards private copying may be established by Member States "without preventing rightholders from adopting adequate measures regarding the number of reproductions in accordance with these provisions".

This clause evidences that the system created by Article 6(4) permits the private copying exception to co-exist with the anti-circumvention protection of technical measures. According to this clause, such co-existence should be achieved through the legal exemption of a number of reproductions that the law may find compatible with the notion of strictly personal use. The explicit reference made by

[669] See §4.5.1., see *supra*.

Article 6(4), §2, to the provision of Article 5(5) of the Directive shows that this solution was intended to make private copying compatible with the three-step test. However, the solution relied upon the availability of technology that was more sophisticated than simple (*i.e.*, rough) anti-copy devices, which only permit the disabling of copying without enabling proper copy-management.

Instead, the trade-off sought by this provision may be perfectly accommodated by today's DRM technology, which provides a much more nuanced and elaborated management of digital content than simple anti-copy devices do.[670] DRM technology may therefore enable a form of user rights management by guaranteeing a limited number of digital private copies identified by legislation (or by an administrative authority, as in the French case) to the user, and imposing this threshold number to DRM technology designers and copyright owners.[671]

The conclusion of the *Mulholland Drive* case shows that the judicial enforcement of the three-step test, in the absence of a balanced statutory interpretation (and implementation) of the "normal exploitation" requirement, may easily lead to the *de facto* elimination of the exception of private copying from the digital environment. The conclusions reached by the French Supreme Court, in contrast with the brave decision of the Paris Court of Appeal, show that the adoption of a far-reaching notion of "normal exploitation" with regard to markets for copyrighted digital works may have the negative consequence of outlawing *all* types of digital private reproductions of copy-protected content, regardless of whether these reproductions are carried out by analogue or digital means.

In the absence of a statutory measure which transposes the solution of Article 6(4), §2, of the Directive, the French Supreme Court followed a very broad notion of normal exploitation. Under this notion, the private copying exception was found to be inapplicable upon the assumption that the normal exploitation of the DVD film would be endangered by risks of digital copyright infringement relating to the removal of anti-copy devices. Moreover, to reach its conclusion, the Supreme Court considered that unauthorised private copying, while depriving the copyright owner of the opportunity of selling additional copies of the work, would have a negative impact on the amount of revenues collected from DVD sales and, as a result, on the coverage of costs to ensure the economic viability of cinematographic production.

Clearly, the wide acceptance of this broad notion of normal exploitation by national courts would mean the *de facto* elimination of the private copying exception in digital settings. When analysing the three-step test, it was emphasised that, if

---

670 In legal scholarship, flexibility of DRM technology was emphasised by Bechtold, 'The Present and the Future of Digital Rights Management – Musings on Emerging Legal Problems', in Becker, Buhse, Gunnewig and Rump (eds), *Digital Rights Management – Technological, Economic, Legal and Political Aspects*, Springer, Berlin 2003, p. 597, at pp. 598-599, who pointed out that important policy and legal values may be preserved in a DRM-protected environment by altering this technology in a "value-centred" design process.

671 The expression "user rights management' is owed to Geiger, 'Copyright and Free Access to Information: For a Fair Balance of Interests in a Globalised World', (28) *EIPR* 2006, p. 366, at p. 372.

the requirement of "normal exploitation" were understood as reserving to the copyright owner *all* types of commercial exploitation of a digitally protected good, no copyright exception would meet this requirement and pass the test.[672] It is evident that, by exempting a certain socially valuable use (*e.g.*, private copying, quotation, parody, *etc*) from copyright's scope, each exception inevitably subtracts a (narrow) market segment from the types of commercial exploitation of the copyrighted work. If the notion of normal exploitation is understood too broadly, this notion may be found to encompass situations in which the copyright owner uses new DRM technology for the commercial exploitation of market segments that are characterised by the uses of the work that the law wishes to remain free. At some point, for instance, copyright owners may find it possible and economically viable to create markets for personal copies or for extracts of the work to enable quotation or parody by a follow-on user. If such commercial practices were found to constitute a "normal exploitation" of the work under the three-step test, copyright exceptions, regardless of the higher or lower social value of the uses that they enable, would always be in conflict with such exploitation.

As argued above, the requirement protecting the normal exploitation of a copyrighted work does not intend to reserve all of the possible market segments to the copyright owner.[673] Instead, the purpose of this requirement is to ensure that free uses of the work do not enter into economic competition with forms of exploitation of the work that have, or are likely to acquire, considerable economic importance.

In this respect, the approach taken by the French Supreme Court in *Mulholland Drive* provides a good example of how the normal exploitation requirement should *not* be implemented. In *Mulholland Drive*, it was evident that the analogue copy of the DVD that the user wished to make for purposes of strictly personal use would not have entered into economic competition with the exploitation of the DVD film, nor could the copy endanger the economic viability of the cinematographic production. This risk may have subsisted if the copy of the copy-protected work had been made on a digital medium, even if the wording of French law did not discriminate between analogue and digital means. The fact that the copy would have been made by analogue means upon which the user paid a copyright levy should have swayed the French Supreme Court that all requirements established by the statutory licence of Article L.122-5 of the French Code had been met.

If the case had concerned a digital copy, instead, a solution would have been more difficult to reach, in the absence of a provision which, under French copyright law, could have provided guidance as to whether or not technical measures could lawfully restrict private copying opportunities.

672 See §4.2.1, see *supra*.
673 *Ibidem*.

7.5.4. The role of national law in the preservation of digital private copying

Notwithstanding the contraction of the market failure rationale in the digital environment, national legislators in the European Union may have good reasons for preserving the exception of private copying under the shield of Article 6(4), §2, of the InfoSoc Directive. Beyond market failure, there are other strong justifications which uphold the preservation of this exception in the presence of DRM and other similar technology.

One of these justifications is the protection of privacy. It was argued earlier that statutory licences which, under certain circumstances, allow the private reproduction of copyrighted works have the effect of protecting the user's privacy in a context in which technical measures may increasingly interfere with the private enjoyment of the work and track its consumption patterns.[674]

Another strong justification stems from the assumption that, in the absence of the private copying benefice, copyright protection would fail the policy objective of stimulating the production of new works. By enabling access to the ideas and information embodied in pre-existing works, the private copying exception allows the user to take account of these works and to draw inspiration from them when creating a new work. In the relevant literature, the crucial importance of private copying for purposes of transformative (*i.e.*, productive) use was emphasised by Senftleben and Geiger.[675] These authors remarked that private copying opportunities serve not only the purpose of mere entertainment, as in the case of a DVD reproduction, but also valuable purposes such as private study and scientific research.

As pointed out by Geiger, in the specific field of scientific research, an enforceable privilege of private copying is highly desirable because private reproduction mainly facilitates private study.[676] In this field, the opportunity of reproducing, by digital or analogue means, pieces of protected works for personal use allows the users/researchers to inform themselves about the current state of science on their particular field of study and to produce new works. This situation is very different from that of the end-user who merely wishes to reproduce a copy-protected film or to download an unauthorised copyrighted song from a peer-to-peer network for sole purpose of entertainment. In these cases, the enforcement of the private copying exception may be easily found to be in conflict with the "normal exploitation" of the work because the user would end up being allowed to watch the desired film or listen to the song without having to purchase an authorised copy of the DVD or the CD embodying the work. Geiger is right when he argues that, if the enforcement of this exception were invoked mainly in order to excuse such con-

---

674 See §2.2.3., see *supra*.

675 See Senftleben, *Copyright, Limitations, and the Three-step Test*, op. cit., pp. 204-206; Geiger, 'Copyright and Free Access to Information', op. cit., pp. 371-372.

676 See Geiger, 'Copyright and Free Access to Information', op. cit., p. 371.

troversial and unproductive cases of unauthorised reproduction, the social desirability of a statutory exception of private copying would then be discredited.[677]

To preserve the exception at issue and foster productive uses of the work, it would be suitable that digital copyright law found a way to differentiate the legal treatment of productive and merely consumptive copies of digitally protected works. In the context created by the InfoSoc Directive, Member State law is free to do this while exercising the above-mentioned policy option provided by Article 6(4). Differentiation in the legal treatment of private reproductions, in accordance with their consumptive or productive purposes, would be very useful in keeping the enforcement of this exception in line with the three-step test, and, in particular, with the requirement of the "normal exploitation" of the work, which aims to secure the copyright owner's predictable revenues from the sale or licensing of authorised copies of the work.[678]

Even if productive purposes are conceivable, in the abstract, in respect of any kind of creative work (*e.g.*, music, novels, films, *etc*), there are fields of human creativity where, due to the type of work that is privately reproduced, productive uses are higher than in other fields. For instance, in the field of scientific research, copying for private study mainly serves the purpose of transformative use by users who are often authors themselves and potential innovators of the state of science.

In academic communities, the problem of private digital copies made for scientific use is normally solved through the publication of copyrighted works under "open access" or "copyleft" licences on the Internet.[679] By virtue of these licences, authors exercise their copyright on scientific works by permitting the user to freely access and copy the work on condition that their right of paternity in the work is respected.[680] In this particular situation, the release of these works on a free basis is due to the fact that academic writers are not motivated by the perspective of enforcing exclusive rights, with the subsequent possibility of economic compensation. Instead, these authors seek to protect the moral aspect of their copyright on the published work.[681]

---

677 See Geiger, 'Copyright and Free Access to Information', op. cit., p. 372.

678 See §4.2.1., see *supra*.

679 A so-called "copyleft" licence defines specific copyright terms applied to works protected under copyright law (*e.g.*, computer programmes, literary and artistic works, *etc*). Whereas copyright law, by default, automatically restricts the right to make and redistribute copies of an author's work, a copyleft licence uses copyright law in order to ensure that every person who receives a copy of a work has the same rights to study, use, modify, and also redistribute both the work, and derived versions of the work as long as the same licence terms apply to all redistributed versions of the work. The term, which derived from a play on the word "copyright", was originally a noun, which meant the copyright licence terms of the GNU 'General Public Licence' (GPL) articulated by Richard Stallman as part of the Free Software Foundation's work. For further information see the entry "copyleft" at http://www.wikipedia.org and the official website of the GNU Project at: http://www.gnu.org/.

680 See, for instance, the standard licence "Attribution/Non-commercial/No Derivatives (by/nc/nd)" made available by the U.S. foundation of Creative Commons at: http://creativecommons.org/about/licenses/meet-the-licenses.

681 See Geiger, 'Copyright and Free Access to Information', op. cit., p. 371.

Where academic works are made available through open publishing systems, private study is encouraged to the highest extent, in a way in which users, who are often follow-on authors, have full freedom of access and private copy in respect of published works. The purpose of preserving freedom of access to and copy of these works through their viral distribution through the Internet is witnessed by the fact that open access licences normally contain contractual clauses that prevent the user from altering the licence terms and using technology (such as DRM) to restrict the licensee's rights under the licence. For instance, the Creative Commons Public Licence 2.5, Article 4(a) ("Restrictions") provides that the user:

"[M]ay not distribute, publicly display, publicly perform, or publicly digitally perform the Work with any technological measures that control access or use of the Work in a manner inconsistent with the terms of this License Agreement."[682]

A basic problem of access to knowledge arises, instead, where scientific works are made available to the public by means of media supporting DRM technology (or by less sophisticated access- or copy-protected formats) and the applicable copyright law does not provide a statutory interface to ensure the enforcement of an exception of private copying for scientific use. In this situation, the user-researcher is not allowed to have access to a copy of the digitally protected work on a free basis and/or to use it outside the right-holder's control. In the logic of unrestricted DRM technology, scientific use becomes subject to the licensing power of the copyright owner so that additional costs for private copying may be charged, which reduces dissemination of scientific works and hinders the incremental nature of scientific innovation.

From a public policy point of view, this still hypothetical but realistic privatisation of the results of scientific research should be avoided, at least for works that are the fruit of publicly funded research. Geiger emphasises that, to avoid the privatisation of access to scientific knowledge, the special provision of Section 53(2)(1) of the German Copyright Act, which has no equivalent in most European copyright laws, provides an exception for copies made for scientific use coupled with a related, enforceable right concerning technical barriers.[683] Interestingly, under German law, the free copying for scientific use takes preference over "generic" private copying of digital works in so far as only the specific exception of personal academic use, unlike the general exception of private copying, is included in the list of enforceable usage rights against technical restrictions.[684] This

682 See Article 4a of the Creative Commons Public License 2.5, available at: http://www.creativecommons.org/licenses/by/2.5/legalcode.

683 See Geiger, 'Copyright and Free Access to Information', op. cit., p. 371. An updated version of the German Copyright Act is available at: http://bundesrecht.juris.de/urhg/__53.html.

684 See §95b(1)(6) of the German Copyright Act. An overview of the different legal treatment of the exceptions of private copying and of "personal academic use" under German law is provided in Appendix II, which shows that, unlike personal reproductions made for academic use, the German exception for private copying by digital means cannot be enforced against restrictions created by technical measures. This exception

regulation may be viewed as a first example of differentiation in the legal treatment of digital private copying, which is defined as an enforceable right in so far as the user shows a scientific use or purpose of use.

Interesting developments in the field of digital private copying may arise in France, where the regime of private copying established by new copyright law seems to facilitate differentiation in accordance with the type of work that a user wishes to copy for his or her private use. As outlined above, the French law which transposed the InfoSoc Directive seeks to implement the three-step test *within* the regulation of private copying by drawing upon and developing the solution of Article 6(4), §2, of the Directive.[685] The special administrative authority created by the French act is given the power to identify the threshold number of permissible digital copies of a protected work, in relation to the type of the work in question and by taking account of its specific modes of communication to the public and of the available measures of technological protection for that specific type of work. This regulation, if applied by the authority in consideration of the above-mentioned distinction between consumptive and productive uses, may ensure a balanced implementation of the private copying exception and compel the enforcement of this exception in fields (*e.g.*, scientific research) where the authority expects transformative uses to prevail on merely consumptive uses. Furthermore, new digital copyright law in France demonstrates that copying for consumptive purposes may not be necessarily abandoned in the face of technical restrictions where the legislator assumes that a certain kind of copy of a digital work does not contradict the three-step test. For instance, the new provision of Article L. 331-11 of the French Intellectual Property Code prevents digital broadcasters from implementing into their broadcasts anti-copy devices that would frustrate the exercise of the private copying exception (*e.g.*, by means of home-taping for mere time-shifting purposes).[686]

Finally, it is worth discussing very briefly the case of Italian law, which follows a unique approach with regard to differentiation in the legal treatment of copies made for personal use. Article 71-sexies, §4, of the Italian Copyright Act provides that, notwithstanding the application of technological measures, copyright owners should allow the lawful acquirer to carry out at least *one* private copy of the protected work, which may also be an analogue copy, on condition that this possibility of copying meets the specific requirements of the three-step test.[687] While transposing the safeguard mechanism of Article 6(4), §2, of the InfoSoc Directive, this provision makes the right of private copying enforceable against technical de-

may be enforced only in respect of reproductions on paper or similar media by photographic techniques.

[685] See Article L.331-8 of the French Intellectual Property Code: see Appendix II, see *infra*.

[686] See Article 16 of the French Law N.2006/961, which added Article L. 331-11 to the French Intellectual Property Code.

[687] See Marzano, *Diritto d'Autore e Digital Technologies*, op. cit., p. 305. An overview of how Italian law implemented Article 6(4), §2 of the Directive, while preserving the possibility of private copying in the presence of technical measures, is provided in the table of Appendix II.

vices only in respect of one (and only one) analogue copy of the digital work. In doing so, the Italian legislator implicitly considered that only analogue copies of the protected work may comply with the requirements of the three-step test, given their old-fashioned, limited possibilities of economic competition with the commercialisation of the work undertaken by the right-holder.

Marzano raised the argument that, due to the restatement of the second and third requirements of the three-step test under Article 71-sexies, §4, the right of *analogue* copying for purposes of personal use may not be enforceable where the making of an analogue copy should contrast with the test.[688] Consequently, under this view, the user's right may prove not to be enforceable if courts should find - on a case-by-case basis - that analogue copies end up conflicting with the normal exploitation of the digitally-protected work or cause an unreasonable prejudice to the right-holder's economic interests. However, as acknowledged by the same author, it seems preferable to conclude that the Italian act, by limiting the right of private copying to the analogue world, has provided a statutory interpretation of the three-step test itself.[689] Under this interpretation, the Italian legislator assessed that analogue copies of a digital work, as such, cannot contrast with the three-step test if the user meets the conditions of exercise established by law for this use to be lawful (that is, the user must have a lawful access to the original copy of the work, has to copy the work for strictly personal use, and has to pay economic compensation under the form of a copyright levy).

By limiting the user's right of private copying to the analogue world, Italian law completely allows copyright owners to restrict the possibility of digital copying through technological measures. The copyright owner is thereby given a great incentive to make analogue versions of the protected work available (*e.g.*, in publicly accessible places: libraries, archives, *etc*) in conjunction with the release of its digitally protected versions. In this way, the availability of analogue copies of the protected work will prevent users from seeking enforcement of the right of (analogue) reproduction from DRM-protected media. This solution draws on the wording of Article 6(4), §2, of the Directive, which empowers Member States to take appropriate measures:

> "[...] unless reproduction for private use has already been made possible by rightholders to the extent necessary to benefit from the exception or limitation concerned and in accordance with the provisions of Article 5(2)(b) and (5) [...]".

This generic description of voluntary measures has the effect of exempting copyright owners from the duty of accommodating private copying opportunities in the presence of technological protection measures and may easily deprive national law of the power to exercise the policy option created by the InfoSoc Directive effectively in respect of copies for personal use.

If, as in the case of Italian copyright law, the fact of spontaneously making available *analogue* copies of the protected work has the consequence of permitting

---

[688] See Marzano, *Diritto d'Autore e Digital Technologies*, op. cit., pp. 305-306.

[689] *Ibidem*.

copyright owners to implement unlimited copy-protection on *digital* formats of the same work, the objective of differentiating the legal treatment of digital private copying, in accordance with the productive or merely consumptive uses that this exception effectively enables, would inevitably be discouraged. The same would occur in respect of the valuable objective of preserving a threshold number of private reproductions with the objective of protecting personal use and user privacy from control opportunities enabled by today's DRM technology.

7.6. Restriction of transformative uses

7.6.1. May DRM technology address cumulative creativity and innovation?

When discussing the suitability of the private copying exception in the digital environment, it was emphasised that this exception should be preserved from the restrictive power of technical measures in so far as, while preserving the user's privacy in the use of the work, it enables (or, at least, facilitates) subsequent productive uses.[690] The implementation of technical measures on hardware and digital media creates a problem of enforcement in respect of transformative uses which is harder to solve than that of private copying. This situation occurs because, in principle, a technical blockage cannot discern whether a user accessing the work is going to make a lawful or an unlawful use of the work.[691] Under EU anti-circumvention law, the circumvention of this technical blockage is unlawful irrespectively of whether circumvention is performed for the purpose of infringing the copyright in the digitally protected work. Hence, this law allows copyright owners to use technology in order to foreclose access to their copyrighted works in an unlimited manner.

In this situation, the only possibility of protecting the statutory rights of the user is that of defining these usages and internalising them into the design of technical blockages. Today's technological scenario shows that DRM technology has become capable of translating traditional usages into digital rights languages or, according to the more recent jargon, "rights expression languages" (RELs). Nonetheless, under the system of safety nets created by Article 6(4) of the InfoSoc Directive, copyright owners have no obligation or incentive to use DRM technology to enable such uses. This solution is obstructed by the requirement of "legal access" to digitally protected works, which allows copyright owners to authorise the user's access in exchange of the contractual promise not to exercise copyright exceptions, including the ones that, under the same Article 6(4), should be guaranteed, notwithstanding the use of technical measures.

When discussing the problem of the enforcement of the user's right of private copying against copy-protection devices, it must be noted that DRM technology,

---

[690] See § 7.5.4., see *supra*.

[691] See Geiger, 'Copyright and Free Access to Information', op. cit., p. 369.

in contrast to simple (or rough) anti-copy devices, is capable of enabling sophisticated copy-management of each type of digital work that the technology protects. In the same way, today's DRM technology and, in the near future, TC platforms, will enable the copyright owner to attach highly flexible and diversified sets of usage permissions to each protected work, so that end-users may carry out several transformative uses. For instance, the XrML rights expression language, which is used as the basis for the standard language of MPEG-21, enables expression in a machine-readable form of the permissions to copy, delete, edit, modify, embed, export, extract, annotate, aggregate, install, backup, transfer, uninstall, verify, save, obtain, issue, possess, revoke, *etc.*[692] The granting of these types of permissions may be conditional on a wide range of circumstances, so that access to and use of digital content may be restricted to certain time periods, locations, devices, and to certain types of users.[693] Moreover, DRM technology allows restrictions of both the quality and the formats in which each digital content can be accessed and the control of the purpose for which access is granted.

Bechtold referred to this flexible technology as "dynamic" DRM systems.[694] This author claims that nothing would prevent DRM systems from addressing cumulative creativity and innovation if this type of creativity were properly expressed into RELs. To this end, Bechtold argued that, to accommodate cumulative creativity completely, these systems should be able to deal with the complex legal relationships that exist among different (and possibly numerous) copyright owners over a multiplicity of pre-existing works used in subsequent works.[695]

Unfortunately, the current standard of REL (*i.e.*, MPEG-21) has not been equipped with adequate tools to deal with the rights of transformative uses.[696] According to the MPEG-21 Overview submitted to the International Organisation for Standardisation, the only user rights that this standard REL intends to support and express are the rights and interests of individuals which address issues of privacy and the use of personal data.[697] In addition, the MPEG-21 standard aims to guaran-

---

692 See the XrML 2.0 Specification & Schema, available at: http://www.xrml.org/get_XrML.asp.

693 See Bechtold, 'The Present and the Future of Digital Rights Management – Musings on Emerging Legal Problems', op. cit., pp. 603-604.

694 See Bechtold, 'The Present and the Future of Digital Rights Management', op. cit., p. 604.

695 *Ibidem.*

696 See Mulligan, Han and Burstein, 'How DRM-Based Content Delivery Systems Disrupt Expectations of "Personal Use"', available at: http://www.law.berkeley.edu/clinics/samuelson/projects_papers/WPES-RFID-p029-mulligan.pdf.

697 See MPEG-21 Overview, published by the International Standard Organisation (ISO: see http//www.iso.org) at Shanghai, October 2002, and available at: http://www.chiariglione.org/mpeg/standards/mpeg-21/mpeg-21.htm#_Toc23297970. Section 5(5) of the Overview states: "The Rights Expression Language is also intended to provide a flexible interoperable mechanism to ensure personal data is processed in accordance with individual rights and to meet the requirement for Users to be able to express their rights and interests in a way that addresses issues of privacy and use of personal data."

tee end-to-end interoperability, consistency and reliability between different systems and services, in a way that content portability may be ensured to the highest extent, thus benefiting end-users.[698]

The main problem that DRM technology raises in respect of cumulative creativity is that this technology turns out to make all transformative uses subject to licensing. The problem is easy to understand. Think of an end-user wishing to reuse pieces of pre-existing works in order to create a new work by means of new technologies such as software enabling "clip-art".[699] In the Introduction, cases of highly appreciated films and songs created by follow-on authors equipped with poor digital technologies who re-used bits and extracts from pre-existing works and inserted them into new films and songs were mentioned as new examples of transformative uses.[700] If the rights on pre-existing songs and films were effectively controlled and managed through dynamic DRM systems, subsequent authors could not use pre-existing content without having to ask the relevant copyright owners for permission. As a result, all would-be creators would be forced to pay for a licence even if their uses (*e.g.*, quotations) or new works resulting from their re-use (*e.g.*, parodies, caricatures, pastiches, extracts made for teaching or educational uses, *etc*) were meant to be assisted by copyright exceptions which exempted these uses or types of works from the scope of copyright on pre-existing works. If so, the free uses of protected works would prove to be converted into pay-per-use permissions by dynamic DRM technology. This conversion would be even more apparent if the logic of DRM technology were transplanted, as in the case of TC platforms, into the end-user's devices (such as personal computers, portable players, *etc*).[701]

In these new circumstances, the crucial issue is that the nature of DRM technology and, even more so, that of TC platforms, disables any sort of *ex post* or case-by-case evaluation of the uses that end-users make of DRM-protected works. Even if one agrees with Bechtold that DRM technology, due to its wide flexibility, cannot be viewed as a blind technical blockage, it seems evident that DRM systems based on RELs are incapable of capturing, or even approximating, the myriad exceptions to exclusive rights as well as the contextual considerations that

698 See MPEG-21 Overview, cit., §5(5): "A standard Rights Expression Language should be able to support guaranteed end-to-end interoperability, consistency and reliability between different systems and services. To do so, it must offer richness and extensibility in declaring rights, conditions and obligations, ease and persistence in identifying and associating these with digital contents, and flexibility in supporting multiple usage/business models."

699 The term "clip-art" originated through the practice of physically cutting images from pre-existing printed works for use in new publishing projects: see the entry "clip-art" at: http://www.wikipedia.org.

700 See §1.4., see *supra*.

701 In this respect, it is worth recalling that the functioning of the MPEG-21 standard relies on the assumption that users who are given usage permissions shall run "trusted" machines, meaning computers that are capable of certifying the identity of an individual by means of authentication mechanisms and private keys of a public/private key pair. The concept and the functions of TC platforms are overviewed in Appendix I, §D, see *infra*.

characterise copyright protection.[702] There are broad categories of transformative use that are and will remain non-manageable even by the most nuanced and sophisticated algorithm. Cohen and Burk note that there are possible uses and outcomes which, to be built-in into the computer code, would require an impossible level of prescience.[703]

As argued above, in a world characterised by DRM protection, the determination of the fairness of a certain use of the protected work must logically take place *ex ante*, given that the setting of usage conditions foregoes the conduct of the user.[704] In DRM technology, the only time when the content management process can foresee and technically accommodate certain transformative uses by exempting them from its permission system is the time in which the technology is coded and its specific REL defines standardised permissions by specifying the terms, conditions and obligations under which usage rights can be exercised.[705]

In my view, a system of standardised user rights (or permissions) to be implemented into DRM technology may be useful only for the purpose of accommodating a few, and not all, of the transformative uses of digital content that copyright law excludes from the scope of copyright. DRM technology may be able to accommodate just the simplest transformative uses of protected works. Think of the case of quotation, for instance. Today, it is easy to express a standardised function enabling the quotation of a literary work or an extract from a film in a DRM system or in a TC platform. A REL may set out the maximum amount of "bits" of the protected work that the end-user is freely allowed to extract in order to exercise his or her quotation right. The same is true for basic functions which enable other legitimate purposes of transformative use. For instance, permissions which allow users to display a work for certain periods of time or partially perform the work a certain number of times. These types of permissions may prove to be indispensable for the purpose of illustration for educational use or scientific research.[706] For these uses to remain free, these standardised permissions should be accompanied by the technical condition that, to a certain extent, acts such as extracts, temporary displays and partial performances are to be exempted from permission and the payment of fees.[707]

In contrast, the most complex lawful transformative uses of pre-existing works are likely to be lost under DRM systems. This is the case of parody, for instance. In no way can the right to parody be expressed in a standardised set of *ex ante*

---

702 This view was expressed by Mulligan, Han and Burstein, 'How DRM-Based Content Delivery Systems Disrupt Expectations of "Personal Use"', op. cit.; and Burk and Cohen, 'Fair Use Infrastructure For Rights Management Systems', (15) *Harvard Journal of Law and Technology* 2001, p. 41, at pp. 55-58.

703 See Burk and Cohen, 'Fair Use Infrastructure', op. cit., p. 56.

704 See §7.2.2., see *supra*.

705 See Burk and Cohen, 'Fair Use Infrastructure', op. cit., p. 55.

706 See Article 5(3)(a) of the InfoSoc Directive.

707 The overview of the MPEG-21 REL standard contemplates situations of free (*i.e.*, unpaid) uses of DRM-protected works when making clear that its REL "[...] is also intended to support specification of access and use controls for digital content in cases where financial exchange is not part of the terms of use [...]".

permissions unrelated to a case-by-case evaluation. Notwithstanding their flexibility, DRM systems are incapable of capturing all the usages that a parodist needs to poke fun at pre-existing works. Moreover, parody is a *free* use, which does not fit the permission system that DRM technology creates. Complex transformative uses such as parody may continue to be allowed in respect of DRM-protected works only if follow-on uses can take place without any technical restrictions.

As explained in greater detail below, this situation may occur if the law allowed transformative uses of digitally protected works through the introduction of an external third party (for example, a decision-maker such as an arbitrator, an administrative authority, a court) whose role would be to govern a so-called "fair use infrastructure".[708] Under this system, the user may, firstly, ask either the copyright owner or the third party for keys to access and use a technically unrestricted copy of the desired work. Secondly, the user may freely access and use the pre-existing work in the manner that he or she likes most. At this point, the user may show to an external third party that his or her subsequent use effectively qualifies for an exemption from copyright under a certain exception.

This oversimplified example intends to highlight that DRM technology is not self-sufficient for the purpose of accommodating complex transformative uses and of preserving their freedom. As emphasised by Burk and Cohen, for these uses to be allowed in a world of DRM-protected works, an externally-mediated mechanism involving the participation of some third party is needed. Otherwise, opportunities of legitimate digital uses of pre-existing works will be left to the partisan decision of copyright owners.[709]

7.6.2. Policy options for the accommodation of cumulative creativity

It was argued above that, with the advent of control and management technologies which foreclose access to the digitally protected work, all *free* transformative use is endangered.[710] Whereas the permission system created by DRM technology may fit the purpose of administering the exclusive right to authorise derivative works ("adaptations, arrangements or other alterations" of the protected work, according to the Berne convention lexicon),[711] the system has negative consequences for subsequent creativity. In the absence of a corrective intervention by the law, DRM systems have the potential to convert rights of use into pay-per-use grants so that

[708] See § 7.6.2.2., see *infra*. See, also, Burk and Cohen, 'Fair Use Infrastructure', op. cit., p. 58.

[709] See Burk and Cohen, 'Fair Use Infrastructure', op. cit., p. 60. The solution of a possible "fair use infrastructure" under EU law will be examined more in depth at §9.2., see *infra*.

[710] See §2.2.1., see *supra*.

[711] See Article 12 of the Berne Convention ("Right of Adaptation, Arrangement or Other Alteration"), which includes control over derivative works within the copyright scope.

the more pieces of protected works the end-user needs to access in order to create a new work, the higher the fees that he or she will be asked to pay.[712]

In the context of the InfoSoc Directive, the problem of transformative uses and, more generally, the stoppage of subsequent creativity raised by technologies which restrict access to information and manage digital content was widely ignored. It was emphasised above that the solution found by European law-makers under Article 6(4) of the Directive does not solve this problem, with regard to both the selection of an unreasonably narrow set of "first-class" exceptions and the creation of an ineffective system of safety nets.[713] As shown by an overview of the transposition of the Directive in a few EU Member States, this system results in divergent national sub-systems where copyright exceptions which enable transformative uses are addressed in very different ways.[714]

In consideration of the unlimited protection of DRM technology established by Article 6 and 7 of the InfoSoc Directive, there are two policy options that the European Commission may consider proposing to the European Parliament and the Council. The first option is that of restricting the scope of the anti-circumvention laws so as to afford legal protection only to technologies that do not protect digital works beyond the limits set out by copyright law.[715] The second option is that of modifying the legal treatment of copyright exceptions by either granting users certain enforceable rights of transformative use against technological measures, or by establishing statutory licences which permit the most important types of subsequent uses.[716]

7.6.2.1. Creating an exception of fair circumvention

As regards the first option, the restriction of the scope of anti-circumvention law may be achieved, as proposed by Samuelson, through the creation in the law of an exception to the circumvention prohibition that may exempt all users engaging in circumvention activities for "legitimate purposes" from liability.[717] Samuelson's proposal referred to the U.S. anti-circumvention provisions created by Section 1201 of the U.S. Copyright Act, whose scope was understood to broaden the legal protection of technical measures required by Article 11 of the 1996 WIPO Copyright Treaty excessively. Samuelson emphasised that the anti-circumvention regulations needed to be revised, given that they ran contrary to the provision of Section 1201(c)(1), which provides that:

---

[712] From an economics-based perspective, the beneficial function of copyright exceptions on transaction costs that would otherwise stifle transformative uses of pre-existing works was discussed above, at §2.2.2.3, see *supra*.

[713] See § 4.5.3, see *supra*.

[714] See § 4.6.2. see *supra*.

[715] See Lessig, *The Future of Ideas*, op. cit., p. 257.

[716] See Geiger, 'Copyright and Free Access to Information', op. cit., p. 372.

[717] See Samuelson, 'Intellectual Property and the Digital Economy: Why the Anti-Circumvention Regulations Need to Be Revised', (14) *Berkeley Technology Law Journal* 1999, p. 519.

"[N]othing in this section shall affect rights, remedies, exceptions, or defenses to copyright infringement, including fair use, under this title."[718]

Samuelson canvasses an exception that should be added to the narrow exceptions to circumvention bans established by the same Section 1201, letters from (d) to (k), for cases of specific legitimate purposes that would otherwise be stifled.[719] This exception would allow the lawful acquirer of a copy of the protected work to circumvent a technical measure for "other legitimate purposes", meaning purposes other than those identified by the current system of very specific exceptions. Clearly, in Samuelson's view, this exception should enable circumvention for the purpose of exercising all the legitimate purposes that U.S. copyright law allows under the fair use doctrine.

If this proposal were accepted under the system created by the EU InfoSoc Directive, the exception would restrict today's unlimited protection of DRM technology by allowing an end-user wishing to carry out a use covered by a copyright exception to reverse-engineer the computer code of a DRM system lawfully. In this respect, this exception would look like the de-compilation exception provided under Article 6(1) of the EC Software Directive. This provision exempts from copyright liability unauthorised acts of reproduction of the code of a protected programme and the translation of its form only for the purpose of obtaining the information necessary to achieve the interoperability of an independently created computer programme with other programmes, provided that the proprietor of the other programmes has not made readily available the interfaces which are needed to support the functionality designed in the independently created programme.[720] The fact that this exception merely covers purposes of interoperability means that the same acts of reverse-engineering are illegal in so far as they are carried out in respect of a DRM programme code for the purpose of accessing the work and to engage in a lawful transformative use (*e.g.*, taking a clip from a digitally protected film for purposes of teaching illustration).

Under the solution proposed by Samuelson, the reverse-engineering of DRM programmes would be allowed on the assumption that the illegality of circumvention would be strictly linked to an effective infringement of copyright law. At the same time, the solution would keep the fair use defence alive while allowing end-users to demonstrate *ex post* the legitimate purpose of their unauthorised use in cases of infringement suits. Moreover, the proposed exception would give developers and users of DRM technology a great incentive to protect digital works only by means of technologies which embody copyright exceptions in their RELs. Under this solution, the (ineffective) system of safety nets created by Article 6(4) of

---

[718] See U.S. Code, Title 17, §1201(c)(1).

[719] See Samuelson, Intellectual Property and the Digital Economy, op. cit., pp. 543-546. As recalled above (at §7.2.4., see *supra*), these exemptions from the U.S. circumvention prohibitions concern certain acts performed by non-profit libraries, archives and educational institutions and other acts of circumvention performed for purposes of law enforcement, intelligence and other government activities, reverse engineering, encryption research, exceptions regarding minors, and security testing.

[720] See Hart, 'Interoperability Information and the Microsoft Decision', op. cit., p. 362.

the InfoSoc Directive may be dismantled. For Samuelson's solution to be effective, nonetheless, a slight re-adjustment (either by legislative amendment or by judicial interpretation) of the "anti-trafficking" provisions which outlaw the production and distribution of circumvention-enabling technologies would be necessary. If these prohibitions were interpreted too broadly, end-users other than experienced hackers would never be able to craft tools with circumvention-enabling uses. In the absence of a legislative re-definition, for users to be able to benefit from the proposed "legitimate purposes" exception, courts must apply these provisions as narrowly as possible, by limiting the enforcement of prohibitions regarding the production and distribution of circumvention-enabling technologies to technology which is primarily designed, produced, adapted or performed for the purpose of committing copyright infringement.[721]

A solution similar to that of Samuelson, though more radical and more difficult to implement in the EU copyright system, was provided in the United States by the "Cohen Theorem".[722] Cohen spelt out this theorem while questioning the constitutional legitimacy of the legislative proposal that, under new Article 2B of the U.S. Uniform Commercial Code (UCC), would have implemented a regime of electronic private ordering in mass markets for information goods.[723] This new law would have permitted contractual agreements to establish "electronic regulation of performance", which could prevent uses of the information which were inconsistent with the agreement of the parties, even if copyright law allowed such uses. Cohen claimed firstly that courts may, and should, have invalidated licence terms based on state legislation designed, in accordance with new Article 2B of the UCC, to legitimate contractual agreements that would enable the wholesale displacement of federal copyright law and policy.[724] In particular, this author emphasised that the U.S. Constitution mandates exceptions on copyright ownership by both the language of the so-called "Intellectual Property Clause" of the U.S. Constitution[725] and the protection of free speech under the First Amendment.[726] With regard to the Intellectual Property Clause, Cohen remarked that the proposed law

[721] See Article 6(2) of the InfoSoc Directive. The same argument was raised by Samuelson, 'Intellectual Property and the Digital Economy', op. cit., pp. 546-549, with regard to the "anti-device" provisions created under §1201(a)(2) of the U.S. Copyright Act.

[722] The denomination of "Cohen Theorem" was invented by Lessig, *The Future of Ideas*, op. cit., p. 257.

[723] See Cohen, 'Copyright and The Jurisprudence of Self-Help', (13) *Berkeley Technology Law Journal* 1998, p. 1089. The so-called UCITA proposal was briefly analysed at §5.4.3.1., see *supra*.

[724] See Cohen, 'Copyright and The Jurisprudence of Self-Help', op.cit., pp. 1128-1137.

[725] The "Intellectual Property Clause" is embodied in Article 1, Sect. 8, Clause 8 of the U.S. Constitution, which provides that the Congress shall have the power "[T]o promote the progress of science and useful arts, by securing for limited times to authors and inventors the exclusive right to their respective writings and discoveries."

[726] The First Amendment to the U.S. Constitution states: "Congress shall make no law respecting an establishment of religion, or prohibiting the free exercise thereof; or abridging the freedom of speech, or of the press; or the right of the people peaceably to assemble, and to petition the Government for a redress of grievances".

would have come into conflict with constitutional policy in so far as it permitted what the referred clause forbade, namely, the protection of facts, ideas, methods of operation, and other elements of "writings" that are not eligible for copyright protection because they do not attain a minimum level of originality.[727] With regard to the First Amendment, Cohen emphasised that freedom of speech would have been threatened if private information providers had been allowed to use non-negotiated, electronic standard forms to enforce prohibitions on a wide range of speech activities.[728] This author developed this argument by arguing that DRM systems which implement (invalid) self-enforcing contracts built-in in the technology should also be considered invalid.[729] Cohen's conclusion was that the invalidity of electronic contracts which override constitutionally-mandated exceptions and the subsequent illegality of DRM systems which enforce these contracts should be meant to provide end-users with a right of "self-help" that authorises users to lawfully circumvent DRM technology restricting fair use opportunities.[730] Cohen reached this conclusion by developing Ginsburg's suggestion that, in some circumstances, the law might afford licensees who engage in contractually prohibited conduct which is permitted by copyright law a "right of fair breach".[731] Cohen claimed that such a right would be meaningless if it did not include a right to carry out the breach, that is, a right to hack the technology that enforces unlawful usage restrictions.[732] Hence, the so-called "Cohen Theorem" postulates that, to ensure that proprietary rights in expression do not frustrate the freedoms of the First Amendment, users must be afforded affirmative rights in order to preserve the fair use privileges established under copyright law and to protect themselves from electronic rights management (*i.e.*, today's DRM) technology. Under this proposal, no legislative revision of anti-circumvention law is required. According to Cohen, under U.S. copyright law a right of fair circumvention against over-restrictive DRM technology can always be invoked by end-users because statutory anti-circumvention provisions are not constitutionally entitled to override mandated copyright exceptions. As explained further in the next chapter, the implementation of such a proposal in the EU copyright system would have to face the

727 See Cohen, 'Copyright and The Jurisprudence of Self-Help', op. cit., pp. 1132-1133, who argued that "[T]he Intellectual Property Clause denies protection to certain subject matter precisely so that it may remain in the public domain, available to all comers. It follows that where unpatentable know-how and uncopyrightable facts or principles are concerned, the same restrictions that bind Congress also bind the states. Any state adopting Article 2B should recognize that it effectively allows information providers to opt out of those restrictions, thereby frustrating constitutional policy."

728 See Cohen, 'Copyright and The Jurisprudence of Self-Help', op. cit., p. 1134.

729 See Cohen, 'Copyright and The Jurisprudence of Self-Help', op. cit., pp. 1140-1142.

730 *Ibidem.*

731 See Ginsburg, 'Copyright Without Walls: Speculations on Literary Property in the Library of the Future', (42) *Representations* 1993, p. 53, at pp. 63-64, available at: http://www.representations.org.

732 See Cohen, 'Copyright and The Jurisprudence of Self-Help', op. cit., p. 1141.

hurdle emerging from the non-recognition of the limited nature of copyright protection at constitutional level.[733]

7.6.2.2. Creating a user rights management infrastructure

A second policy option for the protection of digital transformative uses may be that of converting exclusive rights into remuneration rights whenever the use of a digitally protected work makes it possible to create a new work.[734] A legislative transition from an exclusive right regime to a remuneration right regime (from a "property rule" to a "liability rule" regime, in the language of law and economics)[735] may be suitable, especially in respect of certain types of work for which the opportunities of transformative use are regarded by law-makers as most likely and most important. However, as stated in more depth below,[736] this transition seems to be barred by the legal bounds created by the international copyright law embodied in the Berne Convention. Indeed, Articles 11bis(2) and 13(1) of this Convention have so far been meant to give Contracting Parties the option of determining or imposing non-voluntary licences of exclusive rights *only* in such exceptional cases as the broadcasting of copyrighted works (by any means of communication)[737] and the recording of musical works.[738] Thus, a generalised system of remuneration rights in the face of productive uses of copyrighted works would not be legitimate under international copyright law.

Nevertheless, the distinction between productive and unproductive uses may be a reasonable criterion for copyright policy-makers to decide which rights of use to make enforceable in the digital environment. In this respect, the argument was raised that, notwithstanding its main purpose of protecting personal use from the copyright owner's control, the private copying exception should be preserved in situations where this use fosters the production of new works.[739] The same line of reasoning, *a fortiori* (*i.e.*, with a much stronger foundation), applies to copyright

---

733 See §8.1.2., see *infra*.

734 See Geiger, 'Copyright and Free Access to Information', op. cit., p. 372.

735 According to the law and economics terminology, contrary to *property* rules, *liability* rules establish *mere remuneration* rights. In the presence of certain circumstances identified by the law (*e.g.*, a productive use of a pre-existing copyrighted work, as in the case mentioned in the main text), liability rules allow users to freely use a work without the copyright owner's authorisation, provided that they pay him or her remuneration. The foundational legal entitlements framework in the law and economics analysis was established by Calabresi and Melamed, 'Property Rules, Liability Rules, and Inalienability: One view of the Cathedral', (85) *Harvard Law Review* 1972, p. 1089. For an application of this theoretical framework to the field of intellectual property, see Merges, 'Contracting into Liability Rules: Intellectual Property Rights and Collective Rights Organizations', (84) *California Law Review* 1996, p. 1293.

736 See §8.3.3.2, see *infra*.

737 See Article 11bis(2) of the Berne Convention for the Protection of Artistic and Literary Works.

738 See Article 13(1) of the Berne Convention.

739 See §7.5.4., see *supra*.

exceptions which enable transformative uses, which enjoy a stronger constitutional protection under the democratic principle of freedom of expression.[740]

For the purpose of enabling follow-on creativity and innovation, copyright legislators in the EU may think of creating fully enforceable rights of transformative use, especially in respect of specific types of protected works (*e.g.*, scientific works). This may be sound law and policy, especially where the production of new works is based mainly on iterative patterns, and the expectation of monetary gain is not the key argument giving authors an incentive to create. A perfect example of this situation is given by the licensing practices of authors in the fields of science and research, who often opt for open-publishing systems under copyleft licences. In so far as these systems should continue to proliferate and allow academic users and scientists to be informed about the current state of scientific innovation, as they do now, there may be no reason for implementing a stronger enforcement system for transformative uses. In contrast, the idea of abandoning the logic of mere *exceptions* for the adoption of users' *rights* might be better appreciated in as much as the legislators considered that the "user-friendly" licensing model for scientific works could be stifled by the advent of other, new publishing models in the near future. Digital publishing is likely to change quickly in the light of new business possibilities enabled by pervasive technologies of control and management such as TC systems. As explained in Appendix I to this book, TC platforms promise to make electronic publishing much safer, more sophisticated and more profitable than at present.[741] Therefore, it is not unreasonable to expect that, at some point in the future, authors in the fields of science and academic research may no longer make their most important works available under open (*i.e.*, free) licences. The reasons for this change might be related to the full development of on-line markets for scientific works released in a DRM-protected format or in a "trusted" format. For instance, publishers of scientific journals and academic books selling both on-line and paper versions of these goods may start fiercely opposing the academic writers' well-known practice of disclosing and publishing their working papers on the Internet, on a free and open-access basis, while transferring (after a while) their copyright on the same works to the publishers of journals which sell the same contents on-line.[742] The matter is even more complicated if one considers that universities may intervene in this framework as well, in order to protect their own commercial interests in licensing and marketing their intellectual creations on-line, including, for instance, academic courses and other materials relating to teaching activities. If publishers of scientific works, including universities, started forbidding by contract their authors and employees from engaging in open access practices that have the potential to harm their on-line businesses, scientific works and teaching materials might suddenly become avail-

---

740 See §8.1.1., see *infra*.

741 See Appendix I, §D1.

742 See the Social Science Research Network, available at: http://www.ssrn.com, which is a prominent example of academic network where writers in the social sciences make available their works under (non-exclusive) licences enabling free access and copy of each released work.

able only on the Internet on a pay-per-access and pay-per-use basis (*e.g.*, through individual or university subscriptions) and in a DRM-protected (or similar) format.

In this situation, all opportunities of follow-on creativity through free transformative uses would be objectively frustrated. Copyright legislators may be advised to preserve the most important scientific use of copyrighted works from the permission system enabled by DRM technology. It was made clear above that this technology is largely incapable of capturing and expressing the most complex uses for purposes of teaching and research in RELs.[743] For instance, if a scientific essay were made available under a DRM system, it might become very difficult and expensive for an academic user to access and quote it extensively in order to comment upon it and criticise the original author's ideas.

In this future (though not unrealistic) setting, the adoption of a copyright system based on effective user rights in all cases where a pre-existent work allows the creation of a new work may ensure freedom of access to copyrighted information without requiring the user to hack the technical measure protecting the copyrighted work. However, for the co-existence of this system of user rights with any digital works released under DRM systems, the intervention of an external decision-maker would be needed at some point of the enforcement process. If a copyright exception were created in order to allow users to take a pre-existing DRM-protected work and use it without the technical constraints imposed by the technology, this law should provide the new exception with a viable system enabling the user to access a digitally unprotected (that is, wholly usable) copy of that pre-existing work. This scheme may work well and be desirable for all stakeholders in so far as copyright law established a monitoring mechanism to ascertain whether a specific purpose of transformative use effectively qualifies for the mentioned exception. As explained in more depth below,[744] this result may be achieved through the creation of a so-called "fair use infrastructure" under which a third party, for example, a public agency, could ascertain the identity and the purpose of the requesting user (while somehow preserving his or her privacy, of course) and hand or send electronically a personal cryptographic key or code to the user in order to enable access to a technically unrestricted copy of the requested works. As warned by Burk and Cohen, though, in order to enable a correct functioning of this type of externally-mediated enforcement proceedings and avoid possible abuses, it would be of crucial importance that the mediating party commanded the trust of both the copyright owner and the user of the work.[745] In their proposal of a fair use infrastructure, these authors emphasised that the release of cryptographic keys to enable access to digitally encrypted works does not assure that the humans will employ the keys in a proper or secure way. Thus, the security of these operations could be ensured if the mediating party implemented trusted systems for the purpose of associating access and usage keys with particular users.[746]

---

743 See §7.6.1., see *supra*.

744 See §9.3.2., see *infra*.

745 See Burk and Cohen, 'Fair Use Infrastructure', op. cit., p. 61.

746 *Ibidem*, p. 62.

7.7. Summary

This chapter has focused on how the EU legal protection of DRM technology affects different typologies of free uses of copyrighted digital works. The analysis started by emphasising that DRM technology, while enforcing the access right created by unlimited anti-circumvention law, inevitably alters the way in which the lawful (and possibly free) character of uses of digital works is estimated. It has been shown that the DRM-enabled control of access to and use of protected works compels an *ex ante*, instead of an *ex post* or case-by-case, estimation of fair uses. Due to this change, the only way to make DRM protection compatible with exceptions to the scope of copyright would be that of internalising such exceptions into the rights expression languages (RELs) that DRM technology adopts for controlling and managing permissions for access and usage. The legal tools provided by the InfoSoc Directive are incapable of enabling this solution for two main reasons. On the one hand, the model of copyright exceptions chosen by the Directive has been found to be ambiguous because, while providing a long list of optional "narrow" exceptions for Member State copyright law, it makes the enforcement of these exceptions subject to an unclear possibility of *ex post* judicial review under the three-step test. On the other hand, in the absence of a contract law interface which outlaws the contractual overriding of copyright exceptions, the requirement of "legal access" to DRM-protected works created by Article 6(4) of the Directive allows copyright owners to extract from the user the enforceable promise to give up his or her rights of use when authorising access to their works.

The focus was then shifted to the European Commission's view of DRM technology. It has been recalled that, in its 2004 Communication to the European Parliament and to the Council, the Commission made it clear that DRM systems are not - in themselves - an alternative to copyright policy in setting the parameters either in respect of copyright protection or the exceptions that are traditionally provided by law. On this occasion, the Commission mentioned the establishment of a global interoperable DRM infrastructure to support open standards of communication and encoding, and the enforcement of copyright exceptions as the most important policy objectives to be pursued. In this respect, it has been emphasised that the current market situation concerning DRM solutions and, in particular, the possibly ubiquitous position of Microsoft's proprietary DRM system makes the objective of an open standard of DRM technology very difficult to achieve.

With regard to the effective enforcement of free uses covered by copyright exceptions, the second part of the chapter analysed three different situations in which the implementation of unrestricted DRM technology on digital media frustrates freedom of use. The first situation concerned interoperability. It has been pointed out that the portability of copyrighted digital works from one medium to another may often be frustrated by the technical incapability to interoperate that affects media, software and hardware that support different DRM systems. The analysis has highlighted that this situation is due to private ownership of DRM components and technologies, whose adoption is subject to the licensing power of intellectual property right-holders. This lack of interoperability affects basic rights of access to and use of lawfully acquired works. The examples of the litigation in France and in the United States over the foreclosure of access to digital works enabled by Apple iTunes' DRM system revealed that the intellectual property protection of DRM components and technologies confers legitimacy to the refusal to license raised by property right-holders to suppliers of content and media players who seek the interoperability of their DRM technology with another DRM programme. Then, the example of the new French copyright legislation showed that the creation of an obligation to disclose essential information to enable technical interoperability will remain ineffective in so far as the possibility of requesting this information will be given only to market players, such as content and technology suppliers, and not to end-users or consumer associations. The subsequent remarks on copyright protection and a possible EU interoperability policy have stressed that, in so far as requests of interoperability information are restricted by law to the competitors and the possible customers of the owners of the dominant DRM technology, the room for public disclosure of this information is very small.

The second situation analysed in this chapter concerned the restriction of private copying of DRM-protected works. The *Mulholland Drive* case brought in France by a consumer (joined by an association of consumers) against the producer of a copy-protected DVD film suggested that the implementation of the three-step test, and especially of its second requirement (*i.e.*, the "normal exploitation" requirement), may have the consequence of completely foreclosing the room for the private copying exception in respect of digital media. Criticism has been expressed with regard to the findings that the French Supreme Court reached by applying *in abstracto* a notion of normal exploitation under which *any* unauthorised copy for personal use would be prohibited given the risks of copyright infringement in the digital environment and in consideration of the economic harm caused by each private copy to one of the most important sources of revenues of the protected work (*i.e.*, the sale of DVDs). The Court failed to consider *in concreto* that, under the specific circumstances of the case (*i.e.*, a copy of the movie from a digital to an analogue medium), the user's purpose of private copying would have met *all* the requirements established by the applicable French statutory licence (*e.g.*, payment of fair compensation through a copyright levy). This case has shown that intervention by the legislator in the specific field of digital private copying is needed to achieve a balanced interpretation of the three-step test and to implement policy options which, to some extent, may preserve private copying in the digital environment for the protection of user privacy and for the preservation of the productive purposes enabled by this exception. It has been emphasised that the new French copyright law has exercised the option mentioned in the Directive by conferring the power to regulate and settle impartially the conflict arising between technological protection measures and digital private copying (even in consideration of the specific type of work to be copied) to a new *ad hoc* authority.

The third situation, finally, has shown that DRM technology, notwithstanding its capability of attaching highly flexible and diversified sets of usage permissions to each digitally protected work, is unfit to accommodate the myriad of possible transformative uses that copyright exceptions may prove to allow. It has been noted that DRM systems and, even more so, TC platforms have the effect of disabling any kind of *ex post* (*i.e.*, case-by-case) evaluation of end-user conduct. This effect stems from the technical assumption that the technology and its rights expression languages (RELs) may just encapsulate pre-defined, simple opportunities of transformative uses (*e.g.*, enabling the end-user to extract a certain number of bits from a literary work or film in order to exercise the right of quotation). For the accommodation of the most complex transformative uses (*e.g.*, parody, and various uses for purposes of education and research), the policy options at the copyright legislator's disposal are basically twofold. The first option is that of permitting the circumvention of DRM technology for purposes of legitimate uses, such as that of engaging in fair uses that DRM forecloses. The second policy option for the preservation of cumulative creativity in a world of DRM-protected works may be provided by the creation of an externally-mediated enforcement process. Under this kind of enforcement technique, which Burk and Cohen referred to as "fair use infrastructure", a third party (*e.g.*, a public agency) may ascertain the identity and the purpose of the requesting user (while somehow preserving his or her privacy) and hand or electronically send the user a personal cryptographic key or code which enables access to a technically unrestricted (*i.e.*, completely usable) copy of the requested work (*e.g.*, an analogue copy of the protected work). In this way, the end-user would be free to transform the pre-existing work out of the technical constraints imposed by DRM technology. It has been concluded that, to avoid possible abuses of the system, the third party may ensure the security of these operations regarding cryptographic keys through the implementation of trusted systems which associate the access and usage keys with particular users.

PART IV
WORKING SOLUTIONS IN THE EU COPYRIGHT SYSTEM

8. Copyright policy alternatives for preserving end-user freedom of expression and information

8.1. Addressing the conflict between copyright and freedom of expression

This chapter will consider how the fundamental right of freedom of expression and information embodied in Article 10 of the European Charter of Human Rights (ECHR) may be viewed as an additional legal basis to compel the reconsideration of EU digital copyright law.[747] It was emphasised above that copyright law enacted by the 2001 InfoSoc Directive, while failing to consider and effectively ensure the enforcement of exceptions to digital copyright, ends up running contrary to the clauses of the EC Treaty which aim to preserve national cultural policy and consumer protection.[748] The first part of this chapter provides a brief overview of the legal framework of Article 10 of the ECHR and its influence on the protection of intellectual property. Then, how EU law may be re-adjusted to eliminate copyright-based restrictions that have the effect of depriving end-users of legitimate opportunities of communication over peer-to-peer networks and expression in respect of DRM-protected works will be discussed.

8.1.1. The legal value of Article 10 of the ECHR

Article 10 of the ECHR is particularly relevant because it defines the fundamental right of freedom of expression and information as the right to hold opinions, as

---

[747] See the European Convention on Human Rights (ECHR), signed in Rome on 4 November 1950. Article 10 of the ECHR states: "1. Everyone has the right to freedom of expression. This right shall include freedom to hold opinions and to receive and impart information and ideas without interference by public authority and regardless of frontiers [...] 2. The exercise of these freedoms, since it carries with it duties and responsibilities, may be subject to such formalities, conditions, restrictions or penalties as are prescribed by law and are necessary in a democratic society, in the interests of national security, territorial integrity or public safety, for the prevention of disorder or crime, for the protection of health or morals, for the protection of the reputation or rights of others, for preventing the disclosure of information received in confidence, or for maintaining the authority and impartiality of the judiciary."

[748] See, respectively, §5.3. and §5.4., see *supra*.

well as impart, distribute and receive information without government interference in all the Member States that belong to the Council of Europe.[749] Even though the ECHR is not formally a body of EU law, it is generally accepted that EU legislation and measures need to comply with the fundamental rights embodied in the ECHR.[750] An explicit recognition of the binding character of the ECHR was embodied in Article 6 of the Treaty on European Union,[751] which provides that

> "The Union shall respect fundamental rights, as guaranteed by the European Convention for the Protection of Human Rights and Fundamental Freedoms signed in Rome on 4 November 1950 and as they result from the constitutional traditions common to the Member States, as general principles of Community law."

After having been enforced and recognised as embodying general principles of Community law, this source of law may have a much greater impact on the EU law-making process if these fundamental rights should finally be incorporated into the primary (*i.e.*, constitutional) law of the EU. This process of incorporation has taken place in two steps. Firstly, the Commission, the Parliament and the Council adopted and solemnly proclaimed a Charter of Fundamental Rights which included the Bill of Rights of the ECHR.[752] This document was politically approved by the Member States at the European Council of Nice in December 2000.[753] Secondly, the integration of the Charter into the EU Treaties would have been accomplished by the introduction of the Charter into Part II of the Treaty establishing a Constitution for Europe, which was signed in Rome at the end of October 2004.[754] In 2005, the ratification process of the Treaty failed because of its rejection in the referenda held in France and in the Netherlands.[755] After a period of reflection started in June 2005, and in the aftermath of the negative responses coming from the French and Dutch electorates, the EU Member States brought this institutional crisis to an end at the meeting of the European Council held at Brussels in June

---

749 Especially for non-European readers, it is worth recalling here that the Council of Europe is an international organisation that is separate from and broader (*i.e.*, 46 Member States) than the European Union. The Council of Europe's institutions include a Commissioner for Human Rights and the European Court of Human Rights. For more information, see: http://www.coe.int.

750 The enforcement of the ECHR by the ECJ began by the well-known Case 29/69, *Stauder* v. *City of Ulm* [1969] ECR 419.

751 See Treaty on European Union, OJ C 191, 29.07.1992, in the consolidated version published in the OJ C 325, 24.12.2002.

752 See Charter of Fundamental Rights of the European Union, OJ C 364/1, 18.12.2000.

753 See the EU Charter of Fundamental Rights on the website of the European Commission, Justice and Home Affairs, at: http://ec.europa.eu/justice_home/unit/charte/index/en_html.

754 See the Treaty establishing a Constitution for Europe, OJ C 310/1, 16.12.2004. The fundamental right of freedom of expression and information was included under Article II-11 of the constitutional treaty.

755 See 'French say firm 'No' to the EU Treaty', 30 May 2005, available at: http://news.bbc.co.uk/2/hi/europe/4592243.stm; and 'Dutch say 'No' to EU Constitution', 2 June 2005, at: http://news.bbc.co.uk/2/hi/europe/4601439.stm.

2007 under the auspices of the German Presidency.[756] At this meeting, the Member States finally agreed upon abandoning the project of a Constitution for Europe in order to opt for a more limited (and politically feasible) reform of the two existing Treaties (*i.e.*, Treaty on European Union and the Treaty establishing the European Community).[757] According to the political agreement reached at the Brussels Council, this amendment through a reform treaty will incorporate most of the institutional and legislative changes embodied originally in the single constitutional treaty.[758] In the framework of such an agreement, the European Council conferred upon the governmental representatives of the Member States a political mandate according to which the EU Charter of Fundamental Rights will not be included in the body of the two existing Treaties, as was originally intended. Instead, the Charter will acquire the same legal value as these Treaties through the express recognition of this value in a new provision of the Treaty on European Union devoted to the enforcement of fundamental rights.[759] Consequently, the EU Charter will finally acquire the status of EU primary law and is likely to influence the EU law-making process in a way that would strengthen the case for revision of legislation, like the InfoSoc Directive, that has had a chilling effect on freedom of expression and information.

8.1.2. Copyright *vs.* free expression

It was argued above that, from an economic point of view, one of the main objectives of copyright protection is to foster the production of intellectual works by providing an incentive (or a reward) to would-be creators.[760] By the granting of exclusive rights for the commercial exploitation of creative works, copyright law is designed to allow creators to recoup the investments that they made in the process of intellectual creation. Besides its incentive/reward rationale, copyright law pursues the objective of disseminating intellectual works by limiting the abovementioned exclusive rights both in time and in scope. In particular, copyright exceptions exempt certain socially valuable uses from the copyright scope in order to pursue the objective of the dissemination of copyrighted works while protecting user privacy and stimulating the creation of new works by follow-on authors at the same time.

---

756 See *Verso il nuovo trattato europeo*, Centro nazionale di Informazione e Documentazione Europea (CIDE), available at: http://www.cide.it/Contenuti.

757 See Consolidated Version of the Treaty establishing the European Community, OJ C 325, 24.12.2002.

758 See 'Statewatch Observatory on the EU Constitution and the Reform Treaty', *Statewatch*, available at http://www.statewatch.org/euconstitution.htm.

759 At the time of writing, the above recognition is embodied in Article 6 ("Fundamental rights") of the new version of the Treaty on European Union, as amended by the draft of the reform treaty approved at the Intergovernmental Conference of 18 October 2007 in Lisbon, available at http://www.consilium.europa.eu.

760 See §2.1.2., see *supra*.

As emphasised above, a basic conflict arises between the two policy objectives of *production* and *dissemination* of creative works insofar as exceptions and limitations to property rights on digital information and other opportunities of free use of copyrighted works are eroded by copyright enforcement efforts.[761] The two case studies analysed above showed that copyright enforcement in the digital environment has the potential to frustrate the objective of dissemination of creative works by the wide criminalisation of peer-to-peer (or "point-to-point") transfer of digital works on the Internet and by the lock-up of copyrighted information enabled by DRM technologies.

In my view, these new situations create an evident conflict between digital copyright enforcement and freedom of expression. The conflict originates from the assumption that copyrighted works are both an output of intellectual creation and an indispensable input for subsequent creativity.[762] The purpose of this chapter is to show how today's efforts to enforce copyright, while having the effect of eroding the opportunities of *legitimate* dissemination and the subsequent uses of copyrighted digital works, raise a dilemma that needs to be solved at the level of constitutional law. The basic question is whether the enforcement of property rights on digital information, from a constitutional perspective, is so important as to take absolute priority over the competing objective of preserving user freedom of communication and expression on the Internet and in other new digital settings.

The potential conflict between copyright and freedom of expression was rarely addressed in continental Europe because author's rights (*droit d'auteur*) systems, unlike the U.S. Constitution, reflect no utilitarian considerations of information policy.[763] In contrast to the United States, copyright has no specific constitutional foundation in continental Europe. In most EU Member States, the constitutional basis of copyright law can be found either in provisions which protect personality rights or in those which protect property.[764] In this respect, it is worth recalling that, at the end of July 2006, when reviewing the constitutional legitimacy of the few exemptions from criminal copyright liability contained in the French act which transposed the InfoSoc Directive, the French Constitutional Court (*Conseil constitutionnel*) seized the opportunity to point out that copyright protection is a form of preservation of property embodied in Article 17 of the *Déclaration des Droits de l'homme et du citoyen* of 1789.[765]

---

761 See §2.1.3., see *supra*.

762 See §2.2.1., see *supra*.

763 See Hugenholtz, 'Copyright and Freedom of Expression in Europe', in: Elkin-Koren and Netanel (eds), *The Commodification of Information*, Kluwer Law International, The Hague 2002, p. 239, at p. 241. The Intellectual Property Clause under the U.S. Constitution is provided by Article 1, Sect. 8, Clause 8.

764 See Hugenholtz, 'Copyright and Freedom of Expression', op. cit., p. 242.

765 See Conseil constitutionnel, Decision N.2006-540 DC of 27 July 2006, which addressed the issue of compliance with the French Constitution of the Law on copyright and related rights in the information society, in the version finally approved by the French Parliament on 30 June 2006), paragraphs 30 and 31, available at: http://www.conseil-constitutionnel.fr/decision/2006/2006540/index.htm.

In the context of EU law, neither the EC Treaty nor the ECHR provide copyright protection on an explicitly constitutional basis. Recognition of intellectual property as a fundamental right was embodied in Article 17(2) of the EU Charter of Fundamental Rights, which provides that "intellectual property shall be protected". The recognition of copyright as a fundamental right could be inferred even before the solemn proclamation of the EU Charter from the phrasing of Article 1 of Protocol N.1 to the ECHR:

"[E]very natural or legal person is entitled to the peaceful enjoyment of his possessions."

The settled case law of the European Court of Human Rights has widely admitted that the exclusive rights to use intangible information such as a trademark or a patent constitute "possessions" within the meaning of Article 1.[766]

What is important to emphasise here is that Article 1 of Protocol N.1 of the ECHR (and, seemingly, Article 17 of the EU Charter) makes it clear that the fundamental right to the peaceful enjoyment of possessions, including intellectual property rights, can be made subject to exceptions for the pursuit of the public interest.[767]

The second part of Article 1(1) states that:

Article 17 of the 1789 Declaration of Human Rights provides for the sacred and inviolable character of the right of property and for the condition of fair and preliminary compensation where the proprietor is deprived of the right for the pursuit of a public necessity ascertained by law. The text of the Declaration, which has constitutional value in France, is available in French at: http://www.conseil-constitutionnel.fr/textes/d1789.htm.

766 As remarked by the European Court of Human Rights in the case *Anheuser-Busch Inc.* v. *Portugal*, Application no. 73049/01, Second Section, judgment of 11 October 2005, paragraphs 42 and 43, available at: http://cmiskp.echr.coe.int, "the concept of possessions" has an autonomous meaning which is not limited to ownership of physical goods and is independent from the formal classification in domestic law: certain other rights and interests constituting assets can also be regarded as "property rights", and thus as "possessions" for the purposes of this provision. The issue that needs to be examined in each case is whether the circumstances of the case, considered as a whole, conferred on the applicant title to a substantive interest protected by Article 1 of Protocol No. 1 [...] The Court observes at the outset that intellectual property as such incontestably enjoys the protection of Article 1 of Protocol No. 1." Former cases in which the Court found Article 1 applicable to intellectual property rights were *Smith Kline and French Laboratories Ltd* v. *the Netherlands*, Application no. 12633/87, decision of 4 October 1990; and *British-American Tobacco Company Ltd* v. *the Netherlands*, Series A no. 331, judgment of 20 November 1995.

767 It is worth reminding that the wording adopted by Article 17 of the EU Charter of Fundamental Rights is slightly different from that of Article 1, Protocol N.1 of the ECHR. Article 17(1) is labelled "Right to property" and provides as follows: "Everyone has the right to own, use, dispose of and bequeath his or her lawfully acquired possessions. No one may be deprived of his or her possessions, except in the public interest and in the cases and under the conditions provided for by law, subject to fair compensation being paid in good time for their loss. The use of property may be regulated by law in so far as is necessary for the general interest."

"[...] No one shall be deprived of his possessions except *in the public interest* and subject to the conditions provided for by law and by the general principles of international law."[768]

In addition, Article 1(2) provides that:

"The preceding provisions shall not, however, in any way impair the right of a State to enforce such laws as it deems necessary to control the use of property *in accordance with the general interest* or to secure the payment of taxes or other contributions or penalties."[769]

It is clear that these clauses endorse a system of exceptions on property rights in which such exceptions seek to pursue the public interest. Thus, under the ECHR, the idea of limiting the scope of the property rights created under copyright law does not infringe the fundamental right to property in so far as statutory restrictions on the exercise of copyright have the specific function of protecting public policy objectives such as the dissemination of creative works and the artistic and scientific enrichment of society.

Similar to what Article 1 provides with regard to the right of property, the provision of Article 10(2) of the ECHR clarifies that the fundamental right of freedom of expression and information is not absolute. Article 10(2) of the ECHR provides that the exercise of the freedoms to receive and impart information:

"[...] may be subject to such formalities, conditions, restrictions or penalties as are prescribed by law and are necessary in a democratic society [...] for the protection of the reputation or *rights of others* [...]".[770]

This clause clarifies that the right to freedom of communication can be legitimately limited for the purpose of preserving a wide range of subjective rights and interests which fall within the meaning of "rights of others". In the case law of the European Court of Human Rights, copyrights were found to constitute "rights of others" and thus justify the restrictions of other fundamental rights such as the right to privacy protected under Article 8 of the ECHR, which uses the same expression of Article 10 to limit the protection of privacy.[771] In a case where the right to privacy was invoked against a judicial order of inspection aimed at discovering copyright infringements within a household, the Court held that the protection of privacy found an exception in the protection of "rights of others" such as the exclusive rights created under copyright law.[772]

By virtue of the provisions of Article 10(2) and Article 1 of Protocol N.1, the ECHR sets the stage for a balanced co-existence of the conflicting objectives of

---

[768] Emphasis added.

[769] Emphasis added.

[770] Emphasis added.

[771] Article 8 of the ECHR provides for the protection of privacy from interference by a public authority except for the protection of "rights and freedoms of others".

[772] See the decision taken by the European Court of Human Rights in the case *Chappell* v. *The United Kingdom*, Application no. 10461/83, judgment of 30 March 1989, in which the Court held that copyright constituted "rights of others" within the meaning of Article 8(2) of the ECHR.

copyright (*i.e.*, property) protection and freedom of expression. The recognition of possible mutual restrictions of these prerogatives means that one fundamental right should not be enforced at the expense of the other. It can be concluded that the ECHR mandates a balanced protection of the conflicting interests which underlie the protection of intellectual property and that of freedom of expression and information. As a result, due to the constitutional value of human rights law, the validity of EU secondary legislation that veers away from this balance and stifles one of these fundamental rights for the pursuit of the other might easily be challenged.

8.2. Restrictions on freedom of communication over peer-to-peer networks

This paragraph scrutinises the unsettled issues posed by file-sharing practices from the constitutional perspective of Article 10 of the ECHR. This discussion is followed by proposals for reform of EU digital copyright law that may ensure harmony with the constitutional mandate covering freedom of communication and expression under the copyright system. In my view, this objective may be achieved only in so far as EU law-makers will be able to find a solution to protect the freedom to disseminate free, unprotected works and information over peer-to-peer networks.

8.2.1. Peer-to-peer networking and free communication

The InfoSoc Directive confined its policy solution to the possible conflict of copyright enforcement and freedom of communication through digital media in Recital 22, which seems to reflect the principle that copyright protection should take preference over the competing objective of dissemination of culture. This Recital states that:

> "The objective of proper support for the dissemination of culture must not be achieved by sacrificing strict protection of rights or by tolerating illegal forms of distribution of counterfeited or pirated works."

It seems to me that the policy objective of strict copyright protection, as presented in this Recital, needs to be interpreted and enforced in accordance with Article 10(2) of the ECHR. As pointed out by Hugenholtz, Article 10 is aimed to be interpreted broadly, given that its media-neutral phrasing applies to old and new media alike.[773] Thus, it is reasonable to argue that the rights to impart, distribute and re-

---

[773] See Hugenholtz, 'Copyright and Freedom of Expression in Europe', op. cit., pp. 245-246. In footnote 33, this author recalled, for instance, that the Supreme Court of the Netherlands, 26 February 1999, Nederlandse Juristprudentie 1999, p. 716, held that Ar-

ceive information without government interference applies also to peer-to-peer communication enabled by file-sharing software and networks. Under Article 10, freedom of information in peer-to-peer networking may be lawfully restricted so long as restrictive measures aim at protecting the "rights of others" established by copyright law with regard to the reproduction and making available of creative works through the Internet. Beyond the strict boundaries of copyright protection, therefore, any government interference with end-user opportunities of peer-to-peer networking should be interpreted as violating the constitutional principle of freedom of information.

The analysis of the legal implications of end-user file-sharing of digital works has evidenced that digital copyright enforcement in the EU may have the effect of creating indirect copyright liability on the providers of useful communication technology which is used for both infringing and non-infringing uses.

A first, possible basis of copyright liability for peer-to-peer technology providers was found to be given by Article 8(3) of the InfoSoc Directive. This provision has been used by some national courts in European jurisdictions to issue "shutdown" injunctions against certain user-run websites providing uploading information and search facilities for transmitting unauthorised copyrighted materials through specific peer-to-peer software (*i.e.*, BitTorrent).

A second basis of indirect copyright liability upon technology providers was found in the breach of a general tort law duty of care, which creates an obligation to make peer-to-peer technology more accountable in order to enable the detection of on-line copyright infringements. It was emphasised above that, due to the wording of Article 8 of the IPRs Enforcement Directive, courts might end up reinforcing the obligation of due care upon peer-to-peer software providers by obliging them to opt for a technological design which is capable of seeking information about copyright infringements.[774]

The potential restriction and alteration of the design of peer-to-peer technology stemming from overstretched copyright liability criteria would run contrary to the principle of freedom of communication in so far as end-users would be deprived of the opportunity to disseminate free (*i.e.*, unprotected) information through networks made available by this new medium. Unlike the situation under U.S. law, where the judge-made *Sony* doctrine has immunised "dual-use" technology from indirect liability in as much as the technology is capable of substantial non-infringing uses and is effectively used in that way, EU law has created no clear policy to preserve the availability of technology which enables the free dissemination of unprotected materials, as in the case of peer-to-peer software. When considering the decision of the U.S. Supreme Court in *Grokster* v. *MGM*, it was remarked that none of the opinions delivered by the Court's judges overlooked the relevance of the magnitude of the fair uses of peer-to-peer software in the assessment of the technology provider's liability.[775] Grokster's peer-to-peer provider

ticle 10 of the ECHR was applicable to public telephone network considering its increasing relevance for the exchange of information and ideas.

774 See §6.5.2., see *supra*.

775 See §6.4.2., see *supra*.

was found indirectly liable because of its inducement activities, not because of the mere supply of technology used to infringe copyright. In the same way, in order to reconcile the objective of copyright protection with that of freedom of communication in Europe, courts should be allowed to consider whether and to what extent communication technology is used for legitimate (*i.e.*, non-infringing) purposes.

In spite of evidence of non-infringing uses, the fact of overstretching copyright liability, as the above-mentioned legislation seems to permit, may force technology providers to adopt copyright-protecting architectures. Nevertheless, this approach is likely to fail in a world where peer-to-peer technology increasingly enables completely decentralised transfer of data. Until the moment when all peer-to-peer technology providers comply with their duty of care under tort law and retain some accountability on user-to-user communication, the only restrictive measure that may prove to be effective for protecting digital copyright may be that of altering the end-to-end structure of the Internet and disabling user sharing opportunities from a strictly technical point of view. This situation may be realised in the future if each personal computer connected to an Internet network becomes part of a trusted computing platform in which hardware security components automatically disable access to and use of unauthorised data by the end-user.[776]

Until the moment when most of on-line transfer of unauthorised data is monitored by trusted platforms, the conflict arising between copyright enforcement and freedom of communication over peer-to-peer networks will persist. In this respect, courts are badly equipped to settle the conflict. It is likely that injunctions against developers and suppliers of peer-to-peer technology, or against other categories of on-line intermediaries will provide only a rough and largely unsatisfactory response to the problem. Due to the specificity of this technology, injunctions may result in unproductive measures against intermediaries who have no control over peer-to-peer networking. At the same time, the creation of duties to police ISPs (*i.e.*, hosting providers, network operators, *etc*) may ultimately give these stakeholders a greater incentive to block access to peer-to-peer protocols in order to prevent the risks of criminal and/or civil liability proceedings based on indirect copyright infringement.

Having said this, it can be concluded that a single, clear EU copyright policy in respect of file-sharing practices needs to be developed, given that these practices are inherent to the open structure of the Internet and cannot simply be ignored or criminalised.

8.2.2. How copyleft licences increase the magnitude of *free* information

In today's Internet scenario, the expression "free information" is intended to refer not just to materials such as out-of-copyright works and works that have fallen into the public domain after the expiration of copyright protection. It is reasonable to include in this category of works all copyrighted digital works that are made

[776] See Appendix I, §D.

available to the public under "open access" (or "copyleft") licensing schemes which grant freedom of access and personal use. The inexpensive nature of digital creation and on-line communication has enabled the dissemination of creative works that would probably not have been made available to the public in the absence of the medium of the Internet. To bypass the restrictions that copyright law creates for the dissemination of creative works through the digitally networked environment, a number of legal tools which provide web users with permission to use and share copyrighted works freely under user-friendly conditions have emerged and spread widely. In short, copyleft licences allow users to engage in acts (*i.e.*, reproduction, communication, modification, *etc*) that would normally infringe copyright if not explicitly authorised by the copyright holder.[777] The increasingly popular licences made available by the U.S. foundation of Creative Commons is a prime example of how these licences operate in respect of literary and artistic works which are traditionally protected by copyright.[778] All types of Creative Commons' licences attached to digital content grant basic permission for open access and non-commercial dissemination of licensed works.[779] Instead of the usual "all-rights-reserved" approach, Creative Commons relies on a "some-rights-reserved" approach, which works as an effective slogan to identify the main purpose of the initiative. Given that this licensing model is economically based on solidarity (*i.e.*, on the idea of granting access and use for free), the model mainly attracts copyright owners who do not seek to gain direct compensation from the exercise of their copyrights. This non-profit-seeking purpose is commonly pursued either by creators who are remunerated through financial sources other than licensing revenues (*e.g.*, public funds, as in the case of academic writers, research-

777 In the Free Software Movement's terminology, copyleft is a "general method for making a program free software and requiring all modified and extended versions of the program to be free software as well." See 'What is Copyleft', http://www.gnu.org/licenses/licenses.html#WhatIsCopyleft.

778 See http://www.creativecommons.org. As regards computer programs, the most widely popular and used copyleft licence is the GNU General Public Licence (GPL) of the Free Software Foundation: see http://www.gnu.org. Creative Commons' leader and founding-father Lawrence Lessig has recently pointed out that the idea of the Creative Commons' licence was taken from the GPL. Unlike the Free Software Movement, Creative Commons does not compel the author to adopt a single licence model granting the right to modify the copyrighted work in any way, as the GPL does. While resting upon the proprietary regime of copyright, Creative Commons provides, together with a so-called "share-alike" licence that is identical to the GPL, a flexible range of rights management solutions.

779 Creative Commons makes available six different types of standard permissions which merge legal to symbolic tools in order to market among creators the philosophy of sharing and contributing to the commons. The written form is used for both the whole (and complex) text of the legally enforceable licence and for its short and "human-readable" transposition into a so-called "Commons Deed", which displays a one-page synthetic version of the licence on the user's screen. To the written form Creative Commons couples an effective symbolic description by means of icons indicating the different acts and uses that each licence authorises: see http://creativecommons.org/about/licenses/ meet-the-licenses.

ers, school teachers, *etc*) or by creators who intend to grant free access to their creations so as to achieve a better reputation and subsequently benefit from follow-on remuneration opportunities (*e.g.*, live performances, CD sales, *etc*). In this way, Creative Commons' initiative helps artists, writers and other kinds of creators to gain unprecedented exposure and provides them with opportunities to disseminate their work through the digitally networked environment.

Peer-to-peer networking is an extraordinary medium for spreading copyrighted works licensed under Creative Commons as well as under other open access schemes such as that of the BBC Creative Archive.[780] Authors opting for open access licences can easily use and benefit from peer-to-peer networks as a dissemination channel without losing the original purpose or the advantages of this licensing model. Copyright owners using these licences usually wish to inform users (including potential follow-on creators) about the location of their works on the Internet and about the standardised conditions under which these works can be used and re-used. From a technical point of view, file-sharers obtaining digital works tagged with a Creative Commons or a Creative Archive licence can be informed about the location and the terms of use of each of these works by virtue of a machine-readable translation of the licence code embedded into the metadata of the file in which the work is released.[781] This digital code (the so-called "Uniform Resource Identifier") attached to the work helps search engines and other applications to identify the work by its terms of use and supplies information regarding the copyright holder's identity and the Internet address where the licence embodying the terms of use can be found and read.

The on-line availability of copyrighted works licensed under Creative Commons and other copyleft terms of use has obtained increasing consideration by courts and legislators. As noted above, when delivering his opinion in the U.S. Supreme Court decision on *MGM* v. *Grokster*, Justice Breyer mentioned sharing practices concerning the open content collected and licensed under Creative Commons as one of the most significant non-infringing uses of Grokster's peer-to-peer technology.[782]

Moreover, two courts in Europe recently recognised the enforceability of open content licences. In February 2006, the Spanish Lower Court of Badajoz rejected the claim of copyright royalties by the Spanish authors' collecting society (*So-*

---

780 See http://creativearchive.bbc.co.uk. The BBC Creative Archive Licence Group was launched in April 2005 to make content available for download under the terms of a single, shared user licence scheme. This licence, called the "Creative Archive Licence", has been created for the downloading of moving images, audio, *etc*. The end pursued by the Creative Archive Licence is that of clearing the copyright on TV and radio output so that the public can get creative with it and engage in uses such as non-commercial educational uses, derivative works, *etc*.

781 See "Metadata Embedding", at:
http://creativecommons.org/technology/embedding#1.
In Creative Commons' jargon, this information is called "license verification link", because it points back to a webpage that the licensor herself controls.

782 See Breyer, J., Concurring Opinion, in *Metro-Goldwyn-Mayer Studios Inc.*v. *Grokster, Ltd.*, cit.: see §6.4.2., see *supra*.

ciedad General Autores y Editores: SGAE) against the owner of a disco bar where all publicly performed music proved to be authorised under Creative Commons.[783] According to the Court, the defendant testified convincingly that he was equipped with the technical tools to find the music handled by its authors through these licences. This decision found that, in the absence of contrary evidence, the collecting society was not entitled to ask copyright royalties for public performance of works of music owned by authors not represented by the society.[784] A few weeks later, in March 2006, the District Court of Amsterdam held the publisher of a magazine liable of copyright infringement for having published a few pictures uploaded by a popular MTV video jockey on a well-known photo-sharing website without authorisation.[785] This decision considered that the pictures were uploaded on this website under a "Attribution-Noncommercial-Sharealike" licence by virtue of which the author retained the exclusive right to authorise commercial uses of the pictures, such as publication in a magazine.

Finally, the transpositions of the InfoSoc Directive in France and Spain addressed copyleft licensing practices by affording them special legal treatment or consideration. For instance, new Article L.122-7-1 of the French Intellectual Property Code recognises the social and economic function of the mentioned licensing models while expressly providing that the author is free to make his or her works available to the public free of charge, on condition that the rights of possible co-authors and third parties have been cleared and the author respects the agreements that he or she has concluded.[786] Moreover, Article 21 of the French Act N.2006-961, when creating criminal liability for conduct consisting of supplying peer-to-peer software used in copyright infringements or inducing its use, provided a liability exemption for cases where software was provided and made available to enable "collaborative works", research and exchange of materials not *subject to copyright remuneration.*[787] After constitutional scrutiny, this liability

[783] See Juzgado de Primera Instancia de Badajoz, *SGAE* v. *Ricardo Andres Utrera Fernandez*, Procedimiento Ordinario 761/2005, Sentencia N. 15/2006: see 'Spanish Court recognizes CC-music', at: http://creativecommons.org/weblog/entry/5830.

[784] The Spanish judgment would have been different if the music works publicly performed in the disco bar were licensed under Creative Commons by authors represented by SGAE. This collecting society, as other European collecting societies, takes an assignment (or a "mandate") of public performance rights from the author in present and future works, so that the society effectively becomes the owner of these rights and manages them *on a exclusive basis.* So, Creative Commons licences would have been ineffective had they been adopted by SGAE authors.

[785] See 'Creative Commons licenses enforced in Dutch court', available at: http://creativecommons.org/weblog/entry/5823.

[786] See Article 1-III, Chapter 1 ("Exceptions to copyright and related rights") of Law N.2006-961 of 1 August 2006 on copyright and related rights in the information society, available at: http://www.legifrance.gouv.fr ("L'auteur est libre de mettre ses oeuvres gratuitement à la disposition du public, sous réserve des éventuels coauteurs et de ceux des tiers ainsi que dans le respect de conventions qu'il a conclues.").

[787] See the text of the law which transposed the InfoSoc Directive adopted by the French Parliament on 30 June 2006, available at: http://www.assemblee-nationale.fr/12/dossiers/031206.asp>.

exemption was voided and finally eliminated from the definitive version of the act on the assumption that "collaborative works" was a very unclear expression, which came into conflict with the requirement that criminal sanctions must correspond strictly with the rule of law.[788] Interestingly, the French Constitutional Court also found that the liability exemption nullified the criminal law protection of the moral rights of creators wishing to disseminate their works for free under open access licences. Notwithstanding the outcome of this decision, the debate on the legal treatment of software enabling communication of freely accessible materials under copyright law highlighted that copyleft licensing in the digital environment is decidedly on the map in Europe.

In conclusion, the Spanish law which transposed the InfoSoc Directive enacted a provision (entitled "Promotion of digital works dissemination") which encouraged the government to invest in the development of spaces of public utility where freely accessible materials, including works in the public domain and copyrighted works licensed by their authors under copyleft terms, may be stored and accessed by everyone through digital media.[789]

Due to the increasing consideration of the escalation of on-line sharing practices, policy-makers cannot overlook the impact of these alternative licensing models for digital communication. In the field of peer-to-peer networking, EU policy-makers must consider that the creation of overbroad copyright liability upon providers of peer-to-peer software and the increasing criminalisation of file-sharers is likely to stifle not only flows of unprotected information and public domain materials, but also copyrighted works whose dissemination, access and use is authorised through the legal mechanism of copyleft.

8.3. EU copyright enforcement policy in respect of file-sharing

This section considers the desirability of several policy solutions that might allow EU law-makers to solve (or at least reduce) the problem of on-line copyright enforcement over peer-to-peer file-sharing networks. As pointed out above, legitimate purposes of digital copyright enforcement may easily deprive Internet users

---

788 See Conseil constitutionnel, Decision N.2006-540 DC of 27 July 2006, cit., Recitals 55-57. On this issue, the decision was commented upon by Lucas and Sirinelli, 'La loi n°2006-961 du 1er août relative au droit d'auteur et aux droits voisins dans la société de l'information: premières vues sur le texte promulgué à l'issue de la censure du Conseil constitutionnel', (20) *Propriétés intellectuelles*, July 2006, p. 297, at pp. 334-336.

789 See the Third Additional Provision ("Disposición adicional tercera. Fomento de la difusión de obras digitales") of the Spanish Act N.23/2006 of 7 July 2006, available at: http://www.boe.es. The second part of this provision clearly addresses copyleft licences when it provides that, in the same way as the public domain, publicly accessible digital spaces may include works whose incorporation is expressly authorised by their authors ("Asimismo, a estos espacios publicos podrán incorporarse las obras cuyos autores así lo manifiesten expresamente.").

of technology which permits a faster and more efficient transfer of free, digitised information from individual to individual. In my view, the objective of on-line copyright enforcement must be reconciled with that of preserving the unrestricted availability of peer-to-peer technology and, more generally, the point-to-point (or end-to-end) communication enabled through the decentralised structure of the Internet.

8.3.1. Targeting copyright enforcement at individuals

When reviewing the French case law on end-user liability in cases of peer-to-peer file-sharing, it was concluded that, under today's EU digital copyright law, Internet users indisputably commit a copyright infringement when they share protected works without authorisation.[790] Therefore, EU policy-makers may have to consider the suitability of targeting copyright enforcement at direct infringers by increasing and facilitating the recourse to civil and criminal sanctions against them. In this respect, a brief overview of the recent experience of enforcement proceedings undertaken in the U.S. is a useful point of comparison for equivalent initiatives in the EU.

8.3.1.1. The United States

In the United States, as from 2003, copyright owners in sound recordings and films have increasingly pursued the strategy of filing civil lawsuits against individuals who were found to have uploaded considerable amounts of unauthorised music and film files onto peer-to-peer networks.[791] This strategy was adopted and developed on the technical assumption that perfect decentralisation of peer-to-peer technology deprived technology providers of monitoring capabilities over the enabled transfer of data and made their indirect copyright liability much more unlikely. Notwithstanding its powerful echo in the media and the conviction to pay damages inflicted to thousands of unauthorised uploaders, this type of initiative by the Recording Industry Association of America (RIAA) and the Motion Picture Association of America (MPAA) has resulted only in a slight decrease in infringement activities. Indeed, many of the file-sharers have been able to migrate to more sophisticated peer-to-peer services making illegal downloading more difficult to detect.[792] In the United States, the costs and the length of civil lawsuits against individual file sharers increased considerably after the District of Columbia Court of Appeal's decision in *RIAA* v. *Verizon Internet Services*.[793] This decision held that the RIAA was not entitled to use the subpoena provision of Section

---

[790] See §6.3., see *supra*.

[791] See Groennings, 'Costs and Benefits of the Recording Industry's Litigation Against Individuals', (20) *Berkeley Technology Law Journal* 2005, p. 571.

[792] See Groennings, 'Costs and Benefits [...]', op.cit., p. 600.

[793] See *Recording Industry Association of America, Inc.* v. *Verizon Internet Services*, 351 F.3d 1229, at pp. 1236-1237 (D.C. Circuit 2003).

512(h) of the U.S. Copyright Act to compel ISPs, such as Verizon, to disclose the names of subscribers whom the RIAA had reason to believe were infringing the copyrights of its members. The 1998 DMCA introduced into Section 512(h) special, faster civil proceedings which allowed copyright holders to ask ISPs for the prompt removal of infringing materials that they stored on their systems. In *RIAA* v. *Verizon Internet Services*, the Court of Appeal found that these special proceedings did not apply to cases of infringements committed on peer-to-peer networks on the assumption that such ISPs as Verizon merely routed or transmitted file-sharers' infringing materials without storing them. This meant that RIAA, in order to discover the direct infringer's identity on fully decentralised peer-to-peer networks, would have to resort to ordinary lawsuits against alleged infringers identified by means of anonymous, numerical Internet Protocol (IP) addresses. Since the *Verizon* decision, therefore, copyright enforcement against individuals in the United States has became more costly and time-consuming given that RIAA and other owners of sound recordings can no longer gain access to individuals' identities without filing an ordinary lawsuit and meeting the related costs.[794]

The unsatisfactory response of civil enforcement proceedings against individuals has led some U.S. commentators to argue that, in principle, a higher deterrent may be sought against direct infringers by effectively enforcing the criminal penalties available under Section 506(a) of the U.S. Copyright Act, as amended by the 1997 No Electronic Theft (NET) Act.[795] The NET Act amendment added a criminal provision to the U.S. copyright statute, which was especially designed to punish infringers who, during any six-month period, and regardless of the purposes of commercial advantage or financial gain, reproduce or distribute, including by electronic means, one or more copies or phonorecords of copyrighted works, which have a total retail value of more than $1,000.[796]

To demonstrate that criminal proceedings against individuals may play an important role in the fight against digital piracy, Fisher emphasised that, in the last decade, the U.S. Department of Justice had invested more resources to detect and prosecute intellectual property crimes occurring on the Internet.[797] To this end, the

---

794 See Groennings, 'Costs and Benefits […]', op.cit., pp. 573-574, who recalled that, prior to the *Verizon* case, §512(h) of the U.S. Copyright Act provided copyright owners with a fast and cheap mechanism to discover suspected file-sharers' identities. Indeed, by paying only a $35 fee even for multiple issuances, copyright owners needed to supply a copy of notification, the proposed subpoena and a sworn declaration that the information sought was for the sole purpose of protecting copyright: see U.S. Code, Title 17, §512(h)(2), (A) to (C). After receiving this documentation, courts were used to compel ISPs to disclose subscriber identification information without determining whether the alleged infringer violated any copyright laws.

795 See U.S. Code, Title 17, §506(a)(1) and (2). See Lemley and Reese, 'Reducing Digital Copyright Infringement Without Restricting Innovation', (56) *Stanford Law Review* 2004, p. 1345, at pp. 1395-1399; Groennings, 'Costs and Benefits […]', op. cit., at pp. 594-595; Fisher, *Promises To Keep*, op. cit., at pp. 146-148.

796 See U.S. Code, Title 17, §506(a)(2). See Lemley and Reese, 'Reducing Digital Copyright Infringement […]', op. cit., p. 137; Fisher, *Promises To Keep*, op. cit., p. 146.

797 See Fisher, *Promises to Keep*, op. cit., p. 146.

Justice Department established a Computer Crime and Intellectual Property Section in 1995. As pointed out by Lemley, Reese and Fisher, in the specific field of modern peer-to-peer file-sharing networks, this prosecution strategy might have as its most important targets high-volume uploaders of infringing materials, namely, individuals who knowingly allow their computers to be used as "supernodes".[798] Indeed, due to overcompensatory sanctions under both U.S. civil and criminal copyright laws, these unauthorised uploaders are criminalised as counterfeiters per individual upload.

8.3.1.2. The European Union

In Europe, copyright owners seem far more reluctant to seek copyright enforcement measures against individuals under civil proceedings. The French case law examined earlier reveals that copyright enforcement against individuals resulted mainly from criminal proceedings, in which copyright owners are entitled to participate and seek (even symbolic) damages.[799]

However, this framework may be subject to change in the light of the most recent legislative initiative taken by EU law-makers in respect of civil proceedings regarding the enforcement of intellectual property rights. The adoption of the 2004 IPRs Enforcement Directive has strongly encouraged and facilitated purposes of effective enforcement targeted at individuals. The Directive aimed at providing all EU jurisdictions with effective and harmonised enforcement measures against infringements of intellectual property rights. Article 8 of this Directive ensures that copyright holders are entitled to ask courts throughout the European Union to compel ISPs (and possibly other on-line intermediaries, including certain peer-to-peer software providers) to disclose the identities of Internet users found in possession of infringing goods on a commercial scale or providing services used in infringing activities.[800] These provisions enable judicial authorities, upon request of copyright owners, to identify and prosecute users whose computers are found to work as "supernodes" in fully decentralised peer-to-peer architectures.[801] After having identified direct infringers, copyright owners are given broad and prompt access to civil proceedings which grant interlocutory measures intended to prevent any imminent infringement or continuation of infringements and other measures such as the seizure of goods suspected of infringing copyright.[802]

In this legislative framework, it is unclear how the protection of confidentiality of information sources and the prohibition of the processing of user personal data commanded under Article 8(3)(e) of the IPRs Enforcement Directive will inter-

---

798 See Lemley and Reese, 'Reducing Digital Copyright Infringement [...]', op. cit., pp. 1395-1396; Fisher, *Promises to Keep*, op. cit., p. 148.

799 See §6.3., see *supra*.

800 See Article 8(1) of the IPRs Enforcement Directive.

801 See Article 8(2) of the IPRs Enforcement Directive, which makes clear that information on the origin and distribution networks of infringing goods comprises the names and addresses of distributors and suppliers of infringing goods as well as information on the quantities delivered or received.

802 See Article 9 of the IPRs Enforcement Directive.

play with the powerful measures of investigation and enforcement created by Article 8, paragraphs 1 and 2, of the same Directive.[803] In interim measures proceedings in July 2007, the District Court of Rome held that the protection of confidentiality in electronic communications, as laid down in Article 5 of the Directive 2002/58/EC on privacy and electronic communications,[804] took priority over digital copyright enforcement undertaken through precautionary measures aimed at compelling disclosure of the identity and other personal data of unauthorised file-sharers.[805] The Rome Court rejected the claim of two copyright owners who sought to compel an ISP to reveal the personal data of a few subscribers that were supposedly infringing copyright in their videogames and music works. The Court emphasised that the phrasing of Article 8(3) of the IPRs Enforcement Directive provided explicitly that the civil proceedings remedies made available under Article 8(1) should apply "without prejudice to other statutory provisions which [...] govern the protection of confidentiality of information sources or the processing of personal data."[806] As a result, the Rome Court concluded that, in the EU legal system, access to users' confidential communications and personal data and their retention and processing was permitted only under the exceptional circumstances spelt out under Article 15(1) of Directive 2002/58, which does not include the enforcement of subjective rights (*e.g.*, copyrights) through *civil* proceedings.[807] This provision, instead, makes it clear that national laws may provide for the retention of personal data for a limited period in order to enable prevention, investigation, detection and prosecution of *criminal* offences. Therefore, as suggested by the Rome judgment, courts may recognise the right to information disclosure regarding unauthorised file-sharers' personal data where their conduct is punishable by

---

803 Article 8(3) of the IPRs Enforcement Directive states: "[P]aragraphs 1 and 2 shall apply without prejudice to other statutory provisions which [...] (e) govern the protection of confidentiality of information sources or the processing of personal data".

804 See Article 5 ("Confidentiality of the communications") of Directive 2002/58/EC on privacy and electronic communications, OJ L 201, 31 July 2002, 37, which states: "1. Member States shall ensure the confidentiality of communications and the related traffic data by means of a public communications network and publicly available electronic communications services, through national legislation. In particular, they shall prohibit listening, tapping, storage or other kinds of interception or surveillance of communications and the related traffic data by persons other than users, without the consent of the users concerned, except when legally authorised to do so in accordance with Article 15(1) [...]".

805 See *Techland and Peppermint Jam Records* v. *Wind Telecomunicazioni*, Tribunale Ordinario di Roma, Order at interim measure proceedings. N. 26125/2007, 16 July 2007, available at http://www.altroconsumo.it/images/17/173003_Attach.pdf.

806 See Article 8(3)(e) of the IPRs Enforcement Directive.

807 Article 15 of Directive 2002/58/EC provides that Member States may adopt legislative measures to restrict user privacy-related rights "when such restriction constitutes a necessary, appropriate and proportionate measure within a democratic society to safeguard national security (i.e. State security), defence, public security, and the prevention, investigation, detection and prosecution of criminal offences or of unauthorised use of the electronic communication system, as referred to in Article 13(1) of Directive 95/46/EC [...]".

criminal sanctions under the applicable national laws. Obviously, if this interpretation becomes mainstream in the European case law, the objective of copyright enforcement targeted at individuals by means of the precautionary measures created by Article 8 of the IPRs Enforcement Directive with regard to civil proceedings would largely be frustrated.

In this respect, it must be noted that the European Commission is seeking to strengthen criminal laws by passing a directive "on criminal measures aimed at ensuring the enforcement of intellectual property rights".[808] This directive proposal seeks to create an obligation under which EU Member States should ensure that *all* intentional infringements of an intellectual property right on a commercial scale, as well as the attempting, aiding, or abetting and inciting of such infringements, are treated as criminal offences.[809] The text of the proposal makes it clear that sanctions should include imprisonment (for which a threshold of four-years imprisonment is provided when intellectual property crimes are committed under the aegis of a criminal organisation) and/or monetary fines sufficient to provide a deterrent, consistently with the level of penalties applied for crimes of a corresponding gravity.[810] In the field of on-line copyright enforcement, the adoption of this piece of legislation would have the effect of compelling Member States to adopt criminal penalties against file-sharers who commit copyright infringement "on a commercial scale". As pointed out by the Commission's Explanatory Memorandum attached to the directive proposal, the "commercial scale" requirement is borrowed from Article 61 of the 1994 TRIPS Agreement, which expressly provides for criminal procedures and penalties to be applied in cases of copyright piracy.[811] Therefore, as in the U.S., the new directive proposal on copyright criminal laws, if finally approved, may force EU Member States to prosecute all individuals who are found to have knowingly allowed their computers to be used as high-volume suppliers (*i.e.*, uploaders) of unauthorised materials on peer-to-peer networks. Consequently, the enforceability of criminal penalties in respect of these counterfeiters would remove the hurdle of the above-mentioned prohibitions of retaining and processing user personal data so that copyright infringers' identity and other relevant information could finally be disclosed to copyright holders and used for damages claims in criminal trials.

An interesting exception to the trend toward criminalisation of on-line copyright infringement was created by the recent French transposition of the InfoSoc Directive into national law. Due to much public backlash following the repeal of the proposal of a statutory licence scheme which sought to legalise file-sharing, criminal penalties addressing acts of counterfeit of copyrighted goods committed over peer-to-peer networks were downgraded into (rather low) administrative

[808] See Commission of the European Communities, Amended proposal for a Directive of the European Parliament and of the Council on criminal measures aimed at ensuring the enforcement of intellectual property rights, COM(2006) 168 final, Brussels, 26.4.2006.

[809] See Article 3 of the directive proposal.

[810] See Articles 3 and 4 of the directive proposal.

[811] See the Explanatory Memorandum attached to the directive proposal, pp. 1-2.

monetary fines.[812] In July 2006, before the legislation was finally passed, the French Constitutional Court found the enactment of these administrative penalties to be in contravention of the French Constitution in so far as they would harm the fundamental right to property recognised by the InfoSoc Directive on reproduction and communication to the public of copyrighted works.[813]

8.3.1.3. Why this option would be cost-ineffective and short-sighted

In my view, despite the efforts made in this direction by EU law-makers, and especially by the European Commission, the purpose of strengthening criminal copyright laws to reduce digital piracy over file-sharing networks is likely to result in a rather costly and time-consuming solution. It is indisputable that, under today's digital copyright law, the implementation of effective enforcement measures against file-sharers may have positive effects: it may make clear the illegal nature of unauthorised file-sharing to the benefit of the public opinion; it may deter high-volume uploaders of unauthorised materials from continuing to infringe copyright; and it may facilitate the rise and development of legitimate services of on-line content distribution (*e.g.*, Apple's iTunes, Napster's Rhapsody, the more recent Microsoft's Zune, *etc*).[814]

However, according to an utilitarian argument raised mainly in the U.S. literature, not all direct infringers can be prosecuted. Lemley and Reese stressed that it is highly difficult to estimate how many people governments must prosecute in order to create a credible deterrent to digital copyright infringement.[815] This author noted that, according to the economics of criminal law, rational actors adjust their behaviour in response to *expected* sanctions.[816] Consequently, to create a truly effective deterrent, civil and criminal copyright sanctions should be heavy enough and effectively enforceable to dissuade possible infringers. Contrary to the argument raised by supporters of higher criminal sanctions against digital copyright infringers, it seems persuasive to assume that a wide criminalisation of many Inter-

---

[812] See Article 24 of the text of the copyright statute adopted by the French Parliament on 30 June 2006, at: http://www.assemblee-nationale.fr/12/dossiers/031206.asp. The statutory licence scheme proposed in France before implementation of the InfoSoc Directive is discussed below, see §8.3.3.1.

[813] See Conseil constitutionnel, Decision N.2006-540 DC, cit., *Article premier*. In particular, the Court found that a few exemptions from criminal copyright liability violated the duties of transposition of EU law embodied in Article 88-1 of the French Constitution: see recital 30 of the Decision. For an in-depth examination of this issue, see Lucas and Sirinelli, 'La loi n°2006-961 du 1er août relative au droit d'auteur et aux droits voisins dans la société de l'information', op. cit., p. 301.

[814] See Groennings, 'Costs and Benefits [...]', op. cit., at pp. 591-600.

[815] See Lemley and Reese, 'Reducing Digital Copyright Infringement [...]', op. cit., p. 1399.

[816] See Lemley and Reese, 'Reducing Digital Copyright Infringement [...]', op. cit., p. 1391, drawing on Becker, 'Crime and Punishment: An Economic Approach', (76) *Journal of Political Economy* 1968, p. 169, at pp. 176-177, which is the foundational work in the field of the economics of criminal law.

net users would raise a problem of ethics. Making unauthorised end-users of copyrighted works potential criminals not only creates a problem of proportionality with regard to other criminal sanctions aimed at protecting personal and economic values that are normally ranked in a much higher position than the protection of copyright. The above-mentioned proposals of criminalisation also run the risk that digital copyright enforcement measures may give rise to a sort of random (and rough) justice which makes an example of the very few users caught under criminal proceedings.

In this respect, it is evident that the risk for the user-infringer to be caught under copyright civil and criminal proceedings has decreased dramatically in so far as on-line communication among individuals has become much more difficult to detect. A powerful example of the practical non-viability of copyright enforcement systems based on the identification of direct infringers using their IP addresses is evidenced by the emergence of new modes of connecting to the Internet, which are fast and anonymous. Increasing availability of wireless Internet connections and public Internet access points (so-called "hotspots") have multiplied user opportunities to engage in on-line communication without having to hold a permanent, personal IP address, from which infringers may be identified and, consequently, prosecuted. In these cases, there is no way of identifying and prosecuting individuals. Therefore, whereas the vast array of measures and proceedings granted under the IPRs Enforcement Directive may have a significant impact and act as a deterrent upon direct infringers in the off-line (*i.e.*, real) world, the strategy of prosecuting end-users on an individual basis is likely be insufficient to dissuade on-line infringers from sharing unauthorised materials. Currently, the probability of file-sharers who infringe copyright being detected and prosecuted is so low that tightening civil and criminal sanctions would not create an effective deterrent. In addition to this, it must also be taken into account that it is still unclear how the protection of user privacy in electronic communications under EU law will affect this strategy of enforcement, largely, in the field of civil proceedings.

For these reasons, the targeting of individual offenders is a short-sighted solution. Instead, different, more comprehensive counter-measures should be sought under the law in order to facilitate copyright enforcement without discouraging legitimate uses of peer-to-peer technology or restricting peer-to-peer communication as such.

8.3.2. Copyright levies to compensate creators

In the relevant literature, a number of proposals for reform have been presented to solve the problem of on-line copyright enforcement without criminalising file-sharing and without hindering legitimate purposes of social sharing. The most radical among such proposals is that of replacing exclusive rights of on-line reproduction and communication by means of a regulatory scheme imposing copyright levies on digital media and on-line services. This scheme would aim to permit and to compensate all non-commercial copying, exchange and modification of protected works occurring on the Internet. The most important and renowned versions of this policy solution were presented by U.S. scholars Netanel and Fisher, who developed a plan for the compulsory licensing of copyrighted works aimed at separating authors' compensation from control over digital content, as previously advocated by Lessig.[817]

8.3.2.1. The 'Fisher-Netanel' proposal of a non-commercial use levy system

Fisher and Netanel proposed the enactment of a statutory licence scheme which, while denying copyright holders proprietary control over on-line non-commercial uses of copyrighted works, would grant them mere remuneration rights.[818] The scope of this proposal was not limited to the non-commercial uses of copyrighted works occurring in the realm of peer-to-peer networking, but included making these works available through webcasting and streaming technologies. Netanel's and Fisher's proposals, though fairly similar, were different with regard to one important point. While Netanel's levy for non-commercial use was intended to give individuals an enforceable right, which could not be waived, concerning all kinds of communicative expression (including all types of copyrighted works except for computer programs), Fisher's levy system targeted only entertainment works (*i.e.*, music and movies). Both proposals were based on the idea of a centralised registration system administered by a government agency such as the U.S. Copyright Office.

In Fisher's alternative compensation system, a musician or film-maker wishing to be paid for the uses that others make of his or her work on the Internet would send a copy of the work to a government agency, which would register and store it while providing, in return, a registration number.[819] Each registered work, in Fisher's system, should embody a durable fingerprint that would be replicated in each copy of the original work together with authorship information and standardised author's reports disclosing whether the author has incorporated portions of other recordings into his or her work.[820] Even Netanel's system was somewhat concerned with implementation of fingerprints into digital copies of the licensed works. However, in Netanel's view, fingerprints should mainly serve the purpose of permitting peer-to-peer technologies and ISPs to detect and meter the uses of copyrighted works.[821]

In both the above-commented proposals, copyright management information such as that embedded into each work by means of fingerprinting techniques

---

[817] See Netanel, 'Impose a Noncommercial Use Levy to Allow Free Peer-to-Peer File Sharing', 17(1) *Harvard Journal of Law and Technology* 2003, p. 1; Fisher, *Promises to Keep*, op. cit., p. 199; Lessig, *The Future of Ideas*, op. cit., pp. 241-258.

[818] Using the law and economics terminology, this solution rests upon the substitution of a *property* rule, under which authors hold the exclusive right to authorise or prohibit most uses of their works, with a *liability* rule, under which anyone is free to make use of a protected work on condition that the user pays remuneration: see §7.6.2.2., see *supra*.

[819] See Fisher, *Promises to Keep*, op. cit., p. 203.

[820] See Fisher, *Promises to Keep*, op. cit., pp. 204-205.

[821] See Netanel, 'Impose a Noncommercial Use Levy [...]', op. cit., p. 54.

would also play the important function of allowing users to distinguish original (*i.e.*, authentic) works from versions of the work legitimately modified without the copyright owner's authorisation.[822] Indeed, one of the most important features that would make both these systems different from and far wider than the pre-existing levy schemes adopted in most European countries for legalising unauthorised reprography and private copying is the user right to engage in non-commercial derivative works (*e.g.*, digital re-mixes, or "mash-ups").

Both proposals emphasised that, ideally, the systems they described should be structured so that each copyright owner's share of the overall collected remuneration would be proportional to the total value that, during a given year, consumers derived from the copyright owner's works.[823] To this end, Fisher showed that it would be possible to implement methods for measuring user demand and appreciation of digital works without controlling their effective uses.[824] He explained that this objective could be reached by means of periodic surveys and inquiries seeking to meter activities such as webcasting and CD burning of downloaded registered works. Furthermore, Fisher proposed the establishment of a large-scale sampling system administered by a government agency such as the U.S. Copyright Office. This author pointed out that a sampling system based upon rotating, medium-size samples of households (chosen to be representative of the population as a whole) reporting what they listened to and watched would be the most plausible way to estimate the relative values to consumers of downloaded registered recordings.[825] This system would detect and record what people willing to participate in this reporting activity consume and appreciate most. Netanel, in contrast, proposed to start from estimates of the number of non-commercial downloads, streams and the subsequent uses of the registered works by requiring peer-to-peer software suppliers and ISPs to implement metering technologies into their products and gateways.[826] In this framework, such technologies should include smart software agents which are able to detect fingerprinted contents and count all downloads and uses of the works as an aggregate measure which, in order to respect user privacy, would avoid collecting and indexing this user-related data.

Another interesting point raised by the proposals at issue concerned techniques for measuring the users' effective appreciation of digital works. Fisher argued that, for this purpose, it would be possible to establish voting systems where registered peer-to-peer users could decide, directly or indirectly, which creators should receive funds.[827] Under this system, the calculation of the creators' share of the collected remuneration would also depend on the value effectively derived from the works used. This value, according to Fisher, should be a factor to be considered not only in terms of usage quantity, but also in terms of user preferences

---

822 *Ibidem*, pp. 57-58.

823 See Fisher, *Promises to Keep*, op. cit., p. 223; Netanel, 'Impose a Noncommercial Use Levy [...]', op. cit., p. 36.

824 *Ibidem*, pp. 223-234.

825 See Fisher, *Promises to Keep*, op. cit., p. 229.

826 See Netanel, 'Impose a Noncommercial Use Levy [...]', op. cit., pp. 53-55.

827 See Fisher, *Promises to Keep*, op. cit., pp. 231-232.

among different downloaded materials. He stressed that this system may look like voting systems that have been successfully implemented by Internet websites which have built up social networks in which users subscribing to an account play both the functions of consumers and editors of digital contents.[828] These networks implement automated systems where subscriber preferences have the consequence of increasing or decreasing the rating (and consequently the Internet exposure) of each registered item of content or news.[829]

The most complex aspects of this policy option concerned the problems of determining the amount and sources of monetary compensation due to creators, and the criteria of collection and repartition of such financial rewards among copyright holders. With regard to sources of copyright levies, Fisher proposed, as a first option, a taxation-based funding of this remuneration system.[830] As a second option, Fisher and Netanel argued that digital copyright levies might be imposed on the goods and services used to gain access to the free flows of on-line copyrighted content that the system would legalise.[831] In this respect, Netanel identified four categories of products and services suitable for copyright taxation:

1. equipment used to make copies of digital recordings;
2. digital media used to store such copies;
3. services providing access to the Internet and used either to download files or to stream recordings; and
4. peer-to-peer software and other file-sharing services.[832]

In the above system, all stakeholders providing the above products and services would greatly benefit from the free flow of digital copyrighted works that the system would liberate. As a result, they would be the most suitable stakeholders to be compelled to pay an amount of monetary compensation high enough to offset the losses of net revenues from the markets actually corroded by the legalisation of peer-to-peer file-sharing.[833] According to Netanel, this amount of money might be determined, as an aggregate stock, through negotiations among associations which represent the industries upon which the levy is imposed and the associations which represent the copyright holders in different categories of works.[834] The levies

---

828 *Ibidem*, pp. 253-254.

829 See websites such as slashdot.com, stumbleupon.com, and digg.com.

830 See Fisher, *Promises to Keep*, op. cit., pp. 216-217.

831 See Fisher, *Promises to Keep*, op. cit., pp. 217-221; Netanel, 'Impose a Noncommercial Use Levy [...]', op. cit., p. 43.

832 See Netanel, 'Impose a Noncommercial Use Levy [...]', op. cit., p. 43.

833 See Netanel, 'Impose a Noncommercial Use Levy [...]', op. cit., p. 47; Fisher, *Promises to Keep*, op. cit., pp. 209-210. Both authors emphasised that legalisation of unauthorised non-commercial downloads would potentially supplant markets for hard copies (*e.g.*, CDs and DVDs), consumer-ordered broadcasts such as pay-per-view cable TV, radio broadcasting and web-casting.

834 See Netanel, 'Impose a Noncommercial Use Levy [...]', op. cit., p. 44. This author proposed that, in the absence of agreement, the amount of remuneration fees would be set and periodically revised by means of mandatory arbitration procedure before authorities

thereby calculated would be collected by the public body governing the statutory licence system (*e.g.*, in the U.S., the Copyright Office) and would finally be redistributed among copyright holders in proportion to the appreciation of each copyrighted work by the users.

8.3.2.2. Costs and benefits of a copyright levy system

Choosing the policy solution proposed by Fisher and Netanel and originally advocated by Lessig would undoubtedly bring about a number of benefits. Copyright levies would ensure compensation for creators without incurring the aforementioned social costs raised by copyright-based restrictions on purposes of non-commercial dissemination and modification of the pre-existing works disseminated through the Internet. Indeed, a copyright levy system would legalise the unauthorised non-commercial copying and dissemination occurring on the Internet in such a way as to eliminate all costs of civil and criminal enforcement proceedings. As noted by both the proponents of this system, copyright infringement claims might still occur, but they would be confined to a more limited category of cases.[835] For instance, a person releasing a digital work for unauthorised file-sharing without the copyright owner's consent would continue to infringe the copyright, in the same way as a user creating and releasing a derivative work without mentioning the rightful copyright owner in the original work would do.

The above-described statutory licence would also preserve the point-to-point transmission capabilities of the Internet and, ultimately, using Benkler's lexicon, the wealth of networks.[836] Netanel motivated this proposal of reform by stressing that the non-commercial sharing and reworking of cultural expression is fundamentally speech, not theft. Thus, in his view, the phenomenon of social sharing should be celebrated, not repressed.[837] To this end, the proposed policy solution may be viewed as a middle way between "digital abandon", in which creators obtain no compensation in the face of massive unauthorised file-sharing of their works, and "digital lock-up", in which copyright industries control every use of and access to digital copyrighted works on the Internet.[838] Finally, the above-commented system would avoid the implementation of undesirable, draconian alternatives seeking copyright enforcement at the expense of access to peer-to-peer

---

such as the Copyright Arbitration Royalty Panel (CARP). Under U.S. copyright law, the CARP sets prices that Internet web-casters must pay to copyright owners of sound recordings under the compulsory licence scheme created by the Digital Performance Right in Sound Recordings Act of 1995.

835 See Netanel, 'Impose a Noncommercial Use Levy […]', op. cit., p. 42; Fisher, *Promises to Keep*, op. cit., pp. 204-205.

836 See Benkler, *The Wealth of Networks. How Social Production Transforms Markets and Freedom*, Yale University Press, New Haven and London 2006. An online version of this work is available under a Creative Commons Non-commercial/Share-alike license at: http://www.benkler.org.

837 See Netanel, 'Impose a Noncommercial Use Levy […]', op. cit., p. 83.

838 *Ibidem.*

protocols, and by disabling of the technical possibilities of sharing data between different personal computers.[839]

However, the costs and drawbacks of a levy system could offset these benefits. As pointed out by Hugenholtz, imposing copyright levies on the sale price of multi-purpose personal computers and, possibly, on that of other consumer electronic goods equipped with memory chips (*e.g.*, radio and TV sets; digital cameras, telephones, *etc*) may result in an unjustified and undesirable levying on the copyright system.[840] Hugenholtz claimed that imposing levies on a very wide range of digital copying equipment would ultimately run contrary to the contributory liability rationale underlying any levy system in the analogue world.[841] In this world, levies targeting dedicated equipment allow specific types of copyrighted content to be copied (*e.g.*, photocopying machines for written works, tape recorders for music performances, video recorders for films). In contrast, in the digital environment, the proposed levy system would address digital devices (*e.g.*, personal computers) whose primary purpose is not that of copying, disseminating and editing copyrighted works. This system would, therefore, indiscriminately affect all the consumers of these goods. The same situation would occur with regard to the copyright taxes that this levy system would create upon providers of Internet access services. Indeed, these services would be offered at higher prices in order to subsidise stakeholders harmed by free file-sharing. In this framework, all subscribers of ISPs might be charged with higher fees regardless of whether they accessed and used copyrighted works found on the Internet networks. Thus, the above-mentioned indiscriminate price increases would inevitably distort markets for digital media and Internet services. These distortions would arise in respect of both levy-targeted goods and services, given that people using them for purposes unrelated to the consumption of copyrighted works would end up cross-subsidising the free unauthorised users of these works.[842]

In addition, as suggested by Merges, it must be taken into account that the savings enabled by a copyright levy system with regard to transaction and enforcement costs might be overturned by the high costs of collective administration and repartition.[843] Merges pointed out that existing compulsory licence schemes have clearly shown that administrative proceedings for setting the tariffs of remuneration rights might be so complex and time-consuming as to result in dramatic stagnation at the level of copyright holder compensation.[844] In this respect, Hugenholtz remarked that, in Europe at least, the creators might never have the remuneration they deserved if it was considered that the criteria of repartition adopted by col-

---

839 See Appendix I, §D, where it is explained that the situation described in the text may be achieved through the adoption of TC platforms.

840 Hugenholtz, 'Peer-to-Peer and Copyright, Are Levies a Solution?', paper presented at the 3rd DRM Conference, Berlin, 14-15 January 2005.

841 *Ibidem.*

842 See Hugenholtz, 'Peer-to-Peer and Copyright', op. cit.

843 See Merges, 'Compulsory Licensing vs. the Three "Golden Oldies"', op. cit., pp. 6-10.

844 See Merges, 'Compulsory Licensing', op. cit., p. 9.

lecting societies in administering existing levy systems were mainly opaque.[845] Hence, it is reasonable to be skeptical about the suitability of these kinds of institutions to carry out the sophisticated surveys and metering activities envisaged by Fisher's and Netanel's models.

Last but not least, the described levy system would supplant or irreparably harm the on-line markets on which legitimate or fully licensed content suppliers provide commercially both interactive (*i.e.*, on-demand) and non-interactive services based on the delivery of copyrighted works. Fisher and Netanel were completely aware of this result.[846] This is also the line of argument that would ultimately prohibit the enactment of the described levy system under today's EU digital copyright law.

8.3.2.3. Why this policy option does not fit EU digital copyright law

The adoption of a levy system to legalise the phenomenon of unauthorised file-sharing under EU copyright law is legally unviable for several reasons. In principle, mere downloads from file-sharing networks could be excused under the exception of digital private copying in so far as the Member States exercised the option provided under Article 5(2)(b) of the InfoSoc Directive. Under this provision, national law may limit the exclusive right of digital reproduction for personal uses as long as the copyright holder obtains fair remuneration.[847] In contrast, the Directive does not leave room for any exception to the exclusive right of making content available to the public, which is encroached upon by unauthorised file-sharing uploads. Indeed, the exhaustive list of copyright exceptions provided under Article 5 of the Directive does not foresee any exception to this exclusive right being applied to unauthorised uploading.

Moreover, it must be noted that, even if the Directive had foreseen such a possibility, the legalisation of file-sharing activities in the EU would face an insurmountable hurdle under EU and international copyright laws: the three-step test. The compelling force of the test under international laws such as the Berne Convention and the TRIPS Agreement would prevent even the U.S. legislator from adopting the 'Fisher-Netanel' proposal. In addition, the requirements of the test forbid EU Member States from restricting the legalisation of file-sharing activities to the realm of mere downloads, if these reproductions onto user hardware were considered as copying for personal use under Article 5(2)(b). When analysing the European case law on unauthorised file-sharing, it was pointed out that the three-step test embodied in Article 5(5) of the Directive forbids the application of the

[845] See Hugenholtz, 'Peer-to-Peer and Copyright', op. cit. To clarify this point, it worth recalling that, in the EU Member States which have established levy systems, authors' collective societies are required by law to gather up fees and re-distribute them among their members according to criteria established by each society. In his remarks, Hugenholtz criticised the lack of transparency of these repartition criteria.

[846] See Fisher, *Promises to Keep*, op. cit., pp. 209-215; Netanel, 'Impose a Noncommercial Use Levy [...]', op. cit., pp. 47-52.

[847] See Article 5(2)(b) of the InfoSoc Directive, §4.4.1., see *supra*.

private copying exception to the case of unauthorised downloads.[848] Under the test, a hypothetical national statutory licence which establishes levies to remunerate copyright owners for works downloaded without authorisation would meet the third requirement of the test, but would probably violate the second requirement. Indeed, whereas a levy system might provide fair remuneration to avoid the unreasonable prejudice of the copyright holder interests mentioned under the third requirement, the system would violate the second requirement by irreparably harming today's exploitation of copyrighted works on the Internet. It is clear that a statutory licence which permits all downloading would inevitably corrode today's flourishing markets for interactive (*i.e.*, on-demand) and non-interactive on-line services.[849]

In addition to Article 5(5) of the InfoSoc Directive, the international norms which establish the three-step test for copyright exceptions would forbid the national laws of Member States from replacing the copyright property rule by the enactment of a compensatory regulatory scheme. As pointed out by Ricolfi when he commented upon Fisher's proposal, the enactment of a regulatory scheme for the on-line exploitation of copyrighted works would be in conflict with current international obligations embodied in Articles 11bis(2) and 13(1) of the Berne Convention.[850] As explained in depth below,[851] the prevailing doctrine on the interpretation of the Berne Convention holds that the two above-mentioned provisions constitute the only cases in which the members of the Berne Union are entitled to impose compulsory licences of exclusive rights (which are, respectively, the right to authorise the broadcasting of copyrighted works and the right to authorise the recording of musical works). To overcome this restriction, Ricolfi suggested that all members of the Berne Convention and of the TRIPS Agreement should embark on negotiations in order to obtain a modification of the Berne Convention and of the TRIPS Agreement (which incorporates Articles 1 to 20 of the Berne Convention by reference).[852] As this author remarked, even if the objective to obtain a modification of the Berne Convention on this issue would encounter insurmountable hurdles, it would be worth discussing the proposal of abandoning the copyright property rule in the online environment on its merits, instead of rejecting this solution on the mere grounds of over-restrictive international norms that were adopted ages before the advent of the digitally networked environment and the rise of its new legal challenges.

---

[848] See §6.3.3., see *supra*.

[849] An example of on-demand market for online copyrighted content is given by Apple's, Sony's and Microsoft's on-line music stores. Commercial non-interactive services are exemplified by Internet radio and web-casters of audiovisual works.

[850] See Ricolfi, 'Individual and collective management of copyright in a digital environment', in Torremans (ed) *Copyright Law: A handbook of Contemporary Research*, Edward Elgar, Cheltenham 2007.

[851] See §8.3.3.2., see *infra*.

[852] See Ricolfi, 'Individual and collective management [...]', op. cit., who wrote: "It is a clear invitation to think outside the box. To implement it, treaties have to be amended? So what? Let us amend them; and if this entails a shake up in other issues, as it may well be in a situation where issue linkage prevails, this may even be for the better."

A second line of argument against the adoption under EU law of a levy system such as that proposed by Fisher and Netanel is based on the fact that the European Commission has already started pursuing an opposite strategy. It was emphasised above that the Commission is seeking to abolish levies in the digital environment as long as the implementation of DRM systems and other rights management technologies effectively forbid and control private copying and other unauthorised activities.[853] This action was taken by the Commission in 2006 through the delivery of a roadmap document on the possible reform of copyright levies in Europe.[854] In line with a policy expressed in Article 5(2)(b) of the InfoSoc Directive and re-stated in Recital 35 of the same Directive, the Commission intends to ensure the phasing-out of levies imposed on digital media where private copying is technically prevented by DRM systems and other copy-control devices. To this end, the roadmap document, while urging Member States to monitor the effective implementation of DRM technology on digital media, discloses the Commission's intent of enacting legislative measures which set out objective criteria for the phasing-out of copyright levies. Thus, implementing a levy system for legalising Internet file-sharing would imply a radical change of strategy, which is unlikely to be embraced by the Commission in the short term. In the absence of this strategic change, it would not make sense to enact levy systems whose purposes of legalising file-sharing activities could easily be frustrated by DRM technology with regard to the files to be shared. In this hypothetical situation, users would end up having the right to download for free digital content which, due to the application of DRM technologies, might paradoxically not work or be stored safely on their computers.

8.3.3. Mandatory collective administration of online exclusive rights

This section clarifies whether the objective of legalising unauthorised file-sharing might be legitimately pursued in the EU through statutory regulation of the conditions of exercise of the exclusive rights created by copyright law for the digital environment. To this end, the first section comments upon a system of mandatory collective administration of digital copyright that was proposed and discussed in the preparatory works of the French legislation which transposed the InfoSoc Directive. The second section is devoted to making clear whether this solution may be legitimately undertaken by copyright policy-makers under the frameworks of EU law and international copyright law.

---

853 See §4.4.1., see *supra.*

854 See Commission of the European Communities, *Copyright levy reform, Commission's Work Programme for 2006 – Roadmap*, cit. The Commission undertook this action on the assumption that national levies on digital equipment and media have unequally proliferated, with subsequent distortions in the Community-wide markets for digital media and consumer electronic goods: see §4.4.1, see *supra.*

8.3.3.1. Is mandatory collective management a legitimate policy option?

In 2004, the High Council of Literary and Artistic Property (*Conseil supérieur de la propriété literaire et artistique*), which is a consulting body to the French Ministry of Culture and Communication, established two commissions of study which focused on the impact of new technologies on intellectual property rights. One of these commissions was created in order to find possible solutions concerning the issue of the dissemination of works on the Internet. In December 2005, this commission delivered a report in which a proposal for the legalisation of file-sharing coming from the so-called *Alliance Public-Artistes* (hereinafter *Alliance*) was examined and subsequently rejected.[855] The *Alliance* proposed the adoption of a system of mandatory collective administration, a "global licence" (from the French *licence globale*), for peer-to-peer file-sharing. The proposal was rejected by the majority of the commission's members because it would have provided too weak a response to the problem of on-line copyright enforcement while, at the same time, veering away from the legal boundaries laid down by international copyright law.[856]

The *Alliance*'s central recommendation was the creation of a remuneration system for acts of file-sharing on the basis of a mandatory *contractual* licence to be combined with a *statutory* licence. The practical assumption of this proposal was that, even if direct infringers were legally sued or prosecuted as criminals, such unlawful practices would not cease. Instead, this proposal sought to legalise two distinct acts of unauthorised exploitation exercised by file-sharers: acts of reproduction (*i.e.*, downloads) and communication to the public (*i.e.*, uploads).

In respect of downloading, the *Alliance*'s proposal argued that the existing system of remuneration of private copying should be extended to include and legalise acts of mere downloading from file-sharing networks. In other words, the law should define and treat acts of mere downloading as private copying subject to the existing remuneration system covering copying equipment, recording devices and recordable media.[857] Under this proposal, the range of devices subject to copyright levies would be broadened to cover personal computer hardware and the digital

---

[855] See Sirinelli, 'Droit d'auteur et droits voisins – Chronique', (18) *Propriétés Intellectuelles*, January 2006, p. 58, at p. 65. The Alliance group was interestingly formed, on the one hand, by representatives of performer artists, certain categories of authors and, on the other hand, by associations of consumers and the *Ligue de l'enseignement et les familles*.

[856] See Sirinelli, 'Droit d'auteur et droits voisins – Chronique', op. cit., p. 65.

[857] The relevant legal framework under French law is established by Articles L.122-5 and L.211-3 of the Intellectual Property Code, which provide that authors, performers and producers of phonograms cannot prohibit reproductions of their works, performances and sound recordings so far as these reproductions are carried out for purposes of private use by individuals. Article L.311-1 creates remuneration rights in favour of these right holders for the private copying of phonograms and audiovisual works. According to Articles 311-4 and 311-5, this remuneration originates from the imposition of copyright levies on recordable digital media, which are determined under the supervision of an administrative authority.

equipment used to download works from the Internet.[858] At first sight, this part of the *Alliance* proposal had much in common with Fisher's and Netanel's model of statutory licence.

As far as true "sharing" (*i.e.*, downloading *plus* uploading) is concerned, the *Alliance* proposed the creation of a system of mandatory collective management under which collecting societies, on behalf of different categories of copyright holders, would enter into optional licences with file-sharers who wished to share their materials for non-commercial purposes on peer-to-peer networks. This category of licensees would comprise only those users who paid remuneration for the exercise of the right of making copyrighted content available to the public. In contrast, mere downloaders who only paid copyright levies on their digital copying equipment would be excluded from the scope of the global licence. This contractual system would aim to clear the right of making copyrighted digital works available to the public and would permit all acts of uploading and downloading concerning copyrighted materials. Thus, under the proposed scheme, single acts of downloading performed by licensed users would be automatically cleared by the corresponding (*i.e.*, symmetrical) acts of uploading, which would be legitimately exercised under the mandatory regime of collective administration. According to the *Alliance* proposal, these licences would cover the sharing of all music and audiovisual works, with the exclusion of films whose date of release was older than four years.[859] The proposed global licence would neither cover nor authorise the reproduction and/or the making available of copyrighted videogames and computer programmes.[860] All acts of uploading and corresponding downloading would be legalised where each individual licensee was a natural person sharing his or her materials with other individuals for non-commercial ends. Moreover, each lawful user should pay a certain amount of remuneration fees set out in agreements negotiated by collecting societies (on behalf of copyright holders) and consumer associations (on behalf of file-sharers). In this framework, ISPs could usefully participate in these agreements by acting as intermediaries in the collection of fees from their subscribers who wished to benefit from the global licence.[861] In the absence

---

858 See Bernault and Lebois, *Peer-to-peer et propriété littéraire et artistique*. op. cit., pp. 50-51, who stressed that, in January 2001, the French administrative commission that determines the recordable media subject to levies held that computer hardware should not be included in the list of such media. Obviously, the *Alliance*'s global licence would require modification of this policy.

859 See Sirinelli, 'Droit d'auteur et droits voisins – Chronique', op. cit., p. 65; Bernault and Lebois, *Peer-to-peer et propriété littéraire et artistique*, op. cit., pp. 73-74. In the *Alliance*'s proposal, the "four year" requirement for audiovisual works intended to take into account the usual time frame of commercial exploitation of movies in public performances, broadcasts and in DVD formats. This was an evident attempt by the proponents of the system to seek compliance of the global licence with the second requirement of the three-step test (which protects the "normal exploitation" of copyrighted works).

860 See Sirinelli, 'Droit d'auteur et droits voisins – Chronique', op. cit., p. 65.

861 See Bernault and Lebois, *Peer-to-peer et propriété littéraire et artistique*, pp. 77-78. However, as pointed out by Sirinelli, 'Droit d'auteur et droits voisins – Chronique', op.

of an agreement between stakeholders, a competent authority would intervene to set out the level of remuneration, which should be equally redistributed between authors and publishers of the licensed works.[862]

The *Alliance* proposal, taken as a whole, was very similar in its scope and effects to the proposals of statutory licence formulated by Fisher and Netanel. The French proposal would, therefore, have had the same costs and benefits previously spelt out with regard to the proposal of a statutory non-commercial use levy.[863] The *Alliance* proposal, however, was based on a different legal construction, which might imply a higher degree of legitimacy under the legal framework of EU copyright law.

8.3.3.2. Mandatory collective management, international law and the **acquis communautaire** *on copyright entitlements*

Under the *Alliance* proposal, mere downloaders would reproduce copyrighted works under a statutory licence. In contrast, file-sharers would download and upload copyrighted works under a (mandatory) collective licence, namely, under a contractual (*i.e.*, non-statutory) scheme.

The theoretical distinction between these two distinct parts of the proposal has an important consequence. The statutory licence covering mere downloads would constitute a copyright exception, and it would therefore be subject to the EU regulation of copyright exceptions provided under Article 5 of the InfoSoc Directive.[864] In contrast, the mandatory collective administration of the right of communication to the public would, at least in principle, leave the substance of the exclusive rights intact while merely restricting their exercise in the specific framework of file-sharing activities. This means that a problem of compliance with the EU treatment of copyright exceptions, and, in particular, with the three-step test embodied in Article 5(5) of the Directive, would arise only with regard to the first part of the proposal, and not with regard to its second part.

Even if the enactment of this proposal provided fair remuneration for all unauthorised acts of downloading, the foreshadowed statutory licence would nevertheless conflict with the second requirement of the three-step test, which protects the

---

cit., p. 67, French Internet access providers were against the implementation of the global licence proposal.

862 See Bernault and Lebois, *Peer-to-peer et propriété littéraire et artistique*, op. cit., pp. 72-82, who argued that the practical implementation of a global licence system could have been based on the example of the existing system of mandatory collective administration of remuneration rights established for the case of reprography: see Article L.122-10 of the Intellectual Property Code, as amended by Act N.1995-4 of 3 January 1995.

863 See §8.3.2.2., see *supra*.

864 It must be recalled that, to great surprise, the first part of the *Alliance* proposal was embodied in an amendment approved by one branch of the French legislative assembly (*Assemblée Nationale*) in a resolution of December 2005: see Lucas and Sirinelli, 'La loi n°2006-961 du 1er août relative au droit d'auteur et aux droits voisins dans la société de l'information', op. cit., p. 333.

normal exploitation of copyrighted works at the levels of both EU and international copyright law.[865] As noted earlier, Fisher's and Netanel's proposals are similarly incompatible with the three-step test.[866]

The inquiry about the legitimacy of the system of mandatory collective administration proposed for the clearance of all uploading activities occurring on file-sharing networks is more complex.[867] As Sirinelli noted, the *Alliance* proposed this solution on the assumption that mandatory collective administration does not give rise to a copyright exception and, as such, is not subject to the constraints of the three-step test.[868] As explained by Lewinski and Guibault, under this regime, copyright owners are only restricted in the means of exercising this right, to wit, they are only able to exercise the exclusive right through a collecting society.[869] Lewinski emphasised that the right itself is not limited as such, given that mandatory administration does not protect any interest of the public at large, as copyright exceptions do.[870] This technique has been traditionally used to ensure copyright enforcement in situations in which individual exploitation has proven to be impossible because of the presence of too many protected works and potential users, as in the case of peer-to-peer networks.[871]

---

865 See Article 5(5) of the InfoSoc Directive, Article 9(2) of the Berne Convention, Article 13 of the TRIPS Agreement, and Article 10 of the WIPO Copyright Treaty.

866 See §8.3.2.3, see *supra*.

867 To simplify the analysis, it is assumed here that the mandatory collective licensing of acts of uploading (*i.e.*, making copyrighted works available to the public) effectively extends to and authorise corresponding acts of downloading. This assumption, though, was very controversial. As pointed out by Sirinelli, 'Droit d'auteur et droits voisins – Chronique', op. cit., p. 67, the *Alliance* proposal, which was limited to French law, could only have the effect of legalising acts of uploading originating from the French territory. To the contrary, the proposal could not have the same effect in respect of acts of uploading directed to foreign recipients.

868 See Sirinelli, 'Droit d'auteur et droits voisins – Chronique', op. cit., p. 66.

869 See Lewinski, 'Mandatory Collective Administration of Exclusive Rights – A Case Study on Its Compatibility with International and EC Copyright Law', *e-Copyright Bulletin*, January – March 2004, available at http://portal.unesco.org/culture/en/ev.php, p. 5; Guibault, *Copyright Limitations and Contracts*, op. cit., pp. 26-27, who made clear that "technically speaking, such a measure constitutes a condition to the exercise of a right rather than a exception on that right [...]". While drawing on the disposal of the Council Directive 93/83/EEC of 27 September 1993 on the coordination of certain rules concerning copyrights and rights related to copyright applicable to satellite broadcasting and cable retransmission, OJ L 248, 6.10.1993, 15-21 (hereinafter "Satellite and Cable Directive"), Lewinski pointed out that Recital 28 of this Directive explicitly recognised that, under the regime of mandatory collective administration established by Article 9(1) in respect of the right to authorise or prohibit cable retransmission, the exclusive right "... as such stays intact and only the exercise of this right is regulated to some extent".

870 See Lewinski, 'Mandatory Collective Administration of Exclusive Rights [...]', p. 5.

871 See Guibault, *Copyright Limitations and Contracts*, op. cit., p. 26. The suitability of this technique in the case of unauthorised file sharing might derive from the fact that, due to a far too great number of potential licensees among file-sharers on peer-to-peer networks, the exploitation of online exclusive rights might be better exercised on a *col-*

Even if we took the assumption for granted that mandatory collective administration is not a copyright exception and, as such, is free from the constraints of the three-step test[872], a problem with this policy solution would arise in terms of illegitimate restriction on the exercise of copyright entitlements under both international copyright law and the *acquis communautaire* on the substance of copyright entitlements.

International copyright law embodied in the Berne Convention, and incorporated into subsequent international agreements, provides the legal basis for the implementation of compulsory licences under the law of the countries of the Berne Union (to which all EU Member States are parties).[873]

In this respect, Articles 11bis(2) and 13(1) of this Convention provide that it is a matter for the countries of the Union to determine the conditions under which certain exclusive rights may be exercised. These exclusive rights are, respectively, the right to authorise the broadcasting of copyrighted works by any means of communication[874] and the right to authorise the recording of a musical work.[875] According to Ficsor, by virtue of these two provisions, the Berne Convention covers, in an *exhaustive* way, the cases in which national laws determine or impose non-voluntary licences of exclusive rights, on condition that copyright owners receive fair remuneration.[876] Clearly, given that these provisions were introduced to permit cases of compulsory licensing of the aforementioned rights, *a fortiori* they

lective basis rather than on an *individual* basis. In Europe, this legal technique is well developed in Scandinavian countries (*i.e.*, Denmark, Finland, Sweden, Norway) where the law, since the early 1960s has conferred "extended" effects upon collective agreements which administer certain exclusive rights (*e.g.*, the right to authorize the broadcasting of music works). Under these schemes, the law provides that copyright licences concluded by organisations of right-holders with a user or a group of users shall apply even to right-holders who are *not* members of the contracting organisation.

872 To demonstrate that EU copyright law does not mean mandatory collective administration as a copyright exception, Lewinski, 'Mandatory Collective Administration of Exclusive Rights', op. cit., pp. 13-14, pointed out that the InfoSoc Directive, which strictly regulates the right of communication to the public (see Article 3(1)), includes neither the option of mandatory collective administration nor that of non-voluntary licences in the exhaustive list of exceptions or limitations to this right provided by Article 5(3). According to this author, this provision clearly suggests that cases of compulsory licensing fall *outside* the scope of regulation of the Directive. The same conclusion is derived from the wording of Recital 18 of the InfoSoc Directive, which reads: "This Directive is without prejudice to the arrangements in the Member States concerning the management of rights such as extended collective licences".

873 It is worth recalling that Article 9(1) of the TRIPS Agreement and Article 1(4) of the WIPO Copyright Treaty incorporated the substantive provisions of the Berne Convention by reference. So, what is said in the main text in respect of the Berne Convention applies to the framework of these international agreements alike.

874 See Article 11bis(2) of the Berne Convention.

875 See Article 13(1) of the Berne Convention.

876 See Ficsor, 'Collective Management of Copyright and Related Rights at a Triple Crossroads: Should it Remain Voluntary or May It Be "Extended" or Made Mandatory?', *e-Copyright Bulletin*, October 2003, available at: http://portal.unesco.org/culture/en/ev.php, p. 4.

must be understood to allow the determination and imposition of less restrictive conditions of exercise such as mandatory collective management of the same rights.[877]

That which seems to be the generally prevailing doctrine is that, on the grounds of the *a contrario* principle, beyond the exceptional cases of the rights to authorise the broadcasting of any copyrighted works and the recording of musical works, national laws are *not* entitled to establish restrictions on the conditions of exercise of other exclusive rights under the Berne Convention. As Ficsor argues, this means that mandatory collective administration is not permissible in any case where the international norms on copyright do not explicitly allow it:

> "[...] where the international copyright norms [...] provide for an exclusive right which can be exercised individually and the relevant norms do not allow for the prescription of conditions for its exercise [...] it would be in conflict with those norms to subject the exercise of such a right to the condition that it may only be exercised though collective management."[878]

Such a conclusion was recently advocated in a recommendation released by the *Association Littéraire et Artistique Internationale* (ALAI) in the aftermath of the deliberations in the French legislative assembly regarding the adoption of a system of mandatory collective administration.[879]

In the relevant literature, the above-mentioned prevailing doctrine was strengthened by the observation that the two, supposedly exhaustive provisions of Articles 11bis(2) and 13(1) of the Berne Convention were introduced in order to address and solve potential conflicts arising between broadcasters and record companies on the one hand, and authors' collecting societies on the other, in the exploitation of copyrighted works by means of broadcasts and sound recordings.[880] Accordingly, in no way should these two exceptional cases be interpreted as taking into account the relationship between the author and the end-user, who has

---

877 See Ficsor, 'Collective Management of Copyright and Related Rights at a Triple Crossroads', op. cit., p. 4; Lewinski, 'Mandatory Collective Administration of Exclusive Rights', op. cit., p. 10.

878 See Ficsor, 'Collective Management of Copyright and Related Rights at a Triple Crossroads', op. cit., p. 7.

879 See ALAI, Resolution of 14 January 2006, available at http://www.alai.org, § Publications – Internationals ("Affirmation Droit Exclusif"), which stated:
"Whereas the fundamental rule of copyright, according to the international treaties, is the exclusive right of the author to decide on the principle and the manner of dissemination of the work of authorship, and
Whereas the diminution of exclusive rights is authorised only to the extent set out by those treaties,
Recalls firmly therefore that, beyond the limits expressly provided in the international instruments, any modification of copyright laws, whatever its form or its label, whose result would be to deprive authors of the effective exercise of their exclusive rights is contrary to the spirit and the letter of the international agreements."

880 See Lewinski, 'Mandatory Collective Administration of Exclusive Rights', op. cit., p. 6.

only recently become a possible direct contractor of suppliers of copyrighted works.

In contrast, another view has recently advocated a different interpretation of Article 11bis(2) of the Berne Convention, which would leave wider room for the enactment of a legitimate system of mandatory collective management aimed at legalising file-sharing operations. As argued by Ricolfi, the exception provided by Article 11bis(2) of the Berne Convention in respect of the exclusive rights of broadcasting could also apply to the case of on-line (*i.e.*, "point-to-point") communication to the public, and not only to the traditional "point-to-mass" communication which characterises radio and television broadcasts.[881] Ricolfi found that the provision of Article 8 of the WIPO Copyright Treaty (which provides for the right of making copyrighted content available interactively to the public) was expressly adopted "without prejudice to the provisions of Articles [...] 11-bis(1)" of the Berne Convention.[882] He inferred from this reference to Article 11bis that the possibility of introducing special regimes under the Berne Convention was extended by Article 8 of the WIPO Copyright Treaty to the right of interactive communication to the public, which is actually infringed by uploaders of unauthorised materials on peer-to-peer networks. Ricolfi reached this conclusion on the grounds of the Agreed Statement concerning Article 8 of the 1996 WIPO Copyright Treaty,[883] which would make it clear that the right of interactive communication to the public provided under theTreaty may be made subject to the exceptional regime permitted under Article 11bis(2) of the Berne Convention. However, this author concluded that the creation of a special regime for interactive on-line communication to the public would constitute a copyright exception and, as such, would be subject to the insurmountable barrier of the three-step test.

Given the above-mentioned arguments, it is reasonable to conclude that the implementation of the system of mandatory collective administration proposed by the *Alliance* in France would have been in conflict with the prevailing doctrine of international copyright law regarding the mandatory collective management of copyrights. The French proposal was based on restricting the conditions of exercise of the exclusive right of on-line communication to the public, which would not have been covered by the exceptional provisions regarding the broadcasting and the music recording rights.

As observed by Ficsor in support of the prevailing doctrine on statutory restrictions on copyright management, EU copyright legislation has, so far, carefully re-

---

881 See Ricolfi, 'Individual and collective management of copyright in a digital environment', op. cit.

882 See the initial phrasing of Article 8 of the 1996 WIPO Copyright Treaty ("Right of Communication to the Public"), which states: "Without prejudice to the provisions of Articles 11(1)(ii), 11bis(1)(i) and (ii), 11ter(1)(ii), 14(1)(ii) and 14bis(1) of the Berne Convention, authors of literary and artistic works shall enjoy the exclusive right of authorizing any communication to the public of their works [...]".

883 See the Agreed Statement on Article 8 of the 1996 WIPO Copyright Treaty, available at http://www.wipo.int/treaties/en/ip/wct/statements/html, which reads: "It is further understood that nothing in Article 8 precludes a Contracting Party from applying Art.11-bis(2)".

spected the preservation of the substance of exclusive rights established by international copyright norms.[884] This deference was shown by EU law-makers when enacting Article 9(1) of the Satellite and Cable Directive, which required Member States to create systems of mandatory collective administration for the right to grant or refuse authorisation to a cable operator for a cable retransmission. Such a regime of mandatory collective administration was enacted under the shield of Article 11bis(2) of the Berne Convention, which applies specifically to the licensing of broadcasting rights. The same kind of compliance was shown in other two cases where EU law gave Member States the option of implementing mandatory collective management of mere remuneration rights.[885] This was the case of both the rental right granted under Article 4 of the Rental Right Directive[886] and the resale right provided by Article 1 of the Resale Right Directive.[887] Given that international copyright laws did not recognise any of these rights as *exclusive* rights, no specific exception to the rule of exclusivity was needed to implement such non-exclusive rights under EU copyright law. As pointed out by Ficsor, the fact that the provision of Article 4(3) of the Rental Right Directive found it expressly necessary to provide Member States with *permission* to impose the collective administration of this right to equitable remuneration by the collecting societies of authors and performers implicitly indicates that, under the *acquis communautaire*, the EU legislator understood this permission as being necessary.[888] The same principle was followed by Article 6(2) of the Resale Right Directive, which foresees that Member States *may* provide compulsory or optional collective management of the right to remuneration established to the benefit of the author of an original work of art (*i.e.*, the so-called *droit de suite*), in accordance with Article 14-ter of the Berne Convention.

8.3.4. Seeking complementarity between file-sharing and copyright-protecting technologies

This section scrutinises a final policy option which draws upon the idea that the objectives of on-line copyright enforcement and free dissemination of unprotected

884 See Ficsor, 'Collective Management of Copyright and Related Rights at a Triple Crossroads', op. cit., pp. 5-8.

885 *Ibidem.*

886 See Council Directive 92/100/EEC of 19 November 1992 on rental right and lending right and on certain rights related to copyright in the field of intellectual property, OJ L 346, 27.11.1992, p. 61. The provisions of Article 4(1) and 4(2) of the Rental Right Directive introduced a "non-waivable right to equitable remuneration" in favour of authors and performers on the rental of phonograms and audiovisual works in which their works or their performances have been incorporated.

887 Directive 2001/84/EC of the European Parliament and of the Council of 27 September 2001 on the resale right for the benefit of the author of an original work of art, OJ L 272, 13.10.2001, p. 32.

888 See Ficsor, 'Collective Management of Copyright and Related Rights at a Triple Crossroads', op. cit., p. 5.

works over peer-to-peer networks are not incompatible. The idea is that unauthorised access to and use of copyrighted digital works can be technically impaired without blocking the free dissemination of unprotected information, information in the public domain and copyrighted materials released under copyleft licences. These ends may ultimately be pursued while seeking and imposing technical complementarity between peer-to-peer technologies and copyright-protecting devices such as DRM and fingerprint filtering systems.

Whereas this policy solution would co-exist with the strategy of targeting enforcement measures at individuals,[889] the solution would be logically alternative to the implementation of regulatory models which legalise the file-sharing phenomenon through statutory compensation systems[890] or mandatory collective administration of on-line exclusive rights.[891]

8.3.4.1. Mandating the adoption of copyright-protecting technologies

It was concluded above that, under the EU copyright system, on-line intermediaries such as Internet access and network providers may bear indirect copyright liability for not adopting technical measures capable of detecting on-line copyright infringements over peer-to-peer networks.[892] This conclusion was recently reached in the EU by a few decisions by national courts which, on the grounds of Article 8(3) of the InfoSoc Directive, compelled Internet network and access providers to take appropriate measures to prevent copyright infringement by their subscribers. It was argued that the legal basis of Article 8(3) might be used to extend this positive duty of care to peer-to-peer software providers. If so, both ISPs and peer-to-peer designers may have additional incentives to develop monitoring technologies in consideration of the risks of incurring civil and criminal copyright liability under EU legislation that has recently been enacted or is in the pipeline.[893]

In principle, appropriate measures for protecting copyrighted works without hindering the free communication of unprotected materials over file-sharing networks might be taken by peer-to-peer software providers, Internet access and network providers and suppliers of copyrighted digital content. These measures may include the possible re-design of peer-to-peer networks, the adoption of filtering technologies, and, in particular, the attachment of acoustic fingerprints to each work transmitted over the Internet.

8.3.4.1.1. Re-design of peer-to-peer technology

The most efficient way to ensure the enforcement of the above-mentioned duty of care could be implemented by designers of peer-to-peer software. If copyright law were enforced so as to oblige technology providers to re-design the architecture of

---

[889] See §8.3.1., see *supra*.
[890] See §8.3.2., see *supra*.
[891] See §8.3.3., see *supra*.
[892] See §6.5.4., see *supra*.
[893] See §6.5.2., see *supra*.

their programmes completely, decentralisation of user-to-user communication might be reduced so that the peer-to-peer software provider could retain a certain degree of supervision possibilities on exchanges of copyrighted materials. However, this result could hardly be achieved swiftly and efficiently. It must be considered that most peer-to-peer software programmes are distributed from jurisdictions outside the European Union, where software developers may find it suitable to model their technology architecture on a standard of copyright liability different from that endorsed before European courts. This might be the case of peer-to-peer technologies targeted at the U.S. standard of copyright liability upheld by the decision of the U.S. Supreme Court in the *M.G.M.* v. *Grokster.*[894] Under this standard, a peer-to-peer software provider can be found indirectly liable only for not supervising direct copyright infringements or for culpably inducing them. In the absence of these elements, the developer of software which enables fully decentralised peer-to-peer networking does not bear a duty to modify the technology in order to make it copyright-protecting.

Moreover, it must be always borne in mind that providing today's peer-to-peer networks with a fully decentralised architecture can be strongly justified in terms of efficiency and innovation. Decentralised peer-to-peer networking is the result of years of research aimed at reducing the costs and enhancing the speed of transmission and storage of huge amounts of data across the Internet. An important goal in peer-to-peer networks is that all clients provide resources, including bandwidth, storage space, and computing power. Thus, the total capacity of this communication technology increases proportionally to the number of clients using the technology.[895] The decentralised nature of peer-to-peer networks also increases its robustness in case of failures by replicating data over multiple peers and by enabling peers to find the data without relying on a centralised index server. Thus, it would be unfair to look at the architecture of peer-to-peer networks as something designed only to make copyright infringements easier and more difficult to detect. This conclusion would clearly overlook the benefits of this technology.

Having said this, it is reasonable to conclude that targeting the enforcement of the duty of care of copyrighted digital materials merely at the level of peer-to-peer software developers may not be a good idea, especially if the providers are located outside the European Union. Even if the EU law standard of indirect copyright liability were used to compel peer-to-peer software providers to modify their technology architecture, such complex and time-consuming lawsuits might prove to be ineffective in a borderless environment such as the cyberspace. Indeed, for this solution to be effective, courts should compel peer-to-peer technology providers to take measures such as that of replacing *all* existing copies of their programmes with modified, copyright-protecting versions of the same programmes or, more

[894] See von Lohmann, *IAAL (I Am A Lawyer): What Peer-to-Peer Developers Need to Know about Copyright Law*, op. cit., who intended to provide peer-to-peer software designers with guidelines on how to avoid indirect copyright liability under U.S. copyright law.

[895] This is not true of a usual client-server architecture with a fixed set of servers, in which adding more clients could mean slower data transfer for all users.

unrealistically, that of confining such modified versions to the realm of Internet users located in Europe.

8.3.4.1.2. Adoption of filtering technologies

Unauthorised access to and use of copyrighted materials originating from peer-to-peer networks can be filtered (or blocked) using several techniques and devices. Strowel pointed out that filtering measures may be successfully implemented and supported by Internet access and network providers.[896] These actors may either block subscribers' access to peer-to-peer protocols as such, or filter copyrighted content by detecting it on their networks. Another possibility of filtering unauthorised content would not need the technical support of Internet access providers; instead, it would simply consist of installing technical measures capable of disabling the storage and sharing of certain types of data, for example, MP3 files, on the Internet user's hardware.

Two of these approaches are highly undesirable and legally questionable due to their potential to wholly foreclose legitimate opportunities of using peer-to-peer technology for purposes of free communication and expression. This is the case of both the permanent blockage of peer-to-peer protocols operated by Internet access providers, and the impairment of sharing and storing capabilities of users' hardware. On the one hand, access providers may achieve the objective of permanent blockage of peer-to-peer protocols by detecting and isolating particular "signatures" (*i.e.*, alphanumerical chains) which are contained in packets of information coming from peer-to-peer networks. On the other, users' machines might be technically forbidden from performing activities related to file-sharing (*e.g.*, accessing ports used by peer-to-peer clients; launching peer-to-peer applications; storing particular file formats used and circulated mainly over peer-to-peer networks, *etc*). Clearly, the spread of these technical measures will depend mainly upon the full recognition of the illegal nature of the unauthorised exchange of protected works by both the users and the makers of consumer electronic goods. This type of techniques may include even the draconian measure of installing TC chips or platforms on the hardware of personal computers, with the undesirable consequences detailed in the Appendix I to this book.[897]

The only approach respectful of the constitutionally mandated protection of freedom of expression and communication over peer-to-peer networks is that of implementing filtering devices at the level of protected content. Nevertheless, the objective of detecting and blocking access only to unauthorised copyrighted materials cannot be reasonably pursued by imposing general obligations of on-line surveillance on a unique category of stakeholders. In this respect, an express prohibition of this policy solution is given by Article 15 of the E-Commerce Directive, which makes it clear that Member State law cannot impose on ISPs:

---

[896] See Strowel, 'Le P2P : un problème pressant en attente d'une réponse legislative?', (17) *Propriétés Intellectuelles*, October 2005, p. 428, pp. 430-433.

[897] See Appendix I, §D, see *infra*.

"[...] a general obligation to monitor the information which they transmit or store, nor a general obligation actively to seek facts or circumstances indicating illegal activity."[898]

The objective of filtering unauthorised copyrighted materials could be effectively pursued only through cooperative measures taken by all stakeholders, including information carriers, peer–to-peer software designers and suppliers of copyrighted content. Today's commercial and non-commercial dissemination of content over the Internet shows that suitable "signalling" devices, such as DRM systems and acoustic fingerprints, may be adopted to indicate the specific copyright status of each piece of transmitted content. This suitable form of self-regulation established by stakeholders who occupy different positions and play different roles at different Internet communication levels may originate only from the wide acceptance of single standards of filtering tools. As argued more in depth below,[899] the operation of these technology standards would enable on-line actors to monitor copyright infringements without running the risk of stopping flows of free information.

8.3.4.1.3. On the suitable function of DRM systems and fingerprints

As a general preventive measure against copyright infringement committed through peer-to-peer networks, owners and suppliers of copyrighted digital works have increasingly used DRM technology. So far, this technology has been developed mainly as a technique of content encryption and automated rights management. However, using this technology, file-sharers cannot be prevented from uploading or downloading unauthorised works. Instead, what can be technically entrenched is the possibility of file-sharers to access and use these materials once they have been downloaded and shifted to their computers and media players.

Until recently, no technical measure in the DRM world specifically functioned as a filtering tool in peer-to-peer network settings. Recent developments on the markets for on-line copyrighted content have shown that rights management technologies may soon comprise technology known as "acoustic fingerprinting". Fingerprints can be viewed as individual digital signatures that identify each single piece of work circulated on the Internet by means of authorship and other rights management information to be replicated into each copy of the protected work. Acoustic fingerprints are based on a waveform system that analyses the content of each file, produces a unique fingerprint for that file, and indexes it in a database.[900] This system works by comparing the contents of the transmitted files with the files logged into the databases that index the fingerprints. If the fingerprints match, usage and access restrictions set out by copyright owners can be enforced without

[898] See Article 15 of the E-Commerce Directive. On this issue, see Strowel, 'Le P2P: un problème pressant en attente d'une réponse legislative?', op. cit., p. 433.

[899] See §8.3.4.1.3., see *infra*.

[900] See Einhorn and Rosenblatt, 'Peer-to-Peer Networking and Digital Rights Management. How Market Tools Can Solve Copyright Problems', (534) *Policy Analysis* 2005, available at: http://www.cato.org, pp. 9-11.

restricting the dissemination of other free information.[901] A number of on-line services have been successfully developed by applying acoustic fingerprints to copyrighted content circulated through peer-to-peer networks.[902] Moreover, at the time of this writing, acoustic fingerprinting technology provided by Gracenote, the leading technology producer, is about to be implemented even outside the realm of peer-to-peer networking by one of the most popular websites of social networking in the world, *i.e.*, "My Space".[903] This website is trying to block access to its networked infrastructure to all unauthorised copyrighted works uploaded by its subscribers.[904]

Finally, it is remarkable that even the world's biggest producer of computer programmes, Microsoft, is seeking to explore and take advantage of the beneficial effects of peer-to-peer protocols by developing a new system of "network coding" based on a new peer-to-peer algorithm (called "Avalanche"), which aims to speed up download times.[905] Microsoft's technologists claim that this filtering system will prevent unauthorised distribution of copyrighted materials since content must be digitally signed by the publisher before it can be forwarded.

As with all technology performing tasks of digital rights management, filtering systems such as acoustic fingerprints and network coding technologies have the potential of serving both commercial and non-commercial content dissemination. From a legal perspective, fingerprints can be viewed as technical measures which provide both protection from unauthorised uses of copyrighted works and rights management information under the meaning of Articles 6 and 7 of the InfoSoc Directive. So far, the vast majority of fingerprinting systems has been developed and managed by for-profit corporations, which licence their technologies to on-line commercial services. Thus, each of these services has been provided with a distinct catalogue of fingerprints which correspond to works whose commercial use was licensed by the respective copyright owners (mainly, the recording industry) to the service devisers.[906]

This situation suggests that, until fingerprinting systems are different from one another and are unable to interoperate, they will merely enable copyright enforcement within a limited number of on-line services and in respect of a closed number of works and Internet service subscribers. In such circumstances, file-sharers intending to infringe copyright can always choose to migrate to peer-to-peer platforms where no filtering system is in place.

---

901 See Ganley, 'Surviving Grokster: Innovation and the Future of Peer-to-Peer', op. cit., p. 24; Einhorn and Rosenblatt, 'Peer-to-Peer Networking and Digital Rights Management', op. cit., pp. 12-13.

902 For instance, see web-services such as snocap.com and wippit.com.

903 See http://www.myspace.com.

904 See Rosenblatt, 'MySpace Adopts Acoustic Fingeprinting', *DRM Watch*, 2 Novembre 2006, available at: http://www.drmwatch.com/ocr/article.php/3641591.

905 See Ganley, 'Surviving Grokster', op. cit., p. 24.

906 Besides these for-profit initiatives, open source software such as Digital Media Project's *Chillout* has provided fingerprinting solutions that support the implementation of an open (*i.e.*, non-proprietary), wholly interoperable DRM platform: see http://chillout.dmpf.org/.

Nonetheless, the emergence and spread of acoustic fingerprints and other filtering devices which allow Internet information carriers, copyright owners and end-users to identify and respect the specific management of rights attached to each piece of content will have at least two important consequences. Firstly, in the short term, the emergence and viability of copyright-protecting technologies such as fingerprints demonstrate that peer-to-peer software providers are placed in such a position as to take technical counter-measures against copyright infringements by individuals, which may permit them to continue to operate in a legitimate way without altering the decentralised architecture of their technology. Modern peer-to-peer designers have the possibility of developing (or obtaining in exchange for a licence from producers of this technology) fingerprinting systems that protect copyrighted works from unauthorised downloads and uploads without affecting the architecture of the technology. As a result, judicial orders such as that issued in September 2005 by the Australian Supreme Court against the provider of the Kazaa system, which compelled the provider to adopt unspecified filtering systems, will have a more specific and concrete meaning and a higher possibility of effective performance.[907] This consideration may give peer-to-peer designers an incentive to implement fingerprinting systems into their programmes automatically.

Secondly, in the long term, all stakeholders may find it desirable to endorse the implementation of an open, standardised system of DRM and fingerprinting technologies which ensure interoperability between different platforms of content rights management. As advocated above, the overcoming of a situation characterised by an abundance of proprietary (and often incompatible) DRM and fingerprinting technologies presupposes the creation of a unique (*i.e.*, standard) system of copyright-protecting technology and content rights management devices. These technologies would ultimately pursue the aim of defining what content is free, what is protected, and, in this last case, what the conditions of protection are. In theory, this system may either be left to the self-regulation of the stakeholders, or, as it seems preferable, be subject to the regulatory power of a public institution (*e.g.*, an agency of the European Commission) aimed at setting technology standards in the context of a wider, publicly monitored "user rights management infrastructure".[908]

8.3.4.2. Advantages of this policy option

In my view, complementarity between peer-to-peer technologies and copyright-protecting devices (and, more widely, DRM systems) is the solution that suits the framework of EU law best. This policy option is easier to achieve than the former ones for a number of reasons. First of all, the mandating of the implementation of copyright-protecting technologies in the realm of peer-to-peer networks does not require a reform of the existing copyright law. In contrast to systems which recommend the adoption of statutory licences or mandatory collective management,

---

907 See § 6.5.3.3, see *supra*.
908 See §9.3., see *infra*.

this solution has the advantage of leaving the substance of the exclusive on-line rights of copyright intact.

By following this approach, no concern would arise in respect of both the restrictive criteria of the three-step test and the rule of exclusivity set out for copyright entitlements in international agreements that are binding upon EU Member States. It must be admitted that the choice of this solution is inevitably dictated by the circumstance that alternative proposals of regulatory schemes based either on the assignment of mere remuneration rights, or on compulsory licences administered by collecting societies, would not comply with current international copyright law. It was pointed out that international agreements, beyond a number of explicit exceptions, outlaw both statutory exceptions which veer away from the requirements of the three-step test,[909] and legislative restrictions upon the conditions of exercise of rights which are internationally accepted as exclusive (*i.e.*, privately owned and freely transferable).[910] This lack of flexibility at the level of international copyright law undeniably affects the discussion about the merits of these alternative proposals.

Moreover, the attachment of acoustic fingerprints and other similar devices which embed access and usage restrictions onto contents requires no structural changes of the architecture of peer-to-peer networks. Rights management information working as a filtering tool seeks merely to complement this communication technology without altering its point-to-point structure or losing its technological benefits. Attaching such filtering devices at the level of circulated contents would permit peer-to-peer technology to diversify models of business and non-commercial dissemination, from on-line trading of music downloads to the release of freely accessible copyrighted works published under licences which promote the end of social sharing such as those of Creative Commons.

For this solution to be fully fledged, though, acoustic fingerprinting and other filtering devices should be developed and used beyond on-line businesses. The best option would be that of embedding this technique into a wider, fully interoperable DRM platform that may work as an open, non-proprietary standard of technical protection and rights management information in the digitally networked environment. The development of such an interoperable platform would help to solve both the copyright enforcement dilemma relating to peer-to-peer networking, and the problems created by DRM technology in respect of the statutory rights of users to access and use copyrighted works. In my opinion, it is time to start considering that rights management technologies should not necessarily be viewed as measures to be used by the entertainment industry to enforce technical restrictions that go beyond the legal usage restrictions created by copyright law. Today's research in the field of DRM shows that new types of rights management technologies have the potential to ensure more nuanced and balanced forms of technical protection and rights management information. These new systems of digital protection and management may work as useful tools of rights management information in the peer-to-peer world, too. The insertion of durable, undeletable

[909] See §8.3.2.3., see *supra*.

[910] See §8.3.3.2., see *supra*.

"tags" into files shared on peer-to-peer networks would be beneficial to the enforcement of all usage licences, regardless of their commercial or non-commercial ends. Even Creative Commons' licensing schemes constitute a form of rights management whose enforcement may be ensured through technical measures which instruct file-sharers on the permitted uses of the licensed work and express these uses by means of RELs.[911]

In principle, DRM technology which contains fingerprints may protect even works released under the most permissive copyleft licences against infringement. For instance, DRM technology may be designed to enforce even Creative Commons' "Attribution" licence, which allows any use of the licensed work on condition that the (moral) right of authorship of the work is respected.[912] If digital fingerprints and, more generally, DRM technologies were developed and used as measures to express - in digital means - this very minimal (and, in *droit d'auteur* laws, non-waivable) restriction on use, this technology could secure the "Attribution" clause and let file-sharers know that the digital work is freely accessible, usable and modifiable. Thus, the wide implementation of flexible and interoperable DRM technology may be highly beneficial for the social sharing enabled by Creative Commons and other similar licensing schemes, which are increasingly used to disseminate new works by poorly equipped creators through peer-to-peer networks.

As mentioned above, the best way to combine on-line copyright enforcement with freedom to share unprotected and authorised materials on peer-to-peer networks would be that of defining standards of copyright-protecting technologies in the context of a regulatory framework where a third party institution, preferably an agency of the European Commission, could be assigned governance and supervision powers. This institution would pursue the institutional objective of establishing the technical means aimed at signalling to Internet actors (including users, peer–to-peer software developers, ISPs, *etc*) what content is free and what content is protected by copyright and, possibly, by DRM technology which qualifies for anti-circumvention protection. This public body that would supervise the implementation of filtering tools could also be given the function of third party intermediary in the user rights management infrastructure advocated below.[913]

8.4. The adverse impact of current DRM technology on free uses

It was emphasised above that the kind of DRM technology that is currently implemented on digital media mainly restricts legitimate opportunities of end-users to access, use and re-use digitally protected works, regardless of whether copy-

---

911 See Appendix I, §B, see *infra*.

912 See the licence Attribution ("By") 3.0 at: http://creativecommons.org/licenses/by/3.0/legalcode.

913 See §8.4.2. and §9.3.2., see *infra*.

right exceptions explicitly exempt such uses from the copyright scope.[914] Unfortunately, in practice, this situation is encouraged by the legal treatment of digital copyright exceptions provided under the InfoSoc Directive and by most national transpositions of this legislation. The crucial issue is that EU copyright law does nothing to prevent technical measures, such as today's DRM systems, from converting balanced copyright law into a rough system of pay-per-access and pay-per-use permissions. As emphasised above,[915] such a system is likely to eliminate most opportunities of free use, including both non-transformative uses and subsequent productive uses. Moreover, the lack of interoperability arising between different DRM systems has the consequence of making digital works (even if lawfully acquired or lawfully accessed by the end-user) non-accessible or at least non-usable on a plurality of media.

8.4.1. Collision with the principle of freedom of expression

DRM technology potentially affects the bundle of rights and values that the principle of freedom of expression embodied in Article 10 of the ECHR aims to guarantee. In his study about the relationship between copyright and freedom of expression, Hugenholtz pointed out that the European Court of Human Rights does not treat all content-related speech restrictions equally.[916] In cases not concerning copyright, the Court has tended to grant stronger protection to categories of speech which have a democracy-enabling function.[917] Clearly, the most important values of a democratic society are pluralism and the means by which pluralism can be effectively fostered and preserved, namely, freedom of political speech and artistic expression.

In the field of copyright law, these values will be harmed irreparably in so far as anti-circumvention protection of DRM technology will continue to be unrelated to findings of copyright infringement. Freedom of expression values will be inevitably stifled if DRM technology is not designed to enforce copyright in strict accordance with copyright exceptions and with other limitations such as the time-limited duration of protection.

It is unfortunate that EU law in no way provides that DRM and other technical measures must be dismantled when the time-limited duration of copyright expires. Furthermore, the InfoSoc Directive does not provide that, to be eligible for anti-

---

914 See §7.6.1., see *supra*.

915 *Ibidem*.

916 See Hugenholtz, 'Copyright and Freedom of Expression in Europe', op. cit., p. 262.

917 See Hugenholtz, 'Copyright and Freedom of Expression in Europe', op. cit., p. 262; Burrell and Coleman, *Copyright Exceptions. The Digital Impact*, Cambridge University Press, Cambridge, 2005, pp. 35-41. Burrell and Coleman emphasised that, in the conflict with copyright law, freedom of expression needs to be given much greater weight in the case of copyrighted information relevant to the political process (*e.g.*, information concerning the conduct of politicians and public persons; the policies, funding, structure and behaviour of political parties, trade unions, religious bodies, universities and large corporations; public health and public safety, *etc*).

circumvention protection, technical measures such as DRM systems must comply with a number of indispensable copyright exceptions. The only effort made by the Directive in this direction was that of Article 6(4), which compels copyright owners to make the technical means to benefit from a limited group of copyright exceptions available to the user, and is expressly designed *not* to apply to on-line interactive deliveries of copyrighted works.

As emphasised above, this system failed to protect most of the subsequent, transformative uses of protected works which ensure pluralism and free speech opportunities by successive users-authors.[918] In these circumstances, legitimate uses of digital works, which are an indispensable input for intellectual creation, can be forbidden and wholly commodified, including information in the public domain which, according to the copyright rationale, should remain freely available to anyone for successive uses.

It can be concluded that the systematic restriction of transformative uses enabled by today's DRM technology and, in the near future, the possible transposition of this logic onto personal computers by means of TC platforms, is in conflict with Article 10(2) of the ECHR. This provision makes it clear that the exercise of freedoms of expression may be subject to such restrictions as "... *are necessary in a democratic society* ...". This provision suggests that, in jurisdictions bound by Article 10 of the ECHR, courts may be highly reluctant to endorse copyright-based claims that turn out to be in conflict with the effective exercise of copyright exceptions which aim at protecting democratic values such as freedom of political speech, artistic use and pluralism in the media.[919] By using the principle embodied in Article 10, these courts may challenge national copyright statutes that permit technical devices to impair completely lawful transformative uses (*e.g.*, quotations, educational uses, news reporting, parody, *etc*) which enhance pluralism in sciences and arts.

8.4.2. Chilling effects on follow-on uses: a user rights management infrastructure as a possible way out

The result of the collision between DRM technology and freedom of expression values protected by copyright exceptions may have another significant outcome. Indeed, until the time when DRM technology implemented onto digital media becomes flexible and sophisticated enough to accommodate cumulative creativity, freedom of expression claims may end up having the better of DRM-implemented restrictions.[920]

---

918 See §4.5.3., see *supra*.

919 See Hugenholtz, 'Copyright and Freedom of Expression in Europe', op. cit., p. 263.

920 For instance, when enforcing human rights, courts might understand the principle of free expression embodied in Article 10 as a legal basis for the recognition of a right of "self-help" (*i.e.,* fair "hacking") against DRM technology that restricts legitimate transformative uses which are beneficial to pluralism and free speech. This is the conclusion proposed by the above-mentioned "Cohen Theorem" in the U.S. and by Samuelson's

To resolve this conflict, EU copyright law may prevent the chilling effects raised by DRM technology on follow-on uses of copyrighted works by providing space for free use in order to enable cumulative creativity and freedom of expression. As pointed out above,[921] at a time when digital codes permit the restriction and regulation of uses that were formerly unrestricted and unregulated, the only way to achieve this policy objective is to replace mere copyright exceptions with a system of positively defined and fully enforceable user rights.[922] In this new scenario, rights of access and free use should be automatically expressed into DRM technology in order to ensure a balanced co-existence of copyright protection and opportunities of freedom of expression to the benefit of potential follow-on authors.[923] This is an approach which is usually referred to as "fair use by design"[924] or "automatic fair use"[925] and is based on the notion of dynamic DRM systems.[926]

At the first level of this legal and technical infrastructure, copyright owners wishing to benefit from anti-circumvention laws would be required to build "automatic fair use defaults based on customary norms of personal non-commercial use" into their rights management technologies.[927] As emphasised above, copyright laws allow transformative uses that are so broadly conceived and practically unpredictable that even the most nuanced rights management technology would not be able to accommodate them.

To enable this broader and less defined typology of lawful uses, Burk and Cohen foresaw a second level in their fair use infrastructure. At this level, users wishing to have greater opportunities of transformative use, out of the constraints imposed by rights management technologies, would turn to a trusted intermediary, preferably a government agency.[928] This third party intermediary would administer a system in which access and decryption keys should be deposited into a key es-

proposal of enacting an exception of fair circumvention for legitimate uses of copyrighted works: see §7.6.2.1., see *supra*.

921 See §7.6.2.2., see *supra*.

922 This is what Burk and Cohen called "fair use infrastructure": see Burk and Cohen, ("Fair Use Infrastructure"), op. cit., pp. 54-70. See, also, Geiger, 'Copyright and Free Access to Information', op. cit., pp. 370-372; and Burrell and Coleman, *Copyright Exceptions*, op.cit., p. 279.

923 As proposed by a few commentators, the goal of protecting freedom of expression and encouraging intellectual production in the digital world should also compel legislators to positively map the subject-matter of the public domain, which comprises all information not eligible for copyright protection and that no one should be entitled to make excludable (*i.e.*, inaccessible) by technical means: see Geiger, 'Copyright and Free Access to Information', op. cit., p. 370; Samuelson, 'Mapping the Digital Public Domain', available at: http://www.law.duke.edu/journals/lcp/archive.html.

924 See Burrell and Coleman, *Copyright Exceptions*, op. cit., pp. 308-309.

925 See Burk and Cohen, 'Fair Use Infrastructure', op. cit., p. 65.

926 See § 7.6.1., see *supra*.

927 See Burk and Cohen, 'Fair Use Infrastructure', op. cit., p. 65.

928 Burk and Cohen, 'Fair Use Infrastructure', op. cit., p. 66, argued that a publicly funded institution would be the most suitable choice because the public policies underlying the fair use doctrine require some guarantees of public accountability and institutional longevity.

crow and be granted to the beneficiaries of a fair use exception. As emphasised by Burk and Cohen, the deposit of such keys would be encouraged by conditioning the enforceability of anti-circumvention laws on this deposit. As a result, the user would have the right to circumvent all keys that should not be deposited with the escrow agent.[929]

As noted by Burk and Cohen and, more recently, by Burrell and Coleman, the legal framework of the InfoSoc Directive provides a good starting point from which to build user rights management for the digital environment.[930] They pointed out that, unlike its U.S. analogue, the InfoSoc Directive followed a persuasive approach with regard to the possible and suitable co-existence of copyright exceptions and rights management technologies. Indeed, the system of safety nets envisaged by Article 6(4) of the Directive clearly draws on the idea of a *mixed* fair use infrastructure based, at a first level, on a "fair use by design" solution, and, at a second level, on the implementation of governmental measures aimed to ensure the effective availability of the means to benefit from a certain group of privileged uses.

It was stressed above that, while creating a primary obligation upon copyright owners to build space for users into their strategy of technological protection, Article 6(4) requires Member States to take appropriate measures if copyright owners fail to comply with this duty.[931] Correctly, Burk and Cohen argued that their access key escrow system could be an appropriate tool by which EU Member States could ensure user access or promote the implementation of voluntary measures by copyright holders.[932]

Notwithstanding this possibility, the scope of application of national fair use infrastructures that resulted from the transposition of Article 6(4) of the Directive was dramatically restricted by other mandatory provisions of the Directive which created an inevitable imbalance between the protection of the interests of copyright owners and the interests of users. One of these provisions was the major exception to the field of application of the Article 6(4) system, which does not apply to works made available to the public on the grounds of contractual terms which give rise to on-demand deliveries of copyrighted goods.[933] Another insurmountable restriction was the unreasonably narrow list of exceptions that Article 6(4) permits to enforce.[934] Furthermore, the field of enforceability of this safeguard system is *de facto* weakened by the absence of a statutory interface against the contractual override of copyright exceptions which enjoy a higher ranking from a constitutional perspective. It was emphasised above that, in safeguarding the ef-

---

929 Burk and Cohen's system was designed to apply to anti-circumvention protection of both U.S. and non-U.S. works. Moreover, these authors stressed that, for the self-defence of fair circumvention to be realistic, the so-called anti-device and anti-trafficking provisions would need to be modified: see Burk and Cohen, 'Fair Use Infrastructure', op. cit., p. 66.

930 See Burrell and Coleman, *Copyright Exceptions*, op. cit., p. 276.

931 See §4.5.1., see *supra*.

932 See Burk and Cohen, 'Fair Use Infrastructure', op. cit., p. 70.

933 See Article 6(4), §4, of the InfoSoc Directive.

934 See Article 6(4), §1, of the InfoSoc Directive.

fectiveness of copyright exceptions from attempts of contractual and technical override, the law might afford a higher degree of protection to presumptively productive uses of copyrighted works.[935]

Finally, no single interoperability policy was set out by the Directive in respect of copyrights management technology, with the result that national laws were left with no guidance with regard to measures which aim to encourage (or compel) the adoption of open standards of DRM technology.[936] In my view, what EU copyright policy-makers need to undertake in order to implement a suitable user rights infrastructure is both a change of policy in respect of rights management technologies, and a reform of substantive copyright law.

This action should necessarily be undertaken at the level of EU legislation by amending the InfoSoc Directive. Even if the concerns expressed by Burrell and Coleman with regard to the political impossibility of re-negotiating the Directive are justified and taken into account, it is reasonable to assume that a significantly stronger protection of user rights of access to and use of digitally protected works could *not* be achieved by national laws within the existing legal framework of the Directive.[937]

In my view, working with the Directive without modifying it, as Burrell and Coleman claimed, may produce only minor beneficial effects to the legal condition of the end-users of copyrighted digital works. Indeed, Member States have already taken active steps to supplement the model of the fair use infrastructure proposed by the InfoSoc Directive. While establishing their publicly administered user rights infrastructures, some national legislators have attempted to ensure an effective system of copyright exceptions by defining them as non-waivable user privileges or as provisions that technological measures should necessarily comply with.[938] Other national laws have entrusted administrative or judicial authorities with broad powers to identify and compel the adoption of the most appropriate measures in order to provide users with the technical means necessary to carry out a selected number of unauthorised acts permitted by law.[939]

---

935 See §7.5.4., where it was argued that the law may usefully distinguish between *consumptive* and *productive* copying for personal uses, and afford a higher degree of protection to the latter category of copying.

936 See §7.4.3., see *supra*, where it was emphasised that the isolated attempt by French law to enact a regulation seeking to promote interoperability of DRM technologies resulted in a largely ineffective legislation. It was concluded that this legislation added little to the pre-existing possibility of competitors to obtain essential technical information enabling interoperability under both the EU case law developed from competition law and the de-compilation exception provided by Article 6 of the Software Directive.

937 See Burrell and Coleman, *Copyright Exceptions*, op. cit., p. 281.

938 See the table provided in Appendix II, see *infra*. For instance, Belgian law provided expressly for the non-waivable character of copyright exceptions; German law recognised the imperative nature of the "first-class" exceptions preserved from technical measures under Article 6(4); and French law provided that technical measures cannot lawfully oppose copyright exceptions.

939 See Appendix II, which provides an overview of a few national transpositions of Article 6(4) of the InfoSoc Directive.

Nevertheless, the existing constraints posed by the InfoSoc Directive to the enforcement of user rights against rights management technologies do not leave national laws in a position to reform their copyright systems effectively in a pro-user direction. Last but not least, EU law-makers should never forget that, if Member States were allowed to start implementing more than twenty, different user rights infrastructures on their own, the EU copyright system would become even more fragmented than it already is. If so, the institutional objective of an effective harmonisation of copyright law in the EU Internal Market would definitely be lost.

In consideration of the arguments developed above, the final chapter will propose a possible re-adjustment of the legal relationship between copyright exceptions, anti-circumvention laws and rights management technologies as set out by Articles 5 and 6 of the InfoSoc Directive.

8.5. Summary

This chapter has argued that a correct interpretation of Article 10 of the ECHR sets the stage for a balanced co-existence of copyright protection and freedom of expression and information. It has been stressed that the constitutional mandate of ensuring such a co-existence applies also to the two unsettled, much debated issues analysed in Part III of this book.

With regard to Internet users' freedom of communication on peer-to-peer networks, it has been pointed out that EU law ends up creating an obligation to make peer-to-peer technology, in the same way as all on-line communication services (*e.g.*, ISPs) more accountable in order to enable or facilitate the detection of copyright infringements. In the light of this potential restriction and alteration of peer-to-peer technology, it has been argued that the constitutional mandate of preserving freedom of communication even on peer-to-peer networks compels EU law to develop a copyright policy capable of addressing the new phenomenon of unauthorised file-sharing. My conclusion was that this copyright policy should not have the consequence of stifling the free transfer of unprotected information, works which belong to the public domain, or copyrighted works released under copyleft licences such as Creative Commons'.

While looking for the most appropriate strategy to preserve Internet users' freedom of expression and information, the chapter has examined four possible alternatives proposed in the relevant literature and in the preparatory works preceding the national implementation of the InfoSoc Directive:

1) the targeting of civil and criminal copyright sanctions at individual file-sharers;
2) the abandoning of the proprietary paradigm by the establishment of levies to compensate the economic losses suffered by copyright owners in the light of unauthorised sharing;
3) the legal imposition of mandatory collective administration of the on-line exclusive rights concerned by file-sharing practices;

4) the encouragement of the implementation, and the acceptance by the public, of copyright-protecting technologies which work as filtering tools.

It has been concluded that the fourth alternative seems to be the best one under the current state of the law and in consideration of the available digital technologies aimed at protecting copyright. This conclusion was achieved not only on the grounds of the costs and benefits which, in the abstract, each solution creates. This conclusion was also conditioned by the insurmountable hurdle that international copyright law embodied in the Berne Convention raises for the adoption of the second and the third alternatives. In this regard, it is, in my view, undeniable that the enforcement of the three-step test and the too narrow derogations provided by the Berne Convention from the paradigm of exclusive rights excessively restrict the room for suitable copyright policy alternatives which are capable of providing a legal solution to the problem of file-sharing.

As regards the collision of DRM technology with Article 10 of the ECHR, it has been found that current DRM technology is mainly designed to stifle much of the copyright exceptions which enable end-user freedom of speech, artistic and scientific expression. It has been argued that, due to the constitutional value and democracy-enabling function of certain uses of copyrighted digital works, EU law should promptly be reformed in order to ensure the accommodation of the related copyright exceptions into the digital languages (*i.e.*, RELs) of DRM systems. To this end, it has been explained that a suitable reform of the Infosoc Directive may be inspired by the current "fair use infrastructure" created by Article 6(4) of the Directive. This infrastructure, which would look like the model proposed in the literature by Burk and Cohen, would be based on two levels and could be administered by a newly established trusted third party, preferably a public agency. At the first level of this infrastructure, EU law could condition the applicability of anti-circumvention laws created under Article 6 on the adoption by DRM measures of "fair use by design" techniques. At the second, more complex level, the law should require copyright owners to deposit with copyright public agencies that administer "escrow systems" the technical information (*e.g.*, access and decryption keys, communication interfaces, *etc*) which enable lawful users to exercise broader and less definable legitimate uses of digitally protected works. The chapter has concluded by arguing that, as Articles 5 and 6 of the InfoSoc Directive stand, the creation of a user rights management infrastructure could be achieved only by radically revising the InfoSoc Directive.

9. Conclusion: towards a better EU copyright law

9.1. Introduction

This final chapter will propose reforms of EU copyright law that could solve the problems emphasised in the course of this work with regard to the interests of end-users. The reform package advocated here draws upon the main idea that a legal infrastructure of user rights needs to be created in order to counterbalance the excessively broad scope of protection and excludability enabled by DRM technologies in respect of digitally protected content. The present proposal is inspired by the principle that suitable copyright law and policy should protect only rights management technologies which enable the exercise of *both* exclusive rights and exceptions created under copyright law. In this book, it has been emphasised that the enforcement of copyright exceptions is particularly important for the protection of the end-user's private sphere from external interference, and for the promotion of old and new opportunities of free expression, innovation and cumulative creativity by end-users in the digital world.

Firstly, this chapter will introduce the notion of a user rights infrastructure, which will be developed in the following section. Secondly, the elements of this infrastructure will be identified and located into the legal framework established by the InfoSoc Directive. Finally, special attention will be devoted to the provision of the InfoSoc Directive that embodies the three-step test, which conditions and undeniably affects the concrete enforceability of legitimate uses of copyrighted works.

9.2. Creating a user rights infrastructure

Chapter 8 concluded that EU law-makers must urgently reform the part of the InfoSoc Directive which covers the legal relationship between copyright exceptions, anti-circumvention law and rights management technologies. Current EU copyright law stifles end-user expectations of legitimate use of digital works while overprotecting the interests of copyright owners. This overprotection arises from the unlimited scope of the anti-circumvention laws and the weak, ineffective system of safety nets created by Article 6(4) of the Directive for the enforcement of copyright exceptions.

9.2.1. Legal protection of technical measures should follow copyright law

It was emphasised above that, by seeking copyright protection in the digital environment through the delegation of all regulatory powers to the interplay of usage licences and rights management technology, the InfoSoc Directive has resulted in legislation that disregards the preservation of the exceptions expressly required by Article 11 of the 1996 WIPO Copyright Treaty.[940] This provision reads:

"Contracting Parties shall provide adequate legal protection and effective legal remedies against the circumvention of effective technological measures that are used by authors in connection with the exercise of their rights under this Treaty or the Berne Convention and that restrict *acts*, in respect of their works, which are not authorized by the authors concerned or *permitted by law*."[941]

Article 11 of the WIPO Treaty provides that technical measures should not qualify for legal protection in so far as they restrict acts that the law intends to allow for the pursuit of a number of important public policies. As noted throughout this book, the most important public policies pursued through copyright exceptions are the protection of freedom of expression and information (including the encouragement of scientific and artistic innovation by follow-on creators) and the preservation of the private sphere of the user.

To preserve the pursuit of these public policy objectives, even in the light of the enhanced expressive opportunities provided by the digital environment to the end-user of copyrighted works, it would be highly desirable to revise the EU anti-circumvention regulations created under Article 6 of the InfoSoc Directive. This result could be achieved by confining the scope of application of anti-circumvention law to the field of technical measures that allow *both* the exercise of the exclusive rights of the copyright holders and the exercise – on the part of the users - of the uses permitted by law. This solution would follow the same approach adopted by Article 7 of the Software Directive, which makes it clear that technical measures applied to protect a computer programme must leave the rights and the exceptions created under its provisions intact.[942] As emphasised above, even Article 6(2) of the original version of the European Commission's proposal for the InfoSoc Directive afforded anti-circumvention protection to technical measures in as much as they restricted or prohibited copyright infringement.[943]

A desirable revision of the InfoSoc Directive should thereby draw on the following guidelines:

- Anti-circumvention laws should be designed to apply on condition that technical measures implement "fair use by design" technologies by default. Con-

[940] See Article 11 of the WIPO Copyright Treaty ("Obligations concerning Technological Measures").
[941] Emphasis added.
[942] See §4.5.4., see *supra*.
[943] See § 3.4.2., see *supra*.

sequently, EU law should expressly exclude all technical measures which fail to meet this technical requirement from the scope of the application of anti-circumvention laws, with the consequence that these kinds of measures could be lawfully hacked and removed by users;[944]

- User rights infrastructures should be established at the level of national laws, on the basis of the solution provided by Article 6(4) of the Directive. Each national infrastructure should be administered by a pre-existing or newly established public authority that would be entrusted with the responsibility of storing and managing all technical information (for example, access and decryption keys; interoperability interfaces) that enables users of digitally protected works to benefit from a given copyright exception;[945]
- Open and completely interoperable standards of on-line filtering tools and rights management technologies should be encouraged or required by law for the purposes of:

  i. Creating technical devices that may stop or reduce massive copyright infringement on peer-to-peer networks without restricting technological innovation and freedom of communication;
  ii. Providing technical protection and rights management for the benefit of copyrighted works released under copyleft licences; and
  iii. Fostering publicly mandated opportunities for unauthorised access to and use of digitally protected works, as dictated by a statutory system of user rights.[946]

9.2.2. Replacing copyright exceptions by a law of users' rights

To be effective, all the above-mentioned changes to EU copyright law should be based on an indispensable reform of the legal treatment of copyright exceptions, as provided by Article 5 of the InfoSoc Directive. A law of user rights needs to be established in the EU for the purpose of creating an effective legal infrastructure by which users will be entitled to ask for the administrative or judicial enforcement of acts permitted by copyright law.[947] In this reform package, usage privileges covered by copyright exceptions should be given the status of *subjective rights*, with the consequence that their violation would create liability upon copyright owners, suppliers of protected content, developers of technological protection measures and any other actor who might be in such a position as to frustrate the exercise of statutory exceptions. In this picture, users would have direct access to courts in order to ask for injunctive relief and the reparation of any damages suffered by any user through illegal conduct. Moreover, if the enforcement of user rights were taken as seriously as the enforcement of copyright owner rights, it

---

944 See §9.3.1., see *infra*.

945 See §9.3.2., see *infra*.

946 See §9.3.3., see *infra*.

947 See Burrell and Coleman, *Copyright Exceptions*, op. cit., p. 276; Geiger, 'Copyright and Free Access to Information', op. cit., pp. 370-372.

would not be illogical or exaggerated to think of enacting criminal sanctions against the violation of user rights.

As outlined by Burrell and Coleman, the implementation of a system of user rights would not be in conflict with international copyright law, even though the Berne Convention, the TRIPS Agreement and the WIPO Copyright Treaty do all refer to "limitations and exceptions".[948] The obligations set out in these agreements, mainly through the three-step test, do not prevent national copyright laws from ensuring the effective enforcement of acts exempted from the scope of copyright for specific reasons of public policy.

Even if the change of terminology were a minor reform, the change would nonetheless be relevant from a political and psychological point of view. Speaking of "rights", instead of "exceptions", would place more emphasis on the fact that, in order`to be effectively protected against access and usage restrictions that are enabled by technical measures, uses covered by copyright exceptions should be completely and effectively enforceable.

To this end, it would be of crucial importance for any EU law covering user rights to be based on imperative, non-waivable statutory exceptions to exclusive rights, similar to that provided under the Software Directive in respect of unauthorised acts of back-up copying,[949] observation, study or testing of the computer programme[950] and de-compilation (or "reverse-engineering") for purposes of interoperability.[951]

It was argued above that the Software Directive provides a useful model for the reform of the interface between end-use licences and copyright exceptions under the InfoSoc Directive.[952] The mandatory character of copyright exceptions was achieved in the Software Directive through a simple provision which declared null or void any contractual provisions contrary to the above-mentioned exceptions.[953] In my view, there is a strong need to introduce a similar provision into the InfoSoc Directive in respect of all the exceptions that should be preserved from technical and legal restriction. In this way, end-users would benefit from a higher degree of protection when contracting with the suppliers of copyrighted goods which embody a rights management system. Present-day consumer contract law only provides end-users with a right of information about the application and the effects of rights management technologies on copyrighted goods. In contrast, with my proposed reform, EU copyright law would automatically make any contractual provisions which seek to reduce the legal threshold of user rights null and void.

In undertaking this project of reform, the most complex undertaking would certainly be that of defining which exceptions should be replaced by non-waivable rights of use. Once defined, these uses should be included in the group of guaran-

---

948 See Burrell and Coleman, *Copyright Exceptions*, op.cit., p. 279.

949 See Article 5(2) of the Software Directive.

950 See Article 5(3) of the Software Directive.

951 See Article 6 of the Software Directive: see §3.3.3.2., see *supra*.

952 See §4.5.4, see *supra*.

953 See Article 9(1) of the Software Directive, which states: "[...] Any contractual provisions contrary to Article 6 or to the exceptions provided for in Article 5 (2) and (3) shall be null and void."

teed acts which benefit from the fair use infrastructure developed by broadening and improving the current safeguard system created by Article 6(4) of the InfoSoc Directive. As emphasised above, because Article 5 of the Directive does not harmonise the national laws governing copyright exceptions, it fails to pursue the objective of market integration, which propelled the adoption of the Directive.[954] An appropriate amendment of this provision should fully harmonise *all* the exceptions included in the fair use infrastructure. In contrast to the current form of Article 5, this set of exceptions (*i.e.*, user rights) should be implemented under national laws on a mandatory basis and be expressly protected by the new contract interface which invalidates any contractual provisions that run contrary to any of these exceptions.

With regard to the punctual identification of user rights, the revision of Article 5 may legitimately draw upon the idea that not *all* copyright exceptions need to be legally reinforced and defined as imperative. From a constitutional law perspective, the guiding principle in the definition of completely enforceable user rights may be that of privileging and securing the copyright exceptions aimed at fostering freedom of expression by permitting the creation of new works. These exceptions would correspond to uses that were described earlier as "transformative".[955] However, it must be admitted that limiting the reinforced status of enforceable rights to transformative uses would unduly overlook the function of non-transformative uses such as private copying in fostering cumulative creativity. The distinction between transformative and non-transformative uses was used in this book as a descriptive tool to explain that new rights management technologies affect the legitimate uses of copyright materials in different ways. In this respect, the distinction allows one to reach the conclusion that rights expression languages (*i.e.*, RELs) and rights management technologies are totally capable of encapsulating the exception of private copying, while remaining largely unable to translate into digital languages much of lawful transformative uses.[956]

Apart from this descriptive application, it is my view that the distinction between transformative and non-transformative uses evaporates when copyright policy-makers have to evaluate the classes of unauthorised uses that are socially desirable for the encouragement of cumulative innovation and for the pursuit of other public policies such as the protection of privacy.[957] To evaluate the desirability of private copying properly, EU law-makers must recall that, especially in certain fields of human creativity, copying is an indispensable step toward the creation of new works.[958] Thus, a user rights infrastructure that does not include, or

[954] See §5.2.2., see *supra*.

[955] See §1.3. and §1.4., see *supra*.

[956] See §7.6.1., see *supra*.

[957] See Senftleben, *Copyright, Limitations and the Three-Step Test*, op. cit., pp. 32-33 and 39-41; Geiger, 'Copyright and Free Access to Information', op. cit., pp. 371-372.

[958] See Burrell and Coleman, *Copyright Exceptions*, op. cit., pp. 289-290; Geiger, 'Copyright and Free Access to Information', op. cit., p. 371. As pointed out by these authors, in the field of academic and scientific research, copying occurs at the early stage of research, when a researcher needs to collect copies of articles, extracts from books and other materials informing her or him about the current state of science.

shield against digital locks, private copying for scientific and academic research would therefore stifle the creation of new works. Hence, it is reasonable to be very skeptical about the constitutional legitimacy of all Member State copyright laws that, following the non-mandatory provision of Article 6(4), §2, of the InfoSoc Directive, do not include digital private copying into the list of exceptions that benefit from the fair use infrastructure created by the Directive.

It is suggested here that the EU copyright system would be better off if this optional clause were repealed. The private copying exception needs to be regulated harmoniously at the level of EU copyright law not just for the potential impairment that unrestricted DRM technologies may cause to cumulative innovation in such strategic sectors as scientific and academic research. From the perspective of Article 95 of the EC Treaty, the harmonisation of private copying from digitally protected works is necessary to avoid the adverse impact of different national regulations on the trans-border trade of digitised information taking place on the Internet. The missed opportunity of harmonisation in the field of private copying is even more evident and relevant at a time when the European Commission is trying to foster the implementation of Community-wide licences for the on-line exploitation of copyrighted works (that is, works of music) and to abolish national copyright levies in respect of the technical impairment of private copying by DRM technologies.

Moreover, considering that the exception (or right) of private copying will be accommodated mainly by the technique of fair use by design, the suggested reform would permit and strongly encourage the development of rights management technologies to be used, circulated and recognised as lawful technical measures in all jurisdictions of the EU.

The example of private copying clearly shows that, to build an efficient and constitutionally valid infrastructure of user rights, copyright law would need to retain a certain degree of flexibility in order to identify the most desirable uses. Such uses may need to be set out not only on the grounds of the type of use effectively undertaken (*e.g.*, copying, quoting, *etc*), but also on the basis of the type of work used or in consideration of the field of creativity where the use occurs. In other words, it might be very necessary to shape copyright law in such a flexible way as to enable differentiated legal treatments of the same type of use in respect of different categories works. Whereas a free use may be socially desirable in respect of an article of scientific research, it may not be beneficial with regard to a free copy of a pop song downloaded from a peer-to-peer network.[959]

In my view, an efficient and desirable regime of private copying from digital works should be so flexible as to specify the conditions (*i.e.*, the number of permissible copies, the digital or analogue formats of permissible reproduction, *etc*) under which each category of copyrighted work can be lawfully copied for purposes of personal use without the right-holder's authorisation.[960] Moreover, this

[959] This example is made by Geiger, 'Copyright and Free Access to Information', op. cit., pp. 371-372.

[960] Such an ideal regime of private copying would be similar to that recently created in France by the act of implementation of the InfoSoc Directive. Under this regulation,

legal regime should be based on the legal assumption that copyright owners should always equip their rights management systems with privacy-enhancing technologies, as dictated by the applicable EU regulation on the protection of personal data.[961]

To ensure flexibility of the law of user rights while making copyright harmonisation a reality and abolishing the existing fragmentation, a suitable reform of the InfoSoc Directive should promptly abandon the idea of an *exhaustive* list of permitted uses under Article 5. Flexibility and full harmonisation might be achieved and might co-exist in the field of copyright exceptions in so far as two types of legislative measures were implemented. On the one hand, EU law should compel Member States to transpose harmonised exceptions into national laws by means of legislative phrasings which, where possible, should be identical (or as similar as possible) to those used by the detailed provisions of Article 5 of the Directive. To this end, the European Commission holds the institutional power to pursue infringement proceedings against Member States that enact exceptions which deviate from the models imposed by the Directive. This measure would greatly reduce the risks of divergent interpretations regarding the scope of copyright exceptions in different jurisdictions.

On the other hand, the suggested reform may modify and expand the monitoring system created by Article 12 of the Directive, by entrusting the European Commission with powers of delegated legislation for the enactment of new copyright exceptions (or rights of use) that might turn out to be desirable so long as digital markets and new uses are developed. Like the policies developed by EU law in other sectors such as agriculture and competition law, delegated legislation may be required to specify and quickly adapt the law of user rights to the changing market and to social circumstances, without reference to the standard procedures for the enactment of secondary EU legislation.[962] This delegated legislation would be based on Article 202 of the EC Treaty, which regulates the conditions under which the European Commission is entitled to exercise legislative powers for implementing rules laid down in acts adopted by the Council.[963]

---

flexibility and differentiation of legal treatment for different types of reproductions are sought through the establishment of an administrative authority entrusted with powers of delegated legislation: see §7.5.4, see *supra*.

961 See §2.2.3, see *supra*.

962 See Gatto, 'Governance in the European Union: A Legal Perspective', (12) *Columbia Journal of European Law* 2006, p. 487. The delegated legislative power of the Commission is justified by the fact that there are certain areas of Community policy that require regulations to be passed quickly in order to cope with changing market circumstances.

963 Following the provision of Article 202 of the EC Treaty, the exercise of legislative powers by the European Commission through the appointment of specific committees is now regulated by the 1999 "Comitology Decision" of the EU Council: see Council Decision of 28 June 1999 laying down the procedures for the exercise of implementing powers conferred on the Commission, OJ L 184, 17 July 1999, 23. The enactment of this Decision, while replacing an equivalent Council Decision of 1987, enhanced the degree of democratic participation in this type of law-making process. Indeed, the 1999 Decision recognises to the European Parliament effective powers of information and

Clearly, new user rights stemming from the exercise of this delegated legislative power would be subject to the three-step test, so that the introduction of the test into EU law would provide both the Commission and national courts with additional criteria for reviewing the fairness of new uses not foreseen by the Directive.[964]

9.3. Elements of a user rights management infrastructure

9.3.1. Implementation of the 'fair use by design' requirement

To make sure that all rights management technologies which benefit from anti-circumvention laws do not replace the public law of copyright with private legislation unilaterally imposed by content suppliers, the EU may revise the definition of 'technological protection measure' provided under Article 6(3) of the InfoSoc Directive.[965] It would be highly recommendable to amend this definition by replacing the reference to acts "which are not authorised by the rightholder of any copyright or any right related to copyright" with a phrasing which makes it clear that technical measures wishing to obtain anti-circumvention protection under Article 6 should be technically designed only to inhibit copyright infringement, and, at the same time, to enable user rights by default, as set out under the reformed version of the InfoSoc Directive.

Under the suggested legislative reform, Article 6(3) must make it clear that, to qualify for anti-circumvention protection, technical measures should:

- build space *inside* the technology for free uses provided by copyright law in as much as the state of the art in RELs allows this;
- be submitted for approval and storage to a public copyright agency (*e.g.*, the public agency of the country where the digitally protected work is publicly released for the first time). This public body would be given the institutional tasks of examining, archiving and administering technical information, thus enabling the exercise of user rights when the technical measure is not able to accommodate the requested use by default.

As emphasised above, notwithstanding its potential to accommodate an impressive number of uses by default, the current international standard of REL (*i.e.*, MPEG-21) has not been equipped with adequate tools to enable rights of transformative uses.[966] The only user rights that the MPEG-21 standard supports and expresses properly are the rights of individuals regarding privacy and the use of personal

control over the implementing measures adopted by the Commission and its advisory committees on the grounds of legislation enacted under the so-called "co-decision" procedure: see Gatto, 'Governance in the European Union', op. cit., pp. 500-502.

964 See §9.4.2., see *infra*.

965 See §3.4., see *supra*.

966 See §7.6.1., see *supra*.

data. All other uses enabled by this technology are designed to be made available upon payment of licensing fees; they are not for free. Under the reform of the InfoSoc Directive that is proposed here, such full commodification of uses *freely* permitted by law would prove to be unlawful in the light of its contrast with the imperative character of user rights provided by the new phrasing adopted by Article 5. Thus, due to its structure and ultimate purposes, MPEG-21 would not qualify for anti-circumvention protection under Article 6 of the Directive, with the result that technical measures embodying this specific REL could be legally hacked and removed by end-users. If, following the adoption of the advocated reform package, RELs embodied in DRM technology were not re-designed (or re-programmed) in order to accommodate mandatory user rights, an enforceable right of fair circumvention (such as that advocated by the "Cohen Theorem") would become effective.[967]

Whereas the MPEG-21 and its XrML rights expression language would not meet the mandatory requirement of "fair use by design", the DRM technology developed by the Digital Media Project (DMP) would certainly do so. The DMP is an important research project led by technologist Chiariglione and joined by several firms from the telecommunication, information technology and content industries.[968] This ongoing project is implementing the approach of fair use by design by mapping so-called "traditional rights and usages" (TRUs) within standardised and interoperable DRM technology.[969] It redresses the aforementioned failure of the MPEG-21 standard by accommodating end-user expectations of unrestricted personal use and cumulative creativity.[970] The participation of important industries and research centres from the world of digital media in this project demonstrates that there is a strong interest in the replacement of today's DRM systems with a system of user rights management that makes the implementation of technical measures more acceptable to end-users.[971]

9.3.2. Implementation of a mixed user rights infrastructure

To develop an effective user rights infrastructure from the present, ill-suited system created by Article 6(4) of the Directive, it would be indispensable to broaden

---

[967] See §7.6.2.1., see *supra*.

[968] See http://www.chiariglione.org/project/.

[969] See the Digital Media Manifesto at http://www.chiariglione.org/manifesto/.

[970] In an electronic mail sent on 8 October 2006 to the mailing list of the "Digital Media in Italia" Project (http://www.dmin.it), Chiariglione emphasised that he expects the map of traditional rights and usages developed by the DMP to become so sophisticated and fine-grained as to accommodate even the most complex purposes of transformative use (*e.g.*, parody). Chiariglione argued also that the creation of such highly sophisticated DRM technology would make the possible creation of an exception (or right) of fair circumvention simply unjustified.

[971] See Geiger, 'Copyright and Free Access to Information', op. cit., p. 372. The complete list of members of the DMP can be found at: http://www.chiariglione.org/project/members.htm.

the field of application of this pro-user infrastructure. A suitable development of the fair use infrastructure would necessarily require the repeal of the fourth subparagraph of Article 6(4), which unduly restricts the scope of application of this provision to the off-line world.[972]

Following the rationale spelt out above for the identification of non-waivable end-user rights, the recommended infrastructure of Article 6(4) may include and preserve all unauthorised uses which have the effect of fostering freedom of expression and subsequent creativity. Using the wording of Article 5 of the Directive, the non-exhaustive list of such rights may include all uses which permit or facilitate the creation of new works by the greatest number of users, namely:

- use for the purpose of illustration for teaching or scientific research;[973]
- uses for the benefit of people with disability, which are directly related to the disability and of a non-commercial nature;[974]
- use of works in connection with the reporting of current events, to the extent justified by the informational purpose;[975]
- quotations for purposes such as criticism or review;[976]
- use of political speeches as well as extracts of public lectures or similar works to the extent justified by the informational purpose;[977]
- use for the purpose of caricature, parody or pastiche;[978]
- reproduction for private use and for ends that are neither directly nor indirectly commercial, on condition that the right-holders receive fair compensation;[979]
- reproduction for purposes of personal academic use and of scientific research.[980]

As anticipated above, the proposed infrastructure of user rights management would have recourse to an administrative process of external mediation in all cases where the mandatory adoption of fair use by design technologies by copyright owners were not capable of accommodating one of these enumerated uses.

---

[972] See §4.5.3., see *supra*.

[973] See Article 5(3)(a).

[974] See Article 5(3)(b).

[975] See Article 5(3)(c).

[976] See Article 5(3)(d).

[977] See Article 5(3)(f).

[978] See Article 5(3)(k).

[979] See Article 5(2)(b). To include private copying under the regime of mandatory exceptions advocated in the text, the optional provision of Article 6(4), §2, of the Directive should logically be repealed.

[980] This desirable, specific exception is not embodied in the current version of Article 5 of the InfoSoc Directive. As noted by Geiger, 'Copyright and Free Access to Information', op. cit., p. 371, an exception for copies made for scientific use is provided by Section 53(2)(1) of the German Copyright Act, which may be a useful source of inspiration for EU law-makers.

It was suggested that this process could be managed and coordinated by the European Commission through a copyright agency or committee whose functioning, law-making powers and procedures may be regulated by the 1999 "Comitology" Decision of the EU Council.[981] A higher degree of public participation in delegated law-making activities concerning the setting of new rights of use or new conditions of exercise of pre-existing usage rights could be achieved by requiring the Commission to undertake greater consultation with copyright holders and other parties concerned, including consumer and user associations.[982]

The establishment of a copyright committee to advise the Commission in carrying out tasks of law-making and external mediation in the field of copyright exceptions may be easily accomplished by amending Article 12 of the InfoSoc Directive. In its current version, this provision imposes a duty on the European Commission to examine, every three years, whether acts permitted by law (*i.e.*, copyright exceptions) are adversely affected by the effective use of technical measures. To conduct this periodical examination, Article 12 creates a contact committee which acts as an advisor to the Commission in its monitoring of the evolution of legislation, case-law and technological developments.[983]

It would be highly desirable for this monitoring system to be supplemented by the above-mentioned delegated law-making process and the re-definition of the institutional tasks of the existing contact committee. With the proposed reforms, this committee should be transformed into a dedicated administrative agency that permanently works as a coordinator and advisor of the national copyright agencies which, under the amended wording of Article 6(4), Member States would be required to establish or reform.[984]

Under the suggested reforms, it would be incumbent upon these national agencies to carry out the most complex activities in order to shape an appropriate and cost-effective infrastructure of user rights management. These activities would in-

---

981 See Council Decision of 28 June 1999 laying down the procedures for the exercise of implementing powers conferred on the Commission, cit.

982 Similarly, Burrell and Coleman, *Copyright Exceptions*, op. cit., p. 280, stressed that, in any proposal for reform, "far more effort needs to be made to ensure that a greater range of interested parties are given an opportunity to shape the legislation". If EU lawmakers should follow the option indicated in the main text, a suitable amendment to the InfoSoc Directive may create a duty for the Commission to keep its delegated law-making process in the field of exceptions open to as many groups of interested parties as possible. In this way, the advocated law of users' rights would encourage the achievement of widely agreed legislative solutions. It is worth recalling here that the desirability of this policy is already acknowledged under the current, ambiguous wording of Article 6(4), which refers to "agreements between rightholders and other parties concerned" as a form of voluntary measures to be taken by copyright holders to enable uses permitted by law.

983 See §4.5.5, see *supra*.

984 It must be recalled here that copyright agencies (*e.g.*, authorities, committees, tribunals, *etc*) have already their place in much of the EU Member States' copyright systems. Appendix II to this book provides a table that shows the example of a few Member States' authorities that deal with the task of supervising the enforcement of certain copyright exceptions in compliance with Article 6(4) of the InfoSoc Directive.

clude the maintenance of "escrow systems" for the administration of access and decryption keys (or codes), as well as unprotected (*i.e.*, wholly usable) formats of DRM-protected works.[985] With a view to increasing the efficiency and security of the overall infrastructure, specific duties and day-to-day activities by these agencies might be regulated by legislative measures and codes of best practices implemented and constantly updated by the Commission's copyright committee. For instance, it is foreseeable that, in the management of technical information which enables the exercise of certain rights of use, national copyright agencies should be equipped to send this information electronically to the user through a trusted system protecting the released information from possible misuses. Only administrative bodies would be well placed to provide this kind of highly sophisticated management of fair use rights. In contrast, judicial authorities might be given the tasks of reviewing appeals against decisions issued by copyright agencies and, upon the request of any interested party, examining the lawful character of acts occurring within the administrative process.

To build the infrastructure that was sketched out above, Article 6(4) should be reformed by a punctual identification of the obligations of both the copyright owners and the Member States under the externally mediated process. To this end, the ambiguous legislative expressions of these duties – that exist under the current provision - should be replaced by more nuanced expressions. Article 6(4) must make it clear that copyright owners would be forced to implement fair use by design technologies and to deposit all technical information enabling fair uses promptly with the escrow systems administered by one of the aforementioned copyright agencies.

It should be clear from the proposed amendment to Article 6(4) that failure to comply with requirements concerning the depositing of information and with deadlines regarding the submission of materials would exclude the implemented technical measures from the legal protection granted by anti-circumvention laws. The revised Article 6(4) should make it clear that, instead of the unspecified and

---

[985] The idea of a fair use infrastructure providing a system of publicly-mandated, external mediation and trusted deposit of technical information capable of enabling certain rights of use of DRM-protected content was developed by Burk and Cohen, 'Fair Use Infrastructure', op. cit. The idea of external mediation, however, was developed earlier by Stefik, 'Shifting the Possible: How Trusted Systems and Digital Property Rights Challenge Us To Rethink Digital Publishing', 12(1) *Berkeley Technology Law Journal* 1997, p. 137, at p. 156, in the context of rights management technologies such as trusted systems: see Appendix I, §A, see *infra*. Stefik proposed the establishment of such a dedicated social institution as a "Digital Property Trust", which would interact with government bodies and law enforcement agencies in making available to qualified users the legal and technical means (*e.g.*, an arbitration system; a licensing service, *etc*) for the application of the fair use defence. In a similar way, Sirinelli, 'L'étendue de l'interdiction de contourner les mesures techniques protégeant l'accès aux oeuvres et les droits d'auteurs: exceptions and limitations – Rapport Général', in *Régimes complémentaires et concurentiels au droit d'auteur, Acts of the ALAI Conference, 13-17 June 2001*, New York, ALAI (USA) 2002, p. 415, spoke of "guardians of keys" for institutions which aim at disclosing the information necessary to carry out a specific exception in favour of qualified users such as schools and libraries.

conditional "appropriate measures" provided under the current provision, the Member States should establish (or re-structure) their copyright agencies in order to entrust them with the institutional tasks of archiving, managing and supplying user rights management information. Moreover, under my proposed reforms, all EU copyright agencies would be part of a networked information infrastructure which would operate under the supervision of the European Commission through its specialised advisory committee.

Finally, given the wider ambit that my copyright law reform would leave for lawful acts of circumvention of technical measures which fail to meet the structural and procedural requirements designed to accommodate user rights, it would be fair to ensure greater access by users to circumvention-enabling technologies. To this end, it would suitable to confine the field of application of the bans created by Article 6(2) of the Directive to the manufacture and distribution of devices aimed at and mainly used to circumvent technical measures that qualify for anti-circumvention protection under the amended provision of Article 6(3).[986]

9.3.3. A single EU interoperability policy for DRM technology

The final framework in which the InfoSoc Directive would need to be revised concerns the creation of a single interoperability policy about rights management technologies. Recital 54 of the InfoSoc Directive only overviewed this objective. The wording of this recital reveals the original, though very soft, EU policy-makers' policy in respect of the possible incompatibility between "technical systems of identification of works and protected subject-matter in digital format [...]".[987]

While recognising that important progress had been made in the international standardisation of these systems, this recital of the Directive provided that the compatibility and interoperability of the different systems of identification of copyrighted works should be encouraged, preferably by means of the adoption of global systems.[988] The fact that this recital only refers to systems of "identification" (and not "rights management") is due to the fact that, at the time of the Directive drafting, between 1997 and 2000, policy-makers were largely unaware of

---

986 See Dusollier, *Droit d'auteur et protection des oeuvres dans l'univers numérique*, op. cit., p. 544, who outlined that, even if the legal bans of Article 6(2) were maintained, as it seems desirable, nothing would impede law-makers or stakeholders from agreeing upon and developing circumvention-enabling technologies aimed at facilitating the exercise of copyright exceptions by qualified users such as visually-impaired people.

987 See Recital 54 of the InfoSoc Directive.

988 Recital 54 provides as follows: "Important progress has been made in the international standardisation of technical systems of identification of works and protected subject-matter in digital format. In an increasingly networked environment, differences between technological measures could lead to an incompatibility of systems within the Community. Compatibility and interoperability of the different systems should be encouraged. It would be highly desirable to encourage the development of global systems."

the likely development of the sophisticated RELs which are embedded in today's DRM technology.

As explained above, in its Communication of 2004 on copyright management in the EU internal market, the European Commission defined its purpose for pursuing open standardisation and interoperability in respect of the DRM infrastructure.[989] According to this Communication, the Commission intended to undertake an interoperability policy for the specific purpose of safeguarding the effectiveness of copyright law and of avoiding the progressive erosion of copyright exceptions by DRM technologies. Unfortunately, since that time, no concrete measure has been undertaken by the European Commission in respect of DRM interoperability.

The proposed copyright reform may directly fill this gap and address the issue of interoperability by promoting (or directly imposing) the development and disclosure of an openly accessible and interoperable standard of DRM technology. As emphasised when discussing the most suitable technique for protecting digital copyright on peer-to-peer networks,[990] an ideal DRM infrastructure should be available to anyone wishing to license and distribute copyrighted content under the type of rights management that best fits the copyright owner's purposes. It was stressed that, given the very low cost of publishing in the digital environment, new flows of copyrighted works by unsigned creators have become increasingly available under such copyleft licence terms as Creative Commons'.[991] In principle, DRM technology and the other filtering devices embodied in it (for example, durable fingerprints) may play a key role even in enforcing these user-friendly forms of licensing.

The idea that DRM technology must be open and interoperable "by definition" was upheld by the economist Varian. It was noted above that, as things stand on the markets for DRM solutions, the "nightmare scenario" evocated by Varian may easily come true in the years to come.[992] To facilitate competition in this regard, Varian suggested that open standardisation might be a better alternative to proprietary technologies.[993] He explained that, due to their nature of bottlenecks, it would be highly desirable to adopt technical specifications for DRM technology that were as open and as free as the Internet TCP/IP protocols and the GSM standards in mobile phone technology.[994]

Clearly, the main problem in the pursuit of this policy objective is how to dismantle the proprietary extensions which characterise today's DRM technology or, alternatively, how to make the existence of such proprietary pieces compatible

---

989 See §7.3.2, see *supra*.

990 See § 8.3.4., see *supra*.

991 See §8.2.2., see *supra*.

992 See §7.4.4., see *supra*.

993 See Varian, 'Economics of DRM', op. cit.; Mazziotti, 'Did Apple's refusal to license [...]', op. cit., p. 273.

994 *Ibidem*. The acronym TCP stands for "Transmission Control Protocol", whereas IP means "Internet Protocol". This protocol suite is the set of communication protocols which allow the Internet and most commercial networks to run. GSM stands for "Global System for Mobile communications".

with the policy goal of full interoperability. It was argued above that the most widespread, proprietary DRM technology has been developed for the sole purpose of ensuring the practical enforcement of conditions of access to and use of digitally protected works that have little to do with the balanced law of copyright.[995] DRM technology has become vilified by its opponents because of its perceived unilateral and unbalanced technological development. This opposition is exemplified by the recent boycott campaign launched by the Free Software Foundation against the implementation of what is perceived as a system of digital "restrictions", rather than as a method of "rights management".[996] This situation has been exacerbated by the failure of the copyright industry to implement DRM technology fairly and in a manner more acceptable to consumers.[997]

The proposed reform package may greatly reduce the conflict of an open standardisation policy with intellectual property rights on existing DRM systems. Under the suggested reform of the InfoSoc Directive, most of the existing DRM systems would *not* qualify for anti-circumvention protection. As recommended earlier, the application of anti-circumvention law should be legally conditioned on the adoption of fair-use-by-design technologies.[998] Moreover, as a subsidiary measure, the law should oblige the developers (and also the adopters) of such measures to deposit all technical information enabling the management of user rights with the competent public agencies. Failure to comply with these duties would imply that anyone could lawfully circumvent, through acts of reverse engineering, the computer code of a DRM system in order to make it interoperable with the digital content or hardware that supports another DRM system.[999] Cur-

---

995 See §7.6.1, see *supra*.

996 See http://www.defectivebydesign.org and http://www.drm.info (where DRM stands for "Digital Restrictions Management").

997 One of the most recent scandals in the story of unfair implementation of DRM technologies on digital content took place in November 2005, when one of the majors of the recording industry, Sony BMG, distributed millions of music CDs that embodied two flawed and overreaching technologies that, according to Sony, were designed merely to restrict unauthorised copying of the music on the CDs. In truth, these technologies were found to do much more, while reporting customer listening of the CDs and installing undisclosed and, in some cases, hidden files on users' computers that could expose them to malicious attacks by third parties, all without appropriate notice and consent from purchasers. More information on this case can be found at http://www.eff.org/IP/DRM/Sony-BMG.

998 See §9.3.1., see *supra*.

999 For instance, in August 2004, the online music provider Real Networks announced that it was able to reverse-engineer the encryption system and the computer code of Apple's Fairplay DRM system in order to make Real Networks' music downloads compatible with Apple's iPod portable music player. After this announcement, Apple claimed that Real Networks had violated the anti-circumvention law embodied in Section 1201(1)(A) of the U.S. DMCA: see 'Apple brings discord to Hymn', cit., available at http://www.theregister.co.uk. This dispute, which was never brought to court, showed that U.S. anti-circumvention law applied to DRM software had the potential of frustrating interoperability at the expense of usability of digital content but also to the

rently, the most widely used systems of DRM technology do not comply with copyright exceptions by default, which would make them freely circumventable under revised anti-circumvention laws. Thus, under this reform, the owners of foundational DRM technology would have a greater incentive to re-design their respective technologies to make them compliant with the above-mentioned law of user rights.

The fact that the positive effects of a new law of user rights on interoperability problems might be much greater if it were made clear that technical information which enables interoperability should be submitted to a public copyright agency must also be considered. This information should be disclosed by each agency to any interested party that showed that the lack of compatibility between different DRM systems actually impaired one of the user acts permitted by law. In this way, the EU copyright system would *de facto* pre-empt the acquisition or the exercise of intellectual property rights that had the effect of entrenching the legitimate uses of digitally protected works. By means of this amendment, the legal infrastructure, which aims to provide users with the technical means to enable the exercise of their rights, would require copyright holders to deposit with the competent copyright agencies even the technical interfaces which ensure interoperability with the implemented DRM systems. The inclusion of such interfaces into the set of technical means to be publicly deposited and disclosed by public copyright agencies would be highly beneficial to qualified end-users. This new regulation would progressively discourage the acquisition of exclusive rights (*i.e.*, copyrights, patents) or the maintenance of trade secrets on technical interfaces which enable different DRM systems to interoperate. This duty of preventive disclosure upon owners of DRM interoperability information would ultimately give shape to Varian's idea of establishing a completely open DRM system without proprietary extensions.

If so, the legal protection of the technical information which enables interoperability would inevitably be modified. At present, the only way to obtain this information without the authorisation (and co-operation) of the owner of the information is through the reverse-engineering of the DRM software codes. This activity (known also as "de-compilation") is strictly regulated under Article 6 of the Software Directive, which allows de-compilation for the (sole) purpose of enabling interoperability with independently created computer programmes.[1000] Under this regulation, the reverse-engineering of a DRM software code undertaken for the purpose of enabling interoperability between the DRM programme and digital content other than computer programmes (*e.g.*, music downloads) would be unlawful.[1001]

---

detriment of competition on the markets for on-line music: see Mazziotti, 'Did Apple's refusal to license [...]', op. cit., p. 272.

1000 See §3.3.3.2., see *supra*.

1001 A similar problem was raised also under U.S. anti-circumvention law when, in the above-mentioned case regarding Apple's DRM technology, Real Networks circumvented Apple's proprietary DRM system for mere purposes of enabling interoperability between Apple's software and Real Networks' music.

The advocated legislative change would set aside such uncertainty in the regulation of circumvention acts which aimed to ensure interoperability between digitally protected content, hardware and media players. Indeed, each producer of computer programmes which performed tasks of copyrights management and who wished to benefit from the anti-circumvention laws provided under the amended version of Article 6 of the InfoSoc Directive would be required to make technical information which enables interoperability with DRM computer codes (*e.g.*, programming interfaces, communication protocols, *etc*) accessible on a free and open basis by any interested party through the mediation of a public copyright agency.

A workable alternative to the idea of pre-empting the bottleneck effects of proprietary DRM technologies through the disclosure of technical interfaces was considered by the Italian working group Dmin.it (*i.e.*, "Digital Media in Italia").[1002] This working group has proposed that the law should be reformed to compel the adoption of a single, interoperable DRM system whose technical specifications would be developed and managed under the aegis of a central authority.[1003] Under this proposal, the interoperable DRM system (entitled *iDrm*) would require content providers to make their works available *even* by means of the interoperable technical interfaces developed and specified by the central authority. This means that, under the *iDrm* proposal, the existing DRM systems might be still used and would be legally protected in so far as content providers who implemented proprietary technologies would release their works *also* under the publicly mandated DRM standard.

In my view, if the proposal of open standardisation in the field of DRM technology were endorsed by copyright policy-makers at national or at Community level, the institutional task of defining and supervising the open standard of DRM technology could be easily carried out by the public copyright agencies managing the user rights infrastructure. To this end, it would be sufficient to create a duty of disclosure and public deposit of interoperability information (*i.e.*, rights expression languages, software specifications, *etc*) upon copyright holders. Such duty of disclosure would allow public copyright agencies to receive and store interoperability information at the same time as receiving from copyright holders the above-mentioned set of technical information and materials which enable the exercise of the most complex fair uses. This regulation would look, to a certain extent, like the pro-interoperability legislation enacted under the 2006 French act which implemented the InfoSoc Directive.[1004]

Nonetheless, if the EU law-makers should embark on this desirable modification of the Directive, it would be necessary to establish an effective open standard of DRM technology, thereby avoiding the unfortunate drawbacks of the above-mentioned French legislation. It was pointed out above that this legislation set out conditions which are too narrow for the application of the duty to disclose interoperability information. Indeed, under the French statute, only software developers, other providers of technical measures and adopters of DRM systems can request

1002 See http://www.dmin.it/proposta/index.htm.

1003 See http://www.dmin.it/proposta/proposta-operativa.htm.

1004 See §7.4.3., see *supra*.

this information.[1005] Consequently, EU law should make it possible for copyright agencies to compel the disclosure of interoperability information upon the request of *all* interested parties, including end-users, consumers and their advocates (*i.e.*, consumer associations). Under this proposed reform, enforcement proceedings aimed at disclosing interoperability information would pursue not only the objective of facilitating competition between content and digital media providers, but also the objective of removing obstacles to the free usability of lawfully acquired content by means of different formats and equipment.

Moreover, the proposed reform should make it clear that the existence of intellectual property rights or trade secrets on DRM technologies would *not* constitute an objective justification for refusing to deposit or disclose this information, or, under the second option, for failing to release the protected works under the publicly-mandated standard of DRM.[1006] This last alternative may prove to be useful in as much as EU copyright policy-makers were unwilling to encroach upon or pre-empt intellectual property rights on DRM extensions. If so, new EU copyright law may end up requiring copyright owners to make DRM-protected works available under both a proprietary (possibly non-interoperable) format and a standardised, completely interoperable format which adopts the technical specifications elaborated and made publicly accessible by the European Commission through its copyright committee and the network of national copyright agencies.

9.4. Re-adjusting the three-step test

As explained above, as EU copyright law currently stands, it is unclear whether Article 5(5) of the InfoSoc Directive, which embodies the three-step test, binds national legislators (who are already bound by the test under international copyright laws) or whether the test is supposed to be applied by national courts in a *direct* way. Given the legislative context of the InfoSoc Directive, it would be more appropriate if the test was applied by the judiciary.[1007] However, this conclusion raises a number of concerns with regard to the enforceability of copyright exceptions in the digital environment, especially if exceptions are replaced by completely enforceable rights of use.

In order to achieve these ends, Article 5(5) should be revised. The next section explains why the test is ill-suited for judicial interpretation and how Article 5(5) might be usefully amended in order to uphold the law of user rights that was advocated above.

[1005] *Ibidem.*

[1006] See §7.4.4., see *supra.*

[1007] See §4.2.2., see *supra.*

9.4.1. The flawed function of Article 5(5) under the InfoSoc Directive

When analysing the legal meaning of the three-step test under the InfoSoc Directive law, Cohen Jehoram emphasised that Article 5(5) embodied a considerable deviation from the opening words of the three-step test under international copyright laws. He noted that all provisions, quoting the test under the Berne Convention, the TRIPS Agreement and the WIPO Copyright Treaty, begin by mentioning the addressees of the test.[1008] These wordings make it clear that the test is designed to instruct national law-makers when drafting their statutory copyright exceptions. Thus, within this legal framework, the test is implemented exclusively by national policy-setting institutions such as governments and parliaments, which are bound to develop their copyright policies in harmony with the model of copyright exceptions described by the test.

While agreeing with the conclusion reached by Cohen Jehoram, it was pointed out that, after Article 5(5) came into force, the three-step test could be directly applied by the judiciary in the Member States of the European Union.[1009] The provision of Article 5(5) has the effect of conditioning the effective enforceability of copyright exceptions in that they must meet *all* the requirements of the three-step test. This is a consequence of the structure of the test, whose requirements are designed to be met cumulatively.[1010] In the relevant literature, it was argued that, by permitting the judiciary to implement the test directly, the InfoSoc Directive inevitably disrupted the order of importance underlying the cumulative structure of the test.[1011] Under this structure, each single requirement is understood as a single *decisive* factor.[1012] In this regard, the direct enforceability of the test by the judiciary creates a significant problem in so far as the test is implemented through a merely quantitative assessment of its three factors.[1013] According to this quantitative interpretation of the test, the first requirement, which is designed to protect the public policy objectives underlying copyright exceptions, is decisively conditioned upon the meeting of the second (*i.e.*, the "normal exploitation") requirement. So far, the requirement of normal exploitation has been broadly understood by courts as confining fair uses to the realm of uses which have a very narrow impact on the markets to be exploited by the copyright owner. Under this approach, therefore, the

---

1008 See Cohen Jehoram, 'Restrictions on Copyright and their Abuse', op. cit., p. 363. In this regard, this author pointed out that Article 9(2) of the Berne Convention reads: "It shall be *a matter for legislation* in the countries of the Union to permit […]"; Article 10 of the TRIPS Agreement begins by saying that "*Member States* shall confine […]"; and Article 10 of the WIPO Copyright Treaty states: "*Contracting Parties* may, in their national legislation […]" (emphasis added).

1009 See §4.2.2., see *supra*.

1010 See Senftleben, *Copyright, Limitations and the Three-Step Test*, op. cit., pp. 126-127; Cohen Jehoram, 'Restrictions on Copyright and Their Abuse', op. cit., p. 361. The cumulative structure of the three-step test was discussed under §4.2.1., see *supra*.

1011 See Koelman, 'Fixing the Three-step Test', (28) *EIPR* 2006, p. 407, at pp. 408-409.

1012 See Koelman, 'Fixing the Three-step Test', op. cit., p. 410.

1013 The problem posed by a "quantitative" interpretation of the three-step test was discussed above: see §4.2.1., see *supra*.

protection of the commercial interest to exploit the copyrighted work has the inevitable result of stifling the public interest preserved by a copyright exception, regardless of the importance, from a perspective of public policy, of the special case made by the exception.

This kind of reasoning was evident in the final ruling of the French Supreme Court in the *Mulholland Drive* case.[1014] In the absence of a statutory provision that forbade technical measures from preventing private copying under French law, the Supreme Court found that the copyright owner's interest in protecting a DVD film through anti-copy measures could lawfully prevail over the user's interest to make a copy of the work for the (legitimate) purpose of private use. This controversial decision was based on the argument that unauthorised copying, even if permitted by a statutory exception under certain circumstances, would conflict with the normal exploitation of the film on the market for DVDs. This decision shows that the court's focus on the actual and potential economic losses suffered by the copyright owner may easily undermine the evaluation of the "special cases" which uphold the social desirability of copyright exceptions. It was emphasised above that, under its international understanding, the "special case" requirement was originally designed to accommodate a *normative* interpretation of the test, so that the national legislators could pursue specific public policies through the subtraction of certain uses from the actual and potential markets for copyrighted works.[1015]

In the final decision on the *Mulholland Drive* case, the reasoning of the French Supreme Court used the second requirement of the three-step test to avoid the enforcement *in concreto* of the statutory provision that, under certain circumstances, permitted the reproduction of the copyrighted work within the user's private sphere. If the French Supreme Court had confined its intervention to the enforcement of this statutory exception, the resulting decision should have upheld the former judgment from the Paris Court of Appeal, which ordered the removal of the anti-copy measure from all DVD formats embodying the copyrighted movie. Instead, the Supreme Court gave priority to protecting the economic interest of the copyright holder at the expense of the user's interest in making particular personal use of the copyrighted work in his or her private sphere.[1016]

In my view, the final decision on the *Mulholland Drive* case provides a very good example of how the *normative* interpretation of the test under its first requirement is endangered by a too broad understanding of "normal exploitation" under the second requirement. Similarly, following the WTO's Dispute Resolution Panel on Section 110(5) of the U.S. Copyright Act, if any economic, future loss for the copyright owner were considered to be a sufficient factor for excluding the fair character of the uses exempted by law from the copyright scope for important

1014 See §7.5.3., see *supra*.

1015 See Ricketson, *The Berne Convention for the protection of literary and artistic works: 1886-1986*, op. cit., p. 361.

1016 As pointed out earlier, in the above-mentioned case the user wished merely to copy the digitally protected movie on an analogue format in order to watch it at a place where no DVD player was available: see §7.5.2., see *supra*.

reasons of public policy, copyright exceptions would never be found applicable and would *de facto* be abolished altogether.[1017]

As Koelman has persuasively concluded, the current three-step test is structurally ill-conceived for a balanced assessment of the competing interests of the copyright holder and of the user by the judiciary. Unlike the U.S. fair use doctrine embodied in Section 107 of the U.S. Copyright Act, the three-step test does not give judges sufficient room to consider interests other than those of the copyright holders.

So far, the test has been interpreted both at international and at national levels in such a way as to consider the adverse economic impact of a certain use on the commercial exploitation of the copyrighted work as a decisive factor which impedes the pursuit of a specific public policy objective underlying a certain copyright exception. This situation contrasts with that of the standard of interpretation embodied in the U.S. fair use doctrine, which is much better suited to judicial interpretation, as it gives judges the necessary discretion and flexibility to consider and weigh all factors listed under Section 107 of the U.S. Copyright Act.[1018] In particular, no decisive role is afforded to the evaluation of the fourth factor of the doctrine, which requires U.S. courts to consider "the effect of the use upon the potential market for or value of the copyrighted work".[1019] Even if this factor is very similar to the "normal exploitation" requirement of the three-step test, it is only *one* of the factors to be considered by courts. As a result, U.S. judges, unlike their European counterparts, are entitled to give preference to other factors which cover a pressing public interest behind a certain use and find this use fair regardless of whether it may cause significant harm to the copyright holder.

9.4.2. Suitable revision of the function of the test inside the InfoSoc Directive

In conclusion, for the test to be implemented fairly in respect of the public policies underlying copyright exceptions (and even more so in respect of the system of users' rights advocated here), it would be highly desirable to redesign the test by drawing inspiration from the U.S. fair use doctrine.[1020] Under this proposal made by Koelman, the three requirements of the three-step test should be transformed into factors that both law-makers and courts should weigh together when determining the most appropriate scope of copyright.

Realistically, however, a revision of the three-step test at international level is very unlikely.[1021] The only remote possibility that such a reconsideration of the test may be effectively undertaken by the members of the Berne Convention and of the TRIPS Agreement is related to the fact that the flexibility of the U.S. fair

---

1017 See §4.2.1., see *supra*.

1018 This argument is made by Koelman, 'Fixing the Three-step test', op. cit., p. 410.

1019 See U.S. Code, Title 17, Sect. 107.

1020 See Koelman, 'Fixing the Three-step Test', op. cit., p. 410.

1021 *Ibidem*, pp. 411-412.

use doctrine is found to be at odds with the rigidity of the three-step test. As stressed by Koelman, the United States may have an interest in promoting a revision of the test in international fora, in order to reduce the danger that the U.S. fair use doctrine might be found to be in violation of international copyright law instruments such as the TRIPS Agreement.[1022]

Whereas a re-phrasing of the test under international copyright laws remains unlikely, the objective of reforming Article 5(5) of the InfoSoc Directive is easier to achieve. In principle, the problem concerning the frustration of copyright exceptions underlying public policy objectives could be solved by re-thinking the *function* of the test within the InfoSoc Directive. Cohen Jehoram has emphasised that, because EU copyright exceptions are legally conditioned upon the meeting the three-step test, it is incumbent upon the ECJ to review the legal meaning and the function of Article 5(5) in the near future.[1023] Should the ECJ embark on this review in the future, it could not fail to consider the important function of the speciality (*i.e.*, the first) criterion of the three-step test for the preservation of public policies which uphold copyright exceptions.

Nonetheless, a mere interpretative re-adjustment of Article 5(5) by an intervention by the ECJ would, by and large, be insufficient to accommodate the enforceability of uses covered by the exceptions effectively. In this regard, the proposed replacement of mere exceptions by an effective system of *non-waivable* user rights would set aside the confusion created by the three-step test in respect of the practical enforceability of copyright exceptions under the InfoSoc Directive. The reform of the whole legal meaning of Article 5 of the Directive would inevitably require a substantive modification of the function of Article 5(5). As pointed out above, the open-ended, *ex post* nature of the kind of evaluation required by the three-step test is at odds with the idea of identifying *ex ante* a number of punctual rights of use.[1024] The technical accommodation of these rights in respect of DRM-protected works should logically be undertaken through the implementation of fair-use-by-design techniques. In this regard, it was made clear that only the most complex and technically "unpredictable" uses should have made recourse to the assistance of the user rights management infrastructure managed by public copyright agencies.[1025] It was concluded that, given the choice of this policy alternative, the revised Article 5 of the Directive should specifically define a threshold number of mandatory users' rights.[1026] This set of indispensable rights could be updated periodically by a delegated law-making power entrusted by a new provision of the Directive to the European Commission.

If a law of user rights were established under Article 5 in accordance with the guidelines set out above, the function of Article 5(5) would change automatically. Due to the creation of imperative and fully enforceable rights of use, the speciality criterion of the three-step test would be given preference over the other require-

1022 See Koelman, 'Fixing the Three-step Test', op. cit., pp. 411-412.

1023 See Cohen Jehoram, 'Restrictions on Copyright and Their Abuse', op. cit., p. 364.

1024 See §7.2.2., see *supra*.

1025 See §9.3.2., see *supra*.

1026 *Ibidem*.

ments. Indeed, courts would not be permitted to apply the three-step test by merely using a quantitative analysis of its requirements. Instead, judges would be forced to adopt a *normative* analysis of the test, so that, for example, they could not apply the requirement of "normal exploitation" while prohibiting the enforcement of a statutory exception *in concreto*. Under this approach, the scrutiny of the courts would focus exclusively on the implementation of the punctual statutory provisions that set out copyright exceptions (or, according to a better terminology, "user rights"). Compliance of exceptions with the test would be ensured by the statutory interpretation of law-makers and policy-makers, including the European Commission when exercising its delegated legislative powers.

If so, the test could be usefully applied by courts as a flexible norm of interpretation each time that statutory exceptions should prove to be inapplicable. This may happen either:

- in cases of uncertainty about the qualification of a certain use scrutinised under enforcement proceedings before public copyright agencies; or
- in cases of contested uses manifestly *not* contemplated in the non-exhaustive list of user rights provided by the amended version of Article 5.

From this perspective, the three-step test could be viewed as a useful, supplementary criterion for ascertaining fairness in respect of uses which fall outside the list of statutory rights provided by the Directive or with regard to new rights of use established under the law-making process of the European Commission.

9.5. Summary

This final chapter has drawn on the preceding analysis of the copyright law embodied in the InfoSoc Directive in order to propose a desirable reform of the legal relationship between copyright exceptions, anti-circumvention laws and rights management technologies. It has been argued that, in order to re-establish harmony with the statement of Article 11 of the WIPO Copyright Treaty, the legal protection afforded to technical measures such as DRM systems should follow and strictly comply with *both* the exclusive rights and the exceptions set out under copyright law. In this regard, it has been emphasised that it would be highly desirable to re-define the character of copyright exceptions by replacing them with enforceable rights of use. The suggestion put forward here is that this change of law and policy could only be undertaken at EU level by revising the relevant provision of the InfoSoc Directive. Indeed, as the text of this Directive stands, national law is not in a position to implement the law of user rights that has been advocated in this book.

It has been argued that, to implement this new law, the existing provisions embodied in Articles 5, 6, and 12 of the Directive need to be revised in accordance with the following guidelines:

- User *rights* of access and use which would replace the mere *exceptions* listed under Article 5 of the Directive should be defined as *non-waivable* through contract, in the same way as certain copyright exceptions embodied in the 1991 Software Directive are.
- The above user rights should be set out in accordance with the constitutional principle of Article 10 of the ECHR, which mandates a balanced co-existence of copyright protection and freedom of expression even in the digital environment. As a result, it would be suitable to recognise the nature of *subjective right* to all existing copyright exceptions that have the purpose of permitting (or at least facilitating) the creation of new works. It has been recommended that acts of unauthorised private copying, as defined in Article 5(2)(b) of the Directive, should be included in this set of non-waivable rights of use, especially in fields of creativity (*e.g.*, scientific and academic research) where this particular use serves purposes of follow-on creation.
- The set of the above-mentioned rights of use should be defined broadly to accommodate the preservation of new rights of use that may prove to be necessary for the protection of the fundamental rights of users, such as privacy and freedom of expression. To this end, the European Commission may be entrusted with delegated law-making powers that would be subject not only to parliamentary control on the grounds of Article 202 of the EC Treaty, but also to the requirements of the three-step test.

The enforcement of user rights could be ensured either through solutions of "fair use by design" or, in cases of broader and more complex uses, through the assistance of a trusted (preferably public) intermediary, such as a copyright agency. This agency could carry out the institutional task of administering "escrow systems" in which copyright owners (or even developers of technical measures such as DRM systems) should deposit all technical information (*e.g.*, codes, keys, communication interfaces) and materials (*e.g.*, unprotected formats embodying digitally protected works) permitting qualified users to exercise their rights on a digitally protected work without having to hack any technical device. Consequently, the existing provision of Article 6(4) should be modified in order to afford anti-circumvention protection only to technical measures which accommodate fair uses "by design". Moreover, the same protection would be made conditional upon the submission of all technical information enabling fair circumvention, decryption and interoperability of technological protection measures to national copyright agencies (that the amended version of Article 6(4) should foresee and require to be implemented).

The contact committee created at the European Commission by the existing provision of Article 12 should be transformed into a dedicated copyright committee. This central agency could work as a permanent advisor of the Commission in the above-mentioned law-making process with regard to copyright exceptions and as a supervisor of the administrative activities of national agencies created on the grounds of new Article 6(4).

Finally, it has been observed that the current version of Article 5(5) of the InfoSoc Directive requires judges to implement a standard of interpretation for copyright exceptions (*i.e.*, the three-step test) which inhibits an appropriate appreciation by the judiciary of the public policy objectives which underlie the acts permitted by the exceptions. It has been stressed that specific public policies which justify copyright exceptions (*i.e.*, under the first step) would be severely impeded in so far as the judiciary would be allowed to forego these policy objectives in order to protect the commercial exploitation of the copyrighted work (*i.e.*, under the second step). As a result, the chapter has concluded that the function of the test under the Directive may be revised by expressly confining the applicability of Article 5(5) to law-making activities (including the above-mentioned delegated law-making process governed by the European Commission) and to judicial cases where no user right proves to be applicable.

APPENDIX

Appendix I - Digital Rights Management: The Technological Scenario

A. Historical background to the concept of digital rights language

The birth of the concept of DRM technology in legal scholarship is often associated with the publication of an essay by scientist Mark Stefik in the Berkeley Technology Law Journal of 1997.[1] At that time, Stefik worked as the principal scientist at Xerox's Palo Alto Reserch Center (PARC), in California.[2] As a researcher of Xerox Corporation, Stefik patented a system for controlling the distribution and use of digital works that was regularly improved over years and resulted in a number of patents issued by all the most important patent offices of the world.[3] On the grounds of the radical innovation produced by Stefik's research, Xerox set up a new company (ContentGuard) that acquired the patent portfolio originally owned by Xerox and specialised in the development of what is called today "digital rights management" (DRM).[4] DRM is a general expression that describes a set of combined technologies that may establish a secure distribution channel for digital content. These technologies include measures of encryption, copy-control, digital watermarking, fingerprinting, access control, authentication, key management, revocation, *etc*.[5] Today's idea of bundling technical measures for the purpose to control the distribution and use of digital works is closely linked to the groundbreaking system foreseen by Stefik in 1997. Stefik showed that the association of trusted systems with digital property rights would have compelled a

---

1 See Stefik, 'Shifting the Possible: How Trusted Systems and Digital Property Rights Challenge Us to Rethink Digital Publishing', (12) *Berkeley Technology Law Journal* 1997, p. 137.

2 Mark Stefik is now research fellow at PARC and manager of the Human-Document Interaction Area in the Information Sciences and Technology Laboratory: see http://www2.parc.com/istl/members/stefik/homeinfo.htm.

3 See the Esp@cenet user interface developed by the European Patent Office (EPO), available at: http://v3.espacenet.com. The above-mentioned Xerox's patent portfolio includes a patent family list of 34 members derived from 24 applications under the classification number EP0715245. This data also contains reference to the equivalent patents issued by the U.S. and Japan patent offices.

4 A detailed list of Xerox's worldwide patents, which are owned now by ContentGuard, is available at: http://www.ContentGuard.com/patents.asp.

5 See Bechtold, 'The Present and Future of Digital Rights Management', op. cit., p. 598.

re-consideration of the notion of digital publishing. This new distribution system that connected publishers of electronic materials to content buyers was based on the notion of *trusted* system, which describes a system that can be relied on to follow certain rules.[6] Under this notion, the "trust" of each system is determined and measured according to the rules that the system is ordered to follow by its programmer.[7] Under Stefik's model, these rules to be followed by both the publisher's and the user's computers referred to the terms, conditions and fees for using published materials electronically. To prevent the unauthorised or the unaccounted distribution and usage of these materials over digital networks, Stefik thought of a method in which the owner of a work could attach usage rights to that work. The expression "usage rights" was used to refer to permissions granted through contract by the owner of a digital work to its buyers. In Stefik's mind, each usage permission had associated with it certain optional specifications outlining the conditions and fees upon which the permitted use may be exercised. This way, the publishing system would have resulted in the specification of certain usage rights (*e.g.*, the rights to access, copy, transfer, print, loan and modify the protected content) which came always with the protected work and established what Stefik called a "digital rights language".[8]

In the trusted system model relied on by Stefik for the purpose to establish a secure method of digital publishing, electronic materials are stored in a repository and are encrypted (*i.e.*, translated into a secret code) or made unreadable to unauthorised parties by means of a digital watermark (*i.e.*, a pattern of visible or invisible bits inserted into a file in order to attach copyright information). For the security of their communications, the publisher's system and the user's system rely normally on public key (or asymmetric) systems of cryptography. In these systems two types of keys are used to encrypt and decrypt the content to deliver: a public key and a private key. The keys are designed with a specific mathematical relationship with each other, meaning that anything encrypted in the public key can be decrypted by (and only by) the private key. Usually, the longer is the key, the more difficult is to decode a message without having access to that key. By the combination of trusted systems and the expression of digital rights languages, the publisher's repository is able to process each request to access a digital work by examining the user's corresponding rights. The enforcement of these rights on the user's system is ensured by digital work "playback devices", which are coupled to the repository that contains the work and are used to play, display or print the work. For this system to work, therefore, both the publisher's and the user's repositories which exchange data one another are required to have some part that is trusted by means of DRM technology that uses the same encoding and decoding languages.

---

6 See Stefik, 'Shifting the Possible […]', op. cit., p. 139.

7 See Stefik, 'Shifting the Possible […]', op. cit., p. 139 ("Suppose that you have a digital work stored on a trusted system, and you do not have a right to copy the work. Then if you ask the trusted system to make a copy, it simply will not do it. Instead, it will give you an error message").

8 *Ibidem*, p. 140.

B. The function of rights expression languages (RELs)

Typically, a DRM system protects copyright by either encrypting information so that only authorised users can access it or marking the information with a digital watermark (or a similar method) in a way that the content cannot be freely distributed, copied, shifted, printed, modified, *etc*. These possibilities of control and rights management over any kind of digital representation of text, pictures, databases, music, or video, are conferred by technical means of expressing usage rights. The technical means to express digital rights can be differently combined and implemented into formal languages that DRM systems are able to interpret precisely. At the time of Stefik's aforementioned publication, Xerox's Digital Property Rights Language (DPRL) had developed sixteen distinct kinds of rights. In this language, each distinct "right" was made of a number of permitted acts that a certain user purpose requires to perform. For instance, "transport rights" included the permission to copy, transfer and loan the protected work, whereas "derivative work rights" included the permission to extract, embed and edit the work.[9] Moreover, Stefik explained that Xerox's DPRL empowered the publisher of electronic materials to re-establish "natural" categories of use while regulating the transfer of information between repositories. In this respect, the DPRL was already able to enforce and differentiate the exercise of the rights to copy, transfer and loan a digital work. The digital right to *copy* enabled the making of a new, usable copy on a certain repository without deleting the original copy, with a subsequent increase of the number of usable copies. To the contrary, the exercise of the digital rights to *transfer* and to *loan* implied that, once a repository transferred or loaned a copy to another repository, the original copy of the work on the first repository was no longer available (or could not be used for the time of the loan in favour of the follow-on repository).[10]

For this secure distribution system to function effectively on the widest amount of networked computers, the highest degree of interoperability between publishers' and users' machines was required. To this end, a standard digital rights language needed to be created for the purpose to specify permissions and conditions associated with digital content as well as services. Only a standard digital property language would have accomplished this task. That is why the idea of a standard Rights Expression Language (REL) emerged and developed quickly.

A standard REL provides a *universal* method for specifying associated information necessary to enable e-commerce transactions in usage rights over digitised content (*e.g.*, how to pay fees, secure digital rights, authenticate typologies of users qualified to obtain certain usage rights, and so on). A REL must be viewed as a machine-readable language that can declare rights and permissions by the use of "metadata" (*i.e.*, information that describes how, when and by whom a particular set of data was collected, and how the data is formatted). In his 1997 essay, Stefik addressed the original concept of digital rights language by using the denomination of DPRL. This denomination was subsequently replaced by the currently used

---

9 See Stefik, 'Shifting the Possible […]', op. cit., p. 140.

10 *Ibidem*, pp. 145-46.

expression "eXtensible Rights Markup Language" (XrML).[11] This new denomination witnesses the translation of the original DPRL into the syntax of the eXtensible Markup Language (XML) set out by the World Wide Web Consortium (known under the acronym of W3C) for the primary purpose to facilitate the sharing of data across different systems, particularly systems connected via the Internet.[12] Both the DPRL and the XrML technologies were developed and patented after years of research at Xerox's PARC.

In response to a call for proposals delivered by the Motion Picture Experts Group (MPEG), a working group established under the shield of the International Organization for Standardization (ISO), the new owner of the Xerox technologies (*i.e.*, ContentGuard) proposed the adoption of the XrML for the setting of a universally recognised REL standard.[13] As a result of this initiative, in December 2001 ContentGuard's XrML was selected as the basis for the development of the MPEG-21 REL standard.[14] This process of standardisation has culminated in the formation of an ISO standard of Rights Expression Language.

As from early 2004, the MPEG-21 (officially known as "ISO/IEC 21000-5:2004") has been approved as an ISO standard and has been endorsed by companies such as IBM, Universal Music Group, Reuters, Microsoft, Intel, Philips, Panasonic as well as major content owner organisations such as the Motion Picture Association of America (MPAA) and the Recording Industry Association of America (RIAA), as active participants.[15] Of particular relevance is the endorsement of the quasi-monopolist on the world market for personal computer operating systems, Microsoft, which has expressed its intention to integrate the MPEG-21/XrLM standard into its potentially ubiquitous DRM technology (*i.e.*, Windows Media Rights Manager).[16] The strategic interest of Microsoft in this standard technology was recently evidenced by its acquisition of the ownership of ContentGuard in joint venture with Time Warner and Thomson in March 2005.[17]

---

11 See http://www.xrml.org/index.asp.

12 See http://www.w3.org/XML/.

13 See http://www.chiariglione.org/mpeg. MPEG is a working group of the ISO (http://www.iso.org) in charge of the development of standards for coded representation of digital audio and video. This working group specified the widely adopted standards of data compression and encoding known as "MPEG-1" and "MPEG-2".

14 See MPEG-21 Overview v.5, at: http://www.chiariglione.org/mpeg/standards/mpeg-21. The MPEG describes its REL as follows: "The REL is intended to provide flexible, interoperable mechanisms to support transparent and augmented use of digital resources in publishing, distributing, and consuming of digital movies, digital music, electronic books, broadcasting, interactive games, computer software and other creations in digital form, in a way that protects digital content and honours the rights, conditions, and fees specified for digital contents. It is also intended to support specification of access and use controls for digital content in cases where financial exchange is not part of the terms of use, and to support exchange of sensitive or private digital content."

15 See http://www.xrml.org/xrml_endorsers.asp.

16 See http://www.microsoft.com/windows/windowsmedia/howto/articles/drmarchitecture. aspx.

17 See http://www.microsoft.com/presspass/press/2005/mar05/03-15ContentGuardPR. mspx.

C. Intellectual property protection of DRM technology components

DRM technologies were defined earlier as a compound of technologies including encryption and management devices. To give shape to a certain DRM system, the maker of each system needs to choose between alternative, specific technologies that carry out functions such as digital rights expression, data compression, encoding and transmission, and communication between hardware and software that adopt the same DRM system. Each of these devices may be subject to patent protection, considering that they are very often the fruit of costly research programs funded by private corporations. Examples of patent protection can be found at several layers of the technological chain which permits DRM systems to exist and operate.

C1. Patent protection of RELs

The aforementioned case of MPEG-21, which developed as a *de facto* REL standard using the proprietary format of ContentGuard's XrLM, is a paramount example of how the use of DRM technologies by content traders and media players manufacturers is subject to the licensing power of the patent holders over system components. The recent acquisition of ContentGuard Holdings, the world leader on the market for DRM technologies, by a joint venture of giants from the industries of software (*i.e.*, Microsoft), content (*i.e.*, Time Warner), and hardware and media players (*i.e.*, Thomson), demonstrates to what extent the blocking, exclusionary power conferred by patented DRM standard components on the fast-growing markets for copyrighted digital works is considered crucial.

C2. Patent protection of audio/video encoding technologies

Another DRM-related standard device which is subject to patent protection, and which is consequently not freely available to the content and information technology industries, is the audio/video coding technology known as "MPEG-4", which is a development of the former compression standards known as MPEG-1 and MPEG-2.[18] These encoding standards (which include the well-known "MP3" format used mostly by unauthorised file-sharers on peer-to-peer networks) were developed by the contribution of two dozens of companies under the supervision of the MPEG and approved as international standards by the ISO. The latest MPEG-4, in particular, is a standard used primarily to compress audio and video digital data.[19] Introduced in late 1998, MPEG-4 is the designation for a group of audio and video coding standards and related technology agreed upon by the MPEG.

[18] See the entries "MPEG-1" and "MPEG-2" at http://www.wikipedia.org.

[19] See Overview of the MPEG-4 Standard: http://www.chiariglione.org/mpeg/standards/mpeg-4/mpeg-4.htm

The uses for the MPEG-4 standard are web (streaming media) and CD distribution, conversational (videophone) and broadcast television, all of which benefit from compressing the audio-video stream. MPEG-4 has absorbed many of the features of MPEG-1 and MPEG-2 and other related standards, adding new features including the possibility of supporting externally specified DRM systems.

The fact that MPEG-4 is a *proprietary* technology means that, although software to create and play back MPEG-4 audio and video files may be readily available, a licence is needed to use it legally in the architecture of DRM systems. Patents covering this encoding standard are claimed by multiple holders, which gathered up in the patent pool known as "MPEG Licensing Authority" to provide a one-stop shop for companies using this standard.[20] However, this licensing activity was recently suspended due to much uncertainty arising about the list of companies owning patents covering the technology.[21] Evidence of such uncertainty is given by the patent infringements recently claimed by AT&T Corporation, which is not part of the MPEG-4 patent pool, against several companies including Apple Computer, CyberLink, DivX, InterVideo, *etc.* AT&T warned these companies that the use of the MPEG-4 video technology without its authorisation was infringing a number of patents related to video compression, which AT&T said are an essential component of this standard technology.[22]

C3. Patent protection of communication protocols

For DRM systems to run on all trusted computer systems where content traders want digital works to be distributed and used, computers need to adopt certain application programming interfaces (so-called "APIs"). An API is the interface that a computer system, library or application provides in order to allow requests for services to be made of it by other computer programmes, and/or to allow data to be exchanged between them.[23] One of the primary purposes of an API is to describe how to access a set of functions. For instance, a computer programme can (and often must) use its operating system's API to allocate memory and access files. In the same way as many types of systems and applications that implement APIs (*e.g.*, graphics systems, databases, networks, web services, *etc*), DRM systems may turn out to be accessible and usable only via a particular API. For instance, this is the case of the DRM system created and implemented by Apple Computer on the complementary products of its online music platform. Thanks to patented APIs, Apple's DRM system ("Fairplay") enables a secure transfer of content from the iTunes Music Store to the customers' personal computer (equipped

20 See http://www.mpegla.com/index1.cfm. The purpose of the MPEG-4 Patent Portfolio Licence is that of enabling companies using this standard to obtain access to essential MPEG-4 patents owned by many patent holders in a single transaction rather than negotiating direct licences with each of them individually.

21 See http://www.mpegla.com/m4s/

22 For more information, see 'AT&T Warns Apple, Others, of Patent Infringement', *PC Magazine*, 9.2.2006, available at http://www.pcmag.com.

23 See the entry "Application programming interface" (API) at: http://www.wikipedia.org.

with the iTunes media player), and from the personal computer to the well-known iPod portable media player. In this way, DRM-protected music downloads cannot be legally transferred out of Apple's platform without using Apple's proprietary APIs. This example shows that patented communication protocols have the consequence of making the possibility of accessing DRM-protected materials subject to the licensing power of the patent holder over the protocols.

D. The advent of "trusted computing" platforms

D1. The notion of 'Trusted Computing' (TC)

Today's industrial development of rights management technologies shows that the picture drawn few years ago by Mark Stefik about the possibility of using trusted systems for the purpose to make digital works perfectly excludable and manageable has become more than a theoretical setting. The most important novelty in this field is, by far, the development of the concept of "Trusted Computing" (TC). This expression refers to private initiatives such as the Trusted Computing Platform Alliance (TCPA), established in 1999 by leading firms in the software, hardware and content industries (*e.g.*, Compaq, Hewlett Packard, IBM, Intel, Microsoft, Sony and Sun Microsystems).

In April 2003, TCPA's project was incorporated into a bigger not-for-profit organisation whose creation was promoted by the same group of stakeholders with the denomination of "Trusted Computing Group" (TCG).[24]

As explained by Anderson:

> "[I]in this context, 'trusted' means that software running on a machine can be trusted by third parties, who can verify that a program running on a machine with which they are communicating has not been modified by the machine's owner. Programs will also be able to communicate securely with each other, and with their authors [...]".[25]

Even if TC platforms do not provide all the necessary technical elements required for DRM systems, thc idea of TC can be viewed as an attempt to transpose and develop the logic of DRM technology into hardware architectures. The mission statement of the TCG asserts that the main goal of TC mechanisms is that of protecting data security by creating a standard for a trusted hardware computing platform.[26] Nonetheless, TC platforms can be shaped so as to perform digital rights

---

24 See http://www.trustedcomputinggroup.org. For now the TCG has 125 members, including component vendors, software developers, systems vendors and network and infrastructure companies.

25 See Anderson, ''Trusted Computing' and Competition Policy', op. cit., p. 36.

26 See http://www.trustedcomputinggroup.org. As reported by the mission statement of the TCG, the primary goal of trusted computing is "to help users protect their information assets (data, passwords, keys, *etc*) from compromise due to external software attack and physical theft." The organisation aims "to develop, define, and promote open

management tasks. Indeed, by enabling functions such as the secure attestation of the state of a computing platform, the creation of trusted computer identities and the provision of protected storage, TC mechanisms have the potential to enable control over the conditions of access to and use of data stored and transmitted across hardware, software, peripherals and mobile devices which adopt the same trusted specifications.

What distinguishes TC platforms from DRM technology is that, to ensure trust between third parties wishing to securely transfer data one another (*e.g.*, emails, corporate documents, *etc*), the former rely on a much more pervasive presence of monitoring and reporting devices than DRM systems do. For instance, the set of trusted specifications developed by the TCG includes a Trusted Platform Module (TPM) used in personal computers and other systems; a software interface specification to enable application development for systems using the TPM; a Trusted Server specification; and a specification called Trusted Network Connect to enable protection of the network. Other work groups are addressing storage, peripherals, mobile devices and other aspects of the trusted enterprise.[27]

As critically pointed out by Anderson, the TCG project proposes a re-design of the personal computer hardware in which a hardware security component, known among technologists as "Fritz-chip", monitors what software and hardware are running on a machine.[28] Fritz-chip is a nickname for the hardware component of the software-execution monitoring system that the TCG indicates as TPM.[29] The Fritz chips installed into different machines can communicate one with another and play the role of certifiers assuring third parties that the user's machine is the machine that the user claims it to be, and that this machine is running the software that the user claim it to be.[30] The presence of hardware security components on all machines and applications that support certain TC platform specifications empow-

standards for hardware-enabled trusted computing and security technologies, including hardware building blocks and software interfaces, across multiple platforms, peripherals, and devices. TCG specifications will enable more secure computing environments without compromising functional integrity, privacy, or individual rights."

27 See https://www.trustedcomputinggroup.org/about/faq/.

28 See Anderson, ''Trusted Computing' and Competition Policy', op. cit., p. 36. The above-mentioned nickname refers to former U.S. Senator Ernest "Fritz" Hollings, who sponsored the adoption of the Consumer Broadband and Digital Television Promotion Act, which aimed at mandating the inclusion of such a chip in every computer. See the entry "Fritz chip" at http://www.wikipedia.org.

29 The TCG defines TPM as follows: "The TPM is a microcontroller that stores keys, passwords and digital certificates. It typically is affixed to the motherboard of a PC. It potentially can be used in any computing device that requires these functions. The nature of this silicon ensures that the information stored there is made more secure from external software attack and physical theft. Security processes, such as digital signature and key exchange, are protected through the secure TCG subsystem. Access to data and secrets in a platform could be denied if the boot sequence is not as expected. Critical applications and capabilities such as secure email, secure web access and local protection of data are thereby made much more secure."
See http://www.trustedcomputinggroup.org/about/faq/.

30 See Anderson, ''Trusted Computing' and Competition Policy', op. cit., p. 36.

ers content creators to maintain some control over their digital works, regardless of where the works may subsequently move. This is a consequence of the fact that, by requiring installation of security components (such as the TPM) on personal computers and other devices, TC technology ends up removing effective control of a machine from its owner.

The removal of control can be effectively achieved because trusted platforms need to adopt cryptographic keys to allow the user's hardware, software and data to be certified in terms of identity and authenticity in respect of third parties. Given that, under the trusted platform models that have been developed until now, the certifying parties owing and managing cryptographic keys are either the content owners (*e.g.*, movie, music, software distributors) or developers of particular TC applications (*e.g.*, a media player), the risk that the end-user's machine may be "locked-in" in a particular TC platform is very high. Obviously, the extent to which the owner of a personal computer may be deprived of control over his or her hardware and applications depends largely on the architecture of each trusted platform. For instance, considering that privacy is a necessary element of a trusted system and that the user's privacy is inevitably restricted by the operation of monitoring and reporting components, the TCG assures that its model of trusted platform leaves the system owner with the ability to choice whether to opt-in and use the trusted subsystem or to preserve the machine's openness.[31]

D2. The case of Microsoft: toward integration between DRM and TC systems

According to different tastes of supporters and opponents of trusted platforms, the letter T of the acronym TC has been read alternatively as "trustworthy" or "treacherous". For instance, Microsoft prefers the former denomination because it emphasises that any content or application running on a trusted computer can be certified, in terms of user's security, by its legitimate owner.[32] This certification process is ensured by the operation of the TPM containing the Fritz chip, which receives encrypted data from the content or software distributor and decrypts it by means of a key that is downloaded automatically from a server under the control of the content owner or the software vendor. Opponents such as Richard Stallman of the Free Software Foundation, instead, claimed that "treacherous" computing would be a more appropriate name for a technology that will inevitably deprive computer users of control over their machines.[33] According to Stallman, this technology is specifically designed to make sure that the machine will systematically disobey its user. Indeed, each "trusted" hardware includes digital encryption and

---

31 See http://www.trustedcomputinggroup.org/about/faq/.

32 See Anderson, ''Trusted Computing' and Competition Policy', op. cit., p. 36; Bill Gates, *Trustworthy Computing*, Executive E-mail, 18 July 2002, available at: http://www.microsoft.com/mscorp/execmail/2002/07-18twc.asp.

33 See Stallman, 'Can you trust your computer?', available at http://www.gnu.org/philosophy/can-you-trust.html

signature devices whose keys are kept secret from the hardware owner, so that personal computers will stop from functioning as general-purpose computers.[34] Under this pervasively restrictive communication system, Stallman argued, every operation may require explicit permission, with the consequence that sharing unauthorised data would become impossible, at least with encrypted content acquired by companies that implement TC mechanisms.[35]

With the advent of TC platforms, moreover, another fanciful Stallman's prediction has come true. As considered earlier, Stallman is the author of a science fiction tale (set in 2047) that depicts a future world in which the exercise of the rights to access and read digitised information is kept under the strict control of central licensing "authorities".[36] Under today's TC platforms, this picture comes out of that science fiction setting and enters everyday life. The TC platform implemented by Microsoft as from the launch on the market of the Windows Server 2003 work group operating system had the potential to eliminate unlicensed software directly.[37] By means of this system, owners of proprietary software making available their programmes for Microsoft's platform were enabled to monitor which other programs end-users could run, which documents or data they could access, and what programmes they could pass them to. After having been installed into each computer network, trusted applications supporting Microsoft's platform were programmed to continually download new authorization rules through the websites of the respective software owners, so that those rules could be automatically imposed on the user's work or programme.[38] This online monitoring activity was allowed by the operation of Microsoft's TPM, which registered and maintained a list of the hardware and system components mounted on each trusted machine. In the meanwhile, Microsoft developed a very similar TC platform to be implemented into a future version of its (almost ubiquitous) personal computer operating system (*i.e.*, Windows). This platform was originally called Palladium and now it is known as Next-Generation Secure Computing Base (NGSCB). The content industry has welcomed this new Microsoft project because it will allow them to support stronger DRM technologies.

In the last years, Microsoft has developed its proprietary DRM technology with a view to bundling it with its proprietary media player (*i.e.*, Windows Media Player) and integrating it into the new NGSCB platform. While pursuing this vertical integration strategy, Microsoft has initially developed and improved its own

---

34 See Stallmank, 'Can You Trust Your Computer?', op. cit.

35 *Ibidem.*

36 See Stallman, 'The Right to Read', op. cit.: see §1.5., see *supra.*

37 See Anderson, ''Trusted Computing' and Competition Policy', op. cit., p. 37.

38 Anderson, ''Trusted Computing' and Competition Policy', op. cit., p. 37, explained that Microsoft's Windows Server 2003 inverted the system by which trusted machines were programmed in order to deliver through the Internet hardware and software information that enabled the above-mentioned monitoring system. Whereas, in original trusted platforms, control was exerted "from the bottom up through the TC hardware", the Windows Server platform was designed so that monitoring took place "from the top" (*i.e.*, from websites under the software and content owners' control) "down through the applications".

Windows Media Rights Manager system. As disclosed by a Microsoft's scientist, the main purpose of this DRM system was that of providing owners of digital media supporting the Microsoft platform with the technical opportunity to treat the consumer as *both* a content user and the one that content owners want to protect their content from.[39] More recently, the position of Microsoft in the field of DRM technologies was strengthened by the acquisition of joint ownership of the world leader company on the market for DRM solutions (*i.e.*, ContentGuard). Together with Time Warner and Thomson, Microsoft has consequently acquired joint ownership of ContentGuard's patent portfolio, which includes foundational DRM technology such as the XrML format that is used by today's international standard of REL (*i.e.*, MPEG-21).

The strengthened position of Microsoft following this acquisition raised competition concerns especially in the European Union. In August 2004, after having been noticed under the EU Merger Regulation[40] about a joint venture established by Microsoft and Time Warner for the acquisition and governance of ContentGuard, the European Commission decided not to immediately authorise (and to assess in more depth) this operation.[41] The Commission expressed the concern that the operation might have created or strengthened Microsoft's "already leading position" in the DRM solutions market:

> "Under Microsoft's and Time Warner's joint ownership [...] ContentGuard may have both the incentive and the ability to use its IPR portfolio to put Microsoft's rivals in the DRM solutions market at a competitive disadvantage. This joint acquisition could also slow down the development of open interoperability standards. As such, this would allow the DRM solutions market to "tip" towards the current leading provider, Microsoft."[42]

Following the Commission's objections, the shareholding structure and governing rules of ContentGuard were significantly modified. The Commission considered that Microsoft, Time Warner and the new stakeholder Thomson each held a one third stake and, in the absence of stockholder voting agreements, none of them had control over ContentGuard.[43] In reviewing whether the transaction involving Thomson would fall under the EU Merger Regulation, the Commission concluded that, through the conjunction of Thomson's acquisition of an equity stake, and of changes in ContentGuard's governance structure, no shareholder could exert con-

---

39 See Pruneda, 'Windows Media Technologies: Using Windows Media Rights Manager to Protect and Distribute Digital Media', *MSDN Magazine,* December 2001 ("DRM Security"), available at: http://msdn.microsoft.com/msdnmag/issues/01/12/drm/.

40 Council Regulation 139/2004/EC on the control of concentrations between undertakings, OJ L 24, 29.01.2004.

41 See Case No. COMP/M. 3445 Microsoft/Time Warner/Content Guard/JV.

42 See Press Office of the Commission of the European Communities, *Commission opens in-depth investigation into Microsoft/Time Warner/Content Guard JV*, Press Release IP/04/1044, 25 August 2004, available at http://europa.eu.int/rapid/searchAction.do.

43 See Press Office of the Commission of the European Communities, *Mergers: Microsoft and Time Warner abandon acquisition of control in ContentGuard as Thomson purchases a one third stake*, Press Release, IP/05/295, 15 March 2005, available at http://europa.eu.int/rapid/searchAction.do.

trol over ContentGuard.[44] Therefore, this transaction was deemed not to be subject to EU merger rules so that the involved companies could withdraw their notification under the Merger Regulation.

44 *Ibidem.*

Appendix II - Examples of National Transposition of Article 6(4) of the Infosoc Directive

The following table summaries in a chronological order how a few national legislations that are mentioned in the book transposed Article 6(4) of the InfoSoc Directive. The following table overviews some of the most interesting and recent (*e.g.*, Spain's and France's) implementation of the legal infrastructure aimed at preserving copyright exceptions from the operation of technological protection measures. The different sections of the table can be read as follows:

- The "Member States" column lists the selected Member States and the acts by which they implemented the InfoSoc Directive;
- The "Preserved exceptions" column shows how the concerned legislators interpreted the list of exceptions regarding the end-user that Article 6(4) intended to protect from technical restrictions;
- The "Private copying" column shows whether and how these Member States exercised the option left by the second sub-paragraph of Article 6(4) for the inclusion of the private copying exception into the set of privileged (*i.e.*, preserved) exceptions;
- The "*Ad hoc* Authority" column evidences the establishment or the preexistence of *ad hoc* authorities that supervise (or govern) administrative or judicial proceedings aimed at enforcing rights and duties provided by Article 6(4);
- The "Administrative or judicial remedies" column, finally, shows the legal techniques by which the examined legislations gave shape to the legal mechanism safeguarding the enforceability of certain users' acts.

Member State	Preserved exceptions	Private copying	*Ad hoc* Authority	Administrative or judicial remedies
Denmark (Danish Copyright Act of 17 December 2002)	Reproduction within archives, libraries and museums Production of anthologies for educational use Use of works of fine art in critical or scientific presentations Reproduction for visually handicapped and hearing-impaired persons	Not included	Copyright Licence Tribunal (see the new §75d(1))	The Copyright Licence Tribunal can order the copyright holder to provide the user with the means to benefit from the exceptions. These means may either an analogue copy of the work or codes, keys, equipment for decryption, *etc.* If the right holder does not comply with the Tribunal's order within 4 weeks, the user is entitled to circumvent the technical measure.
Greece (Law 3057/2002, which amended the Greek Copyright Act, *i.e.*, Law 2121/1993)	Reproduction for private use on paper or any similar medium Reproduction for teaching purposes Reprography within libraries and archives Use for the benefit of people with disability	Not included	Mediators selected from a list drawn up by the Copyright Organisation Court of Appeals of Athens	Right-holders and third parties benefiting from the exceptions may request the assistance of one or more mediators selected from the list of mediators drawn up by the Copyright Organisation. The mediators make recommendations to the parties. If no party objects within one month from the forwarding of the recommendation, all parties are considered to have accepted the recommendation. Otherwise, it is upon the Court of Appeal of Athens to settle the dispute.

Member State	Preserved exceptions	Private copying	*Ad hoc* Authority	Administrative or judicial remedies
Italy (Law N.68/2003, which amended the Copyright Act, *i.e.*, Law 633/1941)	Reproduction for private use on paper or similar media Reprography within publicly accessible libraries, museums and archives Reproduction, quotation and communication to the public of the copyrighted work for purposes of review, teaching and scientific research, provided that teaching and research uses have non-commercial ends and serve illustration purposes only Reproduction and communication to the public of certain uses of the copyrighted work made by people with disabilities (See Art.71-quinquies, §2,Copyright Act)	Art.71-sexies, §4, provides that, notwithstanding the application of technological measures, the natural person who acquires lawfully a copy of the work, or who has lawful access to it, shall be able to carry out a private copy, even if analogical only, for personal use, on condition that this possibility does not conflict with a normal exploitation of the work and does not determine an unreasonable prejudice to the right-holder.	Copyright Committee	Where associations of right-holders and beneficiaries of the preserved exceptions fail to find an agreement for the making available of the means to exercise such exceptions, each association can ask the Copyright Committee to undertake the mandatory procedure of conciliation created under Art.194-bis of the Copyright Act. These proceedings foresee the appointment of a special commission that aims at proposing a solution for the settlement of disputes. If the conciliation fails, each party is entitled to undertake ordinary civil proceedings after 90 days from the undertaking of the conciliation procedure (Art.71-quinquies and 194-bis of the Copyright Act).

Member State	Preserved exceptions	Private copying	*Ad hoc* Authority	Administrative orjudicial remedies
Germany (German Copyright Act of 9 September 1965, amended on 10 September 2003)	Exceptions concerning: People with disabilities Collections for school or educational use School broadcasts and works made available for teaching and research Inclusion of the work in personal files, if and to the extent that reproduction for this purpose is necessary and not done for commercial purposes Personal use in teaching or for examinations. (See §95b(1))	The exception of private copying may be enforced against technological protection measures, but only in respect of: Reproduction on paper or similar media by photographic techniques Reproduction for personal academic use Therefore, the right-holder is not obliged to support the user if he or she wants to make a *digital* private copy of the work. (See §53(1))	There is no special authority	Firstly, it is provided that contractual agreements that override right holders' obligations in respect of guaranteed exceptions are null and void (see §95 (b)(1)). Secondly, right-holders who do not make the necessary means available according to §95(b)(1) face an administrative fine of up to € 50.000,00 (see §111(a)(1) no. 2). No special remedy is provided

Member State	Preserved exceptions	Private copying	*Ad hoc* Authority	Administrative or judicial remedies
United Kingdom (Copyright and Related Rights Regulations 2003 of 3 October 2003, which amended Chapter III of the UK Copyright, Designs and Patent Act 1988)	Research and private study Things done for purposes of instruction or examination (See §296ZE; Schedule 5A, Part I)	§296ZE (Schedule 5A, Part I) provides that the private copying exception shall be expressly preserved in respect of: Copying made by a visually impaired person wishing to have access to a single personal copy of the protected work (see §31A) Multiple copies for visually impaired persons (see §31B) Recording for purposes of time-shifting in respect of broadcasts (see §70)	Secretary of State	Either the beneficiary of a preserved exception or a person being a representative of a class of persons prevented from carrying out a permitted act may issue notices of complaints to the Secretary of State. Where the Secretary of State finds that no subsisting voluntary measure or agreement provides the user with means to carry out one of the preserved exceptions, the Secretary may order the owner of the rights in the work to which the measure has been applied to make available to the complainant the means of carrying out the permitted act to the extent necessary to benefit from that act. Failure to comply with his direction will amount to a breach of statutory duty (see §296ZE).
Netherlands	Educational uses Uses by disabled people	Private copying is included among the exceptions for which the Minister of Justice may issue orders in respect of rightholders.	Minister of Justice	Government orders (*i.e.*, Decrees by the Minister of Justice) may establish rules obliging the author or his successor in title to provide the user of a literary, scientific or artistic work with the means necessary to benefit from guaranteed exceptions (see Art. 29(a)(4)).

Member State	Preserved exceptions	Private copying	Ad hoc Authority	Administrative or judicial remedies
Belgium (Law of 22 May 2005, which amended the Copyright Act of 30 June 1994)	Production of anthologies Reproduction for private use on paper or any similar medium Reproduction for purposes of teaching and scientific research Reproduction and communication to the public in respect of uses carried out by people with disabilities	Art. 79bis, §2, al.2, provides that the King, on deliberation of the Council of Ministers, may add the exception of private copying on any medium other than paper to the list of guaranteed exceptions.	President of the Court of First Instance	Belgian law states the imperative (*i.e.*, mandatory) character of copyright exceptions explicitly (see Art.23-bis of the Belgian Copyright Act). Where copyright holders do not comply with the obligation to take adequate and voluntary measures in a reasonable time (see Art.79bis, §2), the President of the Court of First Instance can ascertain the violation of this obligation and order right-holders to make the means to benefit from the preserved exceptions available (see Art. 87bis).

Member State	Preserved exceptions	Private copying	*Ad hoc* Authority	Administrative or judicial remedies
Spain (Law N.23/2006 of 7 July 2006, which amended the Intellectual Property Act of 12 April 1996)	Exceptions to the benefit of people with disabilities Reproduction, distribution and communication to the public of short excerpts from copyrighted works for purposes of teaching illustration, as provided by Art. 32(2) (see Art. 161(1). It is noteworthy that Art. 161(1) does not include and preserve the exception provided under Art.32(1), which allows quotation for teaching and research purposes. To the contrary, it is expressly provided that acts of extraction and quotation for purposes of teaching and scientific research shall be preserved from the operation of technical measures in respect of databases protected by copyright and the so-called *sui generis* right (see Art. 161(1)(d) and (g)).	Art. 161(1)(a) provides that the exception of private copying (see Art. 31(2)) shall be included in the list of preserved exceptions. However, the Spanish Government is entitled to modify, by means of decree, the regime of *digital* private copying by removing it from the range of preserved exceptions in so far as this solution is suggested by consideration of social needs and technological developments (See the First Additional Provision). Consistently with this provision, the Government is also entitled to phase out copyright levies in respect of equipment, hardware and media that prove not to serve purposes of private copying (see Art. 25(7), letter d).	Intellectual Property Commission, whose tasks may include, on determination of (future) Government decrees, the modification and development of functions of arbitration, mediation, determination of compensation fees in respect of private copying; and the resolution of disputes between collecting societies, user associations and broadcasters (see the Second Additional Provision).	Where right-holders and/or agreements between interested parties fail to make available the means to exercise the exceptions preserved by Art. 161(1), the beneficiaries of such exceptions may undertake civil proceedings. Moreover, when the beneficiary of a preserved exception is a consumer under the meaning of the 1984 Spanish Consumer Protection Act, civil proceedings may be undertaken, on behalf of the consumer, by qualified entities (*i.e.*, consumer associations) that are entitled to take action in court for the enforcement of consumer protection regulations (see Art. 161(2)).

Member State	Preserved exceptions	Private copying	*Ad hoc* Authority	Administrative or judicial remedies
France (Law N. 2006-961 of 1 August 2006, which amended the Intellectual Property Code)	Quotation for purposes of review, critic, teaching, and research Performance and reproduction of excerpts from protected works for teaching and research ends, provided that these uses are addressed to school audiences and do not pursue any commercial purpose Personal consultation of works within libraries and archives Uses by non-profit entities and institutions that provide publicly accessible establishments (*e.g.*, libraries, educational institutions) where copyrighted works are made available to people with disabilities Extraction and re-use of protected databases to enable uses by people with disabilities within publicly accessible establishments Extraction and re-use of a substantial part of protected databases for purposes of teaching illustration and scientific research, on condition that these uses are carried out to the benefit of school audiences and have no commercial ends (see Art. L.331-8)	Art.L.331-8, §1, provides that reproduction for strictly personal use shall be included into the circle of preserved exceptions in respect of both copyright and related rights. It is noteworthy that the Authority for the Regulation of Technical Measures is entitled to determine the *minimum number* of personal copies that technical measures must allow to make. This determination shall take place while taking into account the *nature* of the protected work and its possible *types of exploitation* enabled by technical measures (Art.L.331-8, §3).	Art. L.331-17 established the Authority for the Regulation of Technical Measures, which is defined as an independent, administrative body.	The new provision of Art. L.335-1, §6, of the French Intellectual Property Code (enacted by Art.13 of Law N.2006-961) provides that technical measures cannot lawfully oppose copyright exceptions as well as usage rights conferred by the right-holders through contract. Beneficiaries of preserved exceptions can commence proceedings before the Authority for the Regulation of Technical Measures where such exceptions should turn out to be technically restricted. If the Authority fails to propose a solution agreed upon by both the beneficiary of an exception and the copyright owner, the Authority is entitled to either dismiss the claim or order the copyright owner to make available the means allowing the beneficiary to carry out the preserved use (see Articles L.331-12 to L.331-16).

Appendix III - Directive 2001/29/EC of the European Parliament and of the Council of 22 May 2001 on the harmonisation of certain aspects of copyright and related rights in the information society (Official Journal L 167, 22.06.2001, p.10)

THE EUROPEAN PARLIAMENT AND THE COUNCIL OF THE EUROPEAN UNION,

Having regard to the Treaty establishing the European Community, and in particular Articles 47(2), 55 and 95 thereof,

Having regard to the proposal from the Commission (1),

Having regard to the opinion of the Economic and Social Committee (2),

Acting in accordance with the procedure laid down in Article 251 of the Treaty (3),

Whereas:

(1) The Treaty provides for the establishment of an internal market and the institution of a system ensuring that competition in the internal market is not distorted. Harmonisation of the laws of the Member States on copyright and related rights contributes to the achievement of these objectives.

(2) The European Council, meeting at Corfu on 24 and 25 June 1994, stressed the need to create a general and flexible legal framework at Community level in order to foster the development of the information society in Europe. This requires, inter alia, the existence of an internal market for new products and services. Important Community legislation to ensure such a regulatory framework is already in place or its adoption is well under way. Copyright and related rights play an important role in this context as they protect and stimulate the development and marketing of new products and services and the creation and exploitation of their creative content.

(3) The proposed harmonisation will help to implement the four freedoms of the internal market and relates to compliance with the fundamental principles of law and especially of property, including intellectual property, and freedom of expression and the public interest.

(4) A harmonised legal framework on copyright and related rights, through increased legal certainty and while providing for a high level of protection of intellectual property, will foster substantial investment in creativity and innovation, including network infrastructure, and lead in turn to growth and increased competitiveness of European industry, both in the area of content provision and information technology and more generally across a wide range of industrial and cultural sectors. This will safeguard employment and encourage new job creation.

(5) Technological development has multiplied and diversified the vectors for creation, production and exploitation. While no new concepts for the protection of intellectual property are needed,

the current law on copyright and related rights should be adapted and supplemented to respond adequately to economic realities such as new forms of exploitation.

(6) Without harmonisation at Community level, legislative activities at national level which have already been initiated in a number of Member States in order to respond to the technological challenges might result in significant differences in protection and thereby in restrictions on the free movement of services and products incorporating, or based on, intellectual property, leading to a refragmentation of the internal market and legislative inconsistency. The impact of such legislative differences and uncertainties will become more significant with the further development of the information society, which has already greatly increased transborder exploitation of intellectual property. This development will and should further increase. Significant legal differences and uncertainties in protection may hinder economies of scale for new products and services containing copyright and related rights.

(7) The Community legal framework for the protection of copyright and related rights must, therefore, also be adapted and supplemented as far as is necessary for the smooth functioning of the internal market. To that end, those national provisions on copyright and related rights which vary considerably from one Member State to another or which cause legal uncertainties hindering the smooth functioning of the internal market and the proper development of the information society in Europe should be adjusted, and inconsistent national responses to the technological developments should be avoided, whilst differences not adversely affecting the functioning of the internal market need not be removed or prevented.

(8) The various social, societal and cultural implications of the information society require that account be taken of the specific features of the content of products and services.

(9) Any harmonisation of copyright and related rights must take as a basis a high level of protection, since such rights are crucial to intellectual creation. Their protection helps to ensure the maintenance and development of creativity in the interests of authors, performers, producers, consumers, culture, industry and the public at large. Intellectual property has therefore been recognised as an integral part of property.

(10) If authors or performers are to continue their creative and artistic work, they have to receive an appropriate reward for the use of their work, as must producers in order to be able to finance this work. The investment required to produce products such as phonograms, films or multimedia products, and services such as "on-demand" services, is considerable. Adequate legal protection of intellectual property rights is necessary in order to guarantee the availability of such a reward and provide the opportunity for satisfactory returns on this investment.

(11) A rigorous, effective system for the protection of copyright and related rights is one of the main ways of ensuring that European cultural creativity and production receive the necessary resources and of safeguarding the independence and dignity of artistic creators and performers.

(12) Adequate protection of copyright works and subject-matter of related rights is also of great importance from a cultural standpoint. Article 151 of the Treaty requires the Community to take cultural aspects into account in its action.

(13) A common search for, and consistent application at European level of, technical measures to protect works and other subject-matter and to provide the necessary information on rights are essential insofar as the ultimate aim of these measures is to give effect to the

principles and guarantees laid down in law.

(14) This Directive should seek to promote learning and culture by protecting works and other subject-matter while permitting exceptions or limitations in the public interest for the purpose of education and teaching.

(15) The Diplomatic Conference held under the auspices of the World Intellectual Property Organisation (WIPO) in December 1996 led to the adoption of two new Treaties, the "WIPO Copyright Treaty" and the "WIPO Performances and Phonograms Treaty", dealing respectively with the protection of authors and the protection of performers and phonogram producers. Those Treaties update the international protection for copyright and related rights significantly, not least with regard to the so-called "digital agenda", and improve the means to fight piracy world-wide. The Community and a majority of Member States have already signed the Treaties and the process of making arrangements for the ratification of the Treaties by the Community and the Member States is under way. This Directive also serves to implement a number of the new international obligations.

(16) Liability for activities in the network environment concerns not only copyright and related rights but also other areas, such as defamation, misleading advertising, or infringement of trademarks, and is addressed horizontally in Directive 2000/31/EC of the European Parliament and of the Council of 8 June 2000 on certain legal aspects of information society services, in particular electronic commerce, in the internal market ("Directive on electronic commerce")(4), which clarifies and harmonises various legal issues relating to information society services including electronic commerce. This Directive should be implemented within a timescale similar to that for the implementation of the Directive on electronic commerce, since that Directive provides a harmonised framework of principles and provisions relevant inter alia to important parts of this Directive. This Directive is without prejudice to provisions relating to liability in that Directive.

(17) It is necessary, especially in the light of the requirements arising out of the digital environment, to ensure that collecting societies achieve a higher level of rationalisation and transparency with regard to compliance with competition rules.

(18) This Directive is without prejudice to the arrangements in the Member States concerning the management of rights such as extended collective licences.

(19) The moral rights of rightholders should be exercised according to the legislation of the Member States and the provisions of the Berne Convention for the Protection of Literary and Artistic Works, of the WIPO Copyright Treaty and of the WIPO Performances and Phonograms Treaty. Such moral rights remain outside the scope of this Directive.

(20) This Directive is based on principles and rules already laid down in the Directives currently in force in this area, in particular Directives 91/250/EEC(5), 92/100/EEC(6), 93/83/EEC (7), 93/98/EEC(8) and 96/9/EC(9), and it develops those principles and rules and places them in the context of the information society. The provisions of this Directive should be without prejudice to the provisions of those Directives, unless otherwise provided in this Directive.

(21) This Directive should define the scope of the acts covered by the reproduction right with regard to the different beneficiaries. This should be done in conformity with the acquis communautaire. A broad definition of these acts is needed to ensure legal certainty within the internal market.

(22) The objective of proper support for the dissemination of culture must not be achieved by sacrificing strict protection of rights or by tolerating illegal

forms of distribution of counterfeited or pirated works.

(23) This Directive should harmonise further the author's right of communication to the public. This right should be understood in a broad sense covering all communication to the public not present at the place where the communication originates. This right should cover any such transmission or retransmission of a work to the public by wire or wireless means, including broadcasting. This right should not cover any other acts.

(24) The right to make available to the public subject-matter referred to in Article 3(2) should be understood as covering all acts of making available such subject-matter to members of the public not present at the place where the act of making available originates, and as not covering any other acts.

(25) The legal uncertainty regarding the nature and the level of protection of acts of on-demand transmission of copyright works and subject-matter protected by related rights over networks should be overcome by providing for harmonised protection at Community level. It should be made clear that all rightholders recognised by this Directive should have an exclusive right to make available to the public copyright works or any other subject-matter by way of interactive on-demand transmissions. Such interactive on-demand transmissions are characterised by the fact that members of the public may access them from a place and at a time individually chosen by them.

(26) With regard to the making available in on-demand services by broadcasters of their radio or television productions incorporating music from commercial phonograms as an integral part thereof, collective licensing arrangements are to be encouraged in order to facilitate the clearance of the rights concerned.

(27) The mere provision of physical facilities for enabling or making a communication does not in itself amount to communication within the meaning of this Directive.

(28) Copyright protection under this Directive includes the exclusive right to control distribution of the work incorporated in a tangible article. The first sale in the Community of the original of a work or copies thereof by the rightholder or with his consent exhausts the right to control resale of that object in the Community. This right should not be exhausted in respect of the original or of copies thereof sold by the rightholder or with his consent outside the Community. Rental and lending rights for authors have been established in Directive 92/100/EEC. The distribution right provided for in this Directive is without prejudice to the provisions relating to the rental and lending rights contained in Chapter I of that Directive.

(29) The question of exhaustion does not arise in the case of services and online services in particular. This also applies with regard to a material copy of a work or other subject-matter made by a user of such a service with the consent of the rightholder. Therefore, the same applies to rental and lending of the original and copies of works or other subject-matter which are services by nature. Unlike CD-ROM or CD-I, where the intellectual property is incorporated in a material medium, namely an item of goods, every on-line service is in fact an act which should be subject to authorisation where the copyright or related right so provides.

(30) The rights referred to in this Directive may be transferred, assigned or subject to the granting of contractual licences, without prejudice to the relevant national legislation on copyright and related rights.

(31) A fair balance of rights and interests between the different categories of rightholders, as well as between the different categories of rightholders and users of protected subject-matter must be safeguarded. The existing exceptions and limitations to the rights as set out by

the Member States have to be reassessed in the light of the new electronic environment. Existing differences in the exceptions and limitations to certain restricted acts have direct negative effects on the functioning of the internal market of copyright and related rights. Such differences could well become more pronounced in view of the further development of transborder exploitation of works and cross-border activities. In order to ensure the proper functioning of the internal market, such exceptions and limitations should be defined more harmoniously. The degree of their harmonisation should be based on their impact on the smooth functioning of the internal market.

(32) This Directive provides for an exhaustive enumeration of exceptions and limitations to the reproduction right and the right of communication to the public. Some exceptions or limitations only apply to the reproduction right, where appropriate. This list takes due account of the different legal traditions in Member States, while, at the same time, aiming to ensure a functioning internal market. Member States should arrive at a coherent application of these exceptions and limitations, which will be assessed when reviewing implementing legislation in the future.

(33) The exclusive right of reproduction should be subject to an exception to allow certain acts of temporary reproduction, which are transient or incidental reproductions, forming an integral and essential part of a technological process and carried out for the sole purpose of enabling either efficient transmission in a network between third parties by an intermediary, or a lawful use of a work or other subject-matter to be made. The acts of reproduction concerned should have no separate economic value on their own. To the extent that they meet these conditions, this exception should include acts which enable browsing as well as acts of caching to take place, including those which enable transmission systems to function efficiently, provided that the intermediary does not modify the information and does not interfere with the lawful use of technology, widely recognised and used by industry, to obtain data on the use of the information. A use should be considered lawful where it is authorised by the rightholder or not restricted by law.

(34) Member States should be given the option of providing for certain exceptions or limitations for cases such as educational and scientific purposes, for the benefit of public institutions such as libraries and archives, for purposes of news reporting, for quotations, for use by people with disabilities, for public security uses and for uses in administrative and judicial proceedings.

(35) In certain cases of exceptions or limitations, rightholders should receive fair compensation to compensate them adequately for the use made of their protected works or other subject-matter. When determining the form, detailed arrangements and possible level of such fair compensation, account should be taken of the particular circumstances of each case. When evaluating these circumstances, a valuable criterion would be the possible harm to the rightholders resulting from the act in question. In cases where rightholders have already received payment in some other form, for instance as part of a licence fee, no specific or separate payment may be due. The level of fair compensation should take full account of the degree of use of technological protection measures referred to in this Directive. In certain situations where the prejudice to the rightholder would be minimal, no obligation for payment may arise.

(36) The Member States may provide for fair compensation for rightholders also when applying the optional provisions on exceptions or limitations which do not require such compensation.

(37) Existing national schemes on reprography, where they exist, do not create major barriers to the internal market.

Member States should be allowed to provide for an exception or limitation in respect of reprography.

(38) Member States should be allowed to provide for an exception or limitation to the reproduction right for certain types of reproduction of audio, visual and audio-visual material for private use, accompanied by fair compensation. This may include the introduction or continuation of remuneration schemes to compensate for the prejudice to rightholders. Although differences between those remuneration schemes affect the functioning of the internal market, those differences, with respect to analogue private reproduction, should not have a significant impact on the development of the information society. Digital private copying is likely to be more widespread and have a greater economic impact. Due account should therefore be taken of the differences between digital and analogue private copying and a distinction should be made in certain respects between them.

(39) When applying the exception or limitation on private copying, Member States should take due account of technological and economic developments, in particular with respect to digital private copying and remuneration schemes, when effective technological protection measures are available. Such exceptions or limitations should not inhibit the use of technological measures or their enforcement against circumvention.

(40) Member States may provide for an exception or limitation for the benefit of certain non-profit making establishments, such as publicly accessible libraries and equivalent institutions, as well as archives. However, this should be limited to certain special cases covered by the reproduction right. Such an exception or limitation should not cover uses made in the context of on-line delivery of protected works or other subject-matter. This Directive should be without prejudice to the Member States' option to derogate from the exclusive public lending right in accordance with Article 5 of Directive 92/100/EEC. Therefore, specific contracts or licences should be promoted which, without creating imbalances, favour such establishments and the disseminative purposes they serve.

(41) When applying the exception or limitation in respect of ephemeral recordings made by broadcasting organisations it is understood that a broadcaster's own facilities include those of a person acting on behalf of and under the responsibility of the broadcasting organisation.

(42) When applying the exception or limitation for non-commercial educational and scientific research purposes, including distance learning, the non-commercial nature of the activity in question should be determined by that activity as such. The organisational structure and the means of funding of the establishment concerned are not the decisive factors in this respect.

(43) It is in any case important for the Member States to adopt all necessary measures to facilitate access to works by persons suffering from a disability which constitutes an obstacle to the use of the works themselves, and to pay particular attention to accessible formats.

(44) When applying the exceptions and limitations provided for in this Directive, they should be exercised in accordance with international obligations. Such exceptions and limitations may not be applied in a way which prejudices the legitimate interests of the rightholder or which conflicts with the normal exploitation of his work or other subject-matter. The provision of such exceptions or limitations by Member States should, in particular, duly reflect the increased economic impact that such exceptions or limitations may have in the context of the new electronic environment. Therefore, the scope of certain exceptions or limitations may have to be even more limited when it comes to certain new

uses of copyright works and other subject-matter.

(45) The exceptions and limitations referred to in Article 5(2), (3) and (4) should not, however, prevent the definition of contractual relations designed to ensure fair compensation for the rightholders insofar as permitted by national law.

(46) Recourse to mediation could help users and rightholders to settle disputes. The Commission, in cooperation with the Member States within the Contact Committee, should undertake a study to consider new legal ways of settling disputes concerning copyright and related rights.

(47) Technological development will allow rightholders to make use of technological measures designed to prevent or restrict acts not authorised by the rightholders of any copyright, rights related to copyright or the sui generis right in databases. The danger, however, exists that illegal activities might be carried out in order to enable or facilitate the circumvention of the technical protection provided by these measures. In order to avoid fragmented legal approaches that could potentially hinder the functioning of the internal market, there is a need to provide for harmonised legal protection against circumvention of effective technological measures and against provision of devices and products or services to this effect.

(48) Such legal protection should be provided in respect of technological measures that effectively restrict acts not authorised by the rightholders of any copyright, rights related to copyright or the sui generis right in databases without, however, preventing the normal operation of electronic equipment and its technological development. Such legal protection implies no obligation to design devices, products, components or services to correspond to technological measures, so long as such device, product, component or service does not otherwise fall under the prohibition of Article 6. Such legal protection should respect proportionality and should not prohibit those devices or activities which have a commercially significant purpose or use other than to circumvent the technical protection. In particular, this protection should not hinder research into cryptography.

(49) The legal protection of technological measures is without prejudice to the application of any national provisions which may prohibit the private possession of devices, products or components for the circumvention of technological measures.

(50) Such a harmonised legal protection does not affect the specific provisions on protection provided for by Directive 91/250/EEC. In particular, it should not apply to the protection of technological measures used in connection with computer programs, which is exclusively addressed in that Directive. It should neither inhibit nor prevent the development or use of any means of circumventing a technological measure that is necessary to enable acts to be undertaken in accordance with the terms of Article 5(3) or Article 6 of Directive 91/250/EEC. Articles 5 and 6 of that Directive exclusively determine exceptions to the exclusive rights applicable to computer programs.

(51) The legal protection of technological measures applies without prejudice to public policy, as reflected in Article 5, or public security. Member States should promote voluntary measures taken by rightholders, including the conclusion and implementation of agreements between rightholders and other parties concerned, to accommodate achieving the objectives of certain exceptions or limitations provided for in national law in accordance with this Directive. In the absence of such voluntary measures or agreements within a reasonable period of time, Member States should take appropriate measures to ensure that rightholders provide beneficiaries of such exceptions or limitations with

appropriate means of benefiting from them, by modifying an implemented technological measure or by other means. However, in order to prevent abuse of such measures taken by rightholders, including within the framework of agreements, or taken by a Member State, any technological measures applied in implementation of such measures should enjoy legal protection.

(52) When implementing an exception or limitation for private copying in accordance with Article 5(2)(b), Member States should likewise promote the use of voluntary measures to accommodate achieving the objectives of such exception or limitation. If, within a reasonable period of time, no such voluntary measures to make reproduction for private use possible have been taken, Member States may take measures to enable beneficiaries of the exception or limitation concerned to benefit from it. Voluntary measures taken by rightholders, including agreements between rightholders and other parties concerned, as well as measures taken by Member States, do not prevent rightholders from using technological measures which are consistent with the exceptions or limitations on private copying in national law in accordance with Article 5(2)(b), taking account of the condition of fair compensation under that provision and the possible differentiation between various conditions of use in accordance with Article 5(5), such as controlling the number of reproductions. In order to prevent abuse of such measures, any technological measures applied in their implementation should enjoy legal protection.

(53) The protection of technological measures should ensure a secure environment for the provision of interactive on-demand services, in such a way that members of the public may access works or other subject-matter from a place and at a time individually chosen by them. Where such services are governed by contractual arrangements, the first and second subparagraphs of Article 6(4) should not apply. Non-interactive forms of online use should remain subject to those provisions.

(54) Important progress has been made in the international standardisation of technical systems of identification of works and protected subject-matter in digital format. In an increasingly networked environment, differences between technological measures could lead to an incompatibility of systems within the Community. Compatibility and interoperability of the different systems should be encouraged. It would be highly desirable to encourage the development of global systems.

(55) Technological development will facilitate the distribution of works, notably on networks, and this will entail the need for rightholders to identify better the work or other subject-matter, the author or any other rightholder, and to provide information about the terms and conditions of use of the work or other subject-matter in order to render easier the management of rights attached to them. Rightholders should be encouraged to use markings indicating, in addition to the information referred to above, inter alia their authorisation when putting works or other subject-matter on networks.

(56) There is, however, the danger that illegal activities might be carried out in order to remove or alter the electronic copyright-management information attached to it, or otherwise to distribute, import for distribution, broadcast, communicate to the public or make available to the public works or other protected subject-matter from which such information has been removed without authority. In order to avoid fragmented legal approaches that could potentially hinder the functioning of the internal market, there is a need to provide for harmonised legal protection against any of these activities.

(57) Any such rights-management information systems referred to above may, depending on their design, at the

same time process personal data about the consumption patterns of protected subject-matter by individuals and allow for tracing of on-line behaviour. These technical means, in their technical functions, should incorporate privacy safeguards in accordance with Directive 95/46/EC of the European Parliament and of the Council of 24 October 1995 on the protection of individuals with regard to the processing of personal data and the free movement of such data(10).

(58) Member States should provide for effective sanctions and remedies for infringements of rights and obligations as set out in this Directive. They should take all the measures necessary to ensure that those sanctions and remedies are applied. The sanctions thus provided for should be effective, proportionate and dissuasive and should include the possibility of seeking damages and/or injunctive relief and, where appropriate, of applying for seizure of infringing material.

(59) In the digital environment, in particular, the services of intermediaries may increasingly be used by third parties for infringing activities. In many cases such intermediaries are best placed to bring such infringing activities to an end. Therefore, without prejudice to any other sanctions and remedies available, rightholders should have the possibility of applying for an injunction against an intermediary who carries a third party's infringement of a protected work or other subject-matter in a network. This possibility should be available even where the acts carried out by the intermediary are exempted under Article 5. The conditions and modalities relating to such injunctions should be left to the national law of the Member States.

(60) The protection provided under this Directive should be without prejudice to national or Community legal provisions in other areas, such as industrial property, data protection, conditional access, access to public documents, and the rule of media exploitation chronology, which may affect the protection of copyright or related rights.

(61) In order to comply with the WIPO Performances and Phonograms Treaty, Directives 92/100/EEC and 93/98/EEC should be amended,

HAVE ADOPTED THIS DIRECTIVE:

CHAPTER I

OBJECTIVE AND SCOPE

Article 1

Scope

1. This Directive concerns the legal protection of copyright and related rights in the framework of the internal market, with particular emphasis on the information society.

2. Except in the cases referred to in Article 11, this Directive shall leave intact and shall in no way affect existing Community provisions relating to:

(a) the legal protection of computer programs;

(b) rental right, lending right and certain rights related to copyright in the field of intellectual property;

(c) copyright and related rights applicable to broadcasting of programmes by satellite and cable retransmission;

(d) the term of protection of copyright and certain related rights;

(e) the legal protection of databases.

CHAPTER II

RIGHTS AND EXCEPTIONS

Article 2

Reproduction right

Member States shall provide for the exclusive right to authorise or prohibit direct or indirect, temporary or permanent reproduction by any means and in any form, in whole or in part:

(a) for authors, of their works;

(b) for performers, of fixations of their performances;

(c) for phonogram producers, of their phonograms;

(d) for the producers of the first fixations of films, in respect of the original and copies of their films;

(e) for broadcasting organisations, of fixations of their broadcasts, whether those broadcasts are transmitted by wire or over the air, including by cable or satellite.

Article 3

Right of communication to the public of works and right of making available to the public other subject-matter

1. Member States shall provide authors with the exclusive right to authorise or prohibit any communication to the public of their works, by wire or wireless means, including the making available to the public of their works in such a way that members of the public may access them from a place and at a time individually chosen by them.

2. Member States shall provide for the exclusive right to authorise or prohibit the making available to the public, by wire or wireless means, in such a way that members of the public may access them from a place and at a time individually chosen by them:

(a) for performers, of fixations of their performances;

(b) for phonogram producers, of their phonograms;

(c) for the producers of the first fixations of films, of the original and copies of their films;

(d) for broadcasting organisations, of fixations of their broadcasts, whether these broadcasts are transmitted by wire or over the air, including by cable or satellite.

3. The rights referred to in paragraphs 1 and 2 shall not be exhausted by any act of communication to the public or making available to the public as set out in this Article.

Article 4

Distribution right

1. Member States shall provide for authors, in respect of the original of their works or of copies thereof, the exclusive right to authorise or prohibit any form of distribution to the public by sale or otherwise.

2. The distribution right shall not be exhausted within the Community in respect of the original or copies of the work, except where the first sale or other transfer of ownership in the Community of that object is made by the rightholder or with his consent.

Article 5

Exceptions and limitations

1. Temporary acts of reproduction referred to in Article 2, which are transient or incidental [and] an integral and essential part of a technological process and whose sole purpose is to enable:

(a) a transmission in a network between third parties by an intermediary, or

(b) a lawful use

of a work or other subject-matter to be made, and which have no independent economic significance, shall be exempted from the reproduction right provided for in Article 2.

2. Member States may provide for exceptions or limitations to the reproduction right provided for in Article 2 in the following cases:

(a) in respect of reproductions on paper or any similar medium, effected by the use of any kind of photographic technique or by some other process having similar effects, with the exception of sheet music, provided that the rightholders receive fair compensation;

(b) in respect of reproductions on any medium made by a natural person for private use and for ends that are neither directly nor indirectly commercial, on condition that the rightholders receive fair compensation which takes account of the application or non-application of technological measures referred to in Article 6 to the work or subject-matter concerned;

(c) in respect of specific acts of reproduction made by publicly accessible libraries, educational establishments or museums, or by archives, which are not for direct or indirect economic or commercial advantage;

(d) in respect of ephemeral recordings of works made by broadcasting organisations by means of their own facilities and for their own broadcasts; the preservation of these recordings in official archives may, on the grounds of their exceptional documentary character, be permitted;

(e) in respect of reproductions of broadcasts made by social institutions pursuing non-commercial purposes, such as hospitals or prisons, on condition that the rightholders receive fair compensation.

3. Member States may provide for exceptions or limitations to the rights provided for in Articles 2 and 3 in the following cases:

(a) use for the sole purpose of illustration for teaching or scientific research, as long as the source, including the author's name, is indicated, unless this turns out to be impossible and to the extent justified by the non-commercial purpose to be achieved;

(b) uses, for the benefit of people with a disability, which are directly related to the disability and of a non-commercial nature, to the extent required by the specific disability;

(c) reproduction by the press, communication to the public or making available of published articles on current economic, political or religious topics or of broadcast works or other subject-matter of the same character, in cases where such use is not expressly reserved, and as long as the source, including the author's name, is indicated, or use of works or other subject-matter in connection with the reporting of current events, to the extent justified by the informatory purpose and as long as the source, including the author's name, is indicated, unless this turns out to be impossible;

(d) quotations for purposes such as criticism or review, provided that they relate to a work or other subject-matter which has already been lawfully made available to the public, that, unless this turns out to be impossible, the source, including the author's name, is indicated, and that their use is in accordance with fair practice, and to the extent required by the specific purpose;

(e) use for the purposes of public security or to ensure the proper performance or reporting of administrative, parliamentary or judicial proceedings;

(f) use of political speeches as well as extracts of public lectures or similar works or subject-matter to the extent justified by the informatory purpose and provided that the source, including the author's name, is indicated, except where this turns out to be impossible;

(g) use during religious celebrations or official celebrations organised by a public authority;

(h) use of works, such as works of architecture or sculpture, made to be located permanently in public places;

(i) incidental inclusion of a work or other subject-matter in other material;

(j) use for the purpose of advertising the public exhibition or sale of artistic works, to the extent necessary to promote the event, excluding any other commercial use;

(k) use for the purpose of caricature, parody or pastiche;

(l) use in connection with the demonstration or repair of equipment;

(m) use of an artistic work in the form of a building or a drawing or plan of a building for the purposes of reconstructing the building;

(n) use by communication or making available, for the purpose of research or private study, to individual members of the public by dedicated terminals on the premises of establishments referred to in paragraph 2(c) of works and other subject-matter not subject to purchase or licensing terms which are contained in their collections;

(o) use in certain other cases of minor importance where exceptions or limitations already exist under national law, provided that they only concern analogue uses and do not affect the free circulation of goods and services within the Community, without prejudice to the other exceptions and limitations contained in this Article.

4. Where the Member States may provide for an exception or limitation to the right of reproduction pursuant to paragraphs 2 and 3, they may provide similarly for an exception or limitation to the right of distribution as referred to in Article 4 to the extent justified by the purpose of the authorised act of reproduction.

5. The exceptions and limitations provided for in paragraphs 1, 2, 3 and 4 shall only be applied in certain special cases which do not conflict with a normal exploitation of the work or other subject-matter and do not unreasonably prejudice the legitimate interests of the rightholder.

CHAPTER III

PROTECTION OF TECHNOLOGICAL MEASURES AND RIGHTS-MANAGEMENT INFORMATION

Article 6

Obligations as to technological measures

1. Member States shall provide adequate legal protection against the circumvention of any effective technological measures, which the person concerned carries out in the knowledge, or with reasonable grounds to know, that he or she is pursuing that objective.

2. Member States shall provide adequate legal protection against the manufacture, import, distribution, sale, rental, advertisement for sale or rental, or possession for commercial purposes of devices, products or components or the provision of services which:

(a) are promoted, advertised or marketed for the purpose of circumvention of, or

(b) have only a limited commercially significant purpose or use other than to circumvent, or

(c) are primarily designed, produced, adapted or performed for the purpose of enabling or facilitating the circumvention of,

any effective technological measures.

3. For the purposes of this Directive, the expression 'technological measures' means any technology, device or component that, in the normal course of its operation, is designed to prevent or restrict acts, in respect of works or other subject-matter, which are not authorised by the rightholder of any copyright or any right related to copyright as provided for by law or the sui generis right provided for in Chapter III of Directive 96/9/EC. Technological measures shall be deemed 'effective' where the use of a protected work or other subject-matter is controlled by the rightholders through application of an access control or protection process, such as encryption, scrambling or other transformation of the work or other subject-matter or a copy control mechanism, which achieves the protection objective.

4. Notwithstanding the legal protection provided for in paragraph 1, in the absence of voluntary measures taken by rightholders, including agreements between rightholders and other parties concerned, Member States shall take appropriate measures to ensure that rightholders make available to the beneficiary of an exception or limitation provided for in national law in accordance with Article 5(2)(a), (2)(c), (2)(d), (2)(e), (3)(a), (3)(b) or (3)(e) the means of benefiting from that exception or limitation, to the extent necessary to benefit from that exception or limitation and where that beneficiary has legal access to the protected work or subject-matter concerned.

A Member State may also take such measures in respect of a beneficiary of an exception or limitation provided for in accordance with Article 5(2)(b), unless reproduction for private use has already been made possible by rightholders to the extent necessary to benefit from the exception or limitation concerned and in accordance with the provisions of Article 5(2)(b) and (5), without preventing rightholders from adopting adequate measures regarding the number of reproductions in accordance with these provisions.

The technological measures applied voluntarily by rightholders, including those applied in implementation of voluntary agreements, and technological measures applied in implementation of the measures taken by Member States, shall enjoy the legal protection provided for in paragraph 1.

The provisions of the first and second subparagraphs shall not apply to works or other subject-matter made available to the public on agreed contractual terms in such a way that members of the public may access them from a place and at a time individually chosen by them.

When this Article is applied in the context of Directives 92/100/EEC and 96/9/EC, this paragraph shall apply mutatis mutandis.

Article 7

Obligations concerning rights-management information

1. Member States shall provide for adequate legal protection against any person knowingly performing without authority any of the following acts:

(a) the removal or alteration of any electronic rights-management information;

(b) the distribution, importation for distribution, broadcasting, communication or making available to the public of works or other subject-matter protected under this Directive or under Chapter III of Directive 96/9/EC from which electronic rights-management information has been removed or altered without authority,

if such person knows, or has reasonable grounds to know, that by so doing he is inducing, enabling, facilitating or concealing an infringement of any copyright or any rights related to copyright as provided by law, or of the *sui generis* right provided for in Chapter III of Directive 96/9/EC.

2. For the purposes of this Directive, the expression 'rights-management information' means any information provided by rightholders which identifies the work or other subject-matter referred to in this Directive or covered by the *sui generis* right provided for in Chapter III of Directive 96/9/EC, the author or any other rightholder, or information about the terms and conditions of use of the work or other subject-matter, and any numbers or codes that represent such information.

The first subparagraph shall apply when any of these items of information is associated with a copy of, or appears in connection with the communication to the public of, a work or other subject-matter referred to in this Directive or covered by the *sui generis* right provided for in Chapter III of Directive 96/9/EC.

CHAPTER IV

COMMON PROVISIONS

Article 8

Sanctions and remedies

1. Member States shall provide appropriate sanctions and remedies in respect of infringements of the rights and obligations set out in this Directive and shall take all the measures necessary to ensure that those sanctions and remedies are applied. The sanctions thus provided for shall be effective, proportionate and dissuasive.

2. Each Member State shall take the measures necessary to ensure that rightholders whose interests are affected by an infringing activity carried out on its territory can bring an action for damages and/or apply for an injunction and, where appropriate, for the seizure of infringing material as well as of devices, products or components referred to in Article 6(2).

3. Member States shall ensure that rightholders are in a position to apply for an injunction against intermediaries whose services are used by a third party to infringe a copyright or related right.

Article 9

Continued application of other legal provisions

This Directive shall be without prejudice to provisions concerning in particular patent rights, trade marks, design rights, utility models, topographies of semi-conductor products, type faces, conditional access, access to cable of broadcasting services, protection of national treasures, legal deposit requirements, laws on restrictive practices and unfair competition, trade secrets, security, confidentiality, data protection and privacy, access to public documents, the law of contract.

Article 10

Application over time

1. The provisions of this Directive shall apply in respect of all works and other subject-matter referred to in this Directive which are, on 22 December 2002, protected by the Member States' legislation in the field of copyright and related rights, or which meet the criteria for protection under the provisions of this Directive or the provisions referred to in Article 1(2).

2. This Directive shall apply without prejudice to any acts concluded and rights acquired before 22 December 2002.

Article 11

Technical adaptations

1. Directive 92/100/EEC is hereby amended as follows:

(a) Article 7 shall be deleted;

(b) Article 10(3) shall be replaced by the following:

"3. The limitations shall only be applied in certain special cases which do not conflict with a normal exploitation of the subject-matter and do not unreasonably prejudice the legitimate interests of the rightholder."

2. Article 3(2) of Directive 93/98/EEC shall be replaced by the following:

"2. The rights of producers of phonograms shall expire 50 years after the fixation is made. However, if the phonogram has been lawfully published within this period, the said rights shall expire 50 years from the date of the first lawful publication. If no lawful publication has taken place within the period mentioned in the first sentence, and if the phonogram has been lawfully communicated to the public within this period, the said rights shall expire 50 years from the date of the first lawful communication to the public.

However, where through the expiry of the term of protection granted pursuant to this paragraph in its version before amendment by Directive 2001/29/EC of the European Parliament and of the Council of 22 May 2001 on the harmonisation of certain aspects of copyright and related rights in the information society(11) the rights of producers of phonograms are no longer protected on 22 December 2002, this paragraph shall not have the effect of protecting those rights anew."

Article 12

Final provisions

1. Not later than 22 December 2004 and every three years thereafter, the Commission shall submit to the European Parliament, the Council and the Economic and Social Committee a report on the application of this Directive, in which, *inter alia*, on the basis of specific information supplied by the Member States, it shall examine in particular the application of Articles 5, 6 and 8 in the light of the development of the digital market. In the case of Article 6, it shall examine in particular whether that Article confers a sufficient level of protection and whether acts which are permitted by law are being adversely affected by the use of effective technological measures. Where necessary, in particular to ensure the functioning of the internal market pursuant to Article 14 of the Treaty, it shall submit proposals for amendments to this Directive.

2. Protection of rights related to copyright under this Directive shall leave intact and shall in no way affect the protection of copyright.

3. A contact committee is hereby established. It shall be composed of representatives of the competent authorities of the Member States. It shall be chaired

by a representative of the Commission and shall meet either on the initiative of the chairman or at the request of the delegation of a Member State.

4. The tasks of the committee shall be as follows:

(a) to examine the impact of this Directive on the functioning of the internal market, and to highlight any difficulties;

(b) to organise consultations on all questions deriving from the application of this Directive;

(c) to facilitate the exchange of information on relevant developments in legislation and case-law, as well as relevant economic, social, cultural and technological developments;

(d) to act as a forum for the assessment of the digital market in works and other items, including private copying and the use of technological measures.

Article 13

Implementation

1. Member States shall bring into force the laws, regulations and administrative provisions necessary to comply with this Directive before 22 December 2002. They shall forthwith inform the Commission thereof.

When Member States adopt these measures, they shall contain a reference to this Directive or shall be accompanied by such reference on the occasion of their official publication. The methods of making such reference shall be laid down by Member States.

2. Member States shall communicate to the Commission the text of the provisions of domestic law which they adopt in the field governed by this Directive.

Article 14

Entry into force

This Directive shall enter into force on the day of its publication in the *Official Journal of the European Communities*.

Article 15

Addressees

This Directive is addressed to the Member States.

Done at Brussels, 22 May 2001.

For the European Parliament
The President
N. Fontaine
For the Council
The President
M. Winberg

(1) OJ C 108, 7.4.1998, p. 6 and OJ C 180, 25.6.1999, p. 6.

(2) OJ C 407, 28.12.1998, p. 30.

(3) Opinion of the European Parliament of 10 February 1999 (OJ C 150, 28.5.1999, p. 171), Council Common Position of 28 September 2000 (OJ C 344, 1.12.2000, p. 1) and Decision of the European Parliament of 14 February 2001 (not yet published in the Official Journal). Council Decision of 9 April 2001.

(4) OJ L 178, 17.7.2000, p. 1.

(5) Council Directive 91/250/EEC of 14 May 1991 on the legal protection of computer programs (OJ L 122, 17.5.1991, p. 42). Directive as amended by Directive 93/98/EEC.

(6) Council Directive 92/100/EEC of 19 November 1992 on rental right and lending right and on certain rights related to copyright in the field of intellectual property (OJ L 346, 27.11.1992, p. 61). Directive as amended by Directive 93/98/EEC.

(7) Council Directive 93/83/EEC of 27 September 1993 on the coordination of certain rules concerning copyright and rights related to copyright applicable to satellite broadcasting and cable retransmission (OJ L 248, 6.10.1993, p. 15).

(8) Council Directive 93/98/EEC of 29 October 1993 harmonising the term of protection of copyright and certain related rights (OJ L 290, 24.11.1993, p. 9).

(9) Directive 96/9/EC of the European Parliament and of the Council of 11 March 1996 on the legal protection of databases (OJ L 77, 27.3.1996, p. 20).

(10) OJ L 281, 23.11.1995, p. 31.

(11) OJ L 167, 22.6.2001, p. 10.

Reference List

Authors

Anderson, 'Trusted Computing' and Competition Policy – Issues for Computing Professionals', 4(3) *Upgrade, The European Journal for the Informatics Professional* 2003, p. 35, available at: http://www.upgrade-cepis.org.

Arrow, 'Economic Welfare and the Allocation of Resources for Inventions', in Nelson (ed), *The Rate and Direction of Economic Activity: Economic and Social Factors*, Princeton University Press, Princeton 1962, 609.

Barlow, 'The Economy of Ideas. Selling Wine Without Bottles on the Global Net', downloaded at: http://homes.eff.org/~barlow/EconomyOfIdeas.html.

Bechtold, 'The Present and Future of Digital Rights Management - Musings on Emerging Legal Problems', in Becker, Buhse, Gunnewig and Rump (eds), *Digital Rights Management – Technological, Economic, Legal and Political Aspects*, Springer, Berlin 2003, 597.

Bechtold, 'Value-centered design of Digital Rights Management', available at: http://www.indicare.org/tiki-read_article.php?articleId=39.

Becker, 'Crime and Punishment: An Economic Approach', (76) *Journal of Political Economy* 1968, 169.

Bell, 'Fair Use vs. Fared Use: The Impact of Automated Rights Management on Copyright's Fair Use Doctrine', (76) *North Carolina Law Review* 1998, 557.

Benkler, 'A political economy of the public domain: markets in information goods versus the marketplace of ideas', in Dreyfuss, Zimmermann, First (eds), *Expanding the boundaries of intellectual property: innovation policy for the knowledge society*, Oxford University Press, Oxford-New York 2001, 266.

Benkler, 'An Unhurried View of Private Ordering in Information Transactions', (53) *Vanderbilt Law Review* 2000, 2063.

Benkler, 'From Consumers to Users', 52(3) *Federal Communications Law Journal* 2000, 561.

Benkler, *The Wealth of Networks. How Social Production Transforms Markets and Freedom*, Yale University Press, New Haven and London 2006 (available also at http://www.benkler.org).

Bernault and Lebois, *Peer-to-peer et propriété littéraire et artistique. Etude de faisabilité sur un système de compensation pour l'échange des oeuvres sur Internet*, Institut de Recherche en Droit Privé de l'Université de Nantes, June 2005, available at: http://alliance.bugiweb.com/usr/Documents/RapportUniversiteNantes-juin2005.pdf.

Bomsel and Geffroy, *Economic Analysis of Digital Rights Management systems (DRMs)*, MediaNet Project Paper, reviewed version of 10.2.2005, available at: http://cerna.ensmp.fr.

Bonofacio, 'The Information society and the harmonisation of copyright and related rights: (over)stretching the legal basis of Article 95(100A)?', *Legal Issues of European Integration* 1999, 1.

Boyle, '*The Second Enclosure Movement and the Construction of the Public Domain*', (66) Law and Contemporary Problems 2003, 33, available at: http://www.law.duke.edu/boylesite/.

Braun, 'The Interface Between the Protection of Technological Measures and the Exercise of Exceptions to Copyright and Related Rights: Comparing the Situation in the United States and the European Community', (25) *EIPR* 2003, 496.

Breyer, J., Concurring Opinion, in *Metro-Goldwyn-Mayer Studios Inc.*v. *Grokster, Ltd.*, 545 U.S. Supreme Court (2005).

Burk and Cohen, 'Fair Use Infrastructure for Rights Management Systems', (15) *Harvard Journal of Law and Technology* 2001, 41.

Burrell and Coleman, *Copyright Exceptions. The Digital Impact*, Cambridge University Press, Cambridge 2005.

Bygrave, 'The Technologisation of Copyright: Implications for Privacy and Related Interests', (24) *EIPR* 2002, 51.

Calabresi and Melamed, 'Property Rules, Liability Rules, and Inalienability: One view of the Cathedral', (85) *Harvard Law Review* 1972, 1089.

Caron and Gaubiac, 'L'échange d'oeuvres sur l'Internet ou le P2P', in *Mélanges Victor Nabhan – Hors série Les Cahiers de Propriété Intellectuelle*, Edition Yvon Blais, Montréal 2005.

Caso, *Digital rights management. Il commercio delle informazioni digitali tra contratto e diritto d'autore*, Cedam, Padova 2004.

Clark, 'The Answer to the Machine is in the Machine', in Hugenholtz (ed), *The Future of Copyright in a Digital Environment*, Kluwer Law International, The Hague 1996, 139.

Coase, 'The Problem of Social Cost', (3) *Journal of Law and Economics* 1960, 1.

Cohen Jehoram, 'European Copyright Law – Even More Horizontal', (32) *IIC* 2001, 532.

Cohen, 'A Right to Read Anonymously: A Closer Look at 'Copyright Management' in Cyberspace', (28) *Connecticut Law Review* 1996, 981.

Cohen, 'Copyright and The Jurisprudence of Self-Help', (13) *Berkeley Technology Law Journal* 1998, 1089.

Cohen, 'Lochner in Cyberspace. The New Economic Orthodoxy of "Rights Management"', (97) *Michigan Law Review* 1998, 462.

Cooter and Ulen, *Law and economics* (fourth edition), Addison-Wesley, Boston 2004.

Cornish and Llewelyn, *Intellectual Property: Patents, Copyright, Trade Marks and Allied Rights*, Sweet and Maxwell, London 2003.

Cournot, *Recherches sur les principes mathématiques de la théorie de la richesse*, Hachette, Paris 1838.

Czarnota and Hart, *Legal Protection of Computer Programs in Europe. A Guide to the EC Directive*, Butterworths, London 1991.

Demsetz, 'Toward a Theory of Property Rights', (57) *American Economic Review Papers and Proceedings* 1967, 347.

Depoorter and Parisi, 'Fair Use and Copyright protection: A Price Theory Explanation', George Mason Law & Economics Research Paper No. 01/2003, available at: http://papers.ssrn.com/sol3/papers.cfm?abstract_id=259298.

de Witte, 'Non-market values in internal market legislation', in Shuibhne (ed), *Regulating the Internal Market*, Edward Elgar, Cheltenham 2006, 61.

Dowell, 'Bytes and Pieces: Fragmented Copies, Licensing, and Fair Use in a Digital World', (86) *California Law Review* 1998, 843.

Dusollier, *Droit d'auteur et protection des œuvres dans l'univers numérique. Droits et exceptions à la lumière des dispositifs de verrouillage des œuvres*, Larcier, Bruxelles 2005.

Dusollier, 'L'utilisation légitime de l'oeuvre: un nouveau sésame pour le bénefice des exceptions en droit d'auteur?', *Communications - Commerce Electronique*, November 2005, 17.

Dusollier, 'Le dernier tournant de l'affaire Mulholland Drive', note sous Cass. fr., 28 février 2006, (2) *Auteurs et Média* 2006, 177.

Dusollier, 'Technology as an imperative for regulating copyright: from the public exploitation to the private use of the work', (27) *EIPR* 2005, 201.

Easterbrook, 'Cyberspace vs. Property Law?', (4) *Texas Review of Law and Policy* 1999, 103.

Einhorn and Rosenblatt, 'Peer-to-Peer Networking and Digital Rights Management. How Market Tools Can Solve Copyright Problems', (534) *Policy Analysis*, 17 February 2005, available at http://www.cato.org.

Fallenboeck, 'On the Technical Protection of Copyright: The Digital Millennium Copyright Act, the European Community Copyright Directive and Their Anticircumvention Provisions', (7) *International Journal of Communication Law and Policy*, Winter 2002/2003, available at http://www.ijclp.org.

Farchy, *Internet et le droit d'auteur, La culture Napster*, CNRS Editions, Paris 2003.

Ficsor, 'Collective Management of Copyright and Related Rights at a Triple Crossroads: Should it Remain Voluntary or May It Be "Extended" or Made Mandatory?', *e-Copyright Bulletin*, October 2003, available at http://portal.unesco.org/culture/en/ev.php.

Fisher, *Promises to Keep. Technology, Law and the Future of Entertainment*, Stanford University Press, Stanford 2004.

Forrester, 'EC Competition Law as a Limitation on The Use of IP Rights in Europe: Is There Reason To Panic?', paper presented at the Eight Annual EU Competition Law and Policy Workshop, European University Institute, RSCAS (6-7 June 2003).

Gasser and Girsberger, *Transposing the Copyright Directive: Legal Protection of Technological Measures in EU-Member States. A Genie Stuck in the Bottle?*, The Berkman Center for Internet and Society at Harvard Law School, Berkman Publication Series No.2004-10, November 2004, available at: http://cyber.law.harvard.edu/publications.

Gates, *Trustworthy Computing*, Executive E-mail, 18 July 2002, available at: http://www.microsoft.com/mscorp/execmail/2002/07-18twc.asp.

Gatto, 'Governance in the Europen Union: A Legal Perspective', (12) *Columbia Journal of European Law* 2006, 487.

Geiger, 'Copyright and Free Access to Information: For a Fair Balance of Interests in a Globalised World', (28) *EIPR* 2006, 366.

Ginsburg, Jane, 'Copyright Use and Excuse on the Internet', The Center for Law and Economic Studies, Working Paper n.178, Columbia Law School, 2001.

Ginsburg, Jane, 'Copyright Without Walls: Speculations on Literary Property in the Library of the Future', (42) *Representations* 1993, 53, available at: http://www.representations.org.

Ginsburg, Jane, 'From Having Copies to Experiencing Works: the Development of an Access Right in U.S. Copyright Law', Columbia Law School, Public Law and Legal Theory Working Group, 2000, available at: http://papers.ssrn.com.

Ginsburg, Jane, 'Putting Cars on the "Information Superhighways": Authors, Exploiters and Copyrights in Cyberspace', (95) *Columbia Law Review* 1995, 1466.

Ginsburg, Jane, 'Toward Supranational Copyright Law? The WTO Panel Decision and the "Three-Step Test" for Copyright Exceptions', *RIDA*, January 2001.

Ginsburg, Ruth, Concurring Opinion, in *Metro-Goldwyn-Mayer Studios Inc.* v. *Grokster*, Ltd., 545 U.S. Supreme Court (2005).

Goldstein, *Copyright's highway: the law and lore of copyright from Gutenberg to the Celestial Jukebox*, Hill and Wang, New York 1994.

Gordon, 'Fair Use as Market Failure: A Structural and Economic Analysis of the Betamax Case and Its Predecessors', (82) *Columbia Law Review* 1982, 1600.

Groennings, 'Costs and Benefits of the Recording Industry's Litigation Against Individuals', (20) *Berkeley Technology Law Journal* 2005, 571.

Guibault, *Copyright Limitations and Contracts. An analysis of the contractual overridability of limitations on copyright*, Kluwer Law International, The Hague 2002, 16.

Guibault, *Le tir manqué de la Directive européenne sur le droit d'auteur dans la société de l'information*, Institute for Information Law, University of Amsterdam, Publications, available at http://www.ivir.nl.

Hardin, 'The Tragedy of the Commons', (162) *Science* 1968, 1243.

Hardy, 'Property (and Copyright) in Cyberspace', *University of Chicago Legal Forum* 1996, 217.

Hart, 'Interoperability Information and the Microsoft Decision', (28) *EIPR* 2006, 361.

Hart, 'The Copyright in the Information Society Directive: an Overview', (24) *EIPR* 2002, 58.

Heide, 'Copyright in the E.U. and United States: What "Access Right"?', (23) *EIPR* 2001, 469.

Heide, 'Copyright, Contract and the Legal Protection of Technological Measures – Not "the Old Fashioned Way": Providing a Rationale to the "Copyright Exceptions Interface"', 2003, available at http://www.ssrn.com.

Helberger and Groenenboom, *Digital Rights Management and Consumer Acceptability, Legal Aspect*, 17, available at http://www.indicare.org.

Heller, 'The Tragedy of the Anticommons: Property in the Transition from Marx to Markets', (111) *Harvard Law Review* 1998, 621.

Hugenholtz, 'Adapting Copyright to the Information Superhighway', in Hugenholtz (ed), *The Future of Copyright in a Digital Environment*, Kluwer Law International, The Hague 1996, 80.

Hugenholtz, 'Caching and Copyright: The Right of Temporary Copying', (22) *EIPR* 2000, 482.

Hugenholtz, 'Copyright and Freedom of Expression in Europe', in Elkin-Koren and Netanel (eds), *The Commodification of Information*, Kluwer Law International, The Hague 2002, 239.

Hugenholtz, 'Peer-to-Peer and Copyright, Are Levies a Solution?', paper presented at the 3rd DRM Conference, Berlin, 14-15 January 2005.

Hugenholtz, 'Why the Copyright Directive is Unimportant, and Possibly Invalid', (22) *EIPR* 2000, 500.

Hugenholtz, Guibault, and van Geffen, *The Future of Levies in a Digital Environment*, Final Report, Institute for Information Law, Amsterdam 2003, available at http://www.ivir.nl/staff/hugenholtz.html.

Koelman, 'Fixing the Three-step Test', (28) *EIPR* 2006, 407.

Landes and Posner, 'An Economic Analysis of Copyright Law', (18) *Journal of Legal Studies* 1989, 325.

Lemley, 'Beyond Preemption: The Law and Policy of Intellectual Property Licensing', (87) *California Law Review* 1999, 111.

Lemley, 'Property, Intellectual Property, and Free Riding', John M. Olin Program in Law and Economics, Stanford Law School, Working Paper No. 291, August 2004, available at: http://ssrn.com/abstract=582602.

Lemley, 'The Economics of Improvements in Intellectual Property Law', (75) *Texas Law Review* 1997, 997.

Lemley and Reese, 'Reducing Digital Copyright Infringement Without Restricting Innovation', (56) *Stanford Law Review* 2004, 1345.

Lessig, *Code and Other Laws of Cyberspace*, Basic Books, New York 1999.

Lessig, *Free Culture: How Big Media Uses Technology and the Law to Lock Down Culture and Control Creativity*, The Penguin Press, New York 2004.

Lessig, *The Future of Ideas, The Fate of the Commons in a Connected World*, Vintage Books, New York 2002.

Leval, 'Toward a Fair Use Standard', in Merges and Ginsburg (eds), *Foundations of Intellectual Property*, Foundation Press, New York 2004, 388.

Leveque, 'Innovation, leveraging and essential facilities: Interoperability licensing in the EU Microsoft case', available at: http://www.cerna.ensmp.fr/Documents/FL-Ms-WorldCompetition.pdf.

Leveque and Ménière, *The Economics of Patents and Copyright*, Berkeley University Press, available at: www.cerna.ensmp.fr/PrimerForFree.html.

Lewinski, 'Mandatory Collective Administration of Exclusive Rights – A Case Study on Its Compatibility with International and EC Copyright Law', *e-Copyright Bulletin*, January – March 2004, available at: http://portal.unesco.org/culture/en/ev.php.

Lucas, 'Responsabilité des éditeurs de logiciels permettant des échanges de pair à pair', (17) *Propriétés intellectuelles*, October 2005, 444.

Lucas and Sirinelli, 'Exceptions de copie privée et mesures techniques de protection', (16) *Propriétés intellectuelles*, July 2005, 340.

Lucas and Sirinelli, 'La loi n°2006-961 du 1er août relative au droit d'auteur et aux droits voisins dans la société de l'information: premières vues sur le texte promulgué à l'issue de la censure du Conseil constitutionnel', (20) *Propriétés intellectuelles*, July 2006, 297.

Marzano, *Diritto d'Autore e Digital Technologies, Il Digital Copyright nei trattati OMPI, nel DMCA e nella normativa comunitaria*, Giuffré, Milano 2005.

Mazziotti, 'Did Apple's Refusal to License Proprietary Information Enabling Interoperability with Its iPod Music Player Constitute an Abuse under Article 82 of the EC Treaty?', 28(2) *World Competition* 2005, 253.

Mazziotti, 'Il diritto d'autore comunitario nel nuovo ambiente digitale', 7(1) *Ciberspazio e Diritto* 2006, 55.

Mazziotti, 'Utilisations libres des oeuvres protégées dans le contexte numérique européen: d'une regulation publique à une regulation privée', *Petites Affiches*, Numéro Spécial (*Le clivage acteurs publics/acteurs privés à la lumière du droit européen* – Université Paris X-Nanterre, 29 June 2004), N.54, 17 March 2005, 12.

Merges, 'Compulsory Licensing vs. the Three "Golden Oldies"', (508) *Policy Analysis*, 15 January, 2004, available at: http://www.cato.org.

Merges, 'Contracting into Liability Rules: Intellectual Property Rights and Collective Rights Organizations', (84) *California Law Review* 1996, 1293.

Merges, 'The End of Friction? Property Rights and Contract in the "Newtonian" World of On-line Commerce"', (12) *Berkeley Technology Law Journal* 1997, 115.

Merges, Menell and Lemley, *Intellectual Property in the New Technological Age, 2004 Case and Statutory Supplement*, Aspen Publishers, New York 2004.

Mulligan, Han and Burstein, 'How DRM-Based Content Delivery Systems Disrupt Expectations of "Personal Use"', available at: http://www.law.berkeley.edu/clinics/samuelson/projects_papers/WPES-RFID-p029-mulligan.pdf.

Netanel, 'Copyright and a Democratic Civil Society', (106) *Yale Law Journal* 1996, 283.

Netanel, 'Impose a Noncommercial Use Levy to Allow Free Peer-to-Peer File Sharing', 17(1) *Harvard Journal of Law and Technology* 2003, 1.

Nimmer, 'A Riff on Fair Use in the Digital Millennium Copyright Act', (148) *University of Pennsylvania Law Review* 2000, 673.

O'Rourke, 'Copyright Preemption After the ProCD Case: A Market-Based Approach', (12) *Berkeley Technology Law Journal* 1997, 53.

Pardo, *Copyright and Multimedia*, Kluwer Law International, The Hague 2003.

Patrizio, 'Adobe Right Management Server Extends to Office', available at: http://www.internetnews.com.

Pruneda, 'Windows Media Technologies: Using Windows Media Rights Manager to Protect and Distribute Digital Media', *MSDN Magazine*, December 2001, available at http://msdn.microsoft.com/msdnmag/issues/01/12/drm/.

Reichman, 'Legal Hybrids Between the Patent and the Copyright Paradigms', (94) *Columbia Law Review* 1994, 2432.

Ricketson, *The Berne Convention for the protection of literary and artistic works: 1886-1986*, London 1987.

Ricolfi, 'Comunicazione al pubblico e distribuzione', *Annali Italiani di Diritto d'Autore (AIDA)* 2002, 48.

Ricolfi, 'Individual and collective management of copyright in a digital environment', in Torremans (ed) *Copyright Law: A handbook of Contemporary Research*, Edward Elgar, Cheltenham 2007.

Ricolfi, 'Intellectual property rights and legal order', *Il Diritto di Autore* 2001, 132.

Ricolfi, 'Le nuove frontiere della proprietà intellettuale, da Chicago al cyberspazio', in Clerico and Rizzello (eds), *Diritto ed economia della proprietà intellettuale*, Cedam, Padova 1998, 83.

Ricolfi, 'Proprietà intellettuale, antitrust e reti', in Cambini and Valletti (eds), *I mercati della comunicazione nell'era digitale*, Il Mulino, Bologna 2002, 66.

Romano, *L'opera e l'esemplare nel diritto della proprietà intellettuale*, Cedam, Padova 2001.

Rosenblatt, 'France Approves Modified Copyright Bill', *DRM Watch*, 22 June 2006, available at: http:// drmwatch.com/legal/article.php/3615596.

Rosenblatt, 'MySpace Adopts Acoustic Fingeprinting', *DRM Watch*, 2 November 2006, available at: http://www.drmwatch.com/ocr/article.php/3641591.

Samuelson, 'Challenges for the World Intellectual Property Organization', (21) *EIPR* 1999, 581.

Samuelson, 'DRM {and, or, vs.}the Law', (46) *Communication of the ACM*, April 2003, No.4.

Samuelson, 'Fair Use for Computer Programs and Other Copyrightable Works in Digital Form: The Implications of Sony, Galoob and Sega', (1) *Journal of Intellectual Property Law* 1993, 49.

Samuelson, 'Intellectual Property and the Digital Economy: Why the Anti-Circumvention Regulations Need to Be Revised', (14) *Berkeley Technology Law Journal* 1999, 519.

Samuelson, 'Mapping the Digital Public Domain', available at: http://www.law.duke.edu/journals/lcp/archive.html.

Scotchmer, 'Standing on the Shoulders of Giants: Cumulative Research and the Patent Law', (5) *Journal of Economic Perspectives* 1991, 29.

Senftleben, *Copyright, Limitations and the Three-Step Test. An Analysis of the Three-Step Test in International and EC Copyright Law*, Kluwer Law International, The Hague 2004.

Shapiro and Varian, *Information Rules, A Strategic Guide to the Network Economy*, Harvard Business School Press, Boston 1999.

Sirinelli, 'Droit d'auteur et droits voisins – Chronique', (18) *Propriétés Intellectuelles*, January 2006, 58.

Sirinelli, 'Exceptions au monopole – Copie privée – Statuts des reproductions effectuées par l'intermediaire d'échanges de pair à pair à l'issue de ces derniers – La copie privée de *peer* en pire', (15) *Propriétés Intellectuelles*, April 2005, 168.

Sirinelli, 'L'étendue de l'interdiction de contourner les mesures techniques protégeant l'accès aux oeuvres et les droits d'auteurs: exceptions et limitations – Rapport Général, in Régimes complémentaires et concurentiels au droit d'auteur', Acts of the ALAI Conference, 13-17 June 2001, New York, ALAI (USA) 2002, 415.

Sirinelli, 'Monopole d'exploitation-Exception de copie privée – Copie privée ou ayant droit privés du droit de copie?', (14) *Propriétés intellectuelles*, January 2005, 56.

Stallman, 'Can you trust your computer?', available at: http://www.gnu.org/philosophy/can-you-trust.html.

Stallman, 'The Right to Read', in *Free Software Free Society: selected essays of Richard M. Stallman*, GNU Press (Free Software Foundation), Boston 2002.

Standeford, 'France Forges Ahead With Copyright Law', *Intellectual Property Watch*, 16.05.2006, available at: http://www.ip-watch.org.

Stefik, 'Shifting the Possible: How Trusted Systems and Digital Property Rights Challenge Us To Rethink Digital Publishing', 12(1) *Berkeley Technology Law Journal* 1997, 137.

Strachan, 'The Internet of Tomorrow: The New-Old Communications Tool of Control', (26) *EIPR* 2004, 123.

Strowel, 'Le P2P: un problème pressant en attente d'une réponse legislative?', (17) *Propriétés Intellectuelles*, October 2005, 428.

Temple Lang, 'Anticompetitive abuses under Article 82 involving intellectual property rights', paper presented in the Eight Annual EU Competition Law and Policy Workshop, European University Institute, RSCAS (6-7 June 2003), available at: http://www.iue.it/RSCAS/Research/Competition/2003/200306COMP-TempleLang-sIII.pdf.

Ullrich, 'Harmony and unity of European intellectual property protection', in Bently and Vaver (eds), *Intellectual Property in the New Millenium: Essays in Honour of William R. Cornish*, Cambridge University Press, Cambridge 2004, 37.

Ullrich, 'Legal Protection of Innovative technologies: Property or Policy?', in Grandstrand (ed), *Economics, Law and Intellectual Property - Seeking Strategies for Research and Teaching in a Developing Field*, Kluwer Academic Publishers, Boston 2003, 439.

Van Howeling, 'Distributive Values in Copyright', 83(6) *Texas Law Review* 2005, 1535.

Varian, 'Economics of DRM', Presentation made at the 3rd DRM Conference, Berlin, 13-14 January 2005.

Vinje, 'Should We Begin Digging Copyright's Grave?', (22) *EIPR* 2000, 551.

Vollebregt, 'An analysis of the Kazaa case', *E-commerce Law and policy*, December 2003, 14.

Von Lohmann, *IAAL (I Am A Lawyer): What Peer-to-Peer Developers Need to Know about Copyright Law*, Electronic Frontier Foundation, January 2006, available at: http:www.eff.org.

Wagner, 'Information Wants to Be Free: Intellectual Property and the Mythologies of Control', (103) *Columbia Law Review* 2003, 995.

Weatherill, *EC Consumer Law and Policy*, Longman, London and New York 1997.

Weatherill, 'Harmonisation: How Much, How Little?', 16(3) *European Business Law Review* 2005, 533.

Whish, *Competition Law* (fourth edition), Butterworths, London 2001.

Yen, Sony, 'Tort Doctrines, and the Puzzle of Peer-to-Peer', (55) *Case Western Reserve Law Review* 2005, Symposium Issue, available at: http://ssrn.com/abstract=661168.

Table of cases

European Union

Case 62/79, *Coditel and others* v. *Ciné Vog Films and others* [1980] ECR 881.

Case 78/70, *Deutsche Grammophone* v. *Metro-SB-Grossmärkte* [1971] ECR 487.

Case 341/87, *EMI Electrola GmbH* v. *Patricia Im- und Export and others*, [1989] ECR 79

Case 418/01, *IMS Health GmbH & Co. OHG* v. *NDC Health GmbH & Co. KG* (pending).

Case 377/98, *Kingdom of the Netherlands* v. *European Parliament and Council of the European Union* [2001] ECR I-07079.

Case 479/04, *Laserdisken ApS* v. *Kulturministeriet,* C-479-04, Judgment of 12 September 2006, available at: http://www.curia.europa.eu.

Case T-201/04, *Microsoft Corp.* v. *Commission of the European Communities*, Judgment of 17 September 2007, available at: http://www.curia.europa.eu.

Joined cases 241/91 and 242/91, *Radio Telefis Eireann (RTE) and Independent Television Publications Ltd (ITP)* v. *Commission* [1995] ECR I-743.

Case 29/69, *Stauder* v. *City of Ulm* [1969] ECR 419.

Case 238/87, *Volvo* v. *Erik Veng (UK) Ltd.* [1988] ECR 6211.

Case 158/86, *Warner Brothers Inc. and Metronome Video ApS* v. *Erik Viuff Christiansen* [1988] ECR 2605.

United States

A&M Records v. *Napster*, 114 Federal Supp.2d (N.D. Cal. 2000).

A&M Records v. *Napster*, 239 F.3d 1004 (9th Circuit).

American Geophysical Union, et al. v. *Texaco Inc.*, 60 F.3d 913 (2nd Circuit 1994).

BMG Music v. *Gonzales*, N. 05-1314 (7th Circuit 2005).

Campbell v. *Acuff-Rose, Inc.*, 841 U.S. 419 (1994) [114 S.Ct 1164 (1994)].

Feist Publications v. Rural Telephone Co., 499 U.S. 340 (1991).

Harper & Row Publishers v. *Nation Enterprises*, 105 S. Ct. 2218 (1985).

*In re Aimster Copyright Litigatio*n, 334 F.3d 643 (7th Circuit 2003).

*Metro-Goldwyn-Mayer Studios Inc.*v. *Grokster, Ltd.*, 545 U.S. Supreme Court (2005) available at: http://www.eff.org.

Metro-Goldwyn-Mayer Studios, Inc. v. *Grokster*, 259 F.Supp.2d 1029 (C.D. Cal. 2003).

Metro-Goldwyn-Mayer Studios, Inc. v. *Grokster*, 380 F. 3d 1154 (9th Circuit 2004).

Princeton University Press, Macmillan, Inc., et al. v. *Michigan Document Services, Inc., et al.*, 99 F.3d 1381 (6th Circuit 1996).

ProCD v. *Zeidenberg*, 86 F.3d 1447 (7th Circuit 1996).

Recording Industry Association of America, Inc. v. *Verizon Internet Services*, 351 F.3d 1229 (D.C. Circuit 2003).

Religious Technology Center v. *Netcom On-Line Communication Services, Inc.*, 907 F. Supp. 1361 (N.D. Cal. 1995).

Sony Corp. of America v. *Universal City Studios, Inc.*, 464 U.S. 417 [104 S. Ct. 774 (1984)].

UMG Recordings, Inc. v. *MP3.Com*, 92 Federal Supp.2d 349 (S.D.N.Y. 2000).

European Court of Human Rights

Anheuser-Busch Inc. v. *Portugal*, Judgment of 11 October 2005, Application n.73049/01, available at: http://cmiskp.echr.coe.int/tkp197/search.asp?skin=hudoc-en.

British-American Tobacco Company Ltd v. *The Netherlands*, Judgment of 20 November 1995, Series A no. 331.

Chappell v. *The United Kingdom*, Judgment of 30 March 1989, Application no. 10461/83.

Smith Kline and French Laboratories Ltd v. *The Netherlands*, Judgment of 2 October 1990, Application no. 12633/87.

National Case law

Amsterdam Court of Appeal, *BUMA & STEMRA* v. *Kazaa*, 28 March 2002, available at: http://www.eff.org.

Conseil Constitutionnel, Decision N.2006-540 DC of 27 July 2006, available http://www.conseil-constitutionnel.fr/decision/2006/2006540/index.htm.

Conseil de la Concurrence, Décision N° 04-D-54 du 9 Novembre 2004 relative à des pratiques mises en œuvre par la société Apple Computer, Inc. dans les secteurs du téléchargement de musique sur Internet et des baladeurs numériques, available at: http://www.conseil-concurrence.fr/pdf/avis/04d54.pdf.

Cour d'Appel de Paris (4ème Chambre), *Stéphane P., UFC Que Choisir* c. *Universal Pictures Video France and others*, Judgment of 22 April 2005, available at: http://www.legalis.net.

Cour d'Appel Versailles, *EMI Music France* c. *CLCV*, Judgment of 30 September 2004, available at: http://www.legalis.net.

Cour de Cassation, *Société Studio Canal et autres* c. *Perquin et UFC Que Choisir*, Judgment of 28 February 2006.

Danish Supreme Court, *TDC Totallsninger A/S* v. *IFPI Danmark, KODA, Nordisk Copyright Bureau, Danish Musicians' Union, Danish Artists' Union*, Order of 10 February 2006, Case no. 49/2005.

District Court of Munich, *VG Media* v. *Fujitsu Siemens*, Az: 7 O 18484/03, 23 December 2004, available at http://www.juris.de

Juzgado de Primera Instancia de Badajoz, *SGAE* v. *Ricardo Andres Utrera Fernandez*, Procedimiento Ordinario 761/2005, Sentencia N. 15/2006, available at: http://creativecommons.org/weblog/entry/5830.

Supreme Court of the Netherlands, *BUMA & STEMRA* v. *Kazaa*, First Chamber, Order of 19 December 2003, Nr. C02/186HR JMH/AT.

Tribunal Correctionnel de Rodez, *Ministère Public, Fédération nationale de distributeurs de film, Syndicat de l'édition vidéo et autres, Twentieth Century Fox et al.* c. *D. Aurélien*, Judgment of 13 October 2004.

Tribunal de Grande Instance de Nanterre, *Association CLCV* c. *EMI Music France*, Judgment of 24 June 2003, available at: http://www.legalis.net.

Tribunal de Grande Instance de Nanterre, *Francoise M.* c. *EMI France, Auchan France*, Judgment of 2 September 2003, available at: http://www.legalis.net.

Tribunal de Grande Instance de Paris (3ème ch.), *Stéphane P., UFC Que Choisir* c. *Société Films Alain Sarde*, Judgment of 30 April 2004, available at: http://www.legalis.net.

Tribunal de Grande Instance de Paris, *Christophe R. et UFC Que Choisir* c. *Warner Music France et FNAC*, Judgment of 10 January 2006, available at: http://www.legalis.net.

Tribunal de Grande Instance de Paris, *UEJF et Licra* c. *Yahoo! Inc. et Yahoo France*, Ordonnance de référé, 22 May 2000, available at: http://www.juriscom.net.

Tribunal de Grande Instance Paris, *UEJF, SOS Racisme, J'Accuse, MRAP* c. *OLM, Planet.com, France Télécom, Free, AOL France*, Ordonnance de référé, 13 June 2005, available at: http://www.juriscom.net.

Tribunal de Grande Instance de Pontoise, *Ministère Public, SACEM, SDRM, SPPF, SCCP* c. *Alexis B.*, Judgment of 10 March 2005.

Tribunal de Première Instance Bruxelles, *SABAM* c. *Tiscali*, Judgment of 26 November 2004, available at: http://www.juriscom.net.

Tribunale Ordinario di Roma, *Techland and Peppermint Jam Records* v. *Wind Telecomunicazioni*, Order at interim measure proceedings. N. 26125/2007, 16 July 2007, available at http://www.altroconsumo.it/images/17/173003_Attach.pdf.

International case law

Federal Court of Australia, *Universal Music Australia Pty Ltd* v. *Sharman License Holdings Ltd* [2005] 1242 , 5 September 2005.

World Trade Organisation, *United States – Section 110(5) of the U.S. Copyright Act*, Panel Report of 15 June 2000, WT/DS160/R, available at: http:/www.wto.org.

European Commission documents

Amended proposal for a Directive of the European Parliament and of the Council on criminal measures aimed at ensuring the enforcement of intellectual property rights, COM(2006) 168 final, Brussels, 26.4.2006.

Commentaires du Legal Advisory Board sur la Communication de la Commission du 20 Novembre 1996, available at: http://europa.eu.int/ISPO/legal/fr/proprint/labcomment.htm.

Commission opens in-depth investigation into Microsoft/Time Warner/Content Guard JV, Press Release IP/04/1044, Brussels, 25.08.2004, available at http://europa.eu.int/rapid/searchAction.do.

Commission Staff Working Document, *Impact Assessment reforming cross-border collective management of copyright and related rights for legitimate online music services*, Brussels 11.10.2005, available at: http://www.europa.eu.int.

Commission Staff Working Document, *Study on a Community Initiative on the Cross-Border Management of Copyright*, Brussels 7.07.2005, available at: http://www.europa.eu.int.

Commission Staff Working Paper on the review of the EC legal framework in the field of copyright and related rights, SEC (2004) 995, Brussels, 19.7.2004.

Communication from the Commission to the Council, the European Parliament and the European Economic and Social Committee, *The Management of Copyright and Related Rights in the Internal Market*, COM/2004/0261 final.

Competition: European Commission confirms sending a Statement of Objections against alleged territorial restrictions in on-line music sales to major record companies and Apple, Press Release, Brussels, 3.04.2007, available at: http://www.europa.eu/rapid/pressReleasesAction.do?reference=MEMO/07/126.

Copyright levy reform, Commission's Work Programme for 2006 – Roadmap, available at: http://ec.europa.eu/internal_market/copyright/levy_reform/index_en.htm.

Decision of 24 March 2004, relating to a procedure under Article 82 of the EC Treaty, Case COMP/C-3/37.792 (Microsoft Decision), available at: http://europa.eu.int/comm/competition/antitrust/cases/decisions/37792/en.pdf.

First evaluation of Directive 96/9/EC on the legal protection of databases, DG Internal Market and Services Working Paper, 12.12.2005, available at: http://ec.europa.eu/internal_market/copyright.

Follow-up to the Green Paper on Copyright and Related Rights in the Information Society, COM(96) 586.

Green Paper on Copyright and the Challenge of Technology, COM (88), 172, Final of 7.06.1988.

Green Paper. Copyright and Related Rights in the Information Society, Brussels, 19.07.1995, COM (95) 382 final.

Mergers: Microsoft and Time Warner abandon acquisition of control in ContentGuard as Thomson purchases a one third stake, Press Release IP/05/295, 15 March 2005, available at: http://europa.eu.int/rapid/searchAction.do.

Speech by the European Commissioner for Internal Market and Services, Charlie McCreevy, *Address to the European-American Business Council/Business Software Alliance Conference on Digital Rights Management*, High level Industry Seminar/Global Industry Roundtable on Levies and DRMs, Brussels, 12.10.2005, available at: http://ec.europa.eu/internal_market/copyright/copyright-infso/copyright-infso_en.htm.

Reports and studies

ALAI, Resolution of 14 January 2006, §Publications – Internationals (*Affirmation Droit Exclusif*), available at: http://www.alai.org.

Berkman Center for Internet and Society at Harvard Law School – Digital Media Project, *iTunes – How Copyright, Contract, and Technology Shape the Business of Digital Media – A Case Study*, released on the 15 June 2004 by the, available at: http://cyber.law.harvard.edu.

Centro nazionale di Informazione e Documentazione Europea (CIDE), *Verso il nuovo trattato europeo*, available at: http://www.cide.it/Contenuti.

Foundation for Information Policy Research (FIPR), *Implementing the EU Copyright Directive*, available at: http://www.fipr.org.

Institute for Information Law, University of Amsterdam, *Copyright Law and Consumer Protection, Policy conclusions of the European Consumer Law Group (ECLG)*, based on a study carried out by Dr. Lucie Guibault and Ms. Natali Helberger, downloaded at: http://www.ivir.nl/staff/guibault.html.

Institute for Information Law, University of Amsterdam, *Study on the implementation and effect in Member States' laws of Directive 2001/29/EC on the harmonization of certain aspects of copyright and related rights in the Information Society*, Final Report, February 2007, available at http://www.ivir.nl/index-english.html.

Statewatch, *Statewatch Observatory on the EU Constitution and the Reform Treaty*, available at http://www.statewatch.org/euconstitution.htm.

U.S. Department of Commerce, Patent and Trademark Office, Information Infrastructure Task Force, Intellectual Property and the National Information Infrastructure: The Report of the Working Group on Intellectual Property Rights, available at: http://www.uspto.gov/web/offices/com/doc/ipnii/front.pdf.

EU legislation

Council Directive 91/250/EEC of 14 May 1991 on the legal protection of computer programs, OJ L 122, 14.06.1991, 42.

Treaty on European Union, OJ C 191, 29.07.1992.

Council Directive 92/100/EEC of 19 November 1992 on rental right and lending right and on certain rights related to copyright in the field of intellectual property, OJ L 346, 27.11.1992, 61.

Council Directive 93/12/EEC of 5 April 1993 on unfair terms in consumer contracts, OJ L 95, 21.04.1993, 29.

Council Directive 93/83/EEC of 27 September 1993 on the co-ordination of certain rules concerning copyright and rights related to copyright applicable to satellite broadcasting and cable retransmission, OJ L 248, 6.10.1993, 15.

Council Directive 93/98/EEC of 29 October 1993 harmonising the term of protection of copyright and certain related rights, OJ L 290, 24.11.1993, 9.

Council Regulation (EC) No 40/94 of 20 December 1993 on the Community trade mark, OJ L 011, 14.01.1994, 1.

Directive 95/46/EC of the European Parliament and of the Council of 24 October 1995 on the protection of individuals with regard to the processing of personal data and the free movement of such data, OJ L 281, 23.11.1995, 31.

Directive 96/9/EC of the European Parliament and of the Council of 11 March 1996 on the legal protection of databases, OJ L 077, 27.03.1996.

Directive 97/7/EC of the European Parliament and of the Council of 20 May 1997 on the protection of consumers in respect of distance contracts, OJ L 144, 4.06.1997, 19.

Directive 98/43/EC of the European Parliament and of the Council of 6 July 1998 on the approximation of the laws, regulations and administrative provisions of the Member States relating to the advertising and sponsorship of tobacco products, OJ L 213, 30.07.1998, 9.

Directive 98/44/EC of the European Parliament and of the Council of 6 July 1998 on the legal protection of biotechnological inventions, OJ L 213, 30.7.1998, 13.

Directive 98/84/EC of the European Parliament and of the Council of 20 November 1998 on the legal protection of services based on, or consisting of, conditional access, OJ, L 320, 28.11.1998, 54.

Council Decision of 28 June 1999 laying down the procedures for the exercise of implementing powers conferred on the Commission, OJ L 184, 17.07.1999, 23.

Directive 2000/31/EC of the European Parliament and of the Council of 8 June 2000 on certain legal aspects of information society services, in particular electronic commerce, in the Internal Market, OJ L 178, 17.07.2000, 1.

Charter of Fundamental Rights of the European Union, OJ C 364/1, 18.12.2000, available at: http://ec.europa.eu/justice_home/unit/charte/index/en_html.

Council Regulation (EC) N. 44/2001 of 22 December 2000 on jurisdiction and the recognition and enforcement of judgments in civil and commercial matters, OJ L12, 16.01.2001, 1.

Directive 2001/29/EC of the European Parliament and of the Council of 22 May 2001 on the harmonisation of certain aspects of copyright and related rights in the information society, OJ, L 167, 22.6.2001, 10.

Directive 2001/84/EC of the European Parliament and of the Council of 27 September 2001 on the resale right for the benefit of the author of an original work of art, OJ L 272, 13.10.2001, 32.

Council Regulation (EC) N. 6/2002 of 12 December 2001 on Community designs, OJ L 3, 5.01.2002.

Directive 2002/58/EC of 12 July 2002 concerning the processing of personal data and the protection of privacy in the electronic communications sector (Directive on privacy and electronic communications), OJ L 201, 31.7.2002, 37.

Treaty establishing the European Community (consolidated version), OJ C 325, 24.12.2002.

Directive 2004/48/EC of the European Parliament and of the Council of 29 April 2004 on the enforcement of intellectual property rights, OJ L 157, 30.04.2004, 45.

Treaty establishing a Constitution for Europe, OJ C 310, 16.12.2004, 1.

Directive 2005/29/EC of the European Parliament and of the Council of 11 May 2005 concerning unfair business-to-consumer commercial practises in the internal market and amending Council Directive 84/450/EEC, Directives 97/7/EC and 2002/65/EC of the European Parliament and of the Council and Regulation (EC) No 2006/2004 of the European Parliament and of the Council, OJ L 149, 11.06.2005, 22.

Directive 2006/115 of the European Parliament and of the Council of 12 December 2006 on rental right and lending right and on certain rights related to copyright in the field of intellectual property (codified version), OJ L 376, 27.12.2006, 28.

Directive 2006/116 of the European Parliament and of the Council of 12 December 2006 on the term of protection of copyright and certain related rights (codified version), OJ L 372, 27.12.2006, 12.

Reform Treaty approved at the Intergovernmental Conference of 18 October 2007 in Lisbon, available at: http://www.consilium.europa.eu.

U.S. Legislation

U.S. Digital Millennium Copyright Act (DMCA) signed into law by President Clinton on 28 October 1998, which amended the U.S. Copyright Act (see U.S. Code, Title 17).

Library of Congress, U.S. Copyright Office, Federal Register, *Exemption to Prohibition on Circumvention of Copyright Protection Systems for Access Control Technologies*, 27 October 2000, Library of Congress, Federal Register, vol.65, 31 October 2000, Rules and regulations, p. 64556;

Library of Congress, U.S. Copyright Office, Federal Register, *Exemption to Prohibition on Circumvention of Copyright Protection Systems for Access Control Technologies*, 28 October 2003, Library of Congress, Federal Register, vol.68, 31 October 2003, Rules and regulations, p. 62011, available at: http://www.copyright.gov/1201/index.html;

Library of Congress, U.S. Copyright Office, Federal Register, *Exemption to Prohibition on Circumvention of Copyright Protection Systems for Access Control Technologies*, vol. 71, 27 November 2006, Rules and regulations, p. 68472, available at: http://www.copyright.gov/1201/index.html.

International legislation

Agreement on Trade-Related Aspects of Intellectual Property Rights (TRIPS), Annex 1C of the Marrakesh Agreement establishing the World Trade Organisation, Morocco on 15 April 1994, available at: http://www.wto.org.

Berne Convention for the Protection of Literary and Artistic Works of September 9, 1886, available at: http://www.wipo.int/treaties.

European Convention on Human Rights (ECHR), signed in Rome on 4 November 1950.

Rome Convention on the law applicable to contractual obligations, opened for signature in Rome on 19 June 1980 (80/934/EEC), OJ L 266, 09.10.1980.

WIPO Copyright Treaty and WIPO Performances and Phonograms Treaty, adopted in Geneva in December 20, 1996, available at: http://www.wipo.int/treaties.

Electronic press articles

'Apple brings discord to Hymn', *The Register*, 13.01.2005, available at: http://www.theregister.co.uk.

'AT&T Warns Apple, Others, of Patent Infringement, *PC Magazine*, 9.2.2006, downloaded at: http://www.pcmag.com.

'Dutch say 'No' to EU Constitution', *BBC News*, 2.06.2005, available at: http://news.bbc.co.uk/2/hi/europe/4601439.stm.

'French say firm 'No' to the EU Treaty', *BBC News*, available at: http://news.bbc.co.uk/2/hi/europe/4592243.stm.

'Fujitsu Siemens loses German PC levy case', *The Register*, 3.01.2005, available at: http://www.theregister.co.uk.

'German court sets copyright levy on new PCs', *IT World*, 24.12.2004, available at: http://www.itworld.com.

'Tech industry condemns German PC levy', *Out Law News*, 21.01.2005, available at: http://www.outlaw.com.

Websites

www.alai.org

www.apple.com/itunes/

www.assemblee-nationale.fr

www.cato.org

www.cerna.ensmp.fr

www.chiariglione.org/manifesto/

www.conseil-constitutionnel.fr

www.consilium.europa.eu

www.creativearchive.bbc.co.uk

www.creativecommons.org

www.curia.europa.eu

www.cyber.law.harvard.edu

www.dirittodautore.it

www.drmwatch.com

www.ec.europa.eu/internal_market/copyright

www.eff.org

www.europa.eu

www.gnu.org

www.indicare.org

www.ip-watch.org

www.itworld.com

www.ivir.nl

www.juriscom.net

www.law.berkeley.edu

www.legalis.net

www.microsoft.com

www.myspace.com

www.news.bbc.co.uk

www.portal.unesco.org

www.ssrn.com

www.theregister.co.uk

www.tiscali.co.uk/music/

www.uspto.gov

www.wikipedia.org

www.wipo.int

www.wto.org

Index

D

SPRINGER NATURE

GPSR Compliance

The European Union's (EU) General Product Safety Regulation (GPSR) is a set of rules that requires consumer products to be safe and our obligations to ensure this.

If you have any concerns about our products, you can contact us on ProductSafety@springernature.com

In case Publisher is established outside the EU, the EU authorized representative is:

Springer Nature Customer Service Center GmbH
Europaplatz 3
69115 Heidelberg, Germany

FSC
www.fsc.org
MIX
Papier | Fördert gute Waldnutzung
FSC® C083411

Kolibri 360 GmbH
Ferdinand-Jühlke-Straße 7
99095 Erfurt, Deutschland
produktsicherheit@kolibri360.de